THE BRIDE

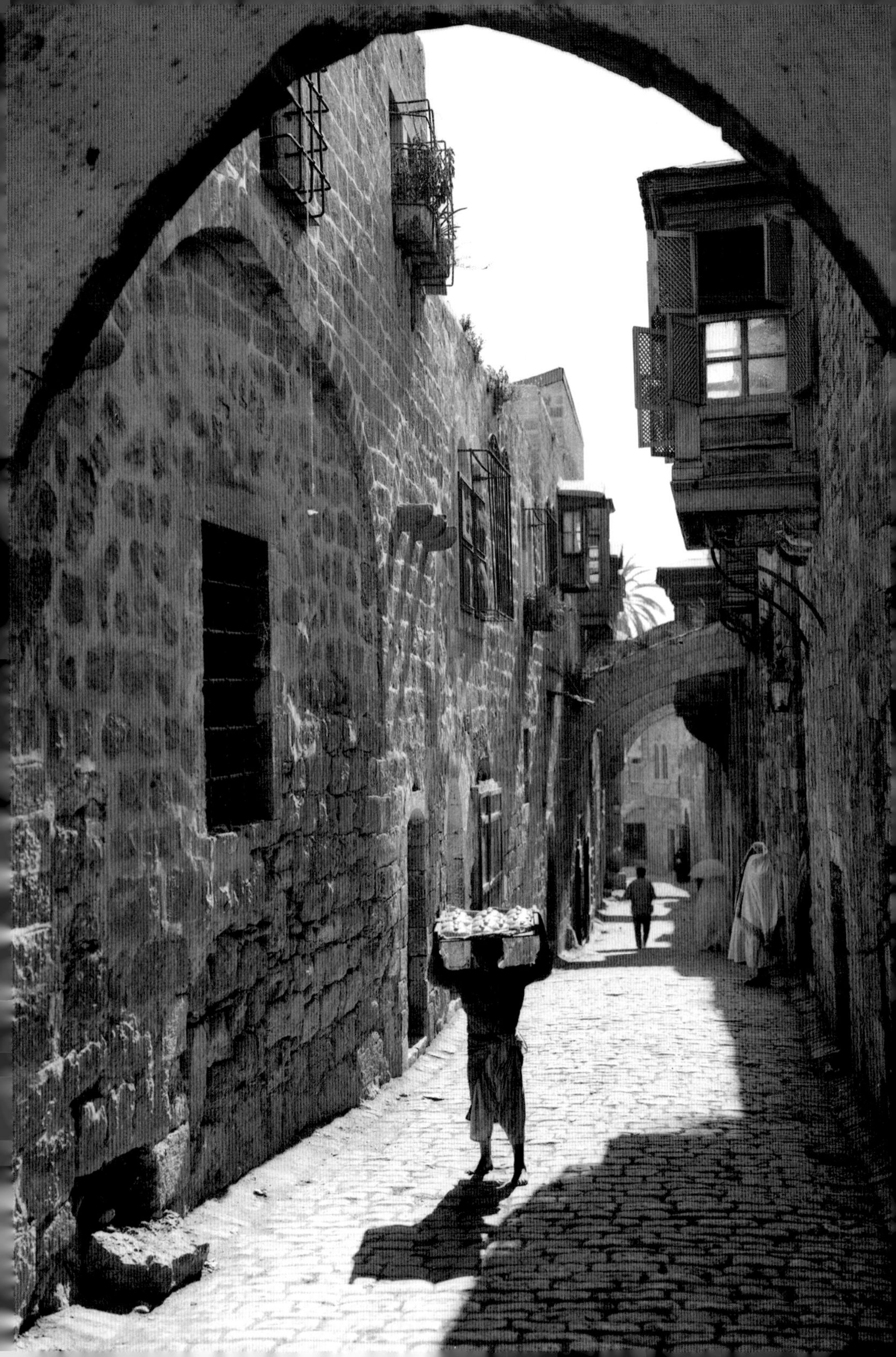

The Bride

An Illustrated History of Palestine
1850–1948

Roger Hardy

Anthony Eyre
MOUNT ORLEANS PRESS

Frontispiece: *The Via Dolorosa, or Street of Sorrows, one of Jerusalem's most popular pilgrim sites; the photograph, from the early 1900s, captures the play of light and shade on the city's ancient walls and cobbled streets.*
(American Colony)

A note on the illustrations
Most of the captions in the book are brief, identifying the image, its date, and the photographer or artist (if known). Further details can be found in the Picture Credits section. While the author has made every effort to identify copyright holders of both texts and images, he would be glad to be informed of any possible errors or omissions.

Published in Great Britain in 2022
by Anthony Eyre, Mount Orleans Press
23 High Street, Cricklade SN6 6AP
www.anthonyeyre.com

Hardback edition: ISBN 978-1-912945-33-7
Paperback edition: ISBN 978-1-912945-34-4

A CIP record for this book is available
from the British Library

Printed in the UK by
Short Run Press

In memory of my brother,

Andrew Hardy,

who did not live to see the book's completion

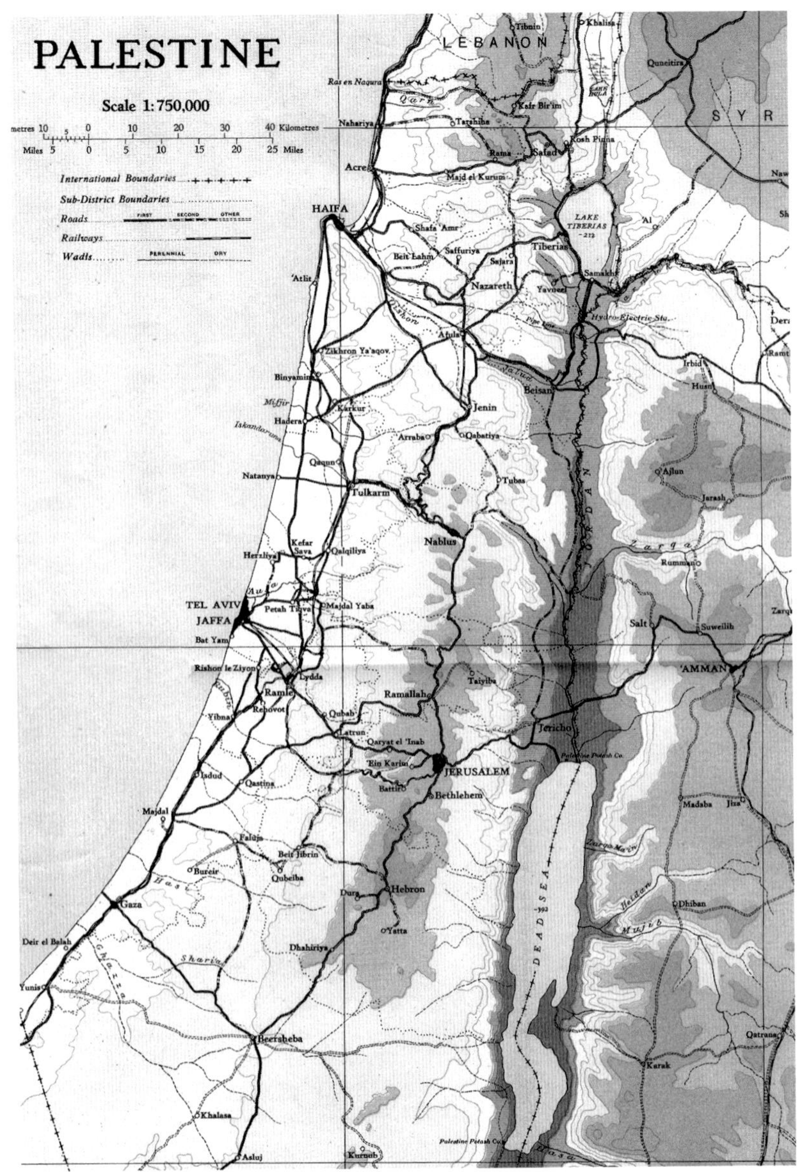

Survey of Palestine, 1946

Contents

Introduction — 9

1   Pilgrims and predators, 1850–1917 — 13

2   Palestine Raj, 1917–1929 — 65

3   Days of rage, 1929–1939 — 113

4   An interlude of war, 1939–1945 — 155

5   Things fall apart, 1945–1948 — 193

Epilogue: the land and the people — 241

Notes — *249*

Select bibliography — *269*

Acknowledgements — *283*

Dramatis personae — *287*

Illustrators & picture credits — *299*

Index — *313*

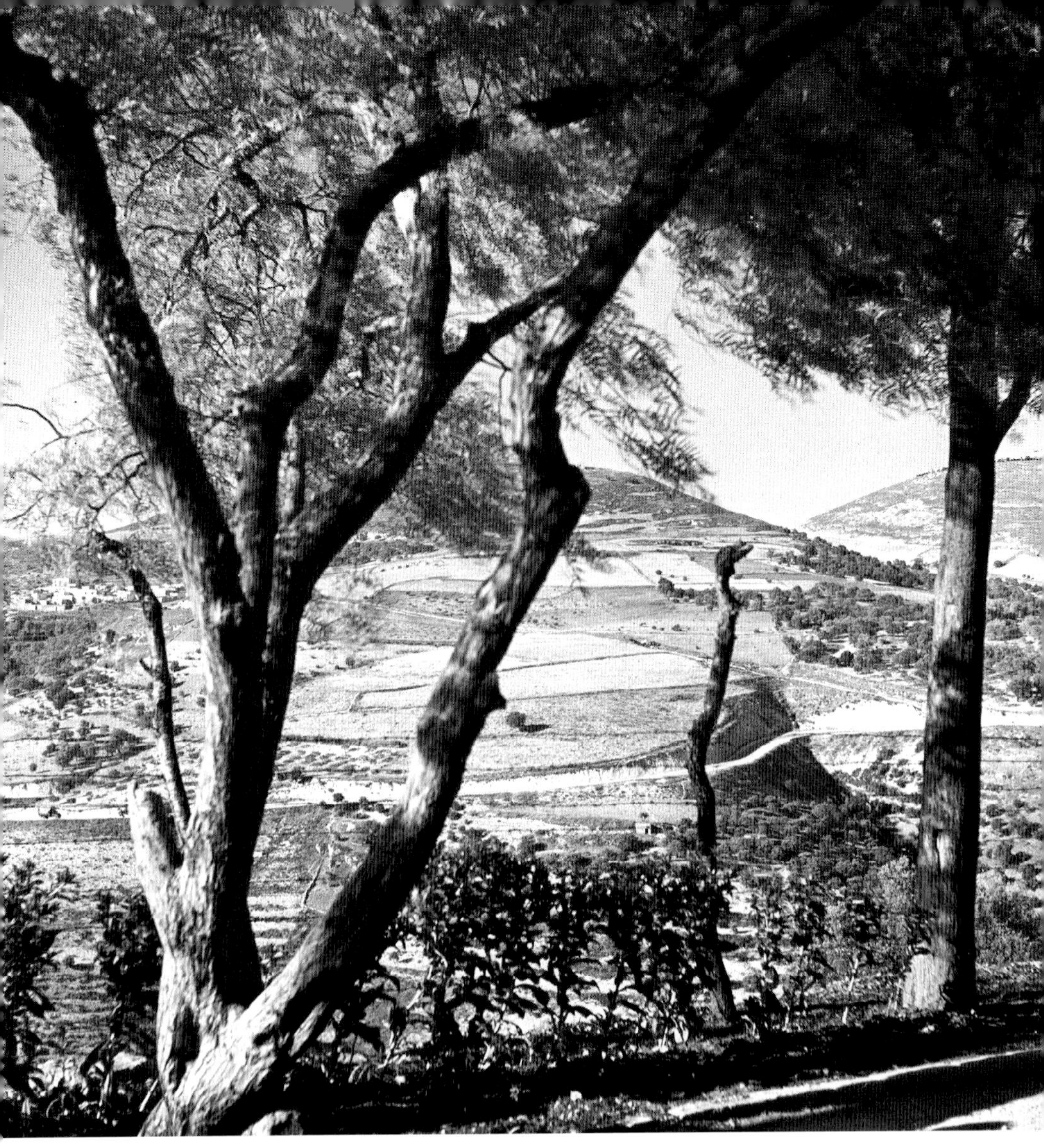

The hills around Safad, northern Palestine, 1947   Zoltan Kluger

Introduction

THIS IS THE story of a bride and an obsession. It describes how, over the course of a hundred years, Palestine was transformed from a backwater of the Ottoman empire into the object of sustained Western ambitions and rivalries; how after the First World War it became part and parcel of the British empire; and how some three decades later, in its final metamorphosis, it was transformed into the state of Israel.

It is, by any standards, an extraordinary and tangled tale. Reflecting on the 'what ifs' of history is often futile but in this case hard to resist. Had the Ottoman Turks not entered the First World War on the side of Germany, had Britain not issued the Balfour Declaration (pledging support for Zionism, the movement to create a Jewish 'national home' in Palestine), had Hitler and Nazism not existed—the outcome might conceivably have been different. As it is, the story can be viewed in very different ways: as a painful episode in the decline of the British empire, as the (improbable) triumph of the dream of a Jewish state, and as the tragedy of the Arabs of Palestine, who paid the price for British failure and Zionist success.

This book has three main features. First, it provides what I hope is a concise and readable narrative of what happened between 1850 and 1948. Second, although I am a journalist not a scholar, I have drawn on the literature of the last thirty-five years which has altered our understanding of crucial events, in particular the conflict of 1948-49.

Third, I use two resources—oral history and photography—to bring the story to life. Photographs, no less then letters, diaries, and memoirs, are a form of testimony. They tell us not only what happened but what it felt like to be there. In choosing texts and images, I have tried to cast a wide net, while remaining conscious of what might be called the 'outsider's gaze'. Many of the diaries and memoirs on which the book draws—I hope not uncritically—are Western sources. Many of the photographs are by Europeans and Americans (even if some of them were resident in Jerusalem). The Arab memoirs I've used, vivid and varied as they are, were written by members of the educated élite, to the inevitable exclusion of the *fellahin*, the Arab peasants who comprised the overwhelming majority of Palestine's population. Despite this limitation, the book employs as broad a palate of written sources—Western, Jewish, Arab—as I have been able to find.

So, too, with the photographs, which include the work of the first Western photographers (mostly British and French) who were active from the middle of the nineteenth century; local practitioners—Armenians, Christian Arabs, and others—who established their studios in the last decades of Ottoman rule; the early Zionist photographers of the 1920s and 1930s; and others—Jewish, Arab, Western—who followed them. I make no apology for drawing heavily on the rich archive of the American Colony in Jerusalem. By way of explanation, I tell the colony's extraordinary story in some detail, and set out why I think the work of its photographic studio has a unique place in the history of Palestine.

The photographers were drawn by a special quality of light which threw into sharp relief the outline of every tree and hill, every building and ruin. Their images capture the play of light and shade on the limestone walls of Jerusalem's Old City, the glistening watermelons on sale at open-air markets, the white apartment blocks of the new metropolis of Tel Aviv, the dusty rubble of houses blown up by soldiers during the rebellion of the 1930s.

Images, like words, need context. The European photographers suffered from both religious and Orientalist prejudices. In the two world wars, photographers working for one side or the other produced war-time propaganda. The early Zionist photographers, employed by Zionist institutions, created and often staged heroic images of pioneers tilling the land—and, later, of soldiers fighting for a Jewish state. None of this necessarily negates the value of their work; but it does mean that we need to tease out, where we can, its purposes and subtexts. Words and images are never entirely innocent; but, taken together, they add new dimensions to our understanding of the history, the geography, and the human reality of Palestine.

Oxford, summer 2021

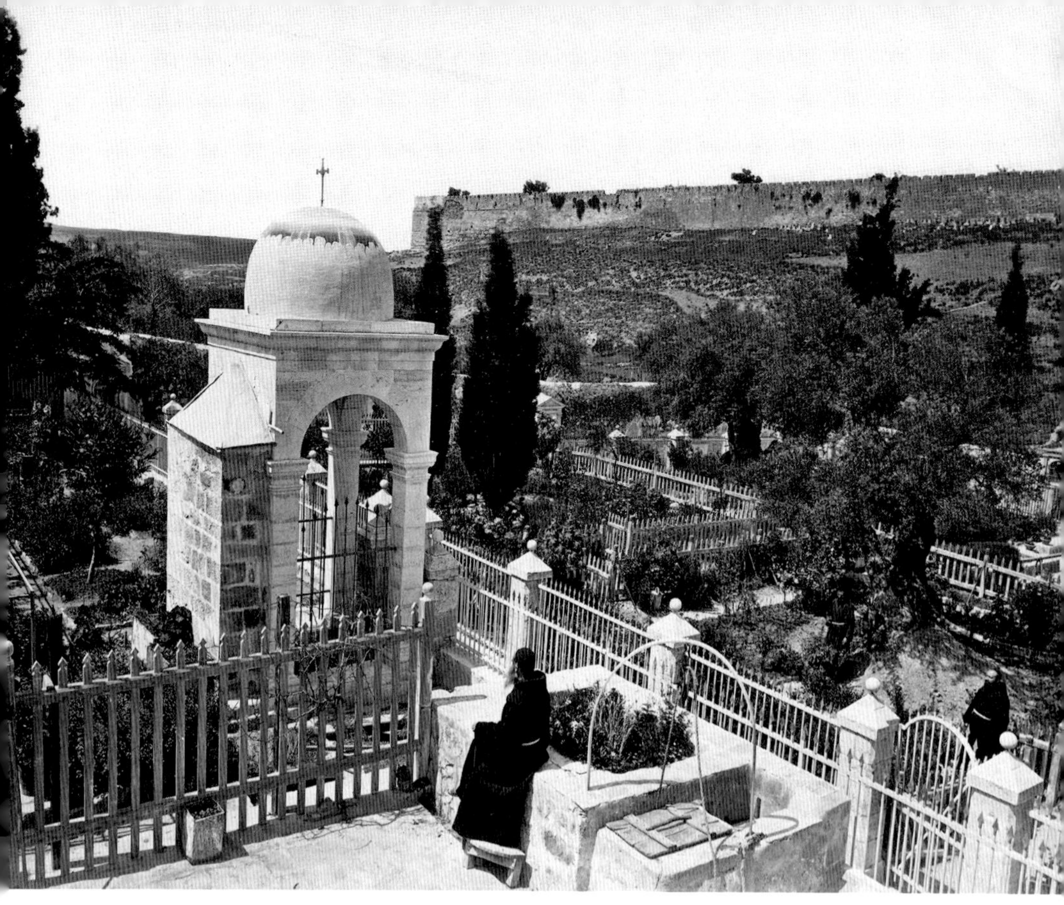

Garden of Gethsemane, Jerusalem, c. 1870 Félix Bonfils

1

Pilgrims and predators, 1850–1917

On 22 June 1865 the great and the good gathered in London for the inaugural meeting of the Palestine Exploration Fund: 'a society for the accurate and systematic investigation of the archaeology, the topography, the geology and physical geography, the manners and customs, of the Holy Land, for biblical illustration'. The society's patron was Queen Victoria, who donated £100—then a considerable sum—to help launch it. The new body had the support of a galaxy of statesmen, scholars, and Anglican clergymen. The meeting's chairman, the archbishop of York, William Thomson, declared in his opening remarks:

> This country of Palestine belongs to *you* and to *me*, it is essentially ours. It was given to the Father of Israel [Abraham] in the words: 'Walk through the land in the length of it, and in the breadth of it, for I will give it unto thee.' *We* mean to walk through Palestine in the length and in the breadth of it, because that land has been given unto us. It is the land from which comes the news of our Redemption. It is the land towards which we turn as the fountain of all our hopes; it is the land to which we may look with as true a patriotism as we do to this dear old England, which we love so

much. [*Cheers*] … It is a sacred duty which we now undertake, to endeavour, by a new crusade, to rescue from darkness and oblivion much of the history of that country, in which we all take so dear an interest.[1]

It is hard to imagine a more forthright expression of Christian imperialism in the Victorian age. In the eyes of the archbishop and his listeners, Christians—and more especially Protestant Christians—had a historic, God-given right to the Holy Land ('that land has been given unto us') and a solemn duty to launch a 'new crusade' to rescue it from 'darkness and oblivion': a civilising mission underpinned by biblical zeal.

In rescuing Palestine they hoped also to rescue Christianity, then under attack from scientific rationalism—Darwin's *The Origin of Species* had appeared in 1859—by producing 'illustration' (meaning concrete evidence) of the Bible's authenticity. To achieve both ends, the fund set in train a series of expeditions to map and excavate Jerusalem and other historic sites in the Holy Land, activities that involved it in political and religious as well as scholarly disputation—and were part and parcel of the West's more active interest and involvement in Palestine in the second half of the nineteenth century. This British role was intensely competitive. Scholarly work was far from disinterested, notwithstanding the assertions of speaker after speaker at the inaugural meeting. As they were well aware, Britain's archaeologists, no less than its diplomats, were constantly on the look-out for opportunities to steal a march on their French, German, and other rivals. With scholarship came power, or the prospect of power.

The bride and the suitors
Palestine's historic misfortune was to be coveted by others who were convinced they had a better right to it than its inhabitants. These devotees of Zion formed a large and motley army:

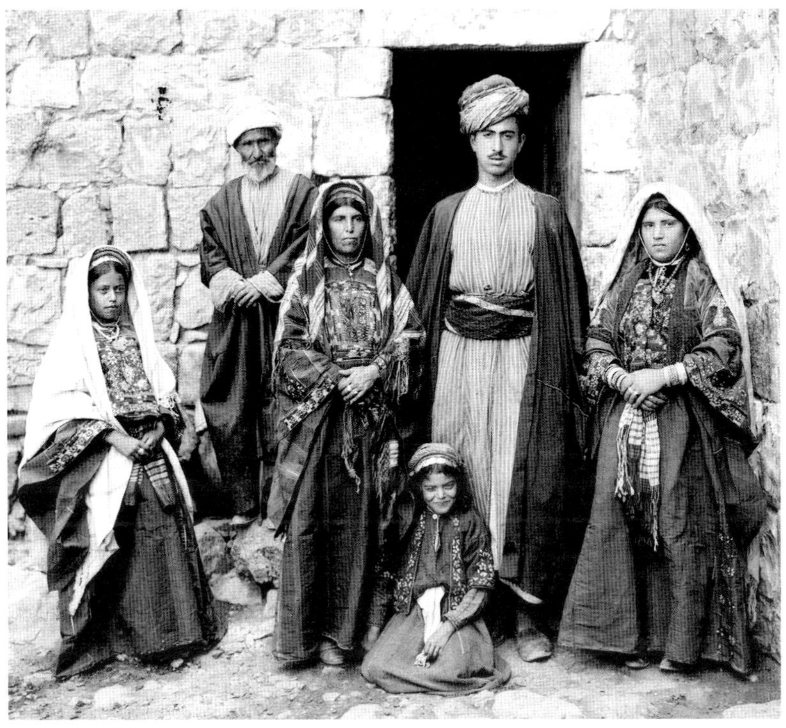

A family in Ramallah, c. 1898-1914   American Colony

clergymen, soldiers, diplomats, and archaeologists from Europe; Orthodox peasants and persecuted Jews from tsarist Russia; born-again fundamentalists from the United States; and an array of zealots, cranks, and misfits from across the globe. Some of them appear in these pages. Many never went to Palestine; for them, it was a country of the mind. Others travelled there but did not stay. A third group came, saw, and conquered. All, in their different ways, were intoxicated with the dream of Jerusalem.

In 1865, as Archbishop Thomson addressed his distinguished audience, the contrast between the Palestine of the imagination and the country's actual condition could not have been more stark. To all outward appearances, it was a small, unprepossessing piece of real estate largely cut off from the outside world. This sliver of land—25,500 square kilometres in area, about the size of Wales—had for three and a half centuries been part of the Ottoman empire. The old idea that it was nothing but desert and desolation is no longer accepted. Nevertheless—with the important exception of the holy places—Palestine in the middle of the nineteenth century had little to commend it. Jerusalem, wrote an English visitor in 1844, was from a practical point of view 'but a paltry inland Eastern town without trade or importance of any kind'.[2]

In Ottoman eyes, Palestine's strategic, economic, and demographic weight—compared with that of Beirut and Damascus to the north and Cairo and Alexandria to the south—was negligible. Its modest export trade consisted of grain, soap (made from olive oil), the much-prized Jaffa orange, and cotton. It was hard to get to. Visitors generally travelled by ship, and when they reached Jaffa (which lacked a serviceable harbour) they found a land with almost no roads, hotels, or amenities. To reach Jerusalem, standing aloof on its hills, required a hard day's journey from the coast. In 1850 the country's population was about 350,000, of whom eighty-five per cent were Muslims, eleven per cent Christians, and four per cent Jews. The majority of the population were Arab *fellahin* (peasants) who lived in some 650 villages and worked the land of local or absentee owners.[3] Village life was close-knit, with a strong sense of loyalty to family and faith. But disease and illiteracy were widespread, and the *fellahin* often struggled with debt. Education was the privilege of a small élite of officials, merchants, and landowners who lived in the coastal towns (Jaffa, Haifa, Acre, Gaza) or in the urban centres of the hilly interior (Jerusalem and Nablus). Prominent families sent their sons abroad to be educated at the

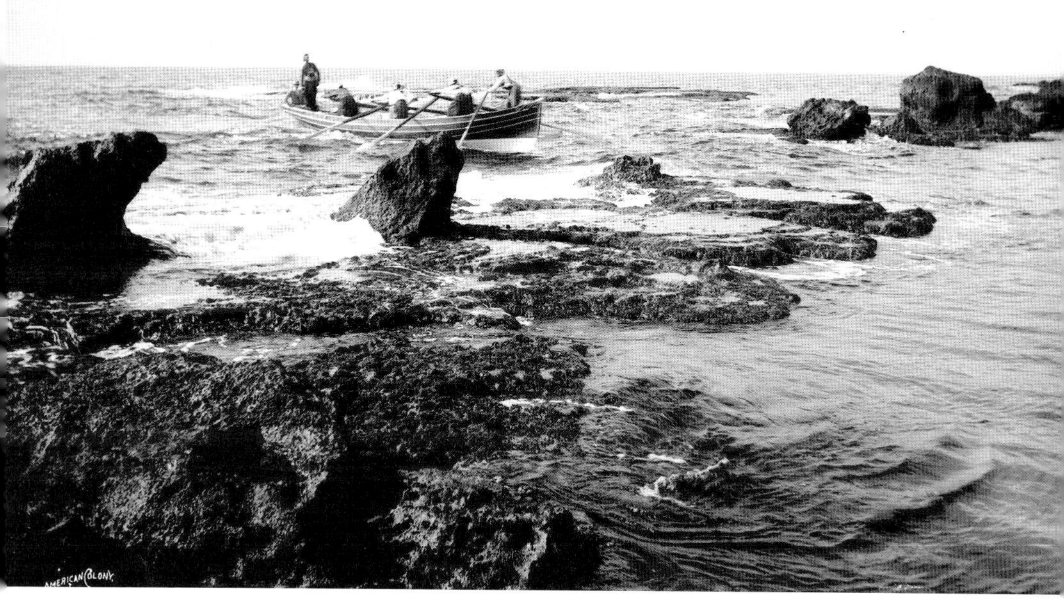

The rocky coast at Jaffa, c. 1898   American Colony

ancient Islamic university of al-Azhar in Cairo or, later in the century, at the new secular universities of Beirut and Istanbul.

The Ottoman Turks had ruled Palestine, as they had ruled much of the Middle East, since the early sixteenth century. Sultan Selim the Grim had conquered Jerusalem in 1517, and his son Suleiman the Magnificent had renovated the city and rebuilt its walls, which had largely been destroyed during the Crusades. The city's history of more than three millennia reflected in microcosm the ambitions, rivalries, and passions of

17

the three great monotheistic religions. For the Jews, it was the city of King David, who had made it his capital around 1000 BC, and the site of the Temple built by his son Solomon (and rebuilt by Herod the Great) which the Romans burnt to the ground in AD 70. For the Christians, it was the city of Jesus's crucifixion and resurrection—a site marked, or so it was believed, by the Church of the Holy Sepulchre inaugurated by the Emperor Constantine in 335.

For the Muslims, who conquered Palestine in the seventh century, Jerusalem was the city of the Haram al-Sharif, or Noble Sanctuary, the 35-acre platform (site of the destroyed Jewish Temple) on which stood Jerusalem's most distinctive landmark, the Dome of the Rock: the faithful believed that, from here, the Prophet Muhammad had ascended into heaven. For Muslims and Christians alike, the city was the focus and prize of the Crusades, the series of wars lasting almost two centuries (1095-1291) during which Europe's Catholic knights established the Latin Kingdom of Jerusalem—a triumph reversed when the renowned Muslim commander Saladin recaptured the city in 1187. From ancient times until 1917, Jerusalem was conquered thirty-five times. It was the common characteristic of those who loved and exalted the Holy City that they built, destroyed, and rebuilt it in a cycle of devotion, zealotry, and violence.[4]

The return of the West

Under Turkish rule, Palestine was not a distinct entity but part of the province of Syria. It was ruled by a handful of Turkish officials and local proxies who kept order, collected taxes, and acted as recruiting-sergeants for the Ottoman army. There were revolts in the eighteenth and nineteenth centuries, usually against conscription and taxation.

A number of developments rekindled Western interest in

Palestine. The first was Napoleon's invasion of Egypt in 1798, which was designed to challenge Britain's position in the Middle East. The expedition ended in failure, but on their way home French troops laid siege to Acre, which was stoutly defended by its governor, Ahmad al-Jazzar. For a moment it looked as if Napoleon had designs on the Holy Land. The moment passed, but it helped put Palestine on the map as a pawn in the game of big-power rivalry in the region.

The second development came in 1831, when Muhammad Ali, the governor of Egypt, broke his ties of loyalty to the Ottoman sultan and sent an army under his son Ibrahim into Syria and Palestine. The period of Egyptian occupation, though much resented by the people of Palestine who saw their sons press-ganged into the Egyptian army, ushered in important changes. In a bid to secure European support, Ibrahim banned discrimination against Christians and Jews, giving them greater security and allowing missionaries more freedom to operate. He also permitted foreign powers to establish consulates in Jerusalem. The first to do so was Britain in 1838. Others followed suit: France, Austria, Prussia, Russia, Italy, and in 1857 the United States.

Egyptian rule ended in 1840 after Muhammad Ali and Ibrahim overreached themselves and threatened Istanbul itself, prompting Britain and France to intervene to rein them in. Ottoman control was restored. But the Egyptian occupation of Syria and Palestine was nevertheless a turning-point which opened up the area to Western influence and Western penetration. The new rights and privileges won by outside powers, and by local Christians and Jews, were maintained when Ottoman rule resumed. Turkish officials and local Muslims resented this intrusion but were powerless to prevent it.

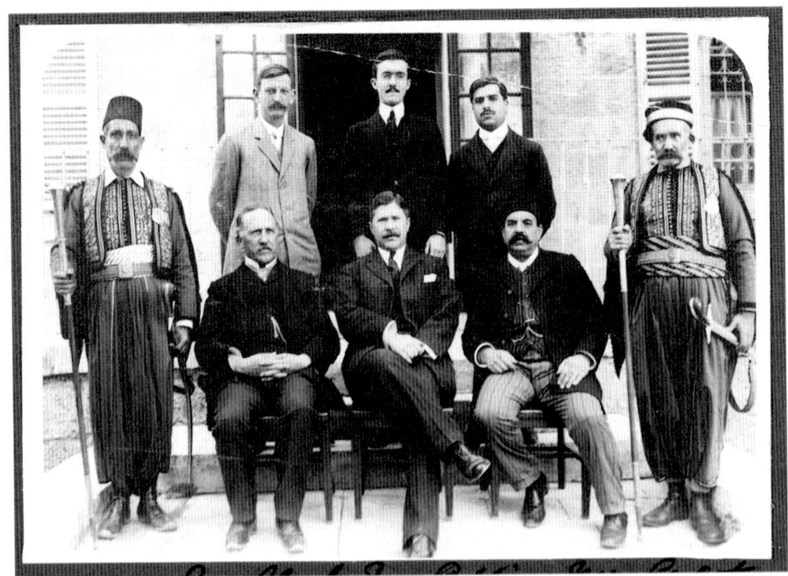

William Coffin, the US consul, centre, with two kavasses (guards), c. 1910

The eagles gather

The age of the consuls began. The West's representatives had a pronounced sense of their own importance, parading through the streets of Jerusalem preceded by elaborately-dressed guards known as kavasses. Through a process of creeping aggrandisement, the consuls extended the rights which Western powers had originally gained under the Capitulations, a series of treaties dating from the sixteenth century under which the Ottomans had granted foreigners immunity from taxation and from the law. Strictly speaking, the consuls were allowed to extend protection only to their own nationals; in practice, they ran much wider networks of protégés whose rights they jealously guarded.

By the middle of the century they had acquired 'the status of virtual colonial governors, each exercising power over his own nationals, institutions, and protected persons, each waging an unceasing struggle against both the Ottoman government and rivals in the consular corps'.[5] In the words of Mrs Finn, the wife of the British consul, 'Thus the eagles were gathering together, or, as the natives express it, the seven nations had come to take possession of Jerusalem.'[6]

Turkish rule was undoubtedly, as Western observers never ceased to point out, harsh, inefficient, and corrupt. But occasionally the tables are turned and we get a glimpse of what Turkish governors thought of these troublesome foreigners.

> Imagine a great city [declared the governor of Acre in 1851] where a hundred thousand individuals are outside the framework of local laws; there isn't a thief, a murderer or a delinquent who does not succeed in putting himself under the protection of some consulate or other. There are twenty police forces which cancel one another out; yet it is the pasha [the Turkish governor] who is supposed to be responsible.[7]

To the frustration of Turkish officials, foreign powers set themselves up as protectors of the country's mosaic of Christian communities—France and Italy of the Catholics; Britain and Prussia of the Protestants; Russia and Greece of the Orthodox, the largest and oldest Christian denomination. (With the addition of Armenians, Copts, Ethiopians, and others, there were some seventeen Christian sects in all.) Political and religious interests were intertwined. France, seeing itself as heir to the Crusaders, aspired to hegemony in the eastern Mediterranean, and to advance its political ambitions promoted itself as guardian of the Catholics of the East. Catholics became involved in a sometimes comic, sometimes sinister, game of one-upmanship with both the Orthodox and the Protestants. Meanwhile the Russian tsars championed Orthodox Christianity and sponsored the annual pilgrimage of thousands of devout Russian peasants to the Holy Land.

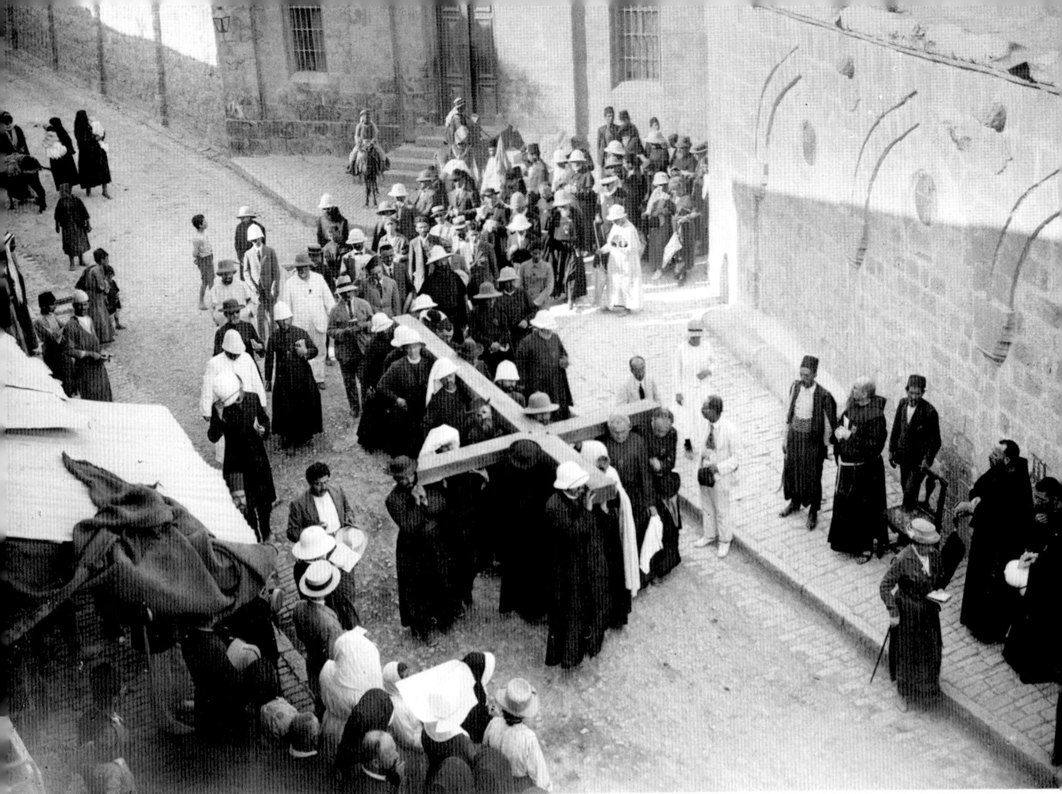

Pilgrims in the Via Dolorosa, Jerusalem, early 1900s

Alarmed by the strength of the position the French and the Russians had established, Britain and Prussia felt the need to catch up. In 1841, at the urging of missionaries and evangelicals, they joined forces to establish an Anglo-Prussian bishopric in Jerusalem. This seemingly odd institution was designed to give Protestantism an institutional base in the Holy Land. In 1849 the first Protestant church was consecrated within the walls of the Old City. An obvious problem, however, was that the number of indigenous Protestants was very small. Hence one of the prime objects of the bishopric was the conversion of the Jews. In Protestant minds the idea of the 'restoration of the Jews', who it was proposed should settle in Palestine under some form of British protection, was the product of both millenarian visions and imperialist designs. Evangelicals were convinced that the return of the Jews, and their conversion to Christianity, were the necessary prelude to Christ's Second Coming. For them, the Jews were to be the instruments of the divine plan. For the more worldly Lord Palmerston—who, as foreign secretary, had authorised the establishment of the British consulate in Jerusalem—they were to be the instruments of British policy. The aim of both bishopric and consulate was to create a community of loyal protégés in the Holy Land—made up of Protestants and converted Jews—and thereby counter the ambitions of tsarist Russia and Catholic France.

In the event, the number of Jewish converts was negligible. The early dreams of Jewish settlement under British patronage came to nothing; but they foreshadowed what was to come.

The bridgehead

Jerusalem's parochial quarrels could on occasion provide the pretext for war. In 1847 the disappearance of a silver star at the Church of the Nativity in Bethlehem escalated into a fierce quarrel between France and Russia, each claiming religious pre-eminence in Palestine. Tsar Nicholas I, demanding the right to protect all Orthodox Christians in the Ottoman empire, invaded the territory of the Turkish sultan, Abdul-Mejid—whom Britain and France (burying for the moment their perennial differences) rushed to defend. This resulted in the Crimean war of 1853-56 which, for the time being, fended off the Russian threat and the danger of Ottoman collapse.

But relying on infidel powers to secure his survival came at a price: Abdul-Mejid felt obliged to repay them by issuing the decree of 1856 known as the Hatt-i Humayün. This was part of a wider series of reforms—the Tanzimat, or Reorganisation—which were designed to strengthen the empire and make its administration more efficient. The decree promised equal rights to Christians and Jews. In practice this meant that churches were allowed for the first time to ring their bells, non-Muslims to visit the Haram al-Sharif, and foreigners to buy land. The big powers were not slow to take advantage of the decree. They bought land in and around Jerusalem's walled city and built convents, schools, and hospitals. There was a construction boom and land prices shot up.

Palestine entered an era of greater economic growth and increasing foreign interference. Between 1850 and 1880 the area of orange cultivation around Jaffa quadrupled; by 1873 there were 420 plantations producing more than 33 million oranges a year.[8] At the same time foreign powers—principally Europe and Russia, and increasingly the United States—established a bridgehead they were never to relinquish. One means of gaining influence was proselytisation, as European and American missionaries stepped up their activities. Since attempting to convert Muslims was fraught with danger and was forbidden by the Ottoman authorities, the missionaries focused their efforts on Jews and Orthodox Christians, stirring up a hornet's nest of opposition as they did so.

A second was archaeology. As foreign archaeologists descended on Palestine, it became a laboratory of biblical investigation. The Palestine Exploration Fund sent specialists to produce maps and excavate historic sites. (The maps came in handy when Britain invaded Palestine during the First World War.) Reporting in 1871 on the fund's activities, a Christian weekly in New York published an article which captured the spirit of the time, entitled 'The Crusade of the Nineteenth Century':

Right: *Jews at the Western, or Wailing, Wall, early 1900s* American Colony

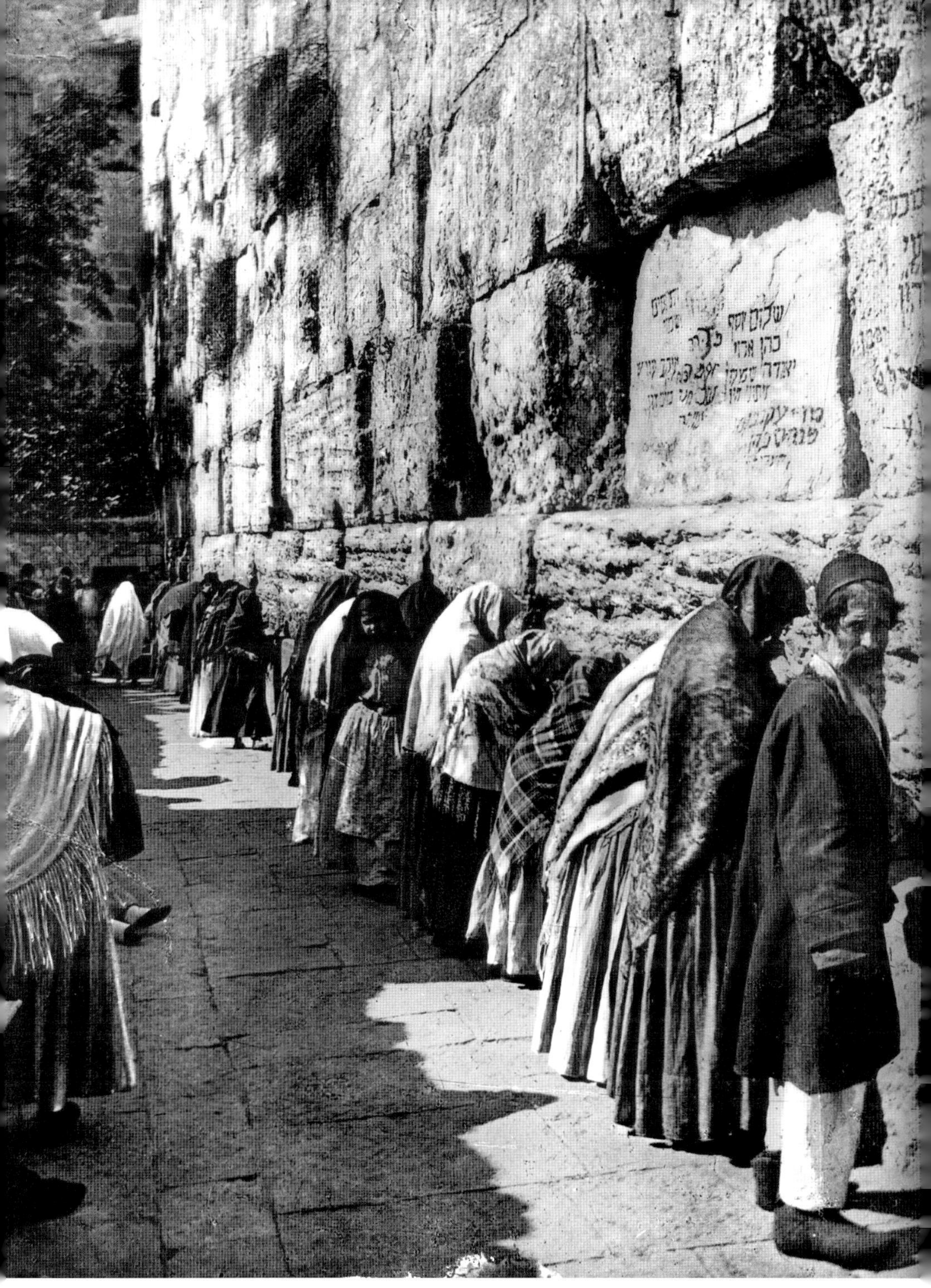

> In the twelfth century [the church] armed itself with sword and
> spear to wrest the city where Jesus Christ was crucified and buried,
> from the unholy hands of the infidel Moslem. In the nineteenth
> century it arms itself with sextant, and theodolite, and compass,
> to wrest from lying priests, and patriarchs, and effendis, the truth
> which the rubbish of ages and the false reverence of superstition
> combine to conceal.[9]

The idea of using what today we would call soft power to 'wrest'
Palestine from the 'infidel Moslem' (and, for that matter, from
non-Protestant Christians) was popular on both sides of the
Atlantic.

A third means of gaining influence was Christian settlement,
though the numbers involved were relatively small. Pious
German Protestants, known as Templers, set up colonies near
Jaffa and Haifa in the 1860s which were admired by foreign
visitors for their neatness and modern agricultural techniques.
Their high-handed behaviour was resented by local Arabs and
Ottoman officials.[10]

Around the same time, Palestine was opened up to popular
tourism. In 1869 Thomas Cook, a young Baptist lay preacher
from Leicester, began offering 'Eastern Tours' to Egypt and
Palestine. Everything was laid on. 'Instead of suspect Oriental
food, Cook's tourists had English ham and Yorkshire bacon,
pickles, potted salmon and Liverpool sardines.'[11]

Travel to the East, whether for religious or secular purposes,
was encouraged by the popularity of painters such as David
Roberts and Edward Lear and writers such as Mark Twain. Twain
realised that the whole phenomenon of Holy Land pilgrimage
was ripe for satire; the result was his irreverent travelogue
The Innocents Abroad (1869). This was Palestine for everyman:
Twain presented himself as an ordinary, down-to-earth traveller,
unwilling to be fooled by the fraud and artifice of a religious
package tour.

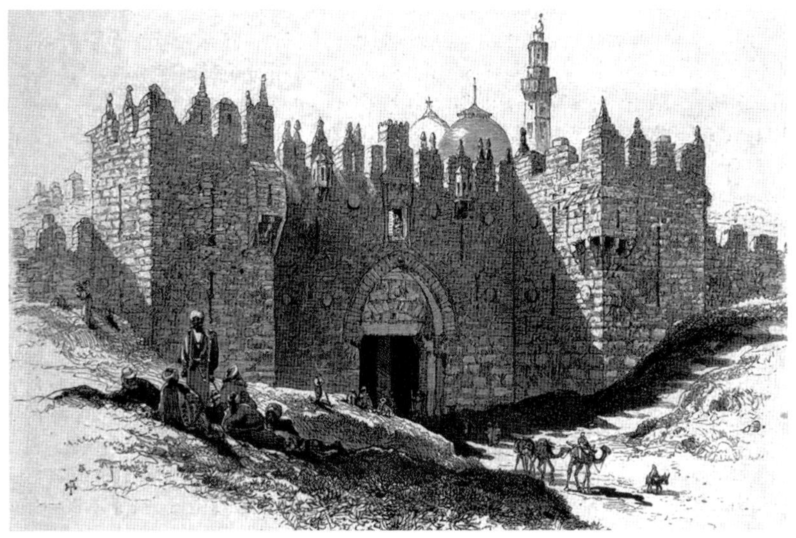

Damascus Gate, Jerusalem, c. 1880   Harry Fenn, *Pictureque Palestine*

The book was highly successful, but it was one of a kind. It did nothing to dethrone the giants of Palestine studies—men such as William McClure Thomson, an American Protestant missionary who had arrived in Beirut in 1833 during the Egyptian occupation and spent twenty-five years in Syria and Palestine. In 1859 his best-known work, *The Land and the Book*, was published in New York in two volumes comprising more than 1,100 pages with over 200 illustrations. Written in the form of a conversation between two travellers, the work was aimed at the general public rather than at scholars. It is encyclopaedic in scope, describing not only biblical sites but flora and fauna and the 'manners and customs' of the people. Thomson was interested in everything, from Palestine's bananas 'with their extraordinary leaves a dozen feet long, and drooping like great pendent ears', to the tax gatherers 'who eat up the people as they eat bread'. Steeped as he was in the beliefs and prejudices of a Protestant missionary, he had nevertheless walked (and ridden) the length and breadth of a country he knew intimately. The book became a runaway bestseller in the United States and Britain.[12]

Imitations followed. One of the most successful was *Picturesque Palestine, Sinai and Egypt,* published serially in New York and London from 1881 to 1883. Edited by Sir Charles Wilson, famous through his work for the Palestine Exploration Fund, and five years in the making, the work comprised some 900 pages and, outdoing Thomson, more than 600 'engravings on steel and wood'. These were from drawings commissioned from the American artist John Douglas Woodward and the British-born Harry Fenn, two highly-regarded landscape artists and masters of the 'picturesque'. (The text, written by American and British contributors, was scholarly and a little dull.)

Artists regarded their work as being superior to photography, but this did nothing to stop the growing popularity of the new medium. The earliest photographic image of Palestine dates from 1839; and in the following decades, as technical quality improved, photographs of the Holy Land were much in demand in Europe and America. At first visiting photographers showed little interest in the country's inhabitants. Caught up as they were in archaeology and the study of the Bible, they regarded the Holy Land as essentially a landscape with ruins. Leading photographers gained the benefit of royal patronage. In 1862, at the bidding of Queen Victoria, the well-known landscape photographer Francis Bedford accompanied her son Prince Albert (the future Edward VII) on a tour of the East. (The hope apparently was that some of the sanctity of the Holy Land would rub off on the playboy prince.) Bedford was given special permission to photograph inside the Haram al-Sharif,

Right: *Pulpit in the Haram al-Sharif, Jerusalem, 1862*   Francis Bedford

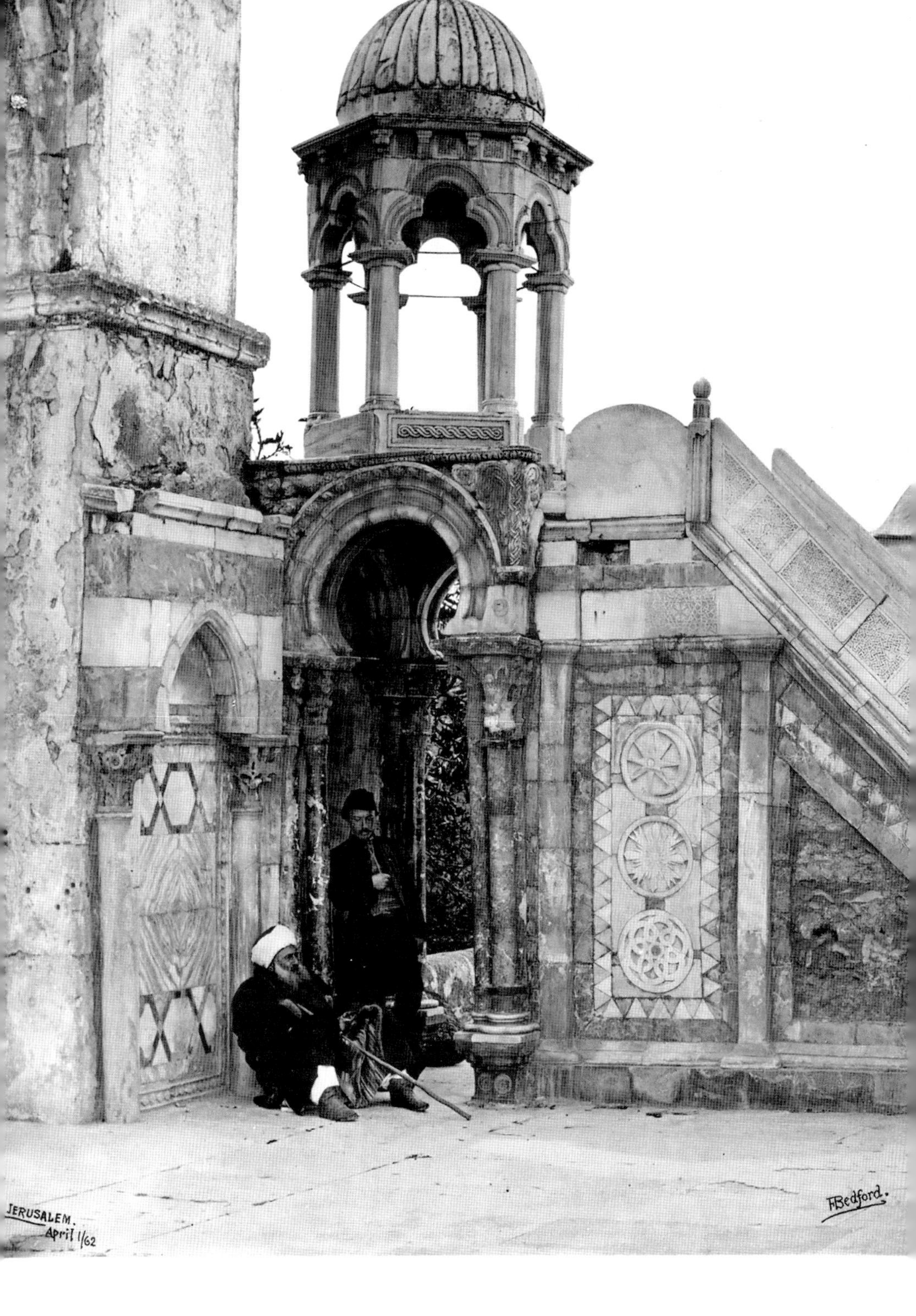

JERUSALEM.
April 1/62
F.Bedford.

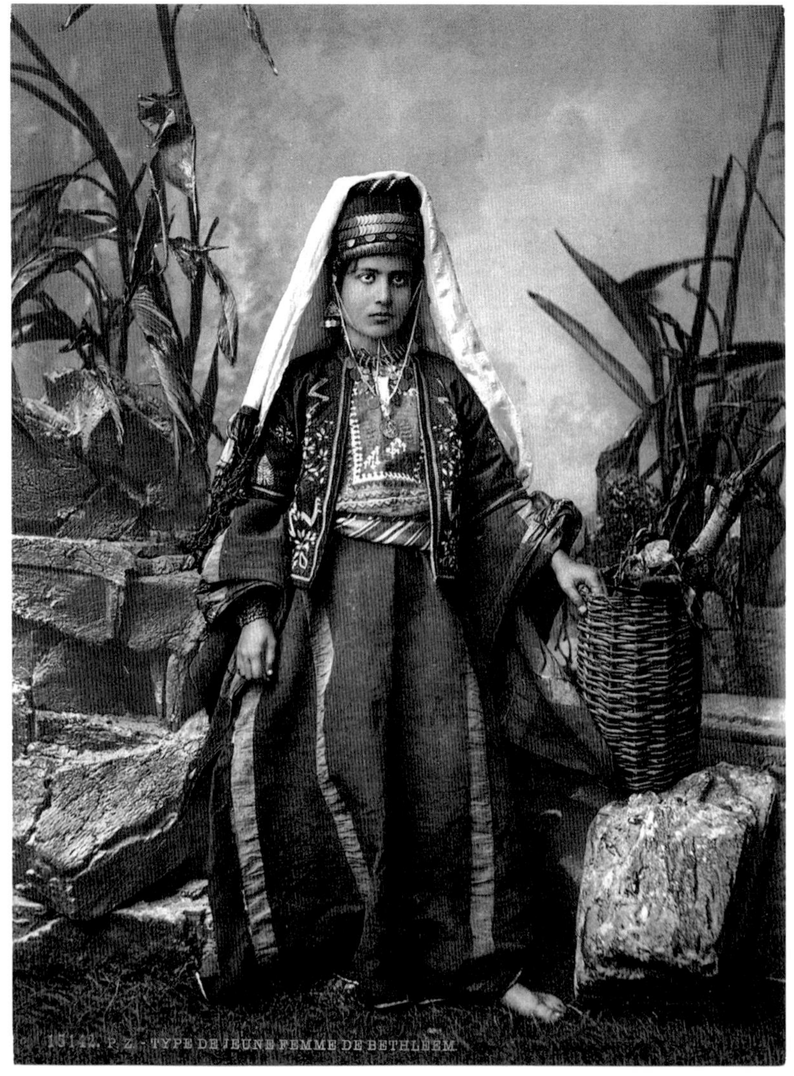

'Young Woman of Bethlehem', c. 1870 Félix Bonfils

something hitherto forbidden. When published on his return, his work was instantly popular.

But when they turned their attention to the people of Palestine, Western photographers—in particular the best-known and most commercially successful of them, the Frenchman Félix Bonfils— produced a set of crude caricatures replete with the cultural prejudices of the age. They focused on certain 'types' (a favourite word) such as exotically-dressed females, bedouin tribesmen, and the dragomen, or interpreters, who acted as local guides for travellers. Moreover, many of their images were staged in the studio, using paid models. Bonfils' highly-exoticised 'Young Woman of Bethlehem' is as fake as the stage props which surround her.

Bonfils and his family had settled in Beirut, where his studio produced an endless stream of such portraits, many of which were sent to Zurich for colour-processing, which enhanced their appeal. It should be added that his best work—enshrined in his five-volume *Souvenirs d'Orient* (1877-78)—was of an entirely different order. His photographs of Jerusalem's churches and mosques and pilgrim sites are among the iconic images of nineteenth-century Palestine.[13]

Court photographers

Abdul-Hamid II, who was Ottoman sultan from 1876 to 1909, was fascinated by photography. 'Every picture is an idea,' he declared to his chief secretary. 'One picture can evoke political and psychological significances which a hundred written pages could not convey. I therefore derive more benefit from photographs than from written papers.'

One potential handicap for a Muslim sovereign was that religious conservatives deemed it blasphemous to produce images of the human form (a view shared by many religious Jews). Perhaps for this reason, the early local photographers were predominantly Armenians or members of other Christian minorities. It is an irony of history that the first patrons of indigenous Middle East photography were the Ottoman sultans and that their principal photographers were members of a Christian minority which was to become the victim of genocide.

The patron-client relationship began in 1863 when Abdul-Hamid's uncle, Sultan Abdul-Aziz, appointed three Armenian brothers—known as Abdullah Frères—as his court photographers. He was conscious that the royal families of Europe were using this new medium to enhance their prestige. The sultan and his young nephew witnessed this for themselves when—in an unprecedented encounter with the infidel world—they visited Paris, London, and Vienna in 1867. During the visit the 25-year-old Abdul-Hamid had his picture taken by Queen Victoria's photographer, W. & D. Downey. The experience seems to have stayed with him. After becoming sultan in 1876 and embarking on an ambitious programme of modernisation, he commissioned a string of photographers to record its achievements in meticulous detail.

The lion's share of the project was carried out by Abdullah Frères, who travelled the length and breadth of the empire photographing palaces, bridges, clock-towers (including those in Jerusalem and Jaffa), military colleges, and schools for girls as well as boys—symbols of both Ottoman power and Ottoman modernity. To the work of Abdul-Hamid's photographers were added collections donated by foreigners (including Bonfils), until the sultan's unique photo-library comprised over 30,000 prints. In 1893 Abdul-Hamid sent selections—each made up of 1,800 photographs in fifty-one ornately-bound albums—to Britain, France, Germany, and the United States. (The British volumes are housed in the British Library; the American albums in the Library of Congress.)

Abdul-Hamid had been quick to grasp that photography could be a valuable tool of security as well as of propaganda:

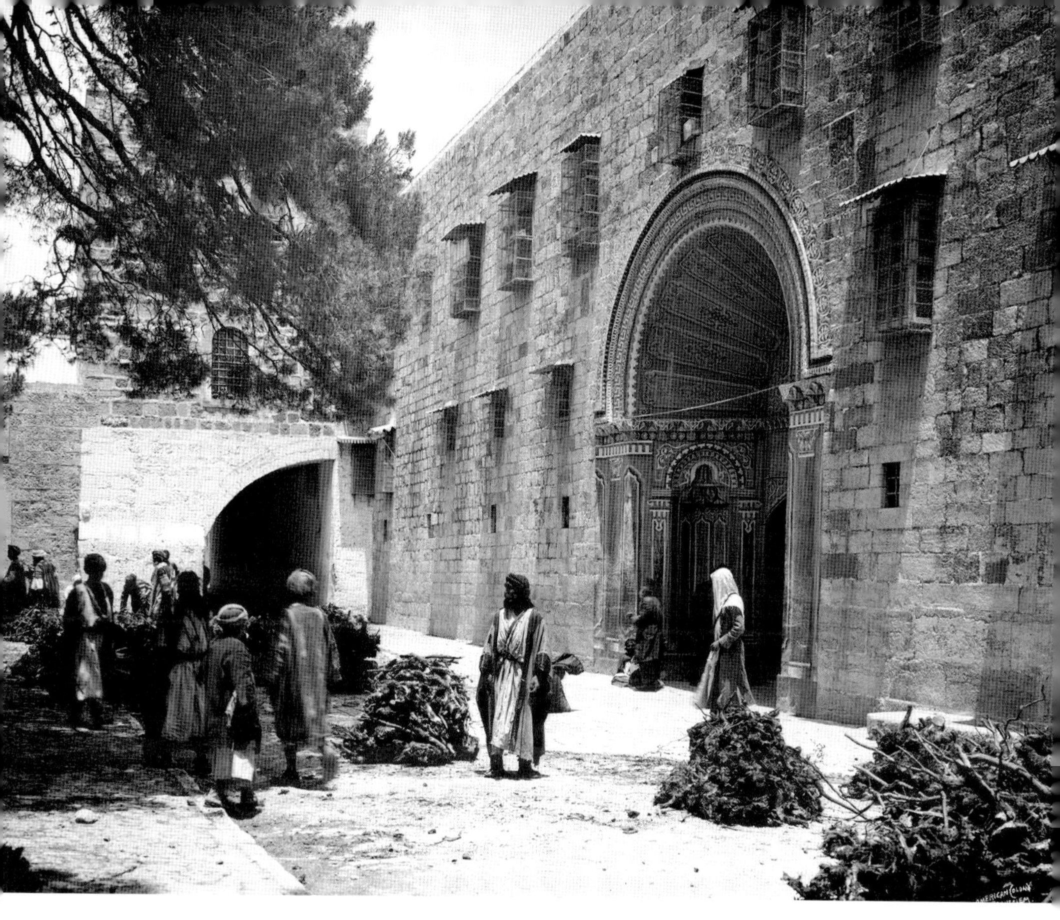

The Armenian Convent in Jerusalem, early 1900s   American Colony

he insisted that photographs should be used in criminal files and in the selection and promotion of officials. For this most reclusive of rulers, fearful of assassination and conspiracy, photography was an indispensable means of intelligence.

The situation of the Armenian brothers could be precarious. Twice they earned the sultan's displeasure: when they photographed a Russian general whose army had just inflicted a humiliating defeat on the Turks, and when it was alleged that women attending their studio were improperly dressed.[14]

Armenian and other local Christian photographers

established studios in Istanbul, Cairo, Damascus, and Beirut, mostly specialising in studio portraits for tourists and the well-to-do. Only gradually did the trend spread to Jerusalem and Jaffa. The first studio in Palestine was established in the 1860s in the compound of the Armenian Convent in Jerusalem, under the aegis of the patriarch, himself a keen photographer. Among his pupils was Garabed Krikorian, who opened his own studio in the city in 1884. Rivals soon appeared—notably Krikorian's former protégé Khalil (or Carl) Raad, a Lebanese Christian—but these early photographers struggled to make their work commercially viable.[15]

Meanwhile Jerusalem's skyline began to change dramatically. The city was no longer confined within its ancient walls. Residential areas sprang up outside the Old City, alongside spectacular structures symbolising the newly assertive presence of the big powers. In the early 1860s the tsars built the 17-acre Russian Compound which housed a consulate, a hospital, an imposing church, and hostels for over 3,000 pilgrims—a little Moscow in the heart of the Holy Land. Other giant buildings followed, including the Russian church of St Mary Magdalene on the Mount of Olives; the hospice of Notre Dame, representing the power of Catholic France; and, a little later, St George's Cathedral and school, products of Anglican Britain. Jerusalem, one consul remarked, was becoming a European city.[16]

The foreign powers saw themselves as a force for modernisation and progress, but they were also a force for discord, vying for power and influence with the Turks and with one another. Yet for all their rivalries and disputes—memorably described by Edward Lear as 'Jerusalem squabblepoison'—they were united in a certain attitude of mind, a conviction that Palestine really belonged not to the Turks or the Arabs, who were unworthy of the charge, but to them.

This attitude found striking expression in a popular book,

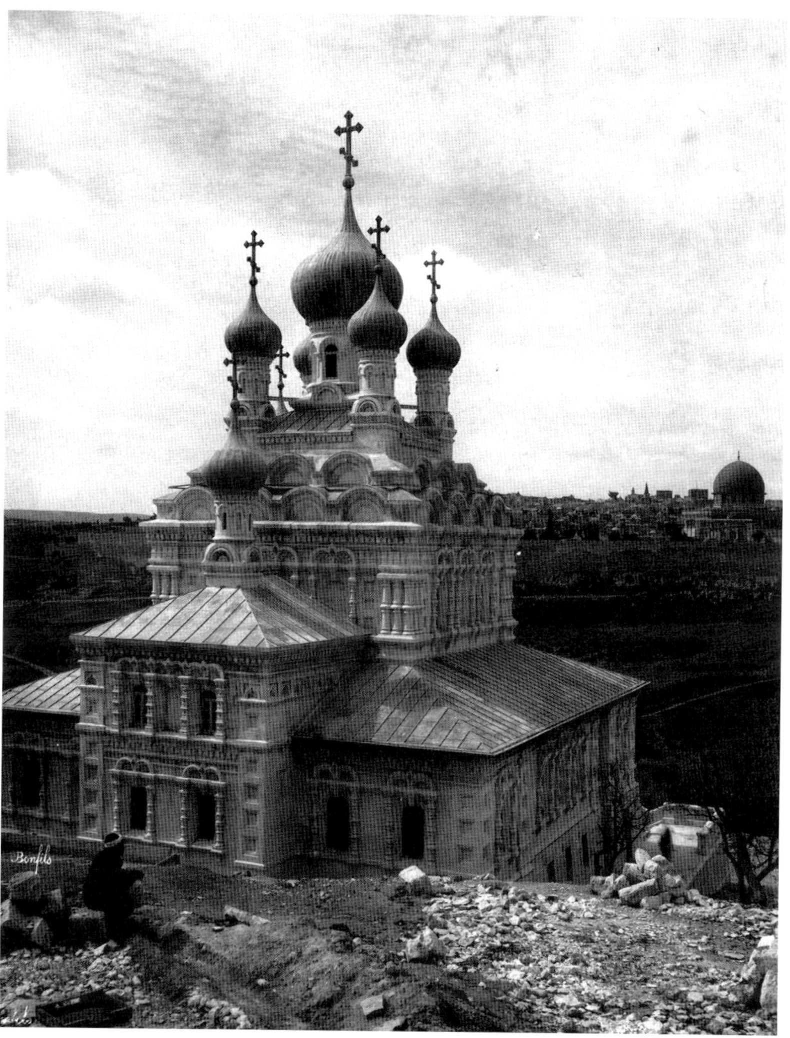

Russian church, Mount of Olives, c. 1870   Félix Bonfils

Underground Jerusalem, published in 1876 by Charles Warren, a young captain in the Royal Engineers who had spent three years in the Holy Land, from 1867, working for the Palestine Exploration Fund. Commenting on the country's puzzling contradictions, Warren wrote: 'King Consul rules supreme, not over the natives of the city, but over strangers; but yet these strangers for the most part are the rightful owners; the natives, for the most part, are usurpers.'[17]

The farmers from Sweden

In fact, whatever Europeans might have thought, the Ottoman Turks were beginning to change the face of Palestine. In the years leading up to the First World War, they built roads and schools and a railway—albeit a slow, single-track railway—from Jaffa to Jerusalem, greatly shortening the journey from the coast. In 1905 they linked Palestine to the Hijaz railway, which brought pilgrims from Damascus to the holy places of Mecca and Medina. They did so for their own reasons. To hold onto their fraying empire, they needed to improve its weak infrastructure and poor communications. At the same time they were anxious to present a more modern and progressive face to their European critics, who constantly carped at their negligent custodianship of the Holy Land.

As the empire weakened and crumbled and the power of the consuls in Jerusalem grew stronger, Ottoman officials became frustrated at their loss of control. Palestine was becoming harder to manage as more and more foreigners arrived from different parts of the world to settle there—all of them demanding consular protection. These now included an esoteric sect which, although dogged by dispute and scandal, was to bear witness to the transformation of Palestine over the next half-century, and which through its gifted photographers was to influence the way in which Palestine was perceived in the wider world.

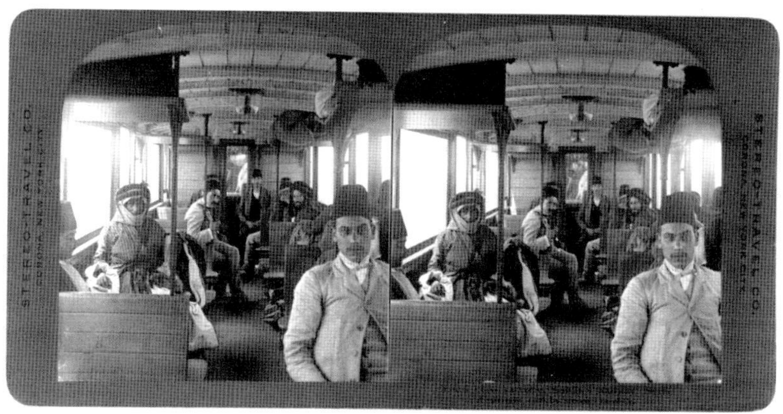

The sultan's railway, third-class carriage, 1904   Photographer unknown

On 23 July 1896 the 15-year-old Lewis Larsson left the village of Nås in central Sweden with his four sisters and widowed mother to make the long and arduous pilgrimage to Palestine. They were part of a group of farming families, pious Protestants who had convinced themselves that the Second Coming was at hand. After selling their farms, the thirty-seven Swedes—fifteen adults and twenty-two children—loaded their belongings (including farm implements and sacks of potatoes) onto a dozen carts and wagons, and set off on their journey. When they boarded a ship bound for Antwerp, most of them had never seen the sea before. From Antwerp they embarked on a three-week voyage to Jaffa, and from there travelled by train on the newly-opened line to Jerusalem.

Their object was to join the American Colony, an eccentric, close-knit, intensely devout group founded fifteen years earlier by an American lawyer from Chicago, Horatio Spafford, and his Norwegian-born wife Anna. Their life in the United States had been dogged by debt and personal tragedy. (Their four daughters had drowned at sea.) When Horatio died in 1888, the charismatic blue-eyed Anna took over the colony and ran it as a religious tyranny.

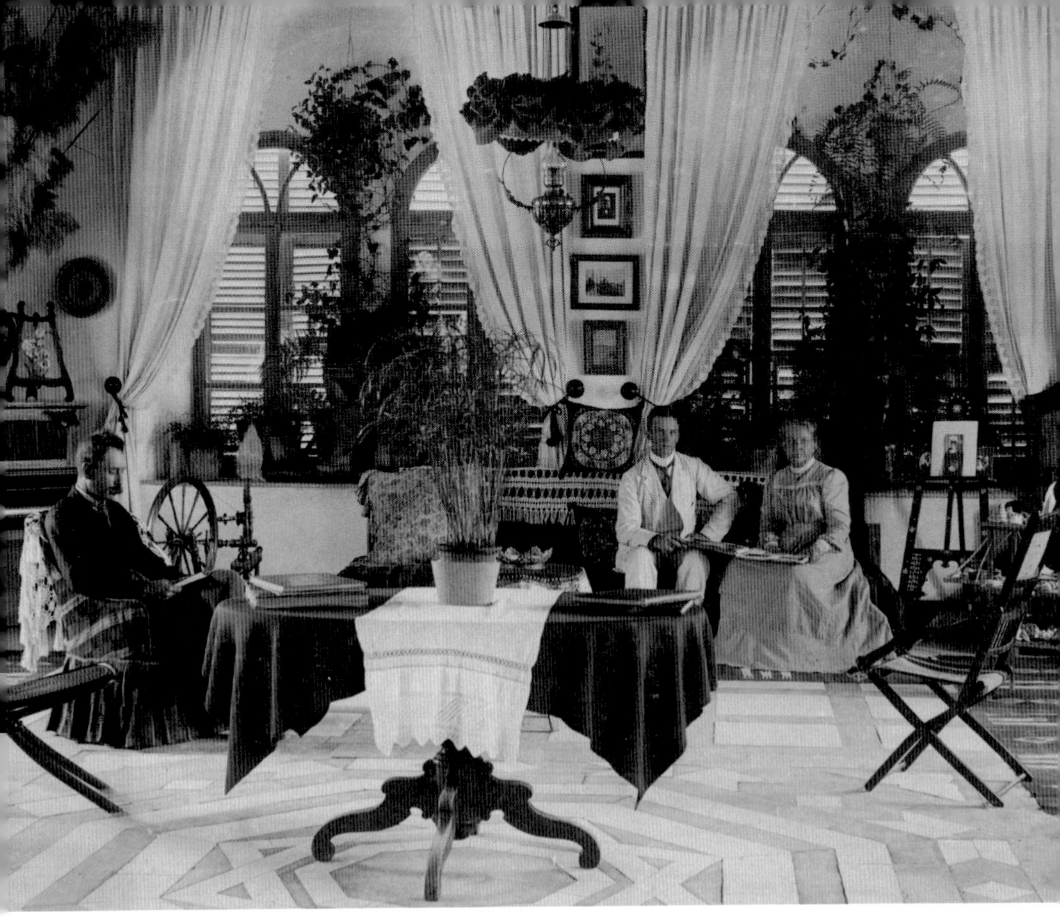

The salon: on the right, Lewis Larsson and Anna Spafford, c. 1900

The colonists' first home in Jerusalem had been an Arab
house rented in the old walled city, but to accommodate the
newcomers they moved to a larger building outside the walls,
with a lovely courtyard, thick walls, and an elegant first-floor
salon. (This building, today, is the American Colony Hotel.) But
while Anna and her daughters lived in some style, the Swedes
found that, after handing over all their assets to the colony,
they had to work hard without pay. They also had to break old
ties. Wives were separated from husbands, and children from

parents. There was a strict rule of celibacy, and no new marriages were allowed. They had to abandon Swedish and speak English. Many fell ill but were denied doctors; six died of malaria and other diseases in the first few months. Anna—whom they were required to call Mother—had complete control; she even read all incoming and outgoing mail. To oppose her was to risk ostracisation or expulsion.

The colonists were part of a wider movement of Protestant millennialism which had taken root in Europe and the United States in the nineteenth century. But even among evangelical Protestants the Spaffords were unconventional: they believed that Christians had a duty to settle in Palestine and prepare for the 'end times' through striving for moral perfection, and convinced themselves that these perfected Christians would be immortal (hence doctors and medicine were unnecessary). They did not believe in hell or the devil. They alienated Jerusalem's missionaries by showing no interest in converting Jews. What's more, Anna believed she had supernatural powers, claiming to receive messages from God which were faithfully recorded and read out every morning to her flock. The colony was involved in a series of disputes with successive American consuls, who believed Anna was holding people against their will, taking their money, and even encouraging sexual immorality. They referred disparagingly to the 'so-called American Colony' (many of whose members were not American) and were not always willing to give it consular support.

If it had been no more than an unconventional religious sect, the colony would probably have collapsed in debt and recrimination. But it was also a kind of NGO, which helped women and children and the sick and the poor, and it was this that endeared it to the people of Jerusalem, whatever they might think of its cranky beliefs and odd behaviour. At the same time, Anna was not averse to making money. The colony rented land

and grew crops, and ran a weaving business, a carpentry shop, a blacksmith's, a bakery, and a souvenir store for tourists. It had plans to open a photographic agency.

The young Lewis Larsson did not embrace the colony's religious ethos. He later recalled the biblical imagery he had imbibed growing up in Sweden: 'As children we understood little of what it was all about … We heard the harps, we saw the powerful arms and flowing beard of God among the clouds. And Jerusalem was a city of gold and mother-of-pearl.'[18] It seems he remained in the colony because he had little choice and because of his new love for the craft that was to make him famous. He was taught the elements of photography by one of Anna's confidants, Elijah Meyers, a 'slightly mad, multilingual Indian Jew from Bombay' who, after converting to Christianity, had arrived at the colony 'clothed in Indian dress with a flowing cloak of finest silk, and his long hair wound into an immense green turban'.[19]

'I work almost daily with photography,' Larsson wrote to his relatives back in Sweden in March 1898. 'We take photographs of all the remarkable places here in this country and sell the pictures to a trading store in town. We have produced around 15,000 photographs this winter, so as you see we've had plenty to do each day.'[20]

The emperor and the sultan

A few months later the little group of photographers had their first big break, with the arrival of an important royal visitor. On 28 October 1898, just two years after Larsson and his family had settled in Jerusalem, the colonists watched an extraordinary spectacle unfold on their doorstep. The German emperor, Kaiser Wilhelm II, grandson of Queen Victoria, rode into Jerusalem on a white horse. With his glittering armour and splendid uniform—he had designed his own distinctive white

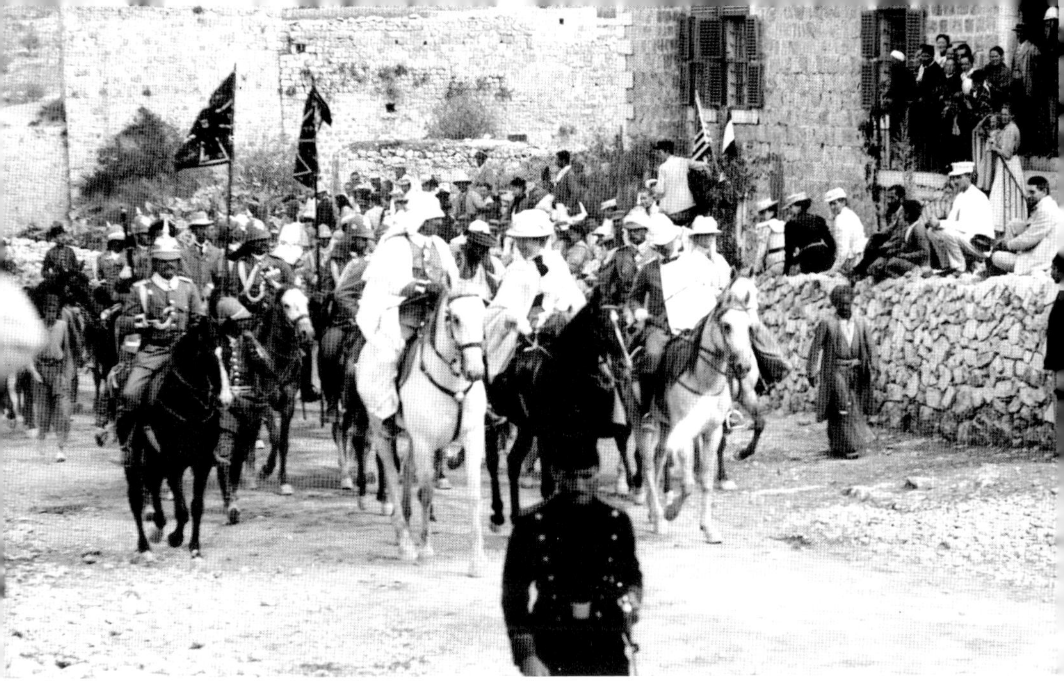

Kaiser Wilhelm passing the American Colony as he entered Jerusalem, 1898

headgear with flowing white veil—he looked like a latter-day Crusader knight.

The kaiser had an entourage of 600 soldiers and twenty-seven senior officials. The travel agent Thomas Cook had supplied him with hundreds of mules, scores of tents, and innumerable translators, servants, and hangers-on. *The Times* reported: 'The superb arrangements for the Emperor's journey to the Holy Land are a triumph of the ingenuity and organisation of Messrs. Cook.' (*Punch*, less charitably, called him 'Cook's Crusader'.)

Wilhelm set up camp in a large tent village on the edge of the walled city. The photographers of the American Colony— together with their rivals, Garabed Krikorian and Khalil Raad— obtained permits to record his triumphal entry and his dizzying round of visits to religious and archaeological sites. Elijah Meyers and his young assistants followed the kaiser's procession accompanied by a 'photo wagon', drawn by two horses, to carry their cumbersome equipment.

After they had taken their pictures, the glass plates were rushed back to the colony, where large numbers of prints were made and posted to newspapers and magazines in London and Berlin, which eagerly awaited them. The colony was soon famous, not as a millennialist cult, but as a successful business enterprise.

The kaiser inaugurated a new Lutheran church, took a polite interest in the affairs of Muslims and Jews, and proclaimed himself 'the knight of peace and labour, interested not in riches but in the healing of souls'. Accompanying the emperor was his wife, Augusta Victoria, and in her honour plans were laid for the construction of a fortress-like building on the Mount of Olives originally designed as a hospice for German visitors. (The Augusta Victoria compound later served as a military headquarters, an official residence, a sanatorium, and finally a hospital.)

Ostensibly about religion, the kaiser's visit was an assertion of German power and influence at a time when the Ottoman empire, under Sultan Abdul-Hamid, was struggling to survive. Abdul-Hamid was deeply ambivalent about the kaiser and his visit. Wilhelm and his wife had begun their Middle East tour in Istanbul as guests of the sultan in his cheerless and elaborately fortified hill-top Yildiz Palace. The kaiser had shown little interest in Abdul-Hamid's lavish gifts, and made no bones about what he was really after: the concession for the Baghdad railway, an ambitious project whose latest phase was designed to link Anatolia to the Gulf. Another (unstated) prize was oil. German geologists, disguised as archaeologists, had informed Wilhelm it was likely there were significant oil deposits in northern Iraq, which was part of the sultan's domain. (Unknown to him, Abdul-Hamid's agents had got hold of the report, so the sultan was under no illusion about Wilhelm's true motives.)[21]

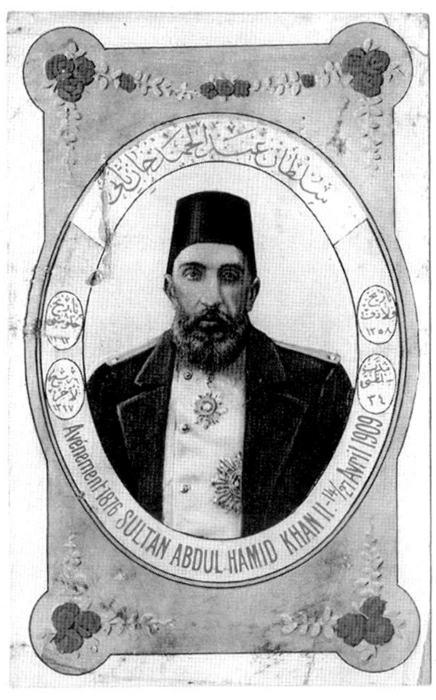

Artist unknown
Sultan Abdul-Hamid, 1909

The two made an odd pair. The bearded, hook-nosed Abdul-Hamid, with dark, heavy-lidded eyes, was gaunt and stooped. (Wilhelm referred to him privately as 'the old spider'.) The young Wilhelm, in contrast, despite having a withered arm, sported martial uniforms and a waxed moustache; and unlike the sultan, who was famously cautious and a master of procrastination, was erratic and impulsive. He was also violently anti-Semitic.

For their own very different reasons, however, the two rulers needed one another. Abdul-Hamid, convinced that Britain and other powers were ganging up on him, wanted a political alliance with Germany and was ready to pay an economic price to get it. (The French ambassador in Istanbul referred scathingly to the German emperor as 'only a commercial traveller who has found in the Sultan the perfect milch cow'.) For his part,

Wilhelm wanted Germany to become a Middle East power and in order to realise his grandiose vision was ready to present himself as the sultan's loyal ally. For both men, the visit to Palestine was highly symbolic.

Mother Russia

The kaiser's Middle East tour and the publicity that attended it were viewed by the other big powers with the deepest misgivings. The last thing they wanted was for Germany to muscle in on a game hitherto dominated by Britain, France, and Russia. The abiding fear of the British and the French was that tsarist Russia would seize Istanbul and the Dardanelles, and so gain access to the Mediterranean. They saw the Ottoman empire, weak and dysfunctional as it was, as a necessary buffer against Russian expansionism.

In Moscow, as in Paris, London, and Berlin, religious and political interests went hand in hand. 'Palestine … is our native land—in which we do not recognise ourselves as foreigners,' declared one nineteenth-century Russian writer, in words which echoed those of Archbishop Thomson in London. 'We must establish our "presence" in the East not politically but through the church,' wrote foreign ministry officials in a report in 1857. 'Neither the Turks nor the Europeans … can refuse us this … Jerusalem is the centre of the world and our mission must be there.'[22] In the eyes of the tsars, the Middle East was not merely a strategic region on their southern flank but the most sacred site of Orthodox Christianity. They saw distinct advantage in promoting themselves as patrons of Orthodoxy (and little disadvantage in pursuing an official policy of anti-Semitism).

For centuries ordinary Russians had had a deep attachment to Christianity and a longing to go on pilgrimage to the Holy Land. From the middle of the nineteenth century, with the advent of steamships sailing from Odessa to Jaffa, the numbers of pilgrims increased significantly. Every year far more came from the tsarist empire to spend Easter in Palestine than from any other country: something the Catholic and Protestant powers observed with disquiet. It was not just that they feared Russian encroachment; they found the Eastern rites—and in particular the age-old Easter ceremony of the Holy Fire—pagan and barbaric.

Most of the Russian pilgrims were poor peasants, men and women, clutching crusts of bread, who often walked hundreds of miles from their villages to catch the boat at Odessa. A young British writer, Stephen Graham, witnessed an elderly Russian trudging through the Holy Land in boots made of birch-bark. He was a 'simple, patriarchal figure ... with long dense hair cut round his head by sheep-shears, and long beard and whiskers ... He was white from head to foot with the dust of the desert.' Far from complaining, the old man remarked, 'Oh, what good is to come [of our pilgrimage] ... if we take no trouble over it?'[23]

The Englishman had joined a group of Russians when their pilgrim ship docked in Istanbul in 1912. Speaking Russian, he managed, remarkably, to pass himself off as one of them. On board their little vessel, 'scarcely bigger than a Thames steamer', were some 500 Russian peasants, dressed as if for a Russian winter.

> The peasants were mostly in sheepskins, and nearly all the time the sun blazed down on them. We had two sharp storms, and the peasants, most of whom had never seen the sea before, were terribly unwell. In one storm, when the masts were broken, the hold where the peasants rolled over one another like corpses, or grasped at one another like madmen, was worse than any imagined pit, the stench worse than any fire.[24]

Graham estimated that sixty per cent of the pilgrims were illiterate. After their ordeal at sea, they found the reality of

Palestine—as did so many foreign visitors—a shock. Jerusalem, wrote Graham, was 'a place where every stone has been commercialised either by tourist agencies or greedy monks'.[25] Like his fellow-pilgrims, he was repelled by 'the loathsome beggary of the East' and by the Turkish soldiers who used whips and rifle-butts to hold back the Easter crowds. (Russians, no less than Western Christians, viewed the 'heathen' Turks and Arabs with the utmost contempt.)

Graham joined a group of a thousand pilgrims who set off from Jerusalem at dawn, led by priests and monks and singing hymns, to walk in procession to the river Jordan.

> They take their death-shrouds to Jordan, and wearing them, bathe in the sacred river. All in white, on the banks where John baptised, they look like the awakened dead on the final Resurrection morning ... They mostly hope to die in the Holy Land ... If indeed they return to their native villages in Russia, it will be to put their affairs in order and await death.[26]

Graham witnessed drunkenness and venality among the

Russian pilgrims in the Jordan, 1899 B. W. Kilburn

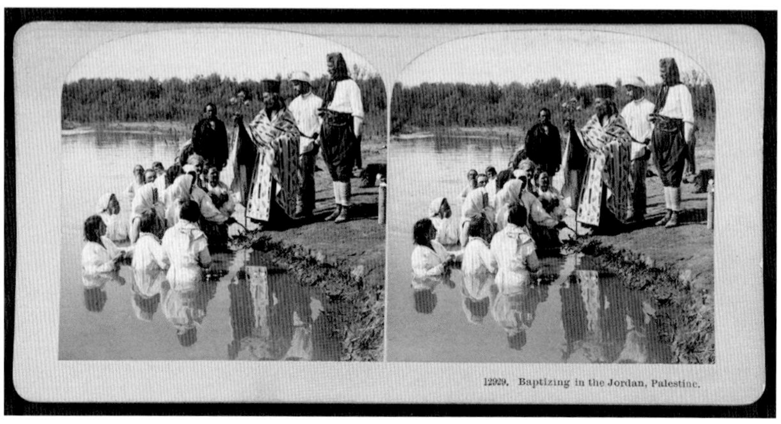

pilgrims, and among the monks who guided and often exploited them. But overall he was struck by their resilience and the intensity of their devotion. He paid tribute to the Russian institution—the Imperial Orthodox Palestine Society, set up under the patronage of the tsars—which had organised their travel and accommodation. Conditions were spartan: in Jerusalem, Graham stayed with his fellow pilgrims at a hostel in the Russian Compound, where they slept on straw pallets and were fed cabbage soup and hunks of bread. But no one complained. The pilgrims were grateful that everything was subsidised. Mother Russia looked after her own.[27]

The secular messiah

On the same steamships from Odessa came travellers from the Russian empire impelled by very different ideas and very different motives. Among them, in 1906, was David Gruen, a young man, not yet twenty, from tsarist-ruled Poland. Growing up in a Yiddish-speaking family in Płonsk, a town north-west of Warsaw, he had been aimless and introverted. His mother, to whom he was devoted, had died when he was eleven. What gave him a *raison d'être*—and at the same time a means of escape from a dull provincial town—was the new and revolutionary creed of Jewish nationalism, or Zionism.[28] For Zionists, Palestine was not a place of religious devotion—though they turned the Jews' spiritual attachment to Palestine to their advantage—but a place of settlement: the site of a future Jewish state.

Between 1882 and 1914 more than two million Jews left the Russian empire fleeing from anti-Semitic pogroms and persecution which convinced them they had no future there. Three-quarters of them emigrated to the United States. For the minority who chose Palestine, there were sometimes practical as well as idealistic reasons. 'The escape route to Palestine was shorter than to America and cost less.'[29] For Gruen and his friends, however, Zionism was much more than a response to persecution. It was an escape *to* as well as an escape *from*. They had the burning desire to create a new Jew and a new society, in sharp rejection of the life of the European diaspora. Zionism was in this sense revolutionary. The young pioneers 'were rebels against every accepted norm of their society, against every institution of authority. They renounced their very obligation to parents and family.' [30]

Early Zionism was markedly Russian in character, and found expression in a movement known as the Lovers of Zion, which had branches across Russia and eastern Europe. But Zionism's founding father was a Western Jew, the young Viennese journalist Theodor Herzl. Born in Hungary and now comfortably assimilated into bourgeois life, Herzl was rudely jolted by the rise of anti-Semitism both in Vienna and in Paris, where it was exemplified by the Dreyfus affair of 1894, which he covered as a journalist. His classic work, *The Jewish State*, came out two years later.

> We have honestly endeavoured [he wrote] everywhere to merge ourselves in the social life of surrounding communities and to preserve only the faith of our fathers. We are not permitted to do so. In vain are we loyal patriots … in vain do we make the same sacrifices of life and property as our fellow-citizens … In countries where we have lived for centuries we are still cried down as strangers.

Herzl argued that the only response to anti-Semitism was to create a Jewish state, either in Palestine or elsewhere. (Both East Africa and Argentina were considered, and only after fierce debate was the matter settled.) *The Jewish State*, a booklet of little more than seventy pages written in German, gave Zionism—a contentious minority movement within world Jewry—a much wider audience and provided activists with a blueprint for action.[31] The first Zionist Congress met in Switzerland the

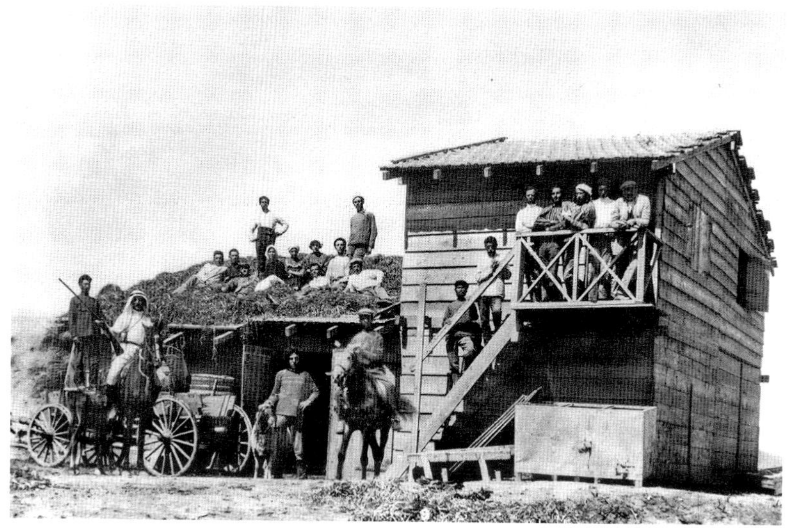

The early Jewish settlement of Degania, 1912   Yaacov Ben-Dov

following year. David Gruen and his friends in Poland regarded Herzl as a secular messiah and were devastated by his death in 1904 at the age of only forty-four.

In the first wave of settlement, from 1882 to 1903, some 25,000 Jews travelled, mainly from Russia, to Palestine. Most but not all were Zionists. Already long established there were some 50,000 religious Jews who lived in the four holy cities of Jerusalem, Hebron, Safad, and Tiberias, subsisting on *halukah* (charitable donations from abroad). The 'new' Jews and the 'old' looked askance at one another. The religious Jews—many of them from Sephardic (or Oriental) communities—mostly spoke Yiddish, and some knew Arabic. The newcomers—mostly Ashkenazi (or European) Jews—made a point of speaking Hebrew, an ancient language in the throes of revival. The religious Jews had known their Arab neighbours for decades and on the whole managed to get along with them; the Arabs did not regard them as a threat. The newcomers, on the other hand, bought land (often from absentee landowners) and treated the Arabs as a reservoir of cheap labour.[32]

The first wave ended in failure. The immigrants were ill prepared for the rigours of life in Palestine. Much of the land they worked was barren or swampy. The climate—so markedly different from Russia's—was for half the year fiercely hot. Many succumbed to malaria. Some of the early settlements were disbanded, and many settlers left the country, disillusioned. But they had put down a marker. The second wave, from 1904 to 1914, brought some 35,000 immigrants to Palestine including the zealous young pioneers who were to lay the foundations of the Jewish state. Among them was David Gruen, who, to celebrate the start of his new life, adopted the Hebrew name Ben-Gurion (Son of a Lion).

The pastor's son

When Tawfiq Canaan established a clinic in Jerusalem in 1905 he was, remarkably, the first Arab doctor to do so. He had been born in 1882, the son of Bishara Canaan, a Lutheran pastor, in Beit Jala, a predominantly Orthodox village a few miles south of the city. Among the Christian sects in Palestine, Lutheranism was a latecomer. When Bishara began holding services in a small room, the Orthodox and the Catholics were not well pleased. But by 1886 the Lutherans had their own church in the village, and their boys' school—and later a girls' school, one of the country's first—attracted children from all confessions.

> Father won the whole village [Tawfiq recalled with pride]. He visited them on feast days, happy family occasions as well as on

American Colony

Right: *Inside Jaffa Gate, c. 1909-1914: the photograph shows the clock-tower, a gift from Sultan Abdul-Hamid; to the right is F. Vester's store, owned by the American Colony, which sold souvenirs—and photographs—to tourists.*

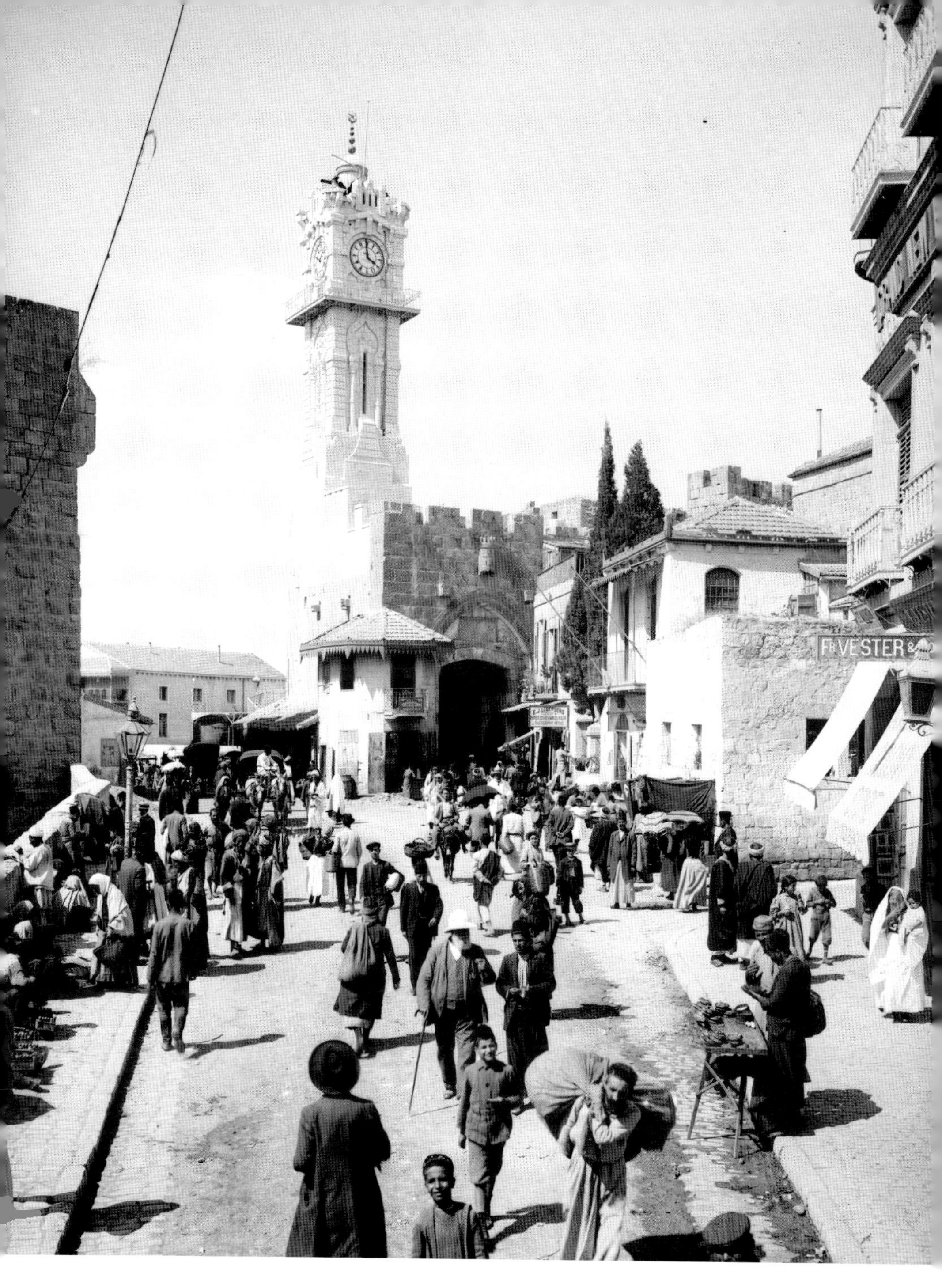
Fr VESTER & Co

mourning days. He went to their houses, vineyards and quarries and took part in every phase of their life. They came to him to take his advice and to pour out their hearts ... He tried everywhere to help: to put a bright child in a boarding school ... to hospitalise the sick, to find a job for those without work, and to settle disputes.[33]

When Bishara went preaching in neighbouring villages, father and son would ride out together on horseback. This kindled in the young Tawfiq an interest in the life of Palestine's *fellahin*—the peasants who formed the great majority of the population—which remained with him for the rest of his life. A hard-working student, he was accepted by the most prestigious secular university in the Middle East, the Syrian Protestant College (later to become the American University of Beirut), to study medicine. But in 1899, a few months after he arrived, his father caught pneumonia and died, leaving the family impoverished. The 17-year-old Tawfiq took any job he could find, including sweeping streets, to pay for his studies. With help from the college, which waived his fees, and from the Lutheran community, he graduated with distinction.[34]

These were years when young men such as Tawfiq began to question whether they were Ottoman or Arab. On university campuses, in coffee houses, and in the newspapers of the day, they had their first exposure to Arab nationalism, then in its formative phase. Its central idea was that all Arabic speakers, Muslims and Christians alike, in a great arc of territory stretching from Morocco to the Gulf, had a common cultural—and potentially political—identity. The Arabs of Palestine initially tended to see themselves as part of *bilad al-sham*, a Greater Syria which embraced Syria, Lebanon, and Palestine. But the appearance of an influential newspaper, *Filastin* (Palestine), in Jaffa in 1911 suggested that there was, even at this early date, an embryonic sense of a Palestinian Arab identity. This was to grow over time, in reaction to European encroachment and Zionist settlement.[35]

Returning to Jerusalem, Tawfiq found that in a city of some 70,000 there were no fewer than eleven hospitals—virtually all of them run by one or other European power. There were so many foreign doctors that it was unheard of for a locally-born doctor to set up his own practice. But by 1913 Tawfiq, still in his early thirties, had become a highly-respected physician and was writing scholarly articles about leprosy and malaria for a journal in Hamburg. Acceptance could not be taken for granted: members of the German community were shocked when the young Arab doctor took a German wife. But before long Tawfiq and Margot moved to a comfortable house in Musrara, a district on the edge of the Old City, which was to serve as both clinic and home for the next thirty-five years. Tawfiq had visited Europe and admired the West's scientific achievements, but regarded himself, proudly, as a 'son of the country'.[36]

Tradition and change

Palestine in 1900 was on the cusp of change. Its isolation was coming to an end, the economy and the population were growing—through immigration as well as natural increase—and a modern infrastructure of roads, railways, schools, and hospitals was starting to be built. At the same time, two rival nationalisms—Arabism and Zionism—were taking root, with far-reaching consequences that no one could then foresee. But change was gradual and uneven. It came more slowly to the remote Arab villages of the interior than to the towns and the coastal plain where the impact of foreigners—merchants, pilgrims, missionaries, consuls—was more pronounced.

Photography both reflected change and was itself an agent of change. It was an intrinsic part of the colonial encounter: 'the introduction of an unknown instrument ... brought by a stranger into a closed society'.[37] The motives of the photographers varied. For the archaeologist-explorers of the Palestine

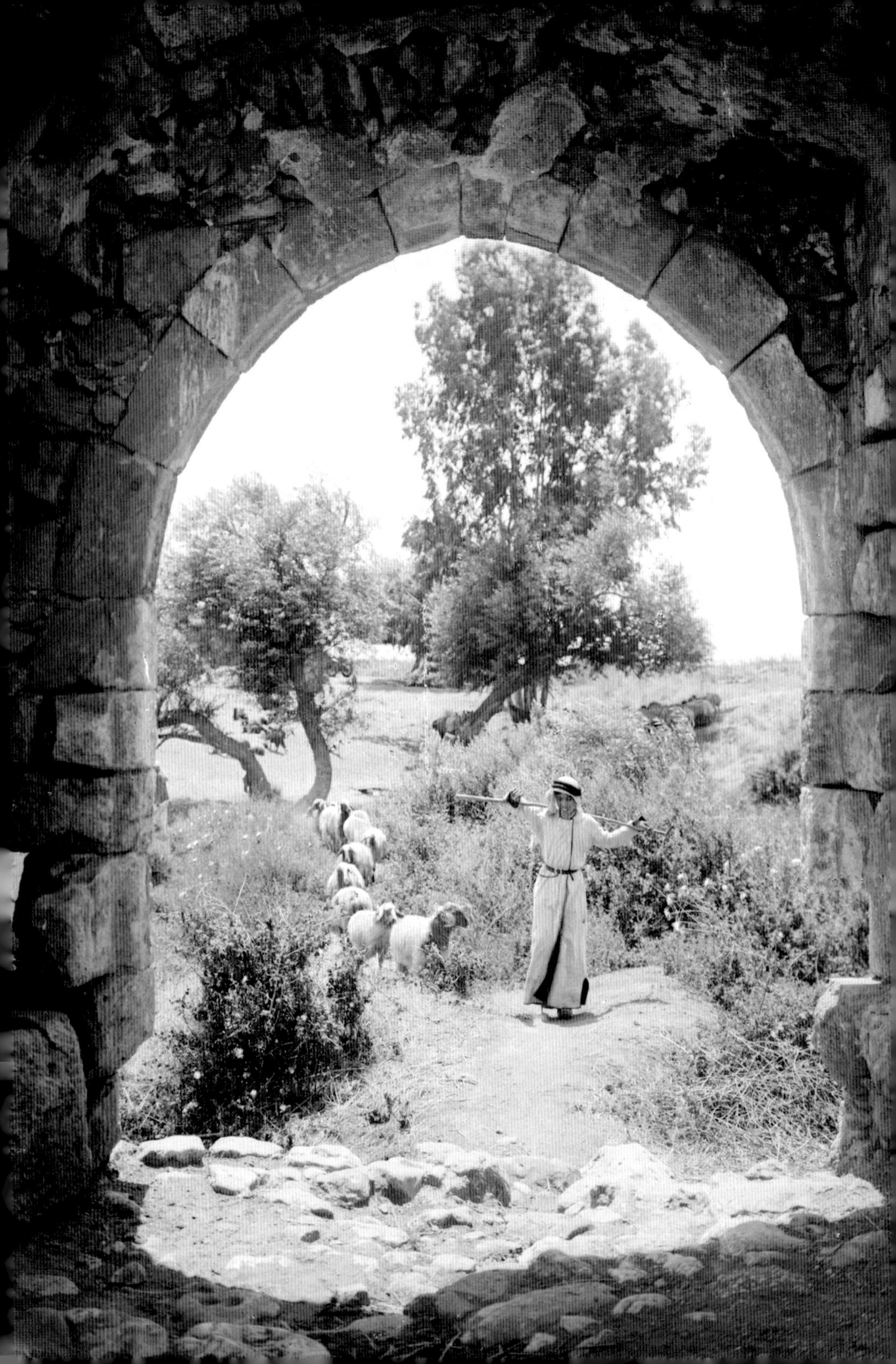

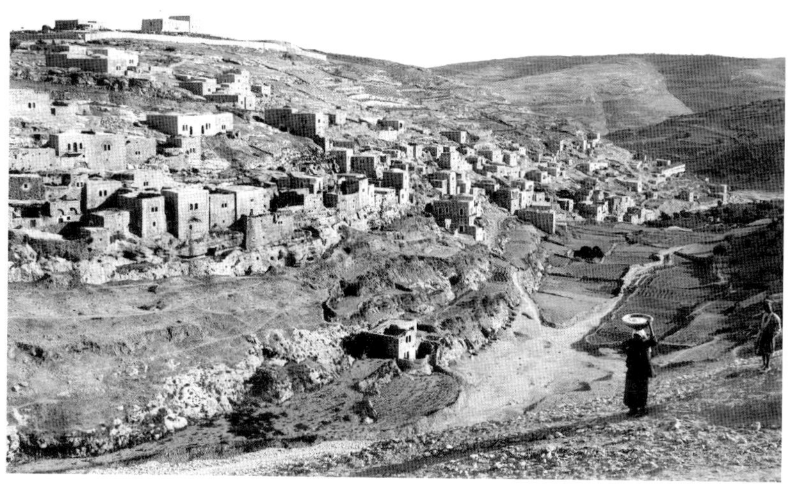

Above: *Village of Silwan, near Jerusalem, early 1900s*   American Colony
Left: *The 'biblical lens': a young shepherd, early 1900s*   American Colony

Exploration Fund, photography was an adjunct to excavation and map-making: a means of identifying biblical sites (often fiercely disputed) and then recording them with the supposedly scientific evidence of the camera. Missionaries took photographs to generate publicity in Europe and America. Their work, like that of the archaeologists, was not commercial.

In contrast, Lewis Larsson and the American Colony photographers produced the largest and most significant body of work on Palestine yet created—and successfully marketed it. To be sure, their membership of a Christian fundamentalist enterprise gave them a predilection for viewing the Holy Land through a biblical lens. For example, to illustrate Psalm 23 ('The Lord is my shepherd') for an article in the *National Geographic,* Larsson took a series of pictures of sheep and shepherds (after his young colleague Eric Matson had gone ahead to pay off the shepherd and the owner of the sheep).[38] In consciously re-enacting biblical scenes, they were peddling the myth that Palestine had remained essentially unchanged since biblical times. This, after all, was what their customers wanted to believe.

Despite this evident flaw, Larsson did something altogether new: he was the first photographer to chronicle, in detail, the life and work of Arab villagers, their weddings and festivals, and the role of women both in the home and in the rural economy. In doing so he also captured the physical reality of the land: its beauty and variety, the sharpness of the light, the way in which the stone of the village houses was often barely distinguishable from the rocky hills around them. He showed how the villagers' lives were governed by hard necessity. Living on the coastal plain was precarious because settlements were traditionally vulnerable to bedouin raids. Hillsides provided both natural protection and the readily available stone the villagers needed to build strong homes. (Throughout Palestine wood was scarce.) Larsson's photograph of men, women, and children coming together to build the roof of a village house captures not just the work but its collective spirit. Clothed as it was in a contrived religious aura, his Palestine was nevertheless real.

The shadow of war
In 1909 Sultan Abdul-Hamid was overthrown by a group of nationalists known as the Young Turks. The object of these ambitious but inexperienced young men was to preserve and reform the Ottoman empire. But they provoked dissent by tightening their grip on the empire's Arab provinces and replacing Arabic with Turkish in schools and government offices, and Arab officials with Turks. In the end, instead of strengthening the empire, they allied themselves with Germany and entered a war that was to destroy it.[39]

The First World War brought about a dramatic transformation

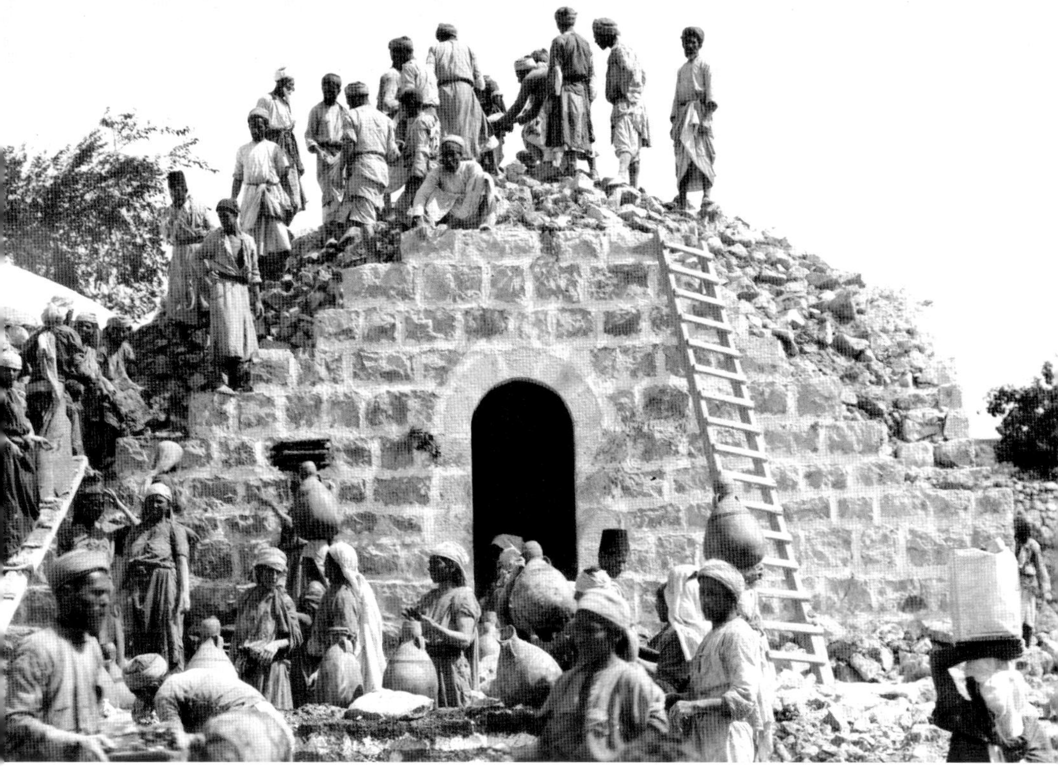

Villagers building the roof of a stone house, early 1900s   American Colony

of the Middle East and its relations with the big powers. Palestine fell under the control of Jemal Pasha, one of the ruling triumvirate of Young Turks, who was appointed military governor of Syria and Palestine and commander of the Ottoman Fourth Army. The 44-year-old Jemal, short and stocky with piercing black eyes, arrived in Jerusalem and took as his headquarters the Augusta Victoria compound, which stood imperiously on the Mount of Olives. Citizens of Britain, France, and Russia—now enemies of the Ottoman empire—were expelled and their property taken over as hospitals and barracks for Jemal's troops. Food, water, and animals were requisitioned.

One of those conscripted into the Ottoman army was Ihsan Turjman, the 22-year-old son of a middle-class Muslim family in Jerusalem. He served initially in Hebron and Nablus, but his

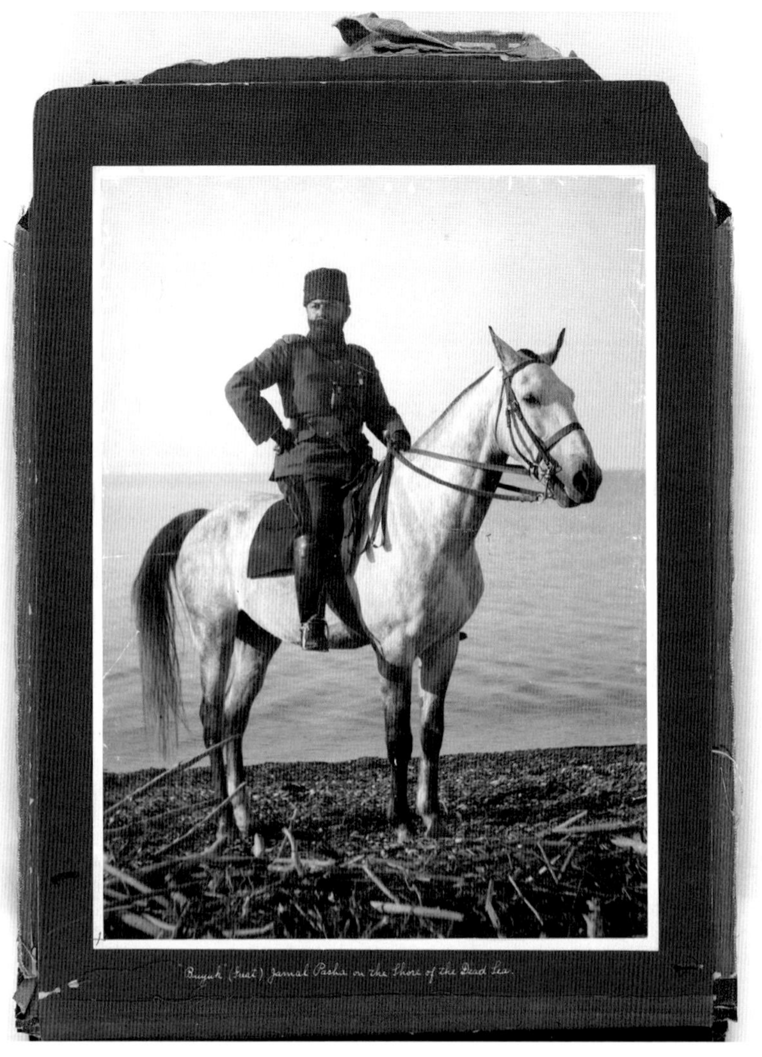

American Colony

Jemal Pasha, posing for the camera by the Dead Sea, c. 1916

family pulled strings to get him posted to his native Jerusalem. Here, through the years 1915-16, he kept a secret diary, written at night by candlelight, which revealed the hopes and fears of a young Arab as he agonised over the dilemmas, both personal and national, that the war had thrown up.[40] Should he fight for the Ottomans? If he was sent to the front, would he survive to marry his beloved Suraya? The Ottomans demanded his loyalty, yet were responsible for Palestine's calamitous state. Was he, then, an Ottoman or an Arab? Living and working in Jerusalem, he was able to discuss such vexed issues with some of the city's leading Arab thinkers, including his teacher and mentor, Khalil Sakakini, himself the author of a remarkable diary of the period.

Turjman's indignation was directed first and foremost at Jemal and his harsh treatment of the population. In enforcing conscription, he had at first allowed exemptions if wealthy Christians and Jews paid to remove their sons from harm's way. But as the war dragged on, the rules were tightened. The Ottomans were heavily dependent on Arab recruits, who comprised a third of all their forces. Draft dodgers and deserters were ruthlessly hunted down and punished. Jemal gained the nickname *al-Saffah* (the butcher).

Locusts, war, and famine
The Turkish governor was harsh but pragmatic. He was ready to seek help even from Western institutions such as the American Colony. Over time Anna Spafford had relented and allowed the colonists to marry. Her daughter Bertha had married a German, Frederick Vester, and together they took over the day-to-day running of the colony. Jemal now called on Anna and Bertha. They took tea and gingerbread, and Jemal bounced Bertha's little daughter on his knee. He had two faces, she recorded: 'We had heard that he was capable of lunching with a man one

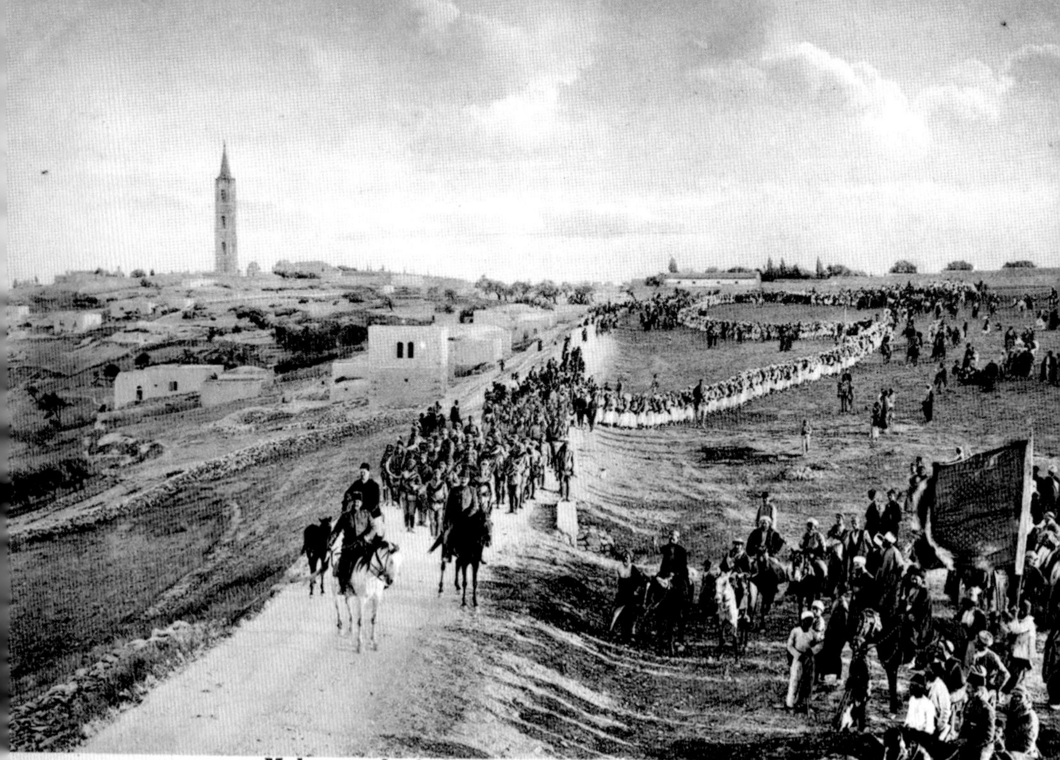

'Muslim volunteers' setting out from Jerusalem, 1915   Khalil Raad

*This is war-time propaganda. Khalil Raad, like Lewis Larsson, was recruited
by Jemal Pasha to record the activities of his army and of the Turkish Red
Crescent. This photograph—a postcard version of one reproduced in a German
newspaper—describes Arab recruits euphemistically as 'Muslim volunteers'.
At bottom left is the censor's mark.*

*In some of his other war-time photographs—for example of sullen-looking
Arab soldiers queuing to be fed—Raad showed that he was alive to the very
real hardships which the war inflicted on Palestine.*

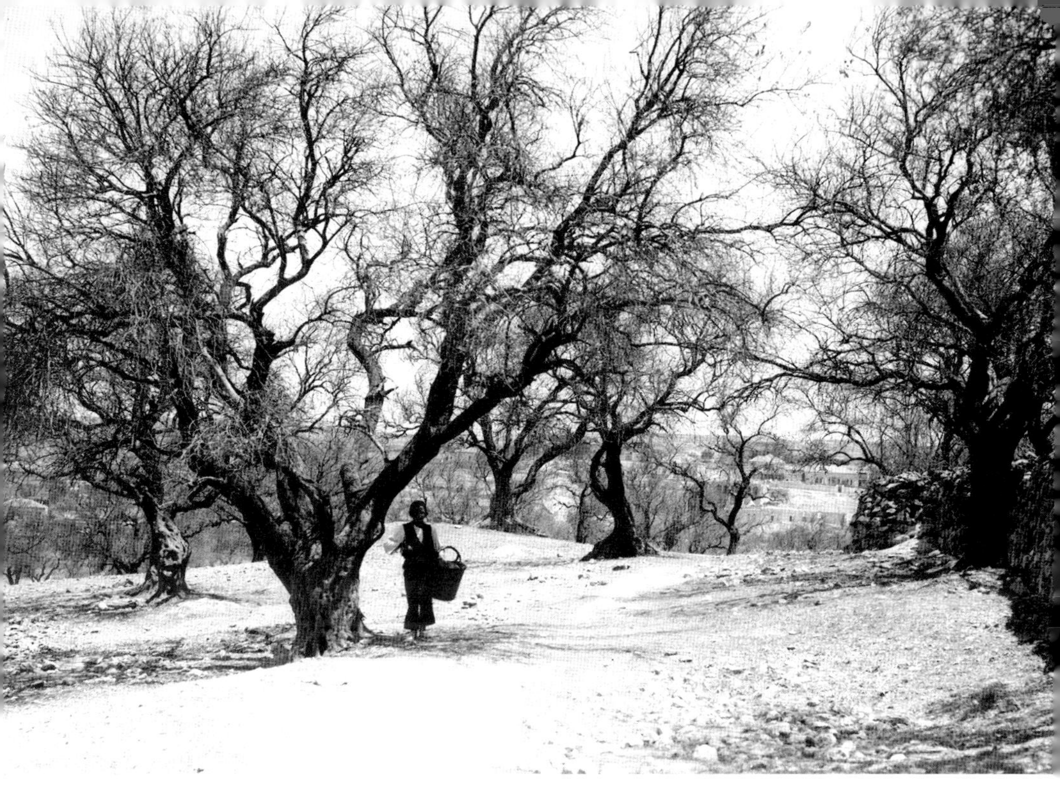

Olive grove stripped bare by locusts, 1915 American Colony

day and hanging him the next.' Anna and Bertha needed his protection and agreed to help him by providing nurses and organising soup kitchens.[41]

Jemal recruited Lewis Larsson and Palestine's first Arab photographer, Khalil Raad, to record the exploits of the Ottoman army. He would summon Larsson to the Augusta Victoria to have his picture taken. In one striking war-time photograph of the military commander on horseback beside the Dead Sea, there is more than a touch of swagger. Larsson also witnessed a new catastrophe that overwhelmed Palestine in 1915. 'Suddenly we heard what sounded like the roar of a waterfall … locusts fell from the sky as thick as snowflakes in a Scandinavian storm.' The young Swede produced a set of photographs documenting

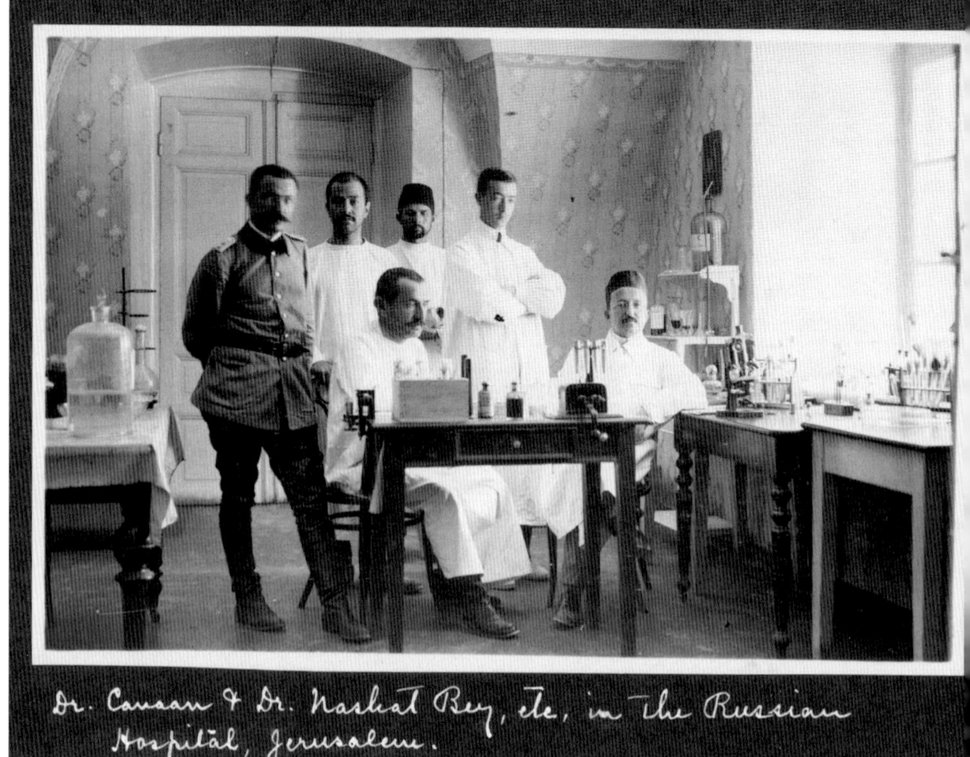

American Colony

Tawfiq Canaan in the uniform of an Ottoman medical officer, c. 1916

in great detail a devastating plague of locusts, which lasted three months, causing havoc and helping turn a food shortage into famine.[42]

Jemal badly needed doctors. Tawfiq Canaan was conscripted as a medical officer and worked with the Ottoman army in Syria and Palestine. At first he tried to buy an exemption, but discovered that doctors were not eligible. In his memoir he reveals that, despite his cultural connections with Germany, his political sympathies were with Britain.[43] At one point the Turks arrested and interrogated him. They needed the Arabs, but could not be sure of their allegiance. Jemal ordered Arab nationalists accused of treachery—including members of prominent families—to be hanged in the public squares of Beirut and Damascus and at the gates of Jerusalem.

Meanwhile, working for Turkish officers who showed him scant regard, Ihsan Turjman was shocked by the contrast between the desperate suffering of the people of Jerusalem and the extravagant—and in his eyes licentious—behaviour of Jemal and his officers who held parties where alcohol flowed and prostitutes were in attendance. As the war dragged on, the cost of food and other essentials shot up; tens of thousands died of disease or starvation; crowds of beggars thronged the streets, including war widows reduced to penury; and the black market flourished. 'Jerusalem has not seen worse days,' Turjman wrote in his diary on 10 July 1916.

> Bread and flour supplies have almost totally dried up. Every day I pass the bakeries on my way to work, and I see a large number of women going home empty-handed. For several days the municipality distributed some kind of black bread to the poor, the likes of which I have never seen. People used to fight over this bread, sometimes waiting in line until midnight. Now, even that bread is no longer available.

When an order was issued which threatened to transfer him to the front in Suez, he wrote:

> I cannot imagine myself fighting in the desert front. And why should I go? To fight for my country? I am Ottoman in name only, for my country is the whole of humanity … Had [the Ottomans] treated us as equals, I would not hesitate to give my blood and my life—but as things stand, I hold a drop of my blood to be more precious than the entire Turkish state.[44]

Turjman did not live to marry Suraya but, in circumstances that are unclear, he was killed by an Ottoman soldier in the closing months of the war.

The United States had at first been neutral, but in April 1917 it entered the war on the side of Britain and France. In Jemal's eyes, Anna and Bertha were now potentially enemy agents: there was a serious risk that he would expel them and take over the American Colony. He called them in and demanded to know where their loyalties lay. To his astonishment, Bertha assured him that they wanted their humanitarian work to go on. The colonists—who had previously shunned medicine—now found themselves running military hospitals for Jemal. Although desperately short of medicines, bandages, and trained doctors, they tended the gangrenous wounds of hundreds of Ottoman soldiers. Amputated limbs were piled high in the colony's court-yard. They managed to hide a few British soldiers whose fate was in doubt as the war drew towards its climax. At the same time, Bertha's soup kitchens kept thousands of Jerusalemites alive.

As Allied forces under General Allenby approached Palestine from the south, everyone waited anxiously to see if Jerusalem would be attacked and its holy sites damaged or destroyed. In the event, under strong pressure from their German allies, the Turks withdrew and the city was spared. On 11 December 1917, Allenby entered Jerusalem on foot, in deliberate contrast to Kaiser Wilhelm's flamboyant arrival almost two decades earlier.

With the defeat of the Germans and the fall of the Ottoman empire, the struggle for Palestine entered a new phase. The age of the consuls was over. A single imperial power now held Palestine in its grasp.

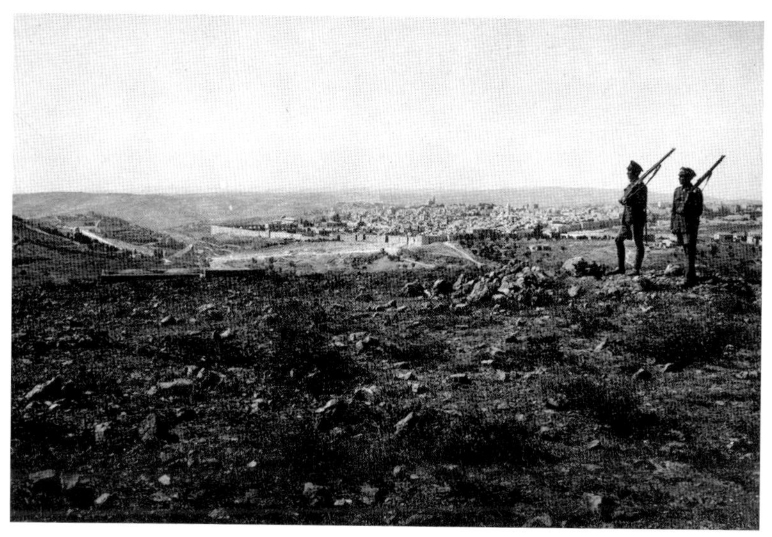

2

Palestine Raj, 1917–1929

'We thought we were witnessing the triumph of the last crusade.'

Bertha Spafford Vester

THE ENTRY OF Allenby's forces into Jerusalem was a moment of high symbolism, an assertion of British power and pride memorialised in film, photography, and painting. For the people of Jerusalem, their long nightmare was over, and now—in the cold, wet winter of 1917—they gradually began to recover. 'Jerusalem was a new city,' wrote Bertha Spafford Vester. 'Strangers greeted and congratulated one another. Faces we had not seen for months and years emerged from hiding.'[1] Groomed in her mother's beliefs, she saw the arrival of the British in glowing religious terms: 'We thought then we were witnessing the triumph of the last crusade.'[2] She proudly

65

wore a ring, given to her by her husband Frederick, bearing 'the Crusader Cross with the date, 9 December 1917, engraved on the inside'—the date the city had surrendered to British forces. Officials in London were anxious to avoid talk of a holy war, but fervent Christians and a jingoistic press had no such inhibition.

For most Jerusalemites, tired, demoralised, and hungry, there were more practical considerations. There was intense relief as Allenby's army imposed law and order and brought in truck-loads of wheat to feed the starving population. The political implications were another matter, and took time to sink in.

The bluff

The Arabs, both inside and outside Palestine, believed that Britain had promised them independence in return for their help in defeating the Turks. But British officials had made other, conflicting, war-time pledges which impinged on Palestine's future. Only a few weeks before Allenby's arrival in Jerusalem, Lloyd George's government had published a letter committing Britain to support a Jewish 'national home' in Palestine. The letter, signed by the foreign secretary, Arthur Balfour, was the product of two converging sets of pressures: from Britain's imperial interests, and from the skilful lobbying of the Zionist movement in London, led by a remarkable Russian, Chaim Weizmann.

Weizmann described himself, self-deprecatingly, as a 'Yid from Motelle',[3] a small town in the Pale of Settlement (the zone in which the tsars had confined the Jews) where he had been born in 1874. He had left Russia to train as a scientist and eventually settled in Manchester. He claimed to have only two passions in life: chemistry and Zionism. One British official recalled his 'almost feminine charm combined with a feline deadliness of attack'.[4] His signal achievement was to help persuade leading statesmen of the day—including Lloyd George,

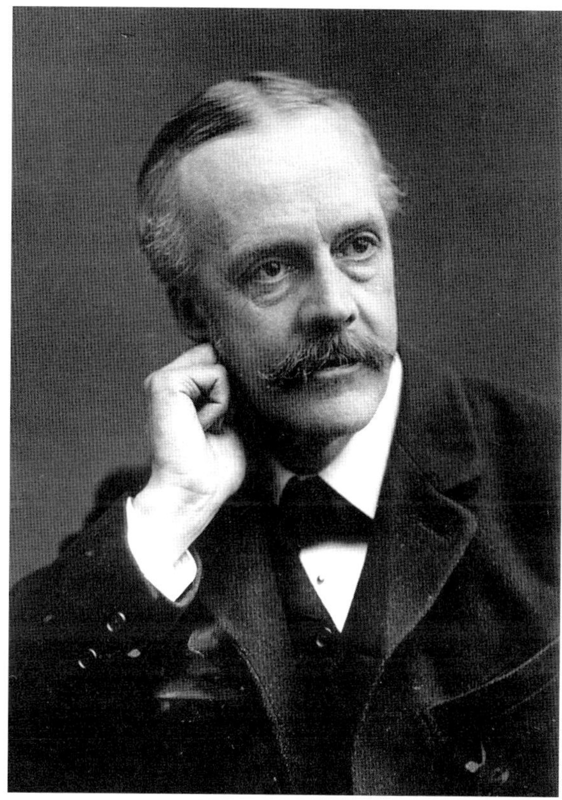

Arthur Balfour,
c. 1917
G. G. Bain

Balfour, and Winston Churchill—that, with British backing, Zionism would provide the British empire with a staunch ally in the new Middle East emerging from the wreck of the Ottoman empire.

'I speak the mind of millions of Jews,' declared Weizmann at his first meeting with Balfour, in 1906.[5] Such were his persuasive powers that his interlocutors regarded him as the leader of world Jewry, and believed he could influence Jewish opinion—not least in Russia and the United States—at a critical juncture in the war. It was a bluff; he was a leader of a movement then in its infancy to which most Jews were either hostile or indifferent.

Foreign Office,
November 2nd, 1917.

Dear Lord Rothschild,

I have much pleasure in conveying to you, on behalf of His Majesty's Government, the following declaration of sympathy with Jewish Zionist aspirations which has been submitted to, and approved by, the Cabinet.

"His Majesty's Government view with favour the establishment in Palestine of a national home for the Jewish people, and will use their best endeavours to facilitate the achievement of this object, it being clearly understood that nothing shall be done which may prejudice the civil and religious rights of existing non-Jewish communities in Palestine or the rights and political status enjoyed by Jews in any other country"

I should be grateful if you would bring this declaration to the knowledge of the Zionist Federation.

The Balfour Declaration, 2 November 1917

But it worked, not least because it played upon the open or latent anti-Semitism prevalent within the British establishment which fostered the myth of a worldwide cabal of Jews pulling the strings of politics, commerce, and the media.[6]

It is sometimes argued that the Balfour Declaration, issued in London on 2 November 1917, was an act of idealism. It is true that, for Lloyd George in particular, support for Zionism was a romantic adventure coloured by biblical sentiment. But British statesmen issued the declaration for hard-headed reasons of imperial self-interest: to create a belt of territory protecting Egypt and the Suez Canal, to thwart French claims to Palestine, which were long-standing and persistent, and to use Jewish money and energy to draw Palestine into the fold (as it was then perceived) of Western civilisation: a novel form of the 'civilising mission'. Weizmann was well aware of Britain's imperial objectives, and much of the success of his assiduous lobbying lay in his skilful identification of British and Zionist interests. Taking the longer view, were British and Zionist interests in fact identical?

> To the Jews who went to Palestine [wrote the historian Elizabeth Monroe], and to many who did not, [the declaration] signified fulfilment and salvation, but it brought the British much ill-will, and complications that sapped their power. Measured by British interests alone, it was one of the greatest mistakes in our imperial history.[7]

Even at the time, there were those who foresaw trouble; among them the powerful figure of Lord Curzon, former viceroy of India and a member of Lloyd George's war cabinet. It was at his insistence that an earlier draft of the declaration was amended with the addition of an important caveat: nothing must be done to prejudice 'the civil and religious rights of existing non-Jewish communities' in Palestine—in other words,

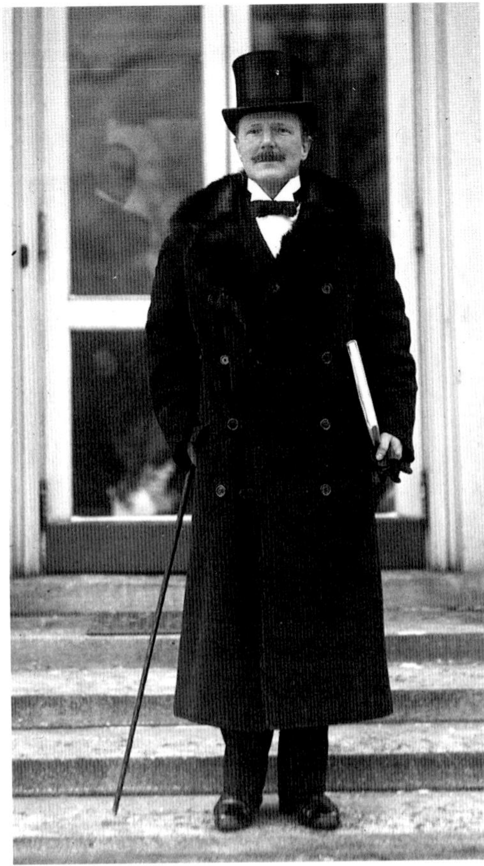

Ronald Storrs, 1923
Harris & Ewing

the Arab majority. This scarcely gave parity to Arabs and Jews: Jews were deemed to have national rights; Arabs were not. But Weizmann was dismayed. He had pinned his hopes on the earlier text of July 1917, drafted by the Zionists themselves, according to which Britain would recognise Palestine as '*the* National Home of the Jewish people', with no mention of the rights of 'non-Jewish communities'. He regarded the changes as a 'painful recession'.[8] This explains his reaction when an excited official, Mark Sykes, emerged from the cabinet office to tell him, 'It's a boy!' 'I did not like the boy at first,' he wrote in his memoirs. 'He was not the one I had expected.'[9] Weizmann saw the essential contradiction in Britain's pledge and feared, correctly, that it would complicate the realisation of Zionist aims. The British were committing themselves, rather clumsily, to being even-handed.

The declaration gave the Zionist movement the backing of the most powerful empire of the day. Pragmatist that he was, Weizmann saw it as a necessary but not sufficient condition for the success of the Zionist project—whose true goal, as Balfour and Lloyd George knew perfectly well, was not a national home but a fully-fledged Jewish state with a Jewish majority. (The only question for debate was how long this might take.) While sharing Zionist euphoria at the publication of the letter, Weizmann had no illusions about the task ahead. To turn the declaration into a reality would require sustained Zionist effort. 'It would mean exactly what we would make it mean,' he wrote; 'neither more nor less.'[10]

A beneficent despotism

Palestine was at first governed by a military administration. This was intended as a temporary expedient but in the event it lasted until 1920. It required prolonged haggling for the peacemakers in Paris to hammer out the destiny of post-war Europe and of the Arab territories of the Ottoman empire.[11] The latter were eventually divided between Britain and France under a system of 'mandates' supervised by the fledgling League of Nations (forerunner of the United Nations). Britain was awarded the mandates for Palestine, neighbouring Transjordan, and Iraq; France, the mandate for Syria and Lebanon. Notionally, mandated territories were held in trust, in parental tutelage, to be prepared for adulthood and eventual independence. This was a sop to the American president, Woodrow Wilson, who was promoting the idea of self-determination. In reality these lands were now subjected to European colonial rule, in a late burst of imperial expansion.

The early years of British rule were an age of innocence. If one man may be said to have epitomised the hubris of the Palestine Raj, it was Colonel Ronald Storrs. Witty and conceited, a lover of music, art, and literature, Storrs was an impresario strutting the Jerusalem stage. He was filled with 'wild exhilaration' when Allenby made him the city's military governor in 1917, although admitting 'I possessed no military competence whatever, and very little administrative experience.'[12] (Despite being given the rank of colonel, his previous work in the Middle East had been political rather than military.) In the early days, he recalled, he ruled as a Beneficent Despot: 'my word was law'. He stayed for virtually a decade, until 1926. 'There are many positions of greater authority and renown within and without the British Empire,' he wrote in his inimitable memoirs, 'but in a sense I cannot explain there is no promotion after Jerusalem.'[13]

Storrs set about the task of restoring Jerusalem's Old City to what he conceived to be its former glory. Employing as his civic adviser Charles Ashbee, a prominent member of the Arts and Crafts movement in Britain (associated with William Morris), he began repairing its walls, renovating the Dome of the Rock, and reviving the traditional crafts of pottery, textiles, and glass-making. He issued a proclamation decreeing that any new building required his personal authorisation, and banning the use of modern materials: only Jerusalem limestone was to be used, in an effort to preserve the city's unique character. To further this work, he created the Pro-Jerusalem Society, a non-governmental body under his supervision which brought together members of the different communities in a show of non-sectarian harmony.[14]

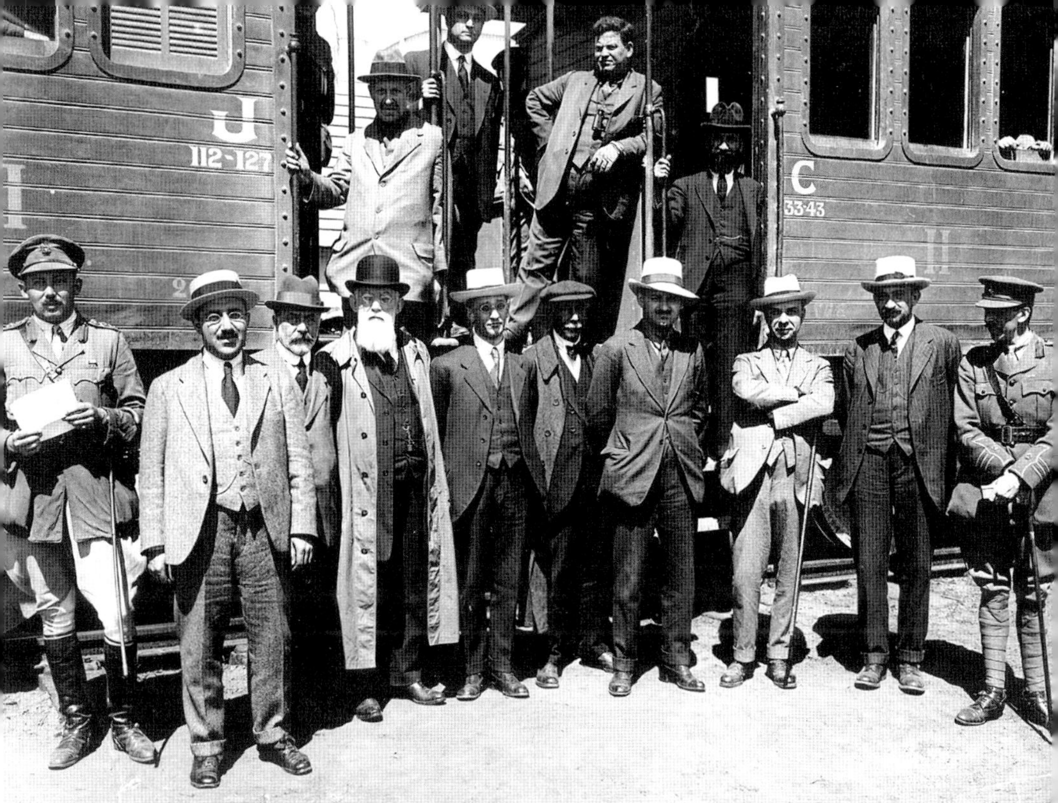

The Zionist Commission, 1918 (Weizmann, second from right)

The first unrest

The military régime—known as the Occupied Enemy Territory Administration, or OETA—was not a success. The soldiers quickly realised they were in an impossible situation—responsible for law and order, but at the same time for implementing the Balfour Declaration in the face of Arab opposition and Zionist impatience.

Weizmann took charge of a newly formed Zionist Commission whose task was to work with British officials to implement the declaration on the ground. When its members arrived in Palestine in 1918, they acted as representatives of a nation-in-waiting,

73

demanding that their national symbols—their blue-and-white flag, their national anthem (the Hatikvah), and their language (Hebrew)—be officially used and acknowledged, regardless of Arab opinion. When British military officials demurred, Weizmann would complain to his highly-placed friends in London that they were anti-Zionist or even anti-Semitic. Some were indeed anti-Semitic, but anti-Semitism does not explain the friction that ensued. The military men wanted to resolve the contradiction in the Balfour Declaration by scrapping it, something officials in London refused to contemplate.

It was an unhappy start to British rule. The *coup de grâce* for the OETA came in April 1920 with the outbreak of the first serious unrest. The occasion was the week-long festival of Nebi Musa, when every year thousands of Muslims converged on Jerusalem and then processed to the site regarded as the burial place of Moses (Musa) near the Dead Sea. It was a lively event, marked by dancing and banners and colourful costumes. But it coincided with the Orthodox Easter and the Jewish Passover, and often sparked political passions. There were four days of violence, and an official report concluded that Storrs had been negligent.

Among the instigators of the unrest were two very different men: a young Arab nationalist, Hajj Amin al-Husseini, and Vladimir Jabotinsky, who was the founder of the Jewish Legion which had fought alongside the British army in the First World War, and later became leader of the right-wing Zionists (known as the Revisionists). Both were given prison sentences, but while Hajj Amin fled the country, Storrs ensured that Jabotinsky was given a comfortable cell and decent food. He was, he acknowledged, politically dangerous, but Storrs found him charming and was impressed that he had translated Dante into Hebrew.

The unrest prompted Lloyd George to wind up the OETA and introduce a civilian administration. He chose as Palestine's

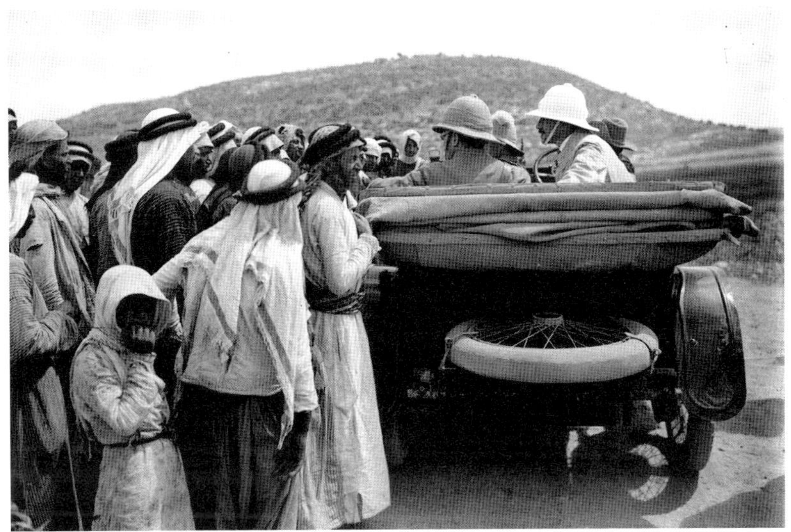

Sir Herbert Samuel, right, meets the people, 1920   American Colony

high commissioner Sir Herbert Samuel, who had been Britain's first Jewish cabinet minister and, unlike most patrician Jews in Britain, was committed to Zionism and the project of a 'national home'. He was initially reluctant to take the job, fearing his background would be an impediment and knowing that Allenby and the generals were opposed to his appointment. But Weizmann and Lloyd George convinced him to accept, and he arrived in Jerusalem, amid tight security, on 30 June 1920. (Unknown to him, Storrs had kept a cocked and loaded Browning pistol by his side during the journey from Jaffa to Jerusalem.)[15]

The Zionists were ecstatic, convinced that the appointment signified an important British concession. Samuel's first steps strengthened this impression. He removed some notably anti-Zionist officials and appointed a committed Zionist, Wyndam Deedes, as his deputy. (He also kept on Storrs, whom the Zionists did not trust, as governor of Jerusalem.) Then, reversing the policy of the OETA, he gave the Zionists the two things they wanted most: the right to settle in Palestine, and the right to buy land.[16]

A little England

'The worst thing here is the everlasting respectability and limelightness of the life,' wrote Helen Bentwich in August 1920.[17] She had arrived in Palestine in 1919, at the age of twenty-seven, and thought it stuffy and provincial. A feminist, she was dismayed to find herself defined by her relationship to two men: she was Herbert Samuel's niece; and her husband, Norman Bentwich, was the administration's senior legal official responsible for supervising the courts and for the sensitive issue of land registration. By Mandate standards, they were an unconventional couple: not only British Jews but Labour-voting Hampstead intellectuals. Both were Zionists, but Norman was more committed to living in Palestine than she was. While he worked long hours drafting new laws, she threw herself into social work, and pined for the concert halls and art galleries of London. (She was not alone: Weizmann much preferred the comforts of England to the austerities of Palestine.)[18]

The little world the British created for themselves in Jerusalem was snobbish, gossipy, and hierarchical. At the top of the pyramid were Samuel and his secretariat who, like the OETA, installed themselves in the imposing Augusta Victoria compound on the Mount of Olives. (Storrs called it 'that gaunt, wind-swept, reverberating prison'.)[19]

English-speakers were much in demand as junior officials and secretaries: the former were recruited largely from the Christian Arab community (which tended to be better educated); the latter from the Evelina de Rothschild School, an Anglo-Jewish establishment run by the remarkable Annie Landau. ('Fifteen typist girls from Miss Landau's … are brought up and down [the

Mount of Olives] every day in a lorry,' reported Helen after her arrival in 1919.)[20] Miss Landau, as she was universally known, had been brought up in Britain as an orthodox Jew, but was not a Zionist. She had arrived in Jerusalem in 1899 and was to stay until her death in 1945. She was a Jerusalem institution, hosting weekly tea parties and popular fancy-dress balls, and was a great gossip (her conversation, wrote Helen, was like a waterfall) and a great match-maker (she had handpicked Tawfiq Canaan's future wife).

Starved of good conversation, Helen found Storrs lively company. He was also a good pianist who took part in the musical soirées organised by the Bentwiches at their home in the German Colony, a fashionable area on the south side of the city. But she thought him a snob and considered his views pro-Arab. Her sharp tongue did not spare the Zionists, either. She thought they lacked a sense of humour.

Building a state

What the Zionists were serious about was creating the building-blocks of a state. Here the key figure was not Weizmann but the young Ben-Gurion, who in 1920 helped create the most important of these building-blocks, the Histadrut. This was a trade-union federation, but a highly unusual one. It not only championed workers' rights but promoted immigration and land settlement and provided crucial services, including health and insurance, for the immigrants when they arrived. It set up a workers' bank, a construction company, and an embryonic defence force, the Haganah.

Ben-Gurion was determined to persuade Jewish businesses to use only Jewish labour, despite the obvious fact that Arab labour was cheaper. This entailed a prolonged fight, in which he was never entirely successful. Ben-Gurion was short and rough-edged and, with his squeaky voice, no great orator. But

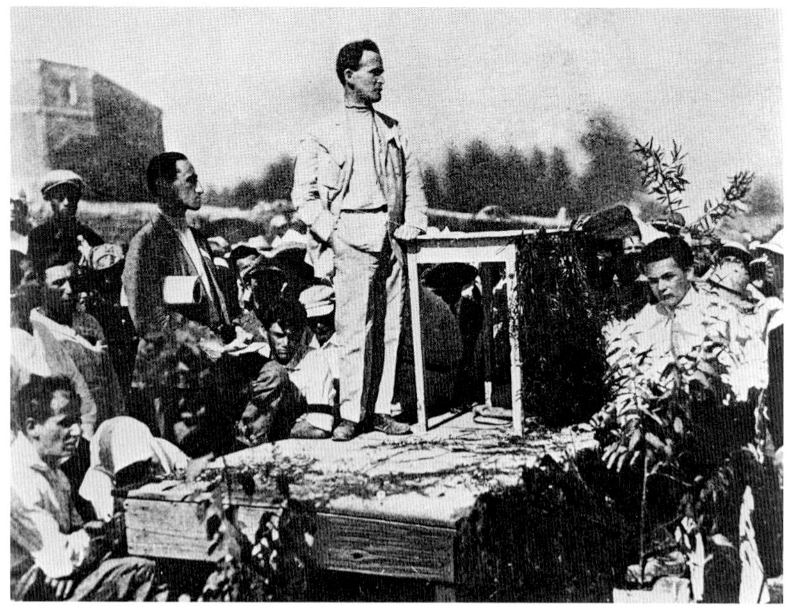

Ben-Gurion addressing Jewish workers, 1924   Photographer unknown

he was a brilliant labour leader and at this stage in his career a firebrand socialist who aspired to be a 'Zionist Lenin'.[21] With great single-mindedness and an intolerance of opposition, he made the 'conquest of labour' a central issue in the struggle for statehood.

Since the Zionist settlers mostly lacked capital of their own, the Jewish National Fund (set up in 1901 with Herzl's support) bought land to be held in trust, for all time, for the Jewish people. In September 1920, in the largest purchase of its kind, the fund bought from the Sursuq family of Beirut a large tract of land in the valley of Jezreel, an area of plains and malarial marshes south-east of Haifa. The local *fellahin* were evicted. Negotiations for the sale had begun before the First World War and had elicited angry protests in the Arab press. The fund

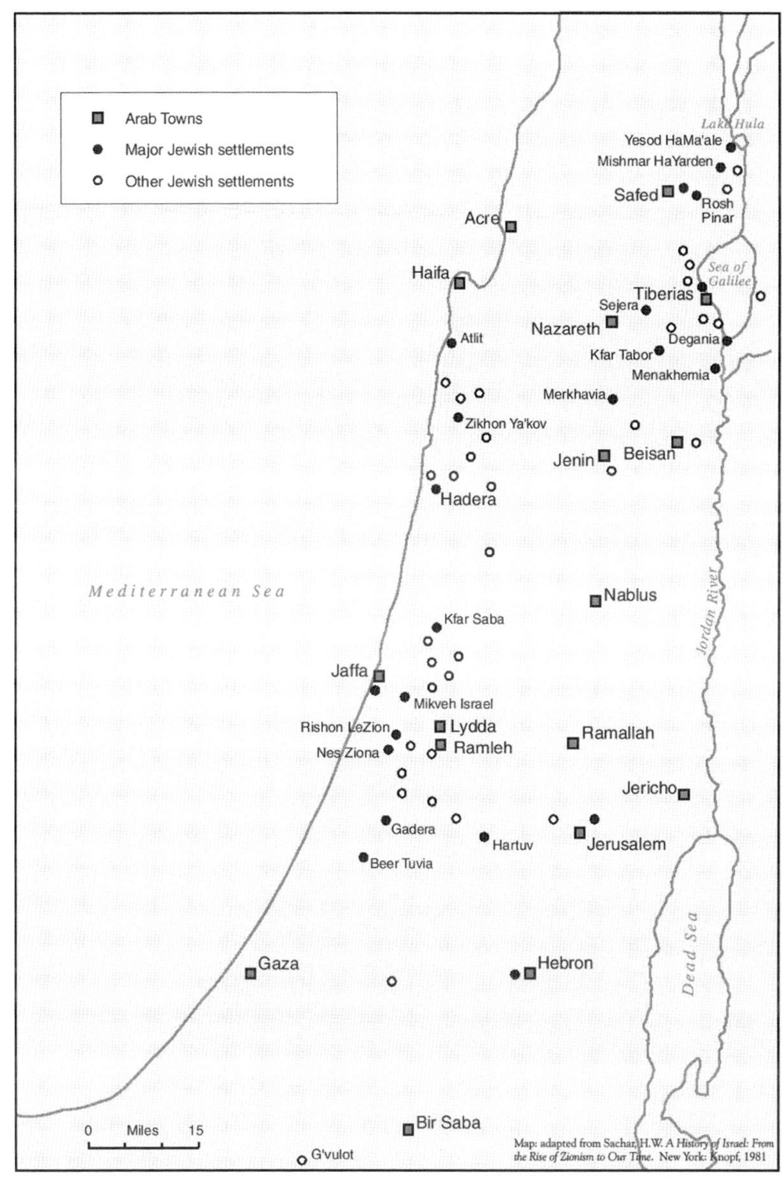

Passia

Settlement of Palestine, 1880-1917

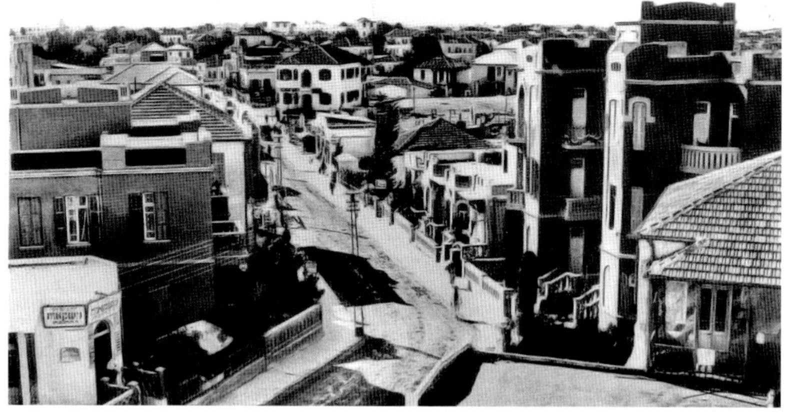

Tel Aviv, 1920   Abraham Soskin

eventually paid the Sursuqs the considerable sum of £700,000. In the years that followed, the valley became the heart of Zionist agricultural settlement in Palestine.[22]

On 21 September 1921—a day that was to enter Zionist folklore—a convoy of seventy-four young Zionist pioneers arrived in the valley, pitched their tents, and founded one of the first kibbutzim, Ein Harod. They began to plough the land, drain the marshes, and establish a quarry and a dairy farm. Within months their numbers had grown to over 200.[23] The kibbutzniks were not simply pioneers of state-building but symbols of the Zionists' determination to make a radical break with the past: through creating a new class of Jewish men and women (wholly unlike the Jews of the diaspora), through their novel collective organisation, and through their doctrine of strict self-reliance. Unlike the first wave of settlers, who had employed Arab workers, they adhered to Ben-Gurion's principle of using only Jewish labour. They considered their claim to the land to be based not on a bill of sale but on the fact that they had *worked* it and, in the language of Zionism, *redeemed* it. Ben-Gurion wanted to create nothing less than a socialist Jewish workers' state.

That at least was the ideal. In reality the kibbutzniks were, and remained, a minority, albeit one with pride of place in the Zionist firmament. To Ben-Gurion's frustration, most immigrants preferred to settle in the towns and cities rather than undertake the back-breaking toil of the kibbutz. Tel Aviv (Hill of Spring), founded on the edge of Jaffa in 1909 as an all-Jewish city, was built to house the immigrants of the second wave. It grew rapidly and by 1925 had a population of 34,000. Many had mixed feelings about the 'white city', as it was called. Storrs admired its energy but wrote, 'The concentration of Judaism, body, mind and soul can … be overpowering.'[24] 'It's hideous,' wrote Helen Bentwich in 1923, 'but it's very alive & modern & free.'[25]

The 1920s witnessed the emergence of a distinctively Zionist genre of photography, much of it sponsored by the Jewish National Fund, which wanted to present a positive image of Zionist state-building and thereby attract both immigrants and funds. The earliest photographers were Russians—Yaacov Ben-Dov, who took pictures of Degania and other Jewish colonies; Abraham Soskin, who recorded the early growth of Tel Aviv; and Joseph Schweig, who was commissioned by the fund to travel the country recording the life of the new settlements.[26]

The Zionists, preoccupied with their own affairs, gave little thought to the Arabs of Palestine. The idea that they comprised a nation—or, like them, a nation-in-the-making—was one that simply never occurred to them; or, if they thought of it at all, was one they rejected out of hand. Hence, when the first violence broke out in the early 1920s, they came up with various responses. One was to explain it away as the work of a few malcontents among the urban élite who could be bribed or fobbed off with minor concessions. (The majority, the *fellahin*, were

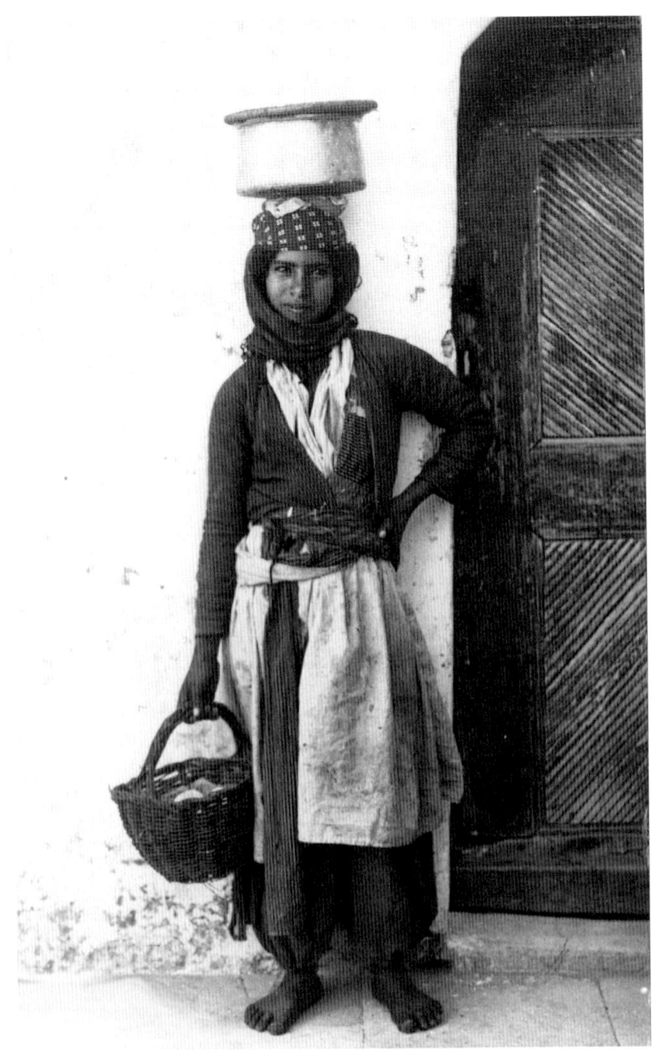

Peasant girl, Nazareth, 1920s   Karimeh Aboud

The first Arab photographers in Palestine were Christians; they included the country's first female Arab photographer, Karimeh Aboud, who in the 1920s produced sets of postcards of Nazareth, where she had her studio.

regarded as inert.) Another was to persuade the Arabs that, thanks to Zionist enterprise and investment, their standard of living would rise significantly. If that argument failed, as it invariably did, a third response was to go over their heads and attempt to reach some form of accommodation with the leaders of neighbouring Arab states. (In one form or another, these attitudes have survived to the present day.)

What the Zionists failed to see was the intensity and the fundamentally *political* character of Arab opposition to the Zionist project. Ben-Gurion was virtually alone among Zionist leaders in realising that this opposition was both authentic and deep-rooted. 'There is no solution,' he declared as early as 1919. 'There is an abyss and nothing can fill that abyss. We want Palestine to be ours ... the Arabs want it to be theirs.'[27] Compromise was an illusion. The only answer to Arab opposition was military strength.

The Syrian option

1920 was a transitional year not only because of the demise of the military administration and the building-up of the Yishuv (the Jewish community in Palestine). The political landscape changed significantly under the influence of events in neighbouring Syria. The hopes of the Arabs of Palestine rose when, in March 1920, Emir Faisal—the Arabian prince who had led the British-backed Arab revolt against the Turks—was proclaimed king of a Greater Syria notionally embracing Lebanon and Palestine. (After the war Weizmann had held two meetings with Faisal and believed he had found an Arab partner ready to accept Zionist settlement in Palestine; but the agreement they signed was to prove a dead letter.) Now, after only four months, the prince was ousted by the French, who set about ruling Syria and Lebanon themselves. Palestine's Arabs felt their options closing: once union with Syria was no longer possible, the goal of an independent Arab Palestine began to seem the only alternative.

During his five years as high commissioner, Herbert Samuel tried to encourage Arabs and Jews to come together, through a series of gradual steps, in self-governing institutions. But the Arabs, through newly-formed Muslim-Christian Associations, made clear their adamant opposition to the Balfour Declaration and all that it entailed. In May 1921, riots in Jaffa left almost 100 dead (forty-seven Jews and forty-eight Arabs) and led to an exodus of the city's Jews to neighbouring Tel Aviv. In response, Samuel temporarily suspended Jewish immigration and shortly afterwards made a speech assuring the Arabs that the Palestine government would never 'impose on them a policy ... contrary to their interests'. The Zionists' opinion of him changed overnight.[28]

British policy-makers were wriggling on a hook of their own devising. Unwilling to abandon the Balfour Declaration, which as even Curzon acknowledged would have entailed an unacceptable loss of face, they attempted to reinterpret it. In June 1922, a White Paper—known as the Churchill White Paper but in fact drafted by Samuel—declared that the government 'do not contemplate that Palestine as a whole should be converted into a Jewish National Home, but that such a Home should be founded in Palestine'. It decreed that no Jewish settlement could be undertaken in Transjordan (the territory to the east); and it affirmed that future immigration to Palestine would depend on 'the economic capacity of the country to absorb new arrivals'.

Weizmann and his colleagues were indignant at what they regarded as this 'serious whittling-down of the Balfour Declaration'.[29] But, under pressure from British officials, they had little choice but to acquiesce.

Right: *The hills around Nablus, c. 1910* G. G. Bain

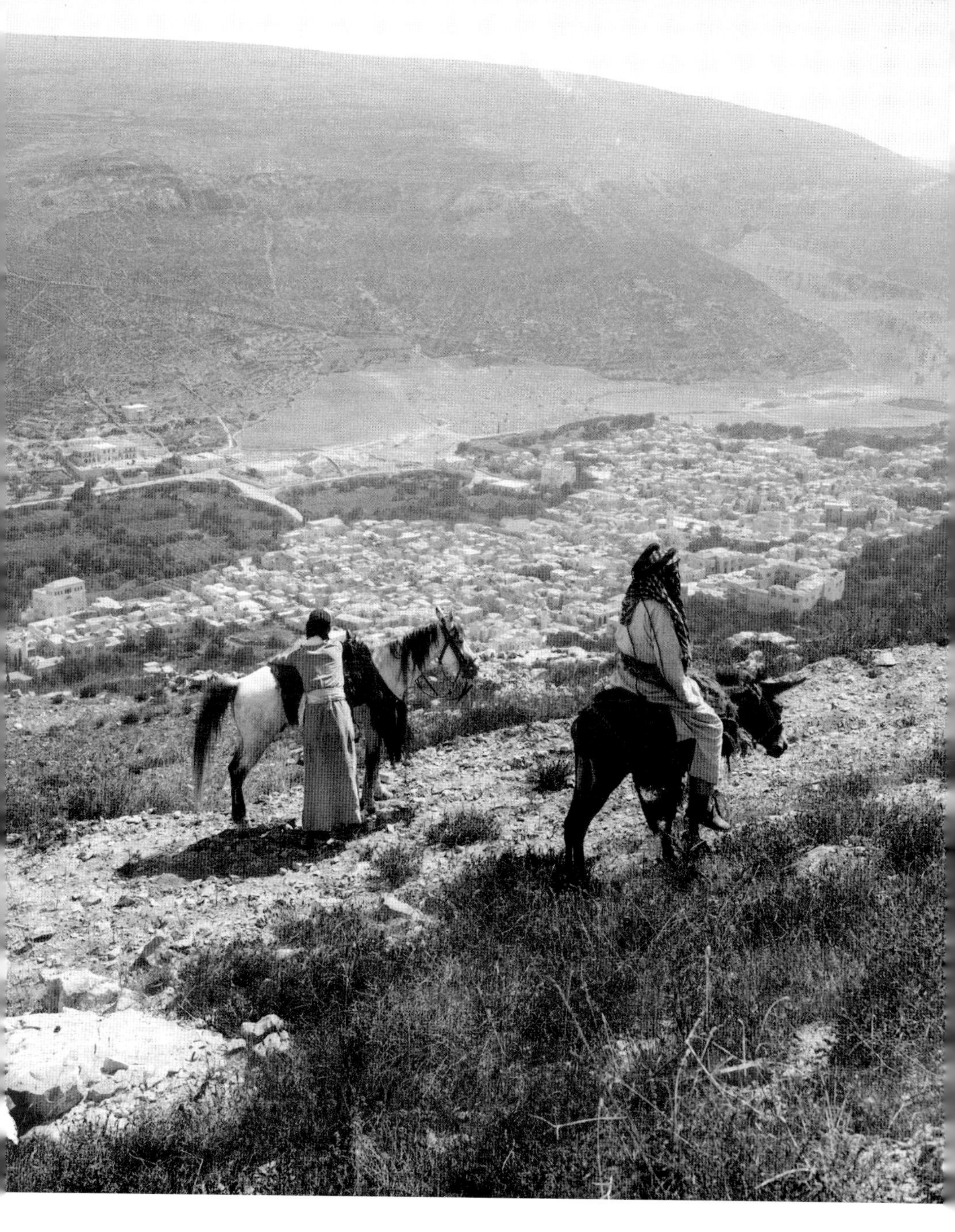

Mountain of fire

One of Fadwa Tuqan's earliest memories, growing up in Nablus in the 1920s, was of the British arresting her father for his political activities and deporting him to Egypt. She had been born in the year of the Balfour Declaration and brought up in a strictly conservative Muslim household, one of ten children. Malaria, she recalled, was the 'constant companion of my childhood': other children made fun of her sallow complexion.[30]

Nablus had long been an important trading centre well known for its cotton and textile industry and for its olive-oil soap, which was highly prized throughout the Middle East. Nineteenth-century travellers remarked on the city's wealth, its solidly-built houses, and its attractive location, situated between two mountains at the end of a fertile valley.

> Its beauty can hardly be exaggerated [wrote a British traveller] ... Clusters of white-roofed houses nestling in the bosom of a mass of trees, olive, palm, orange, apricot ... There is a softness in the colouring, a rich blue haze from the many springs and streamlets, which mellows every hard outline.[31]

The largest building, the palace of the Tuqan family, was a fortress which it was said could accommodate a thousand soldiers. The Tuqans, grown wealthy from trading, were one of the most prominent families in the life of a city which, because of its nationalist sentiment, was known as the 'mountain of fire'.

A girl of independent spirit, Fadwa languished under the stern authority of her father, while secretly yearning to write poetry and go to university like her brother Ibrahim. She briefly attended school, but when a boy gave her a flower she was abruptly taken home, where her confinement resumed. There were only brief moments of escape. One of the few occasions when her mother left home was to go to the *hammam*, the Turkish bath. The young Fadwa accompanied her and was amazed at the freedom and spontaneity of the women, rich and poor mingling without inhibition.[32]

The new Jerusalem

Ronald Storrs did not allow political or security concerns to distract him from his higher mission of restoring and reviving Jerusalem's Old City. When Ashbee resigned, his successor was the Yorkshire-born architect Clifford Holliday, who arrived in Palestine with his wife Eunice in 1922. They had met as architecture students at Liverpool University. Eunice, pregnant with their first child, worked as his assistant, and in spare moments wrote lively letters home to her relatives in Lancashire. Both were in their twenties. Storrs was 'a superior bugger', Clifford recalled later, but working for him was an adventure.

Having trained as a town planner, Clifford regarded Storrs and Ashbee as amateurs. They wanted to preserve the Old City as a kind of museum, rather than having any coherent plan for its future. 'Can one make of Jerusalem (I am speaking always of Jerusalem within the walls) a modern city?' Storrs had asked rhetorically, addressing the council of the Pro-Jerusalem Society. 'Yes, gentlemen, one can; but on one condition, by its destruction.'[33] The society's work, however well intentioned, was heavily dependent on the energy and personality of Storrs, and by 1922 it was in disarray.

When we arrived [wrote Eunice on 7 October 1922] everything was in a most hopeless muddle. Ashbee was evidently the kind of man who liked to look important and be a kind of Lord High Everything and who spent a lot of money and did no work. For instance he had a craze for planting trees because they would make Jerusalem look fresh and pretty and so when you walk along suddenly you come upon a row of miserable looking grey stragglers trying their best to grow and looking very unhappy and all covered with dust. That's just an example of the kind of thing he did so Cliff found the Pro-Jerusalem Society about bankrupt and all the members fed up to the teeth.[34]

(Most of this passage was omitted from the published version of Eunice's letters.)

Clifford Holliday set about producing a new town plan, one of a series drawn up during the Mandate, and only partially implemented. Storrs also gave him other tasks: protecting a Crusader's tomb which lay in front of the Church of the Holy Sepulchre, and removing a Turkish clock-tower—a gift from Sultan Abdul-Hamid which the governor considered an eyesore—from its prominent position at Jaffa Gate. Under the terms of his contract, Clifford was free to take on private commissions. He was soon asked to design a church to commemorate the Scottish soldiers killed in the First World War. This was to be one of his most important projects.

The Hollidays, like all visitors, soon discovered Jerusalem's perennial water problem:

> All the streets in the old city [wrote Eunice in November 1922] are being taken up, and pipes laid down, to carry government water to the public taps. And new taps are being put up; you see so many of the poor people have to fetch their water, just as they used to draw it from wells in the Bible. It's queer to see the old water jars being superseded by petrol tins.[35]

But the 'government water' was never enough. 'The much-needed rain has come at last, in the nick of time,' Eunice reported in January 1923. 'It's poured for three days.'[36]

Tim Holliday, one of their four sons, all of whom grew up in Palestine, remembered their father as a 'restless, dynamic' figure going off to work in 'white suit, floppy bow-tie, and big hat'. Notwithstanding the occasional violence which served as a backdrop to their lives, Palestine was 'singular and unique for us'. Tolerant, sociable, and politically left-wing, Clifford and

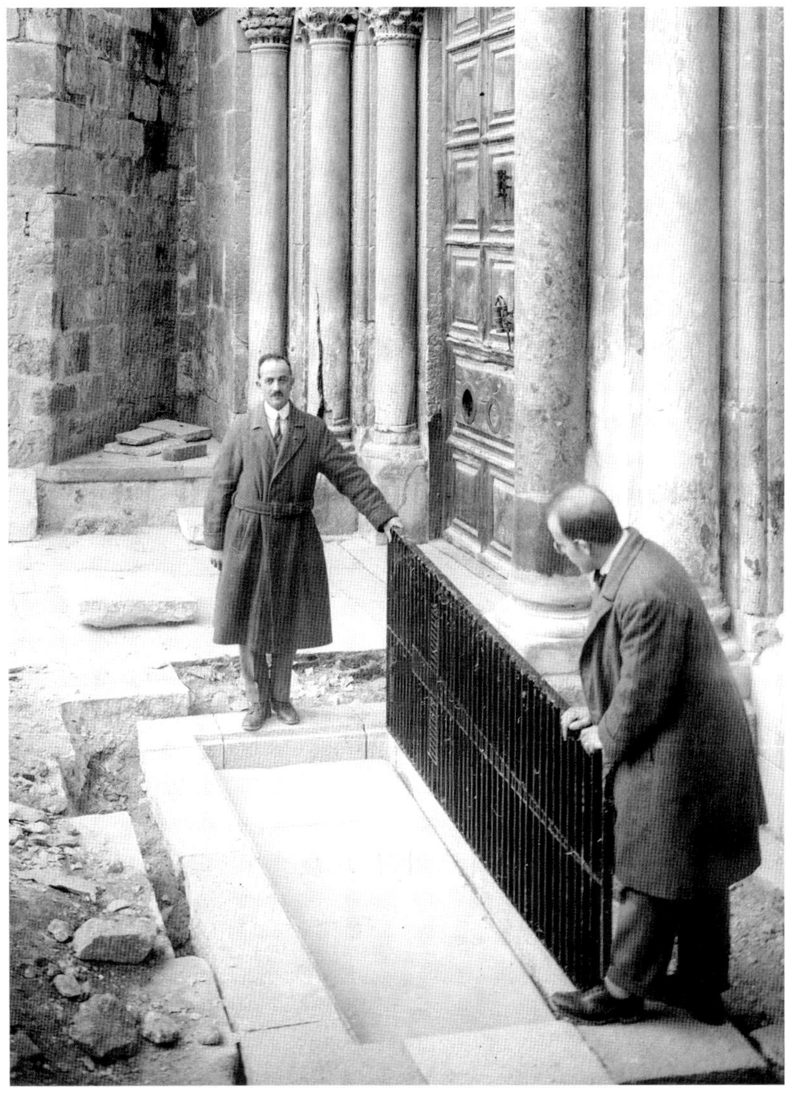

Clifford Holliday, right, restoring a Crusader tomb, 1925   American Colony

Eunice often found it easier to mix with Jews and Arabs than with the stiff-necked British establishment. They did not know it then, but they were to stay in Palestine for thirteen years. For Clifford it was a place of work; for Eunice it was to become 'her spiritual home'.[37]

Light and landscape

Storrs' 'beneficent despotism' had its advantages. In his self-appointed role as patron of the arts, he took under his wing the avant-garde British painter David Bomberg. The son of Jewish parents from Poland, Bomberg had grown up in the East End of London, studied at the prestigious Slade School of Fine Art, and served in Flanders during the First World War. After this traumatic experience, and in search of a new direction for his work, he set off for Jerusalem with his wife Alice in 1923. Here they were met by Clifford Holliday, who took them up onto the walls to see the Old City. 'I was a poor boy from the East End,' Bomberg recalled later, 'and I'd never seen the sunlight before.' Its intensity was 'something quite unbelievable for me'.[38] Eunice visited the couple in their tiny home in the Old City.

> The Bombergs have a little Bohemia all of their own in two rooms in the old city, and a gorgeous high roof overlooking the whole of Jerusalem. I go to have my picture done, and to drink coffee out of little bowls and eat brown bread and butter made of sheep's milk … They are funny people, absolutely on their last crust, literally living on tea and toast …[39]

Bomberg had been commissioned by a Zionist organisation in London to produce uplifting paintings of Jewish life and work in Palestine. Although deeply conscious of his Jewish heritage, he was indifferent to Zionism and struggled to fulfil the commission. Instead he produced a series of naturalistic landscapes—in marked contrast to his earlier work—which depicted the Old City and its surrounding hills in sharp detail and with a brilliant ability 'to transmit the full force of … dazzling white light'.[40] In the end it was Storrs who rescued the impoverished couple by paying £100 for Bomberg's painting 'Mount of Olives'. (Photographs of it survive, but the original was destroyed in a fire.) Another of his paintings in a similar vein, 'Jerusalem, Looking to Mount Scopus' (1925), was bought by Norman Bentwich (see back cover).

Storrs was quick to see that Bomberg's Zionist sponsors 'were hardly receiving the sort of value they had reason to expect for their money', but thought Bomberg's paintings 'were at least as likely to attract the world to Palestine as the mechanised sower going forth sowing, or groups of merry immigrants dancing round Old Testament maypoles'.[41] When Bomberg did finally visit the Jewish settlements, they failed to inspire him.

His experience of Palestine, from 1923 to 1927, is sometimes seen as a diversion from his career as a modernist painter. But it taught him about light and about a Mediterranean world which was a revelation to him.

The man who loved power
The Zionists had their own representative body in Palestine, the Jewish Agency, and Samuel was determined to set up a matching Arab institution. But the Arabs resisted any measure which implied acceptance of the terms of the Mandate, in which the Balfour Declaration had been formally embodied. Moreover the one step Samuel took in an attempt to foster a responsible Arab leadership was to backfire. This was the installation in 1921—technically the election, but the election was rigged—of the young nationalist Hajj Amin al-Husseini to the important position of Mufti of Jerusalem. A striking figure with blue eyes, reddish hair, and a trimmed beard, Hajj Amin had served under Faisal in his short-lived government in Syria.

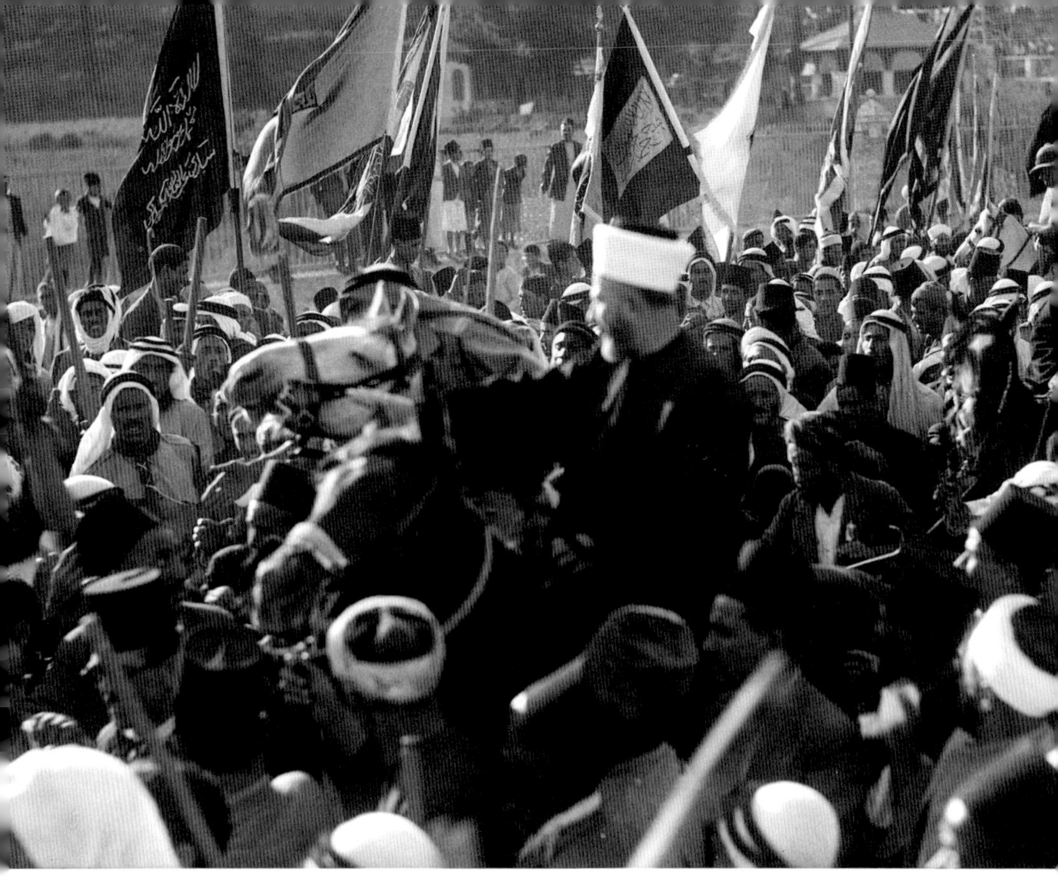

Hajj Amin al-Husseini leading the Nebi Musa procession, 1937

But because he had been convicted *in absentia* for his role in the riots of 1920, officials were divided over the wisdom of the appointment. What's more, he was still relatively young and his religious credentials were weak. But the prevailing view was that, coming from a prestigious Jerusalem family, he could help the Mandate government gain the co-operation of the Arabs and avoid further outbreaks of violence.

The following year Hajj Amin was appointed head of the Supreme Muslim Council, the body responsible for Palestine's mosques and Islamic institutions and the wealth that accrued from them. This gave him money and power and networks of patronage. But while offering the British a show of moderation, he shrewdly exploited the position to which they had elevated him.

> He is one of the ablest politicians that the Near East has produced in recent years [wrote an early historian of the Mandate] … one of those uncomfortable people who love power for its own sake … [a] very able and a very dangerous man, whom the British made the mistake of underestimating until it was too late.[42]

Although Hajj Amin was to act in an increasingly independent way, and eventually become a bitter enemy of Britain, it is striking to note that for well over a decade he was a paid British government employee. The *Palestine Civil Service List*—a kind of official Who's Who of Mandate Palestine—contains the following entry:[43]

Haj Amin Eff. El Husseini (b. 1893)
President and Rais El Ulema [head of the religious establishment], Jerusalem
Salary, £P. 600 [then equivalent to 600 British pounds]
Apptd. Mufti, Grade IV—10 May 1921
Apptd. Pres. and Rais—1 May 1922

Before long the Mufti became the pre-eminent Arab political leader in Palestine. He campaigned to internationalise the issue of Jerusalem and its holy places by turning it into a pan-Islamic cause. At the same time, a bitter rivalry developed between the Husseinis and a rival clan, the Nashashibis, who were readier for compromise with both the British and the Zionists. This dispute was to poison Arab politics for the duration of the Mandate.

In 1923, in an attempt to introduce an element of self-government, Samuel organised elections for a legislative council in which Muslims, Christians, and Jews would be represented. But the Arabs boycotted them and the scheme had to be dropped.

The harsh reality, as the high commissioner was forced to realise, was that if the two communities could not develop together, they would develop separately—and in competition with one another.[44] The idea of a single, shared Palestine with a single, shared identity was one to which the British clung; but it was probably doomed from the start.

A *test of loyalty*

Britain ran Palestine with a civil service of some 2,500 people, the majority of whom were Jews or Arabs. Their loyalties during the course of the Mandate were to be severely tested. From the moment he arrived, Norman Bentwich strove to be impartial but found himself under constant attack not only from the Arabs but from some of his British colleagues and from sections of the press in London. 'The Arabs say *of course* he favours the Jews,' wrote his wife Helen, '& the Jews say they expect him to but he doesn't.'[45] Under Samuel, his position was secure (if often uncomfortable); later, it was to be undermined.

For Arabs, too—like the young, Cambridge-educated Musa Alami—working for the Mandate authority posed inescapable and sometimes insoluble dilemmas. Alami had been born into privilege as a member of one of Jerusalem's leading Muslim families. During Ottoman rule both his grandfather and his father had served as the city's mayor. He had studied at Anna Spafford's American Colony school, with private tutors (including the respected writer and educator Khalil Sakakini), and at the Ecole des Frères. When at the start of the First World War the 17-year-old Musa was conscripted into the Ottoman army, his father, Faidi, pulled strings to get him a safe job in Damascus, where he joined the censorship department. But in 1917 he returned late from leave, was accused of being a deserter, and spent six nerve-racking months hiding in the home of his old tutor, Sakakini.

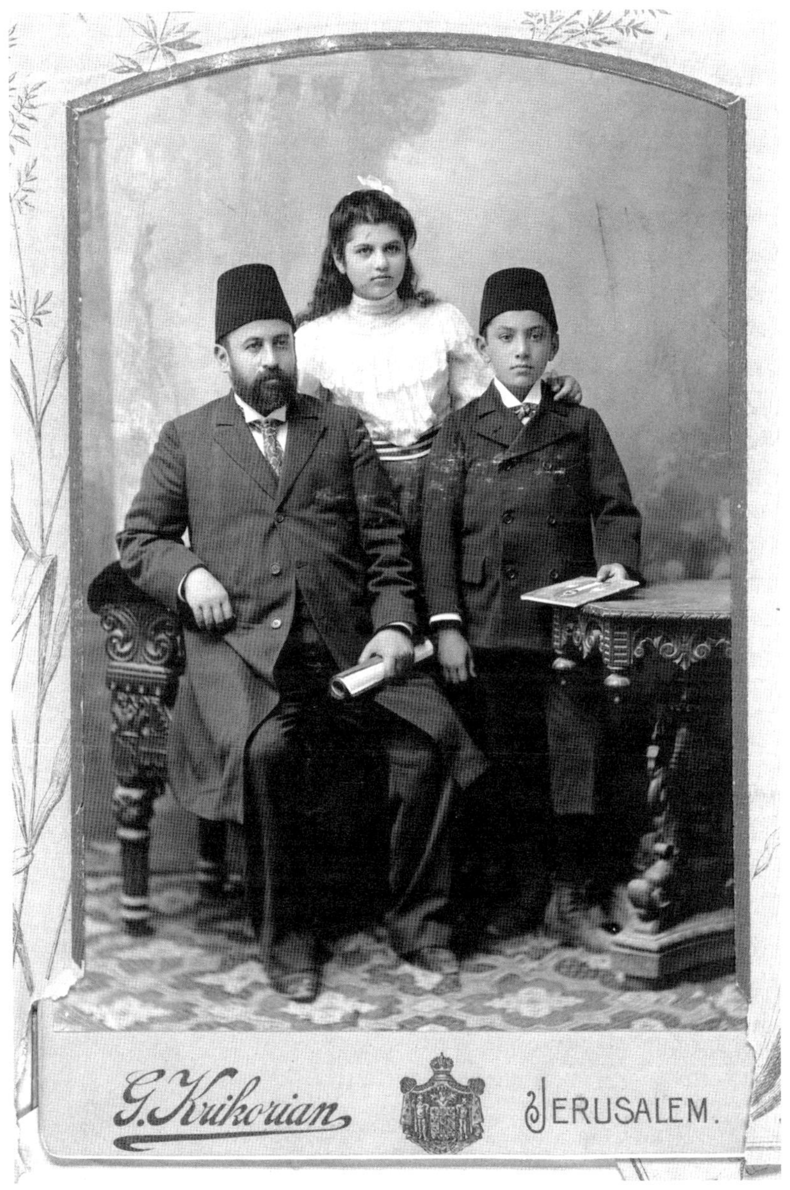

Musa Alami with his father and sister, early 1900s   Garabed Krikorian

After the war, despite Arab misgivings about Britain's new role in the Middle East, Faidi remained a committed Anglophile and arranged for his only son to study law at Cambridge. For Samuel and Bentwich, Musa was accordingly quite a catch—a young, personable, British-educated Arab from a leading Muslim family. (They were conscious of the criticism that they were employing a disproportionate number of Christian Arabs.) But when in 1925 they proposed appointing him to the important position of government advocate, working with Bentwich, officials in London blocked the appointment on the grounds that such a post should be given to an Englishman. He was

An imported Dodge, 1920s   American Colony

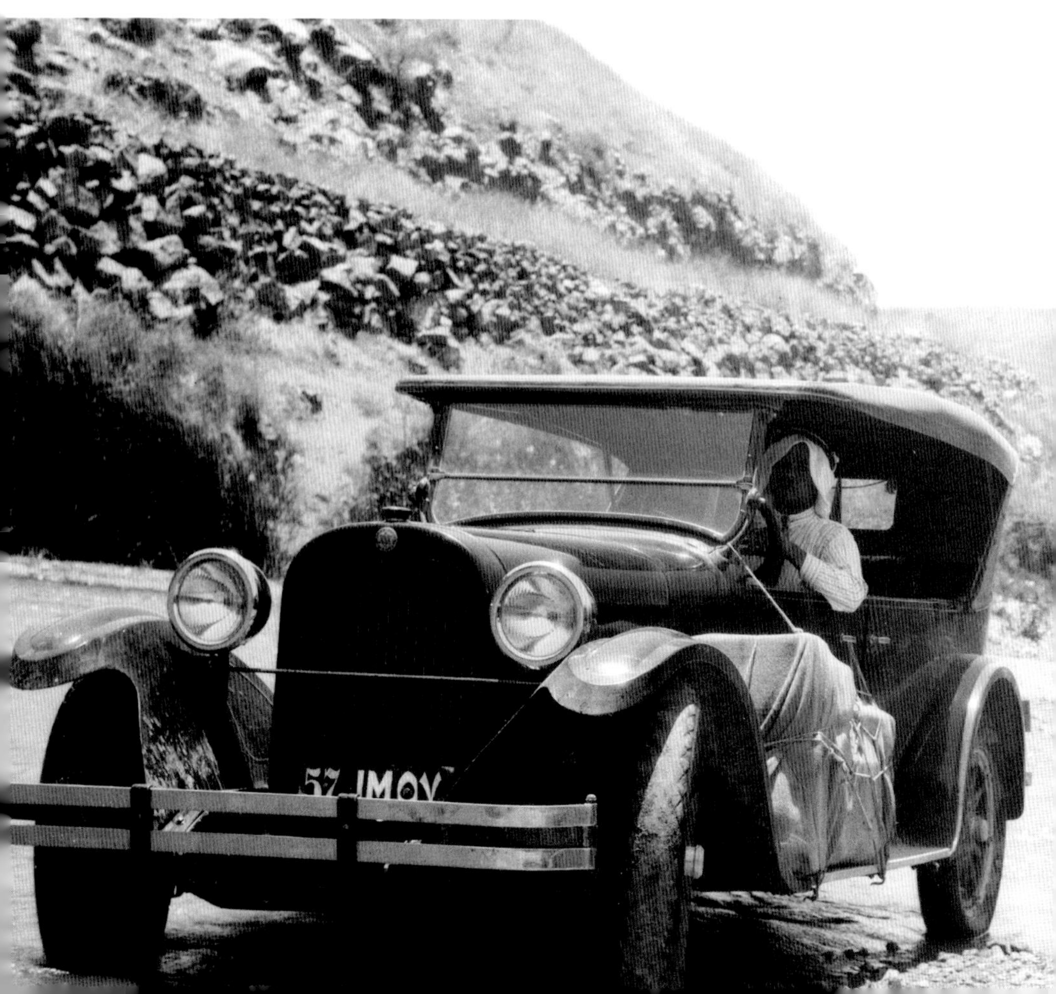

instead appointed to the less sensitive position of junior legal adviser, gaining a reputation for knowledge and impartiality. But remaining impartial in a climate of increasing polarisation was to prove more and more exacting.[46]

Death of a matriarch

In April 1923 Anna Spafford had died. She was eighty-one, and was given the magnificent send-off she would have wanted. Without her, the American Colony was never the same again. Her daughter Bertha had her mother's strength of character but lacked her religious fervour. She liked luxuries that had previously been denied the colonists such as parties and cocktails and jewellery. Under Bertha, the colony had a continuing social and humanitarian role—she set up a children's hospital which survives to this day—and enhanced its money-making activities by importing Dodge automobiles from the United States. But it was no longer a religious cult, and within a few years the rifts within it were to tear it apart.[47]

Meanwhile the photographic business flourished and had become the colony's most profitable activity. By now Lewis Larsson was the colony's principal photographer and his work was known well beyond the Middle East. The thousands of photographs he and his colleagues produced during these years—many of them preserved in the Library of Congress—provide an important visual record of Palestine under British rule.

After the capture of Jerusalem, Bertha and her husband had been quick to ingratiate themselves with Allenby and Storrs. ('Uncle Ronald' had read *Alice through the Looking-Glass* to their six children.)[48] They did the same when Herbert Samuel arrived. But, as Helen Bentwich was quick to notice, they were not enamoured of Zionism.

Culture and change

Tawfiq Canaan's reputation as a doctor was growing. In 1919 he took over the running of a leper home in Talbieh, on the western edge of Jerusalem, which the British decided should house all Palestine's lepers, both Arabs and Jews. He was soon a specialist in the control and management of the disease. He also became an acknowledged authority on Arab folklore, building up a unique collection of the amulets and talismans which were used by villagers to ward off disease and bring good luck. In 1920 the Palestine Oriental Society was founded under British auspices, bringing together Arab, Jewish, and European scholars. Canaan was an active member and contributed to its journal, which from 1924 to 1927 published what was to become his best-known work, *Mohammedan Saints and Sanctuaries in Palestine*. At the same time he worked as the trusted family doctor of many European residents, including British officials. As both physician and scholar, he became an accepted member of the Jerusalem establishment.

Canaan's approach to medicine and tradition was set out in June 1923 in a speech at a graduation ceremony at his *alma mater*, the American University of Beirut (the former Syrian Protestant College). He roundly criticised such superstitions as belief in jinns (spirits) and the evil eye, and practices such as arranged marriage, and argued that greater priority had to be given to family health and in particular infant mortality. It was the clarion call of a modernist. He saw the danger that modernisation might sever the Arabs from their cultural moorings, but had no nostalgic affection for traditional culture, advocating a vision based on change, not on clinging to the past.[49]

For modernists such as Canaan, the future of Palestine had to be secured—as his own future had been—through education. To this the British were committed, but within distinct limits. They acknowledged that Arab illiteracy was widespread and that schools

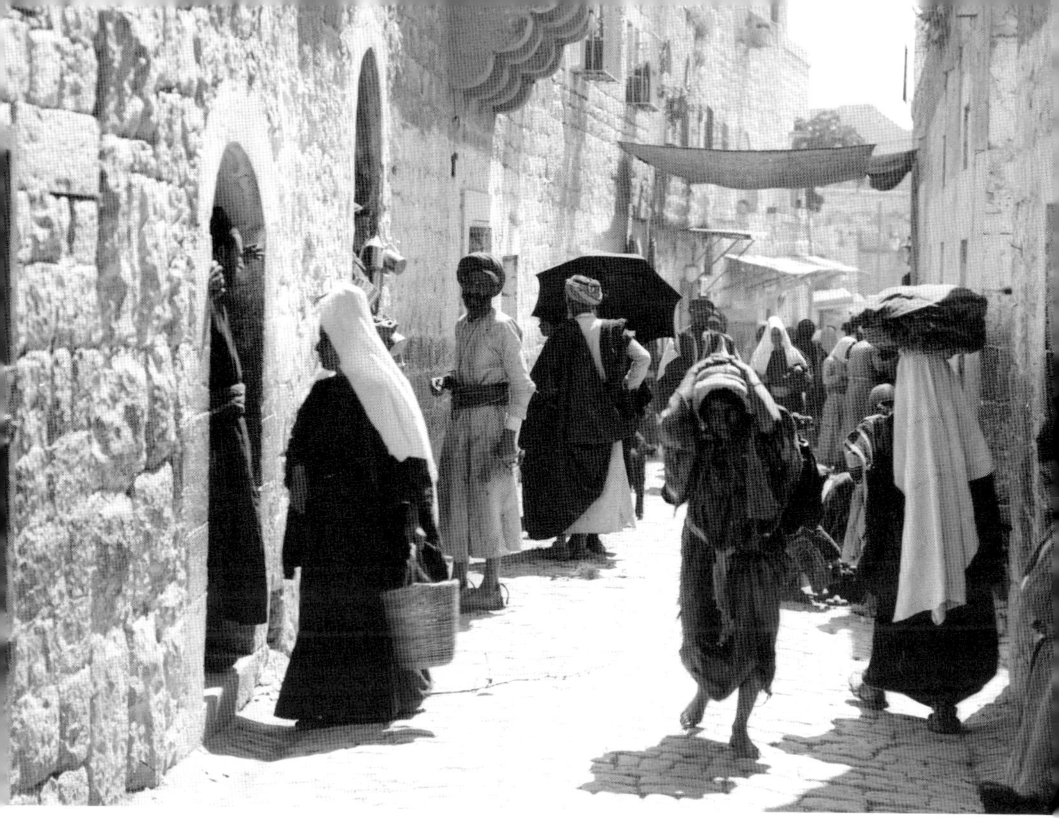

and colleges were badly needed—not only because the Arabs demanded them, but because they themselves needed a cadre of educated Arabs to help them run the country. But they resisted the idea of mass education, partly because of lack of money—officials in London insisted that as far as possible British-run territories should be financially self-sufficient—and partly through fear that schools would spread the contagion of nationalism.

The boy from Bethlehem

Jabra Ibrahim Jabra grew up with the sweet smell of incense wafting down from the floor above. His family's first home—or the first he remembered—consisted of a single room on the ground floor of an old Ottoman building in Bethlehem. The room was 'deep, dank, and dark'. It had no windows: the sun entered it only when the big iron door was opened. Above them lived a friar, and above the friar was a makeshift church where the choir sang in the ancient language of Syriac and 'the scent of incense lingered … all the days of the week'.

Here Jabra lived with his mother, father, grandmother, and elder brother. They were Christian Arabs. A barefoot boy, growing up in the 1920s, he loved climbing trees and flying kites and chasing lizards. His father Ibrahim, dogged by ill health, had a succession of jobs as a cobbler, a gardener, and a construction worker. One day he brought home an old tyre and cut it up to make a pair of shoes. The family kept moving house to save money. Later to become well known as a writer, critic, and translator, Jabra never forgot the meaning of poverty. 'I realised that hunger was pleasurable when you knew there was food waiting for you, and that it was terrifying when you knew there was no food waiting for you.'[50]

The outside world occasionally intruded on the children's lives.

> We went running out of the playground gate to Manger Square. There were cars parked there from which tall, blonde, elderly men and women got out carrying cameras. They spoke to us in a language we did not understand, and they gestured to us to stand in front of them with the Church of the Nativity in the background so that they might take our picture. [51]

Although the British had begun opening schools in the towns and villages, education in Bethlehem—a mainly Christian town of some 5,000 people—was still largely in the hands of the churches, monasteries, and convents. Jabra went to a succession of church schools, fell in love with the sounds and shapes of Arabic, and watched Charlie Chaplin films on Father Domaggi's improvised cinema screen.

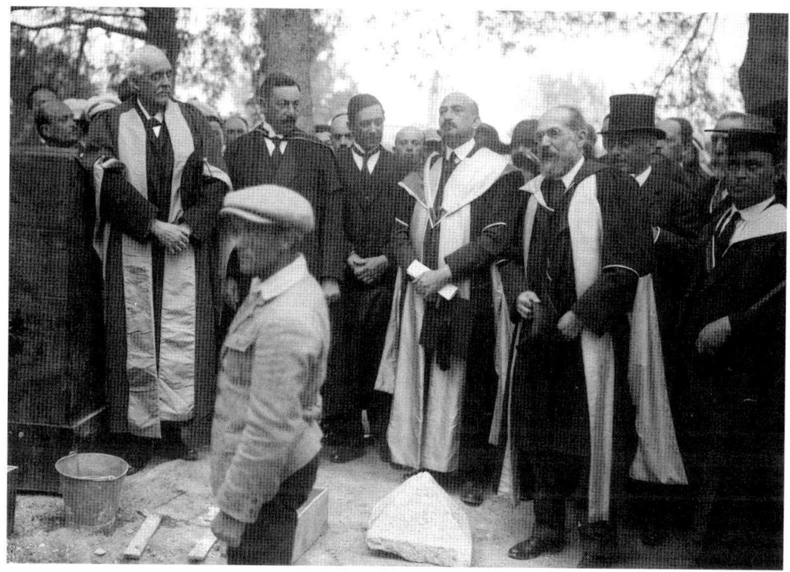

American Colony

Balfour, left, at the opening of the Hebrew University, 1925: beside him, from left to right, Herbert Samuel, Judah Magnes, Chaim Weizmann

Samuel's swansong

The Yishuv, meanwhile, was building up an impressive and largely autonomous network of Hebrew-speaking schools. (Not all immigrants were happy to abandon the languages of Europe, and Hebrew had triumphed only after a bitter *Kulturkampf*.) Illiteracy was virtually unheard of. The Zionists' greatest cultural achievement was the opening of the Hebrew University of Jerusalem, at its site on Mount Scopus, in 1925. Among the visiting dignitaries was the elderly Arthur Balfour, visibly proud of the infant national home.

'There were 12,000 people there,' Helen Bentwich recorded, '& a more orderly crowd you couldn't conceive … All the English & quite a number of non-Jewish Palestinians were there, including a number of Bedouin sheikhs.' But she found the speeches interminable (apart from Samuel's) and Balfour's extempore remarks disappointing. (Eunice Holliday reported that Clifford, too, was bored stiff and fell asleep.) Despite the attendance of those 'non-Jewish Palestinians', the Arabs of Jerusalem organised protests at Balfour's presence, decking the city in black flags. Storrs was delighted at the visit, but admitted it had 'put the clock of reconciliation back by at least a year'.[52]

The president of the new university was a Reform rabbi from California, Dr Judah Magnes. A pacifist, Magnes favoured Jewish settlement in Palestine but argued that the drive for a Jewish state would inevitably lead to violence. He was a prominent supporter of Brit Shalom (Covenant of Peace), a group formed in 1925 which believed Arabs and Jews should work together to create a state of the two nations. The bi-nationalists were always a fringe movement, but they had moral authority. They included another prominent American, Henrietta Szold (founder of the Hadassah hospital), and the philosopher Martin Buber, and enjoyed the quiet support of Norman Bentwich. Acting as the conscience of Zionism, they were a thorn in Ben-Gurion's side.

The inauguration of the Hebrew University marked the climax of Samuel's period in office. It has been remarked that his abilities were those of a civil servant rather than a politician.[53] But despite the suspicion of the Arabs and the scepticism of the Zionist leadership (Ben-Gurion was particularly scathing), he had established Palestine's first civilian administration, while struggling against considerable odds to be even-handed.

Right: *Plumer with his grandson and a French visitor, 1926: Plumer's tenure as Palestine's second high commissioner, from 1925 to 1928, was a rare period of tranquillity in the history of the Mandate.*

American Colony

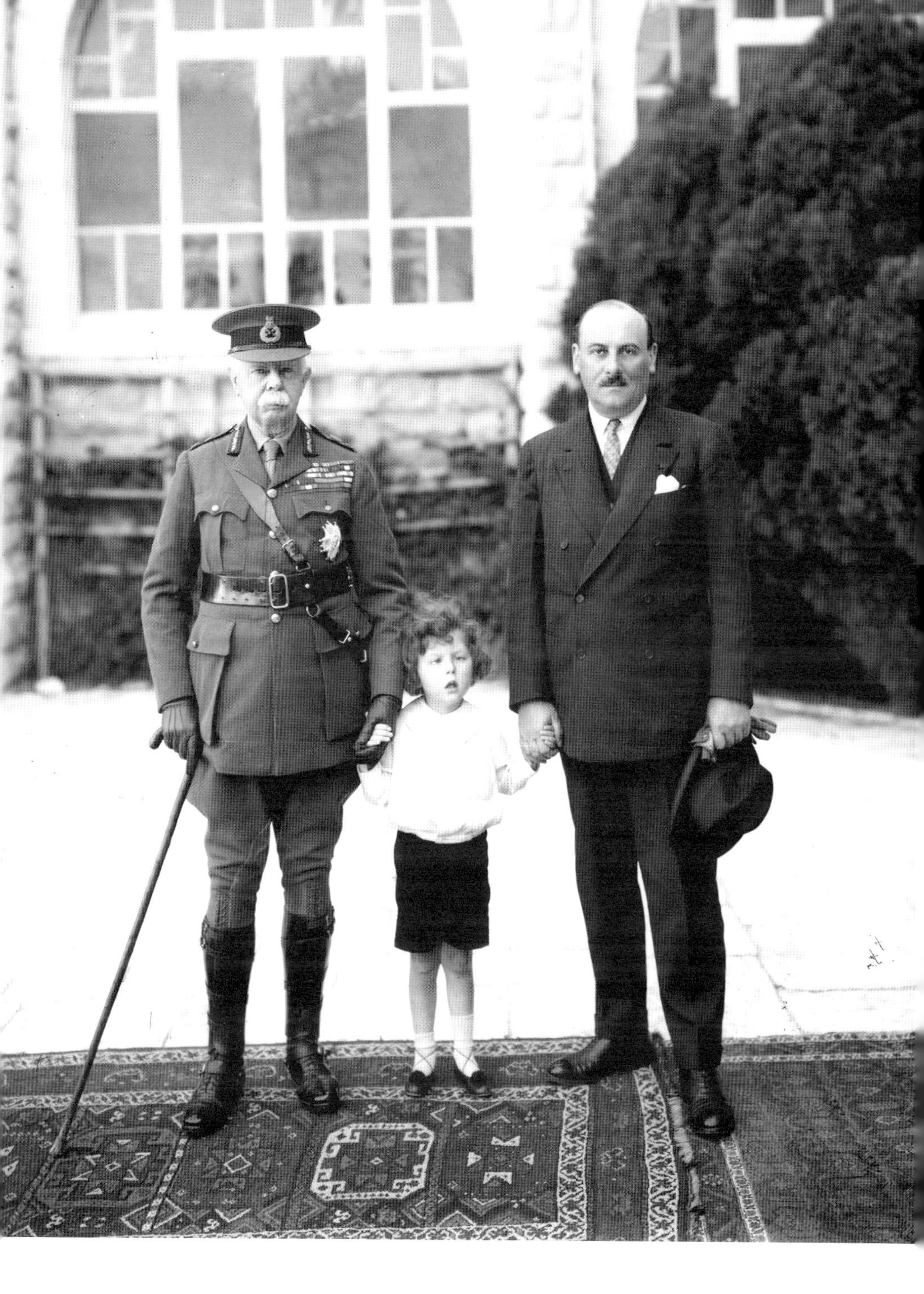

An interlude of calm

Samuel's successor, like all but one of Palestine's subsequent high commissioners, was a military man. Lord Plumer, a 68-eight-year-old veteran of the First World War, was small and outwardly unprepossessing, with a walrus moustache. (He was said to be the model for Colonel Blimp, a cartoon character and later the subject of a popular film.) The Bentwiches did not at first warm to him. Helen feared he would be a crusty old reactionary, and described Lady Plumer as 'very thin & scraggy with a high voice'.[54] Bertha Spafford Vester, a snob, regarded her as a *grande dame,* and was intrigued by her 'strings and strings of irregular pearls'.[55]

The Bentwiches had not planned to stay on after Samuel's departure, but quickly came to like the new high commissioner's strength of character and down-to-earth manner. 'The Plumers are marvellously energetic,' wrote Helen in November 1925, expressing astonishment at 'the old lady's itinerary':

> One day: starting at 8, & seeing all the notables of Nazareth & 3 schools; then lunch at our [Zionist] farm school at Nahalal ... then back to Nazareth for a tea-party, an inspection of the hospital, & more notables ... She has no maid on these tours.[56]

Helen's letters record the distinguished visitors who came to Palestine in the years of Zionism's infancy. There was 'great excitement', she wrote in April 1926, over the visit of the young Lithuanian-born violinist Jascha Heifetz. Music was very important to the Yishuv, not only in the cities but in the agricultural settlements. Heifetz 'played in Tel Aviv 3 times—once to workers, where he had an audience of 6,000—& at Haifa, & to the workers in the Plain of Esdraelon, 2,500 of them'. These were the kibbutzniks of Ein Harod and neighbouring settlements who left their work and flocked to hear him play.[57]

In November 1926 Ronald Storrs made an emotional

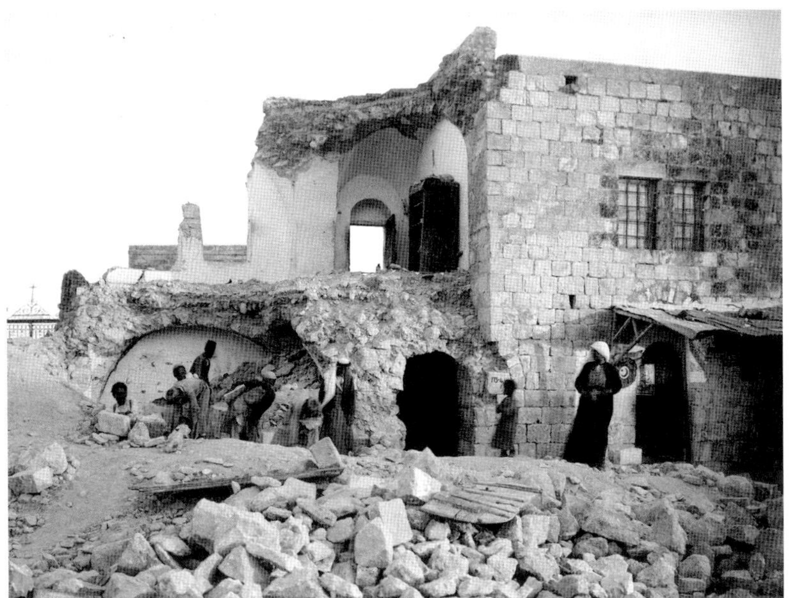

Aftermath of the earthquake of 1927   American Colony

farewell to the city he loved, and went off to become governor of Cyprus. The Pro-Jerusalem Society, which without him lost its *raison d'être,* was wound up. Much of its work was carried on by the government's town-planning department, with Clifford Holliday retained as an adviser.

The following year Palestine experienced a devastating earthquake which killed some 300 people. The young Jabra felt its effects in Bethlehem, where 'countless houses were destroyed … especially the dilapidated ones, and many others were cracked. The earth split open in different places and caused much fear.'[58] But it was Nablus which felt the full force of the quake. 'It's a pitiful sight,' recorded Helen Bentwich after visiting the city:

In the main bazaar were houses three stories high, every room of which was built by and belonged to a different man. They all collapsed—and the chaos about new building permits, loans, etc. may be imagined ... All the houses leaned against each other—& even now, when they take out a dividing wall, others still collapse.[59]

Clifford Holliday was sent to assess the damage. Among the buildings affected was the Augusta Victoria compound, which could no longer be used as the high commissioner's official residence. While the Plumers decamped to an uncomfortable convent, the architect Austen Harrison was commissioned to build a new Government House, on the southern side of the city, on the Hill of Evil Counsel.

Now in his seventies, Plumer's health began to deteriorate, and after three years his term came to an end. The rare period of tranquillity that Palestine enjoyed from 1925 to 1928 was only partly the result of his firm management. Jewish immigration had declined because of the economic depression in Europe. In one year, 1927, more Jews left than entered—a sign that the success of the Zionist project was far from assured. But the consequent easing of tension led Plumer to take the fateful decision to scale back the size of the security forces.

Year Zero

Plumer's successor was Sir John Chancellor, a former army officer and colonial governor who was never comfortable in the post. Norman Bentwich found him 'detached'. Helen, less inhibited, wrote after one dinner party, 'It's like sitting next to a leg of mutton.'[60]

Chancellor's misfortune was to arrive in the middle of a simmering controversy involving the holy places of Jerusalem. In the summer of 1928 a fierce dispute erupted when a British policeman ordered the removal of a screen put up at the Wailing Wall to separate male and female Jewish worshippers. (In the Holy City, such apparently trivial matters often escalated

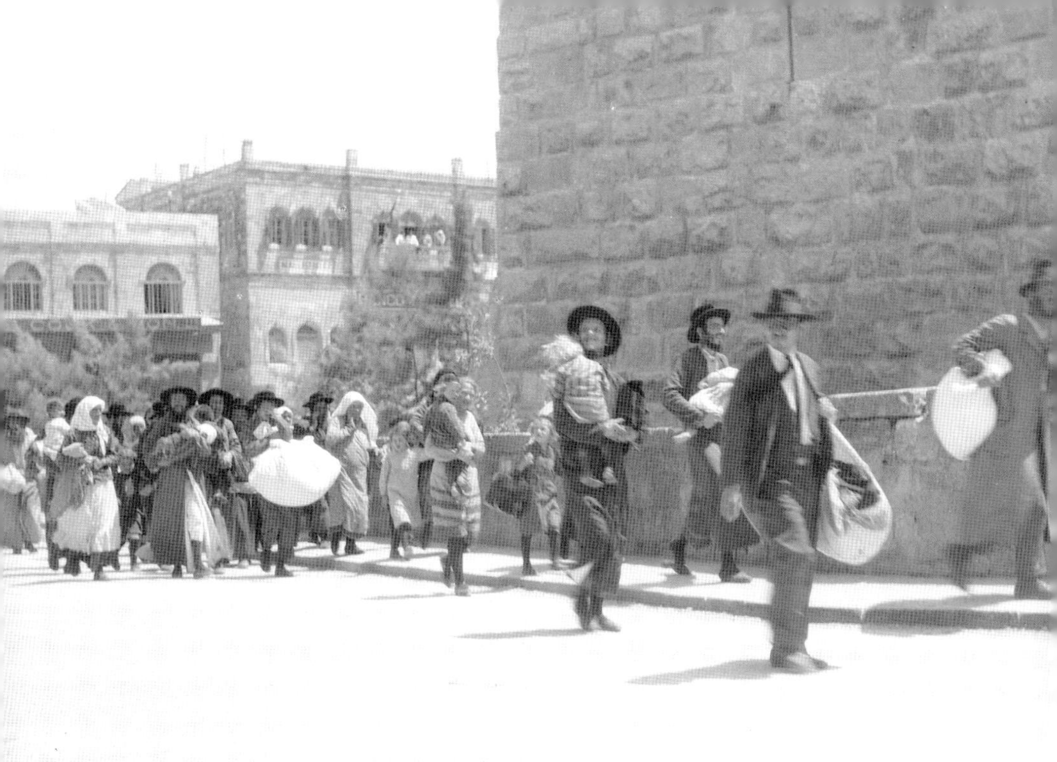

Jerusalem, 1929: Jews fleeing from the Old City

into crises.) The dispute continued into the following year, and finally exploded in August 1929 in a wave of violence which began in Jerusalem and quickly spread to other parts of the country.

According to Eunice Holliday, 'anybody with a Muslim servant knew something was going to happen'.[61] With their growing family, the Hollidays had moved to a larger house on the Street of the Prophets (just north of the Old City). The trouble began after Muslims had attended Friday prayers.

> I don't know what they were told in the mosque on Friday [wrote Eunice], but they all came out determined to kill Jews … It is rumoured that the Grand Mufti [Hajj Amin] told the villagers that

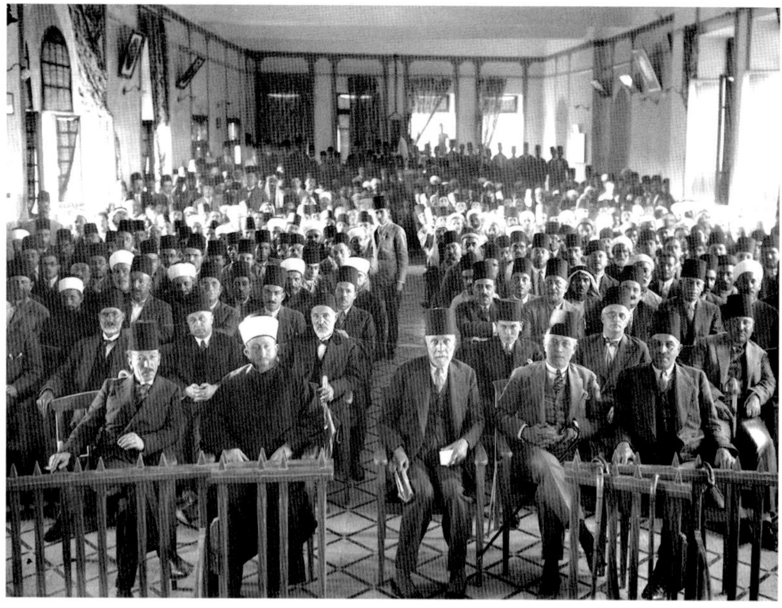

Arab protest meeting in Jerusalem, 1929   American Colony
Hajj Amin is in the front row, second from left

the British would not interfere! The first thing we heard was at 12.30 on Friday. Shouting ... followed by a shooting, a car-load of police going down the road, then the Jews: there were hundreds of them all with sticks, stones, pieces of iron, even bottles, anything to hit with. They all went rushing down the Street of the Prophets ... [62]

The worst of the violence was in Hebron, in southern Palestine, where sixty-seven men, women, and children—part of a small community of religious, non-Zionist Jews—were brutally massacred. The death toll would have been even higher but for the actions of the town's British police chief, Raymond Cafferata, and of local Arabs who protected their Jewish neighbours. 'It's amazing,' wrote Helen Bentwich, 'how many of the Jews—even in Hebron—were saved by Arabs.' [63]

Religious Jews were also the target in the northern town of Safad. Sydney Moody, previously a political officer there and now a senior official in the Jerusalem secretariat, rushed back to the town to see for himself the results of the violence. He found the market in the Jewish quarter a scene of devastation, as his wife Flora recorded in a letter to her family:

> Little booths overturned, stools lying on their sides, and everywhere scattered far and wide all the grapes and tomatoes and fishes and meat, all kicked and trodden and now rotting fast. The stench and flies were abominable … The little shops had been smashed and emptied. The floors were strewn with wreckage thrown down in the mad search for loot …

Their friends, the Semples, Scottish missionaries who ran a school in the town, witnessed how the Jews had been attacked.

> The mob rushed up the hill into the town from the villages. The Semples saw them from their windows, scrambling up the slopes, waving axes, knives, sticks and stones, howling horribly … they swept down the Jewish quarter killing and looting … the native police didn't fire at all. They are accused of helping the rioters …

The Jewish death toll in Safad was twenty-six. When her husband returned to Jerusalem, Flora found him demoralised and disillusioned: 'Jew, Arab and Government alike, he has lost faith in them all.' She also recorded how the European children, including their own, had a new game. Instead of playing cowboys and Indians, they played Arabs and Jews.[64]

The violence spun out of control because, thanks to Plumer's cuts, the country was poorly protected. The police force was hopelessly inadequate and, in times of crisis, its Arab and Jewish

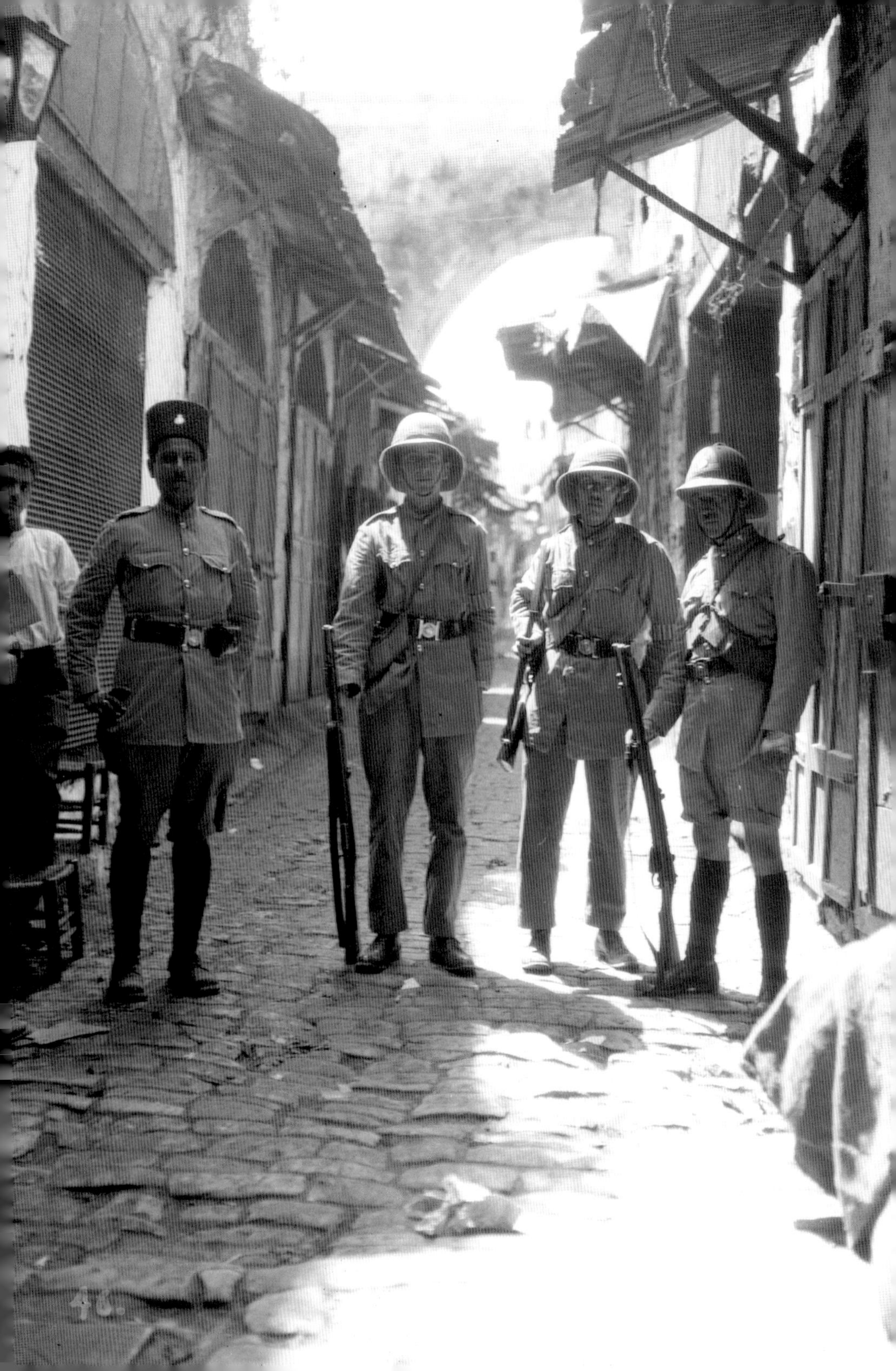

members tended to throw off all semblance of impartiality. Troops had to be rushed in from Egypt. Eunice Holliday was struck by how innocent they seemed. 'They were all very small, fair, blue-eyed, and young.'[65] In addition, Clifford and other civilians were recruited as 'specials', members of a volunteer force brought in to help restore law and order. He wore khaki and, against his will, was issued with a revolver. Eunice waited anxiously when he went out on night patrols. In her letters she tried to keep the worst of the news from her parents in Lancashire, but commented laconically, 'there is a little quiet murder nearly every day'.[66]

Earlier violence in Palestine had been sporadic and contained, allowing complacency to return. There would be an official inquiry, recommendations would be made, and normal life would resume. This time was different. In a week of violence across the country, 133 Jews were killed by Arabs; of the Arab death toll of 116, most were killed by the security forces. It was the ferocity of the violence, as well as its scale, which shook the British authorities. 1929 has been dubbed Year Zero, the moment at which the Arab-Jewish conflict began in earnest.[67]

Left: *Volunteers guarding the Old City, 1929.* American Colony

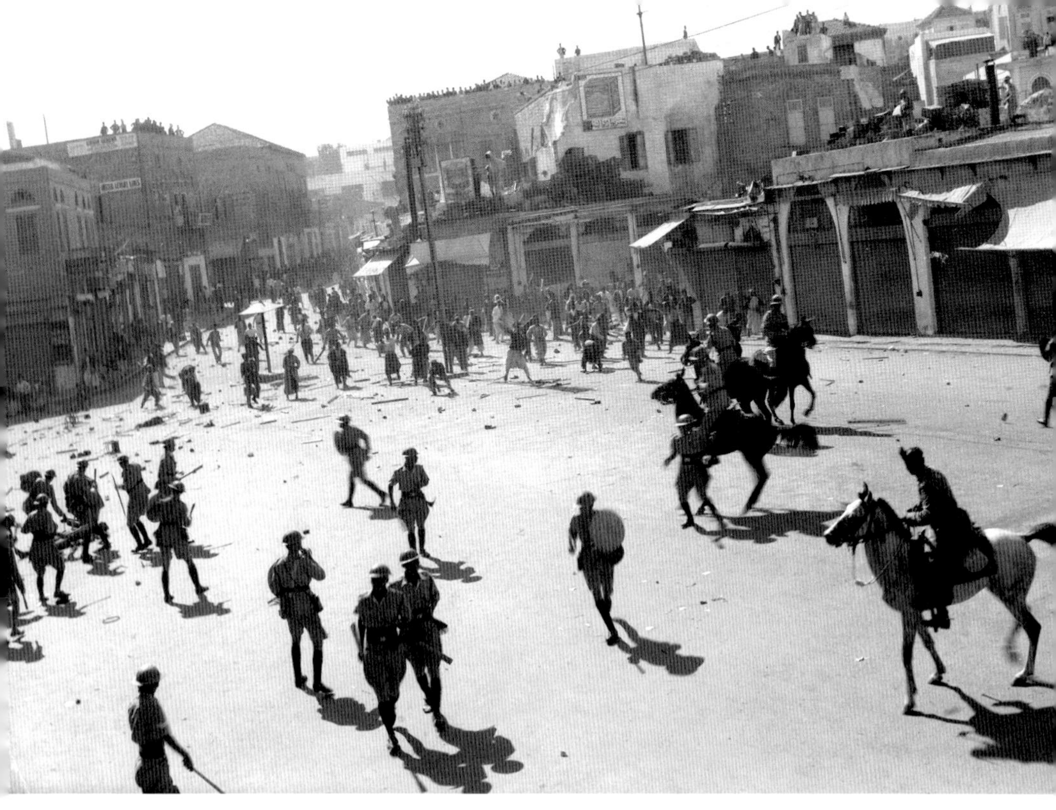

Arab riots in Jaffa, October 1933 American Colony

3

Days of rage, 1929–1939

'An irrepressible conflict has arisen between two national
communities within the narrow bounds of one small country.'

Lord Peel, July 1937

THE TRAUMA OF 1929 was followed, as day follows night, by a commission of inquiry. A team of experts under Sir Walter Shaw concluded that the fundamental cause of the Arabs' resort to violence was 'the disappointment of their political and national aspirations and fear for their economic future'. The commission did not believe the Mufti had instigated the unrest—despite persuasive evidence that he had fanned the flames. More broadly, the Shaw commission's report prompted one of those moments of painful introspection when a British government felt obliged to admit that its Palestine policy had failed.

Shaw put his finger on the two central issues of immigration and land. On his recommendation, another inquiry followed under Sir John Hope Simpson, who was set the task of estimating how many people Palestine could absorb. His conclusion was that the choice lay between introducing costly development projects to the tune of £6-£8 million to enable the land to accommodate a large influx of immigrants—or stopping immigration altogether. The Treasury balked at such expenditure, and instead the government published a proposal—known as the Passfield White Paper of 1930—which recommended the restriction of Jewish immigration and land purchases.[1]

This unleashed a storm of protest from the Zionists and in the British parliament that Ramsay MacDonald's minority government felt too weak to resist. Among those who opposed the White Paper were Lloyd George, Winston Churchill, and Herbert Samuel. In a letter to Weizmann the prime minister withdrew its most sensitive proposals. It is true that he was constrained both politically and legally, with prominent lawyers arguing that the White Paper infringed the terms of the Mandate. But he had nevertheless given the impression of surrendering to Zionist pressure and of carrying out one of the many U-turns which characterised policy-making throughout British rule in Palestine.

As Sir John Chancellor's term drew to a close, one of its least creditable episodes was the campaign of denigration against the attorney-general, Norman Bentwich, in the aftermath of the unrest of 1929. This was led by the chief justice, Sir Michael McDonnell, who did his utmost to persuade Chancellor that having a Jew and a Zionist in this prominent position was detrimental to the government's standing. In November 1929 Bentwich was shot in the leg by a young, possibly deranged Arab (whom he defended when the case came to court), and the incident gave Chancellor the opportunity to argue that Bentwich's life was in danger. While on leave in London, he was dissuaded from returning and was offered posts elsewhere, all of which he turned down. Since he refused to resign, he was sacked. He had the consolation of being appointed to a chair at the Hebrew University, but as he wrote to Chancellor, '[M]y fifteen years' service for Palestine has ended in disgrace.'[2]

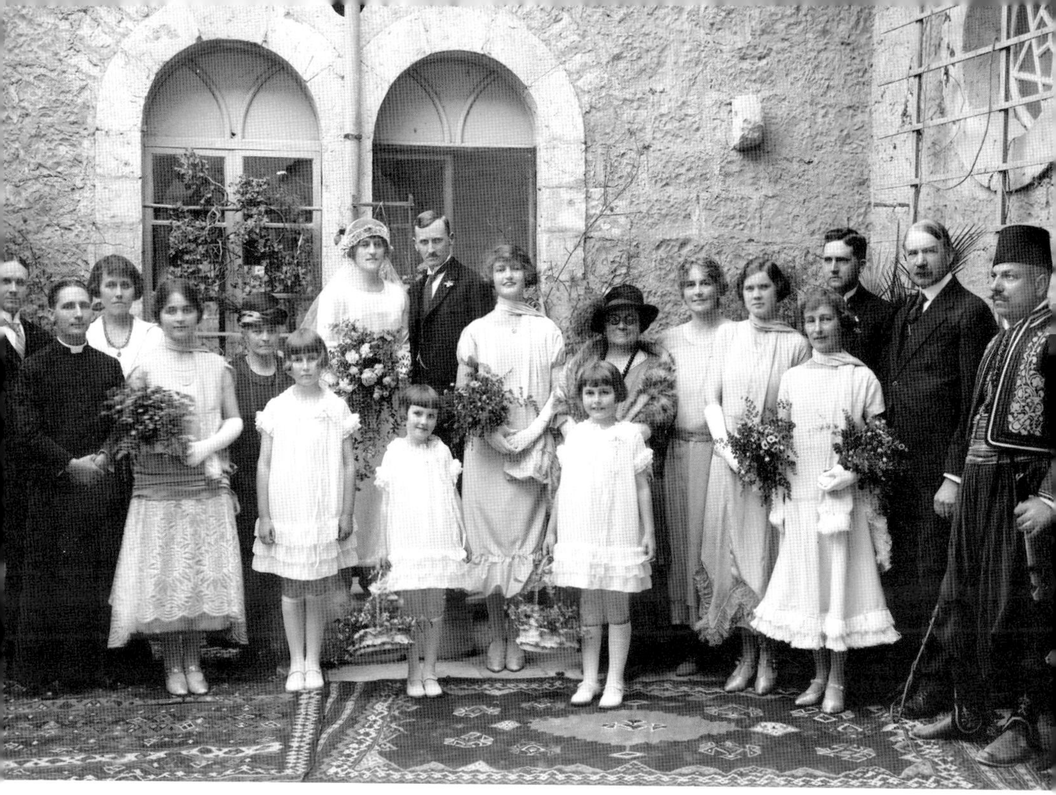

The American Colony in happier times:
Eric Matson's wedding, 1924

American Colony

Death of a dream

One of Bentwich's last and most unpalatable duties as attorney-general had been to oversee the acrimonious break-up of the American Colony. The grievances of the younger Swedes, including Lewis Larsson, against Bertha and Frederick Vester came to a head in a prolonged and bitter feud in which the Mandate authorities and the American consul both became entangled. Essentially, Bertha and Frederick tried to put the colony and its assets, whose legal status had always been undetermined, into their family's hands. This the younger Swedes, who had worked so hard for so little reward, refused to countenance. The colony 'was soon hopelessly split between the

Vester-led majority of old Swedes and the dissident younger minority. Appalling accusations were hurled, every remembered injury, every old grudge, jealousy, or petty quarrel was aired vindictively'.[3]

Bentwich asked a senior British lawyer, C. H. Perrott, to come from Egypt to adjudicate the claims. After a year of wrangling, the assets were finally divided up and the parties to the divorce went their separate ways. The Vesters kept the biggest of their properties which was in time to gain fame as the American Colony Hotel. As compensation Lewis Larsson was given Bertha's house, which later became the Swedish consulate. The photographic agency went to Eric Matson, who henceforth ran it under his own name (so that today the collection of some 20,000 prints in the Library of Congress is known, a little misleadingly, as the Matson collection). 'Never in all my life,' Perrott declared, 'have I had a more distasteful arbitration to perform and never have I dealt with such impossible people.'

As a commercial enterprise, the colony lived on; but its fifty-year history as an eccentric, quarrelsome religious community, imbued with the dream of Jerusalem, was at an end.

A changing skyline

The 1930s got under way as a period of growth and modernisation. Among the innovations that appeared in the late 1920s and now spread more widely were electricity, radio, elevators—and, for those who could afford it, air travel as an alternative to long voyages home. The architectural face of Jerusalem, and with it the city's social life, changed dramatically. A new landmark was the King David Hotel, which provided Jerusalem with a world-class standard of luxury. 'We are invited to the inauguration,' wrote Eunice Holliday on 23 December 1930. 'It is a most marvellous hotel of a new kind for Jerusalem. Tourists are paying £2 to £3 a day there.'[4] Built by a consortium led by

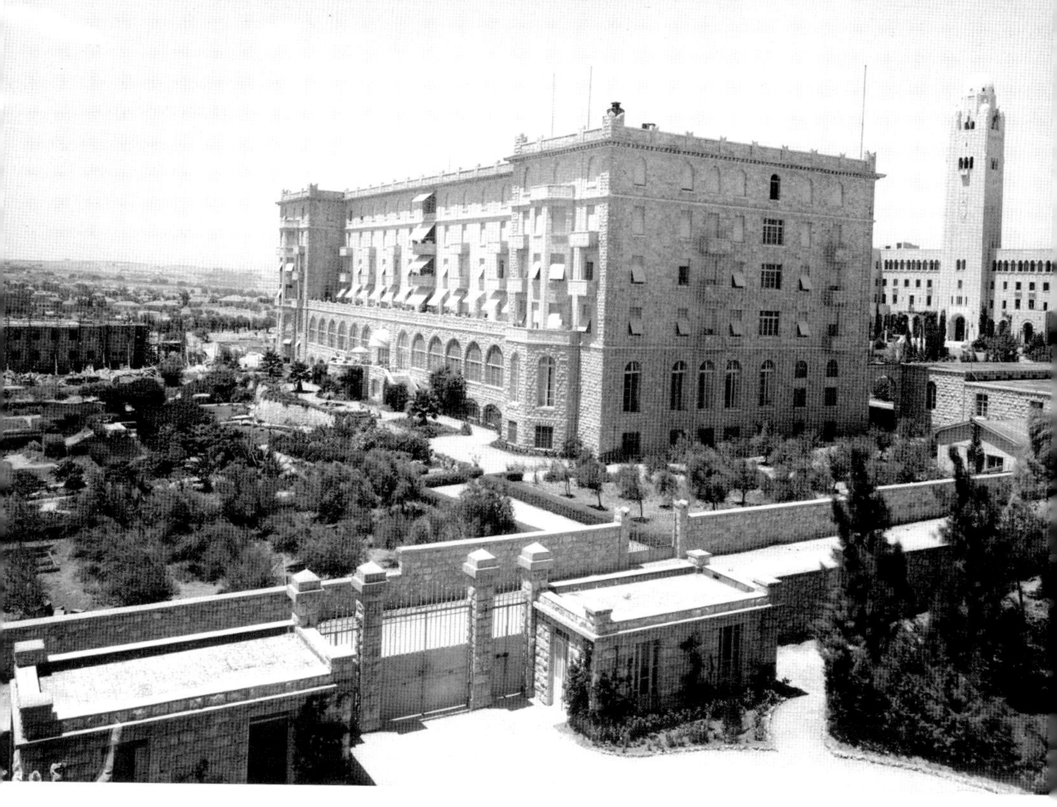

King David Hotel, with the YMCA
in the background, 1930s

the Mosseris, wealthy Egyptian Jews, the hotel became famous throughout the Middle East and beyond. Directly opposite it, and completed in 1933, was the YMCA, funded by American Christians, with a striking tower, an auditorium, a library, and impressive sports facilities: proof that, in transforming the city's skyline, Europe no longer had a monopoly.

By 1932, after ten years in Jerusalem, Clifford Holliday's thoughts were turning to home. He had not intended to stay so long. But there was work in Palestine, and little prospect of it in recession-hit Britain. In 1930 his Scottish church, St Andrew's, had been completed. 'It is plain stone,' wrote Eunice, 'and the

117

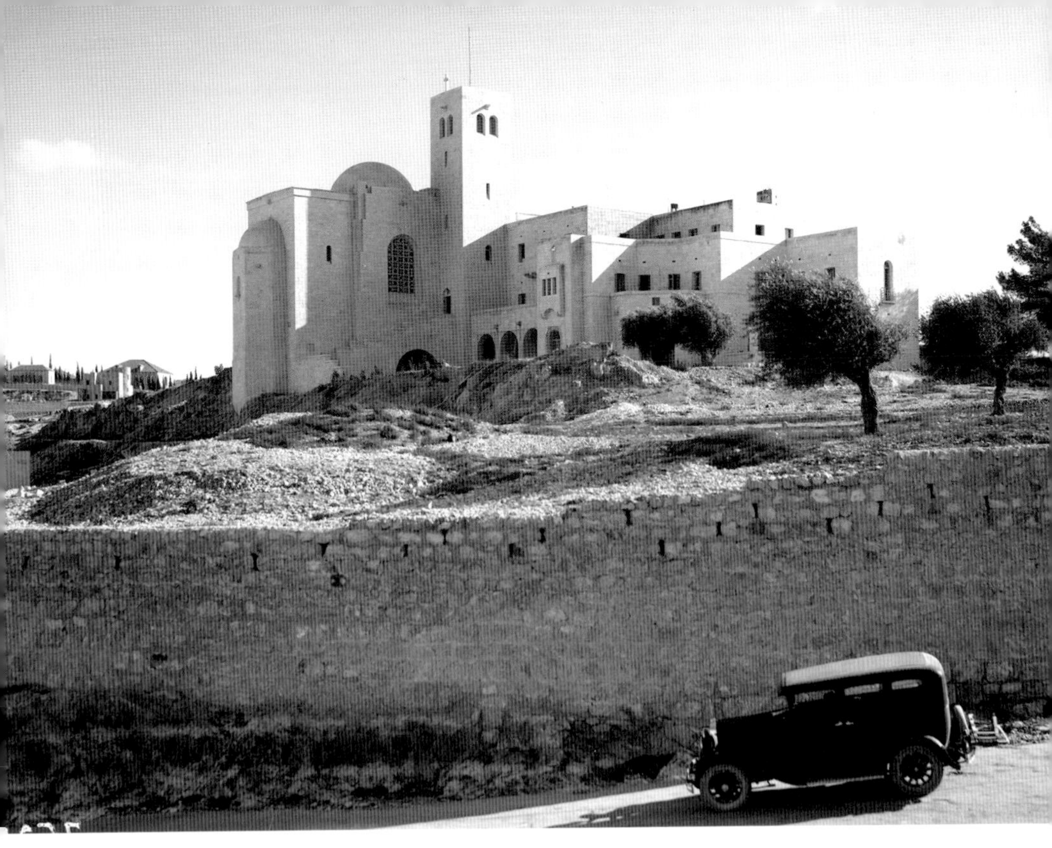

St Andrew's Church, Jerusalem,
designed by Clifford Holliday, 1930s

one colour is blue: blue stained-glass windows, blue (and gold) cloth on the altar table'.[5] Of all his buildings in Palestine, this was by common consent his masterpiece. Among other commissions he went on to build three banks for Barclays, the first in the centre of Jerusalem, which had the novelty of a revolving-door, and the others in Tel Aviv and Haifa.

That same year, 1930, the Hollidays had moved to a new home, Beit Nassar, near Bethlehem, which came with four acres of fields—with pines, almond trees, and olive trees—which the boys treated as a garden. Tim Holliday remembered it as 'a big

Arab house … large and square with a flat roof [and] verandahs with arches above'.

> We had no neighbours that I can remember but there was life and movement on the road beyond the front door. A few cars and lorries would go back and forth on the road but mostly it was donkeys with their heavy loads and people walking, and sometimes herds of goats or camels. The animals had bells about their necks and the melancholy clink, clink of metal on metal is another early memory.

It was a rather lonely spot, and the boys were alert to the snakes and scorpions in the nearby quarry—and dimly aware of what their parents called the 'riots'. They sometimes saw soldiers and armoured cars, and knew their father kept a gun under his bed and that he 'was shot at trying to deliver water to a besieged village'. (This was probably in 1929, and the 'village' may have been a Jewish settlement.) But the 'riots' would subside and 'we travelled about in our old Fiat more or less as we wished'. Their happiest memories were of trips to the sea and to the Crusader castle of Athlit and of picnics ('always sumptuous') by the Dead Sea.

Sixty years later, as a painter living in France, Tim would use the same colour scheme in his work—a landscape that was 'grey rather than green … almost monochromatic'—that he had grown up with as a child. And there were still certain sensations—'insect noises, the smell of bread as it comes out of the oven, walking under pine trees and listening to the sighing of pine needles in the wind'—that unfailingly reminded him of Palestine.[6]

The little Scotsman

Chancellor's term had ended unhappily. 'I came hoping to increase the country's prosperity and happiness,' he declared at

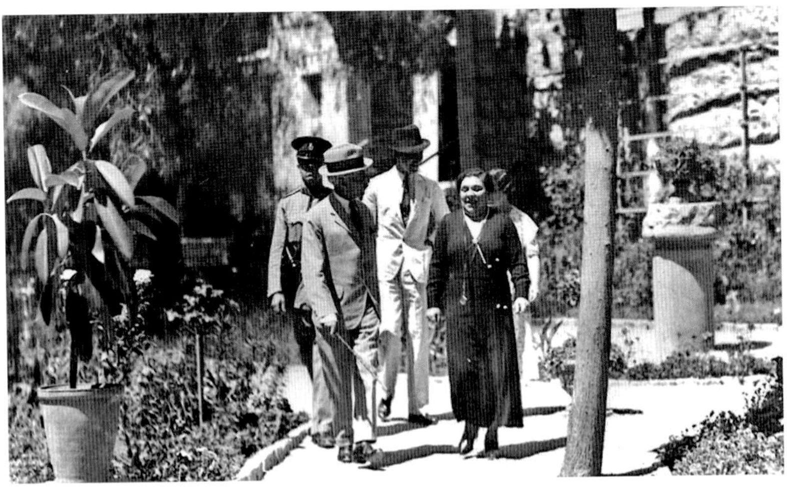

Sir Arthur Wauchope with Annie Landau   Zvi Oron-Orushkes
at her school, 1935

a farewell banquet. 'I am leaving with my ambition unfulfilled. Conditions were against me.'[7]

He was succeeded in 1931 by Sir Arthur Wauchope, whose seven-year reign made him the longest-serving of all Palestine's high commissioners. A Scottish bachelor, small and outwardly un-military, Wauchope was in fact a distinguished general who had been wounded in the Boer war and in the First World War. He is described in the *Dictionary of National Biography* as 'a man of high ideals, cultivated tastes, tireless energy, and considerable personal fortune'. One Englishman recalled him 'eating his breakfast porridge, like a good Scot, walking round the room, which slightly disconcerted his hostess'.[8] Although he could be demanding and irascible, Wauchope was devoted to Palestine and 'determined to see everything with his own eyes and hear everything with his own ears'.[9] He regarded his role as that of a kindly father figure of the two communities.

A vivid picture of what it was like working for Wauchope is

provided by his young private secretary, Thomas Hodgkin:

> The morning parade.
> The royal barouche [His Excellency's Rolls] arrives, flying its Union Jack. HE, ADC [aide-de-camp] and I inside. I have the red box with files HE has read—or hasn't—lots of little bits of paper with his thoughts on various subjects. 'Now, Thomas, what's my programme for this morning?' I rummage. HE smiles benevolently. Here it is, thank God: '11 a.m. Dawe. 11.30 Men of the Trees, Pirie-Gordon. 12.00 Husain Khalidi, mayor of Jerusalem, acting DC in attendance.' 'Now, Thomas, just find my notes about the Jaffa Gate—what is Johns up to there?' Oh dear! I saw them such a little time ago. And what are all these bits of typescript? Top-secret reports from Domvile, and secret service, go to no one but me. 'You'll be losing them in a moment—don't worry.' HE is in a gay and chaffing mood …
> And so the day begins. 'What's the little man like today?' 'Rather chirpy, I'm glad to say.' It ends, with luck, with pleasant talk of love, life, poetry, music, after snoozing through a dinner party for thirty. The ADC is mildly bored, but the loyalties of the Seaforth Highlanders keep him [Wauchope] going until bedtime, and HE doesn't like to stay up after 11 p.m. as a rule …

An innocent abroad

Hodgkin had first visited Palestine in 1932 to join an archaeological expedition in Jericho. He was twenty-two, from a gregarious family of liberal writers and academics, and uncertain of his future. He quickly found archaeology dull, but in the words of his younger brother Edward:

> He fell in love with the country, with the play of light over the mountains of Transjordan, with the flowers that shot up everywhere after the winter rains, and with the mysterious wadis leading up into the Judaean hills. He liked trying to organise gangs of labourers. He began to make friends and to learn Arabic.

He accordingly jumped at the chance to return to Palestine when offered a junior post in the Mandate administration, at a salary of £400 a year. It was to prove a brief but eventful experience.

Politically innocent, but beginning to flirt with left-wing opinions, Hodgkin found he could not escape Palestine's passions, even at the cinema.

> When the Roman officer Massala remarked to Ben Hur: 'You are a snivelling sneaking Jew and your race will always be trodden, as it has always been trodden, in the dirt,' all the Arabs shouted and stamped … But when Ben Hur with flashing eyes replies: 'My afflicted nation has shaken off its other persecutors before now, and the day will come, be sure, when it will rise up and shake off the yoke of Rome,' then all the Jews in the audience joined in a splendid seditious cheer.[10]

Hodgkin underwent a rather unusual political awakening. A natural rebel, he disliked the pretentiousness of British rule—the Rolls-Royces, the top hats and tails, the elaborate protocols of Government House—and, more important, began to perceive the inherent injustice of imperialism. According to his own account, an important influence on his political thinking was his friendship with George and Katy Antonius, well known in Jerusalem for hosting dinner parties that attracted the city's Anglo-Arab élite. They were both from Lebanese Christian families which had settled in Alexandria. George Antonius had studied at Cambridge (where his friends included E. M. Forster) and in the First World War worked for the British in Egypt as a press censor. In 1921 he joined the education department in Palestine, where a few years later he took Palestinian citizenship. The British appreciated his services as translator and mediator—for example, in helping settle border disputes in Arabia, for which he was awarded the CBE—but, like his friend

Musa Alami, he fell victim to the discrimination and back-biting which bedevilled the Mandate administration. He resigned in 1930, and by the time Hodgkin met him he was working as an independent writer—building up material for his classic book *The Arab Awakening*—and as a freelance mediator. Like others, Antonius had at first got on well with Wauchope, with whom he had a series of private meetings, but before long was alienated by his policies.

Hodgkin admired Antonius for his gifts as a go-between who seemed to know everyone—including the Mufti, for whom he acted as an adviser—and for his wit and intelligence and ability to see both sides of an argument. Meanwhile the vivacious Katy took the rather lonely Englishman under her wing. 'Dear Mr Hodgkin,' she wrote to him in May 1933, 'I'd love to go to the pictures with you one night—1st house and we will eat sausages at the Vienna or German Café.'

A time of prosperity

The early 1930s saw the country prosper, as the economy, dominated by citrus exports, enjoyed a boom. The Palestine Electric Corporation, under the dynamic Pinchas Rutenberg, a former Russian revolutionary, inaugurated a large hydroelectric project which brought power to Palestine and neighbouring Transjordan. Haifa became a strategic hub on the imperial map. As its port expanded, with the completion of a terminal and refinery for oil brought 600 miles by pipeline from Iraq, it became a major centre for industry and communications. Its population had grown from 18,000 in 1918 to over 100,000 by 1939. With roughly equal numbers of Arabs and Jews, the city prided itself on developing a model of coexistence.[11]

Wauchope liked Clifford Holliday's work and commissioned him to help design the new Haifa harbour and the adjoining Kingsway development. Here he set up an office and

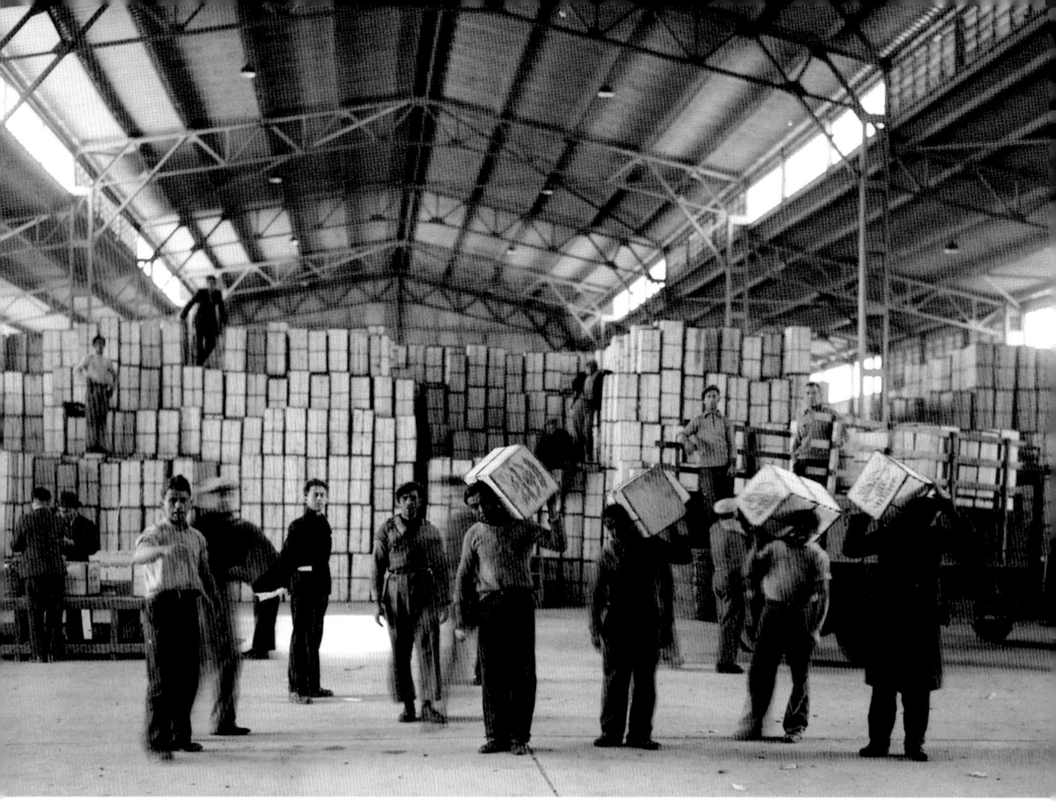

Arab and Jewish orange packers, Tel Aviv, 1930s   American Colony

spent much of 1934. (At one point he was summoned to see Rutenberg, who wanted to build a power station in Haifa. But the Russian was notoriously hard to please; Clifford thought him 'a Mussolini'.)[12] This was to be his last project in Palestine. The Hollidays finally left in August 1935, after thirteen happy years. For Eunice especially, the memory of the land where her children had grown up, with its hills and flowers and rich diversity of people, stayed with her for the rest of her long life.

A new underclass

Palestine's new prosperity was not shared. On the outskirts of Haifa and other towns and cities, shantytowns sprang up housing unemployed *fellahin* who had left the countryside to find work. Their anger was directed not only at the British and the Zionists but at the Arab notables who sold land to the Jews. At first these had mainly been absentee landowners, but by now it was common knowledge that local Arabs—including prominent nationalists—were making fortunes through such sales, which they concealed through the use of middlemen.

The poet Ibrahim Tuqan, Fadwa's elder brother, wrote scathingly of those who undermined the nationalist cause they claimed to lead.

> *You are so sincere in your patriotism,*
> *You are bearing the burden of the cause,*
> *You are men of action, without words;*
> *May God give His blessing to your strong arms!*
> *A statement from you is as good as an army,*
> *Fully equipped, marching forward for freedom,*
> *And a public meeting of yours restores to us*
> *The bygone glories of Umayya's victories.*
> *The salvation of our country is on our doorstep*
> *And the great celebrations draw near.*
> *We do not deny your fine works, and yet*
> *In our souls one wish still lingers on:*
> *We have in our hands the remains of a country,*
> *So retire, or else you will lose what is left.*[13]

For Fadwa, meanwhile, growing up in Nablus, the events of 1929 had marked the first glimmerings of political awareness. Ibrahim took her under his wing, encouraging her to write poetry and inviting her to live with him and his wife in Jerusalem. But the moment of freedom was brief. Back in the family home, she was plagued by depression, even contemplating suicide. She could not bear the double standards practised by the men of her family. '[They] dressed in European style [she wrote later]; they spoke Turkish, French, and English; they

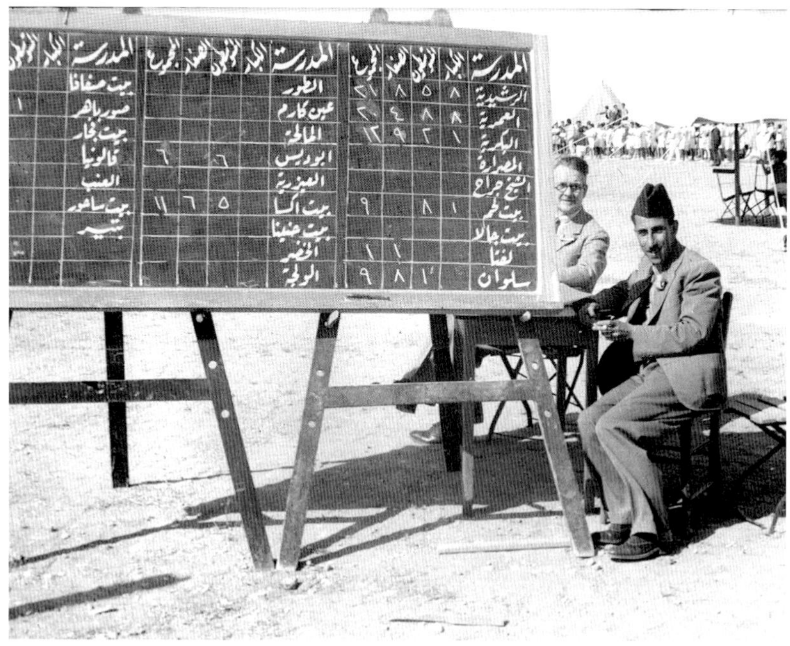

Sports Day at the Arab College, Jerusalem, 1940   American Colony

ate with knives and forks; they fell in love'—yet they kept their womenfolk in virtual servitude and confinement. For Fadwa, the dream of personal liberation became intertwined with that of national liberation.[14]

Of books and Beethoven

The Bethlehem boyhood of Jabra Ibrahim Jabra ended in March 1932 when his family moved to Jerusalem.

> On the morning of a heavily clouded day [he wrote] a large truck came to the road near the entrance of our house's courtyard. We began to move onto it our bedding, mats, bags of provisions, cans of olives, copper utensils which were our mainstay for cooking and

washing, the cans we needed to carry water, and the large water jar which always occupied the most important corner of the house. [15]

His father sat with the driver, and the five others huddled with their belongings—including Jabra's much-prized crate of books—in the back of the lorry. Their new home, just outside the walls of the Old City, consisted of a single basement room. Jabra transferred to the Rashidiyya secondary school, where he did well and gained admission to the government-run Arab College, whose principal was the formidable educator Ahmad Samih al-Khalidi.

He was by now writing stories and drawing and painting and had developed a passion for Beethoven. In the memoir he wrote half a century later, in exile in Iraq, he recalled Khalidi's 'stentorian voice' and 'strong presence' and his insistence that the pursuit of knowledge was a patriotic, as well as an individual, duty. 'We read and studied with passion and perseverance all day long,' he wrote, 'and then all night to the point of sickness.' When he graduated from the college in 1937, he was chosen by Khalidi for a scholarship to study at Cambridge. He set sail for England in the first days of the Second World War.

The rowdies and the swots

'I like having Isaiah here,' wrote Thomas Hodgkin in September 1934. 'He speaks Zionist opinions (without quite calling himself a Zionist) and I try to answer with British official opinions (without in the least calling myself a British official).' This was Isaiah Berlin, a friend from Oxford days. Berlin was indeed a Zionist but not an uncritical one. He thought Tel Aviv 'dreadful', Ben-Gurion a 'demagogue', and Jewish officials 'the rudest people on earth'. But he reserved his severest criticism for British officialdom. 'The English lower officials are a poor tired washed out lot, the upper, patient, disillusioned, uninterested policemen.' He compared Palestine under British rule to a large and dysfunctional school 'staffed by public school men—of an inferior brand'. The headmaster (Wauchope) was old and suffered from 'excessive high-mindedness'. The Arab boys were 'high spirited and tough', liable to 'break the skulls of a few Jews or an Englishman', while the Jews were 'abler & richer than the other boys ... rude, conceited, ugly, ostentatious ... always saying they know better, liable to work too hard & not to play games with the rest'.[16]

Hodgkin showed him round and introduced him to his friends, including George Antonius. Berlin regarded Hodgkin as kind and generous but hopelessly naïve in his left-wing, pro-Arab sentiments. It was around this time that Hodgkin underwent a political conversion when, in the company of Judah Magnes, he visited a group of some thirty communists who were on hunger strike in a Jerusalem jail—Christian and Muslim Arabs, Jews, Armenians, all crammed into a single cell. Their internationalist solidarity impressed him. This, he wrote later, was his road to Damascus.[17]

The politics of radio

In March 1936 Wauchope launched the Palestine Broadcasting Service. This was one of his notable achievements and a sign of the idealistic paternalism which animated him. Bringing news, music, and educational programmes to the country's different communities in the three official languages—Arabic, Hebrew, and English—the station would, he declared, eschew politics in favour of 'knowledge and culture'. He singled out two groups of particular interest to him—farmers (by which he principally meant the Arab *fellahin*) and music lovers (which, although he mentioned 'both Oriental and Western music', essentially meant the Jews of the Yishuv). Radio was entering its heyday, and would soon supplant newspapers as the principal source of news and entertainment. Given the predominantly rural character of the

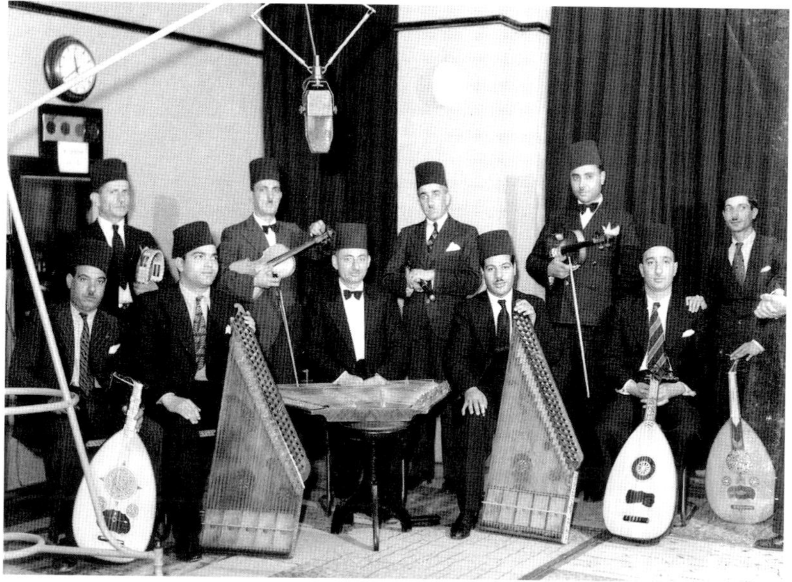

Musicians of the Palestine Broadcasting Service,
c. 1936-1946

Matson Photo Service

Arab population and its high level of illiteracy, Wauchope saw the new station as having an important dual role as a means of communication and as an instrument of modernisation. With its educational programmes on helping the Arab farmer and on the importance of health and hygiene for the Arab mother, as well as its (carefully chosen) talks on history and religion, the service addressed itself to citizens rather than to consumers. It was, in intention at least, a nation-building exercise.

Modelled on the BBC, the new station was designed to be non-political and a force for unity, but ended up being neither. However hard they tried, the British could not keep nationalism out of broadcasting. Soon after the launch, there was a row over the Hebrew section's attempt to call itself Kol Eretz Israel (the Voice of the Land of Israel). This was politically unacceptable,

and to get round the problem all announcers were told to introduce their programmes with 'This is Jerusalem' or 'Jerusalem
Calling'. There was sensitivity about the playing of national
anthems (which, with some exceptions, were discouraged). Two
senior figures in the Arabic section—the poet Ibrahim Tuqan
and Ajaj Nuwayhid, who was Lebanese—were avowed nationalists, which it was hoped would give the station credibility with
Arab audiences. But there were inevitable tensions with British
officials, and Tuqan eventually resigned after accusations of
bias. One of the station's most lasting effects on Palestine was,
through the use of language, 'to reinforce the idea of two separate communities'.[18] Moreover the timing of the launch was
unfortunate, coming as it did on the eve of the most sustained
insurrection British-ruled Palestine had thus far experienced.

From Berlin to Tel Aviv
The underlying causes of the 'disturbances', as officials insisted
on calling them, were the familiar, long-standing grievances
over land and immigration. In addition, Arab fears that the
Zionists were secretly arming themselves gained credence when,
in October 1935, barrels of cement arriving at Jaffa broke open
to reveal a large cache of weapons and ammunition. There
was also a growing conviction among the Arab underclass that
Palestine's growing prosperity benefited the Zionists and the
wealthy Arabs who sold land to them, leaving the *fellahin*—the
majority—poor, destitute, and frequently landless. Moreover,
after the boom years of the early 1930s, there was a slump in
1935 which caused a sharp increase in Arab unemployment.

Aggravating all of this was the policy Wauchope chose to
pursue which, whatever his intention, brought these grievances
to a head. He believed that the way to resolve the Arab-Jewish
problem was to create two communities of roughly equal size
which, through a process of self-government in stages, would

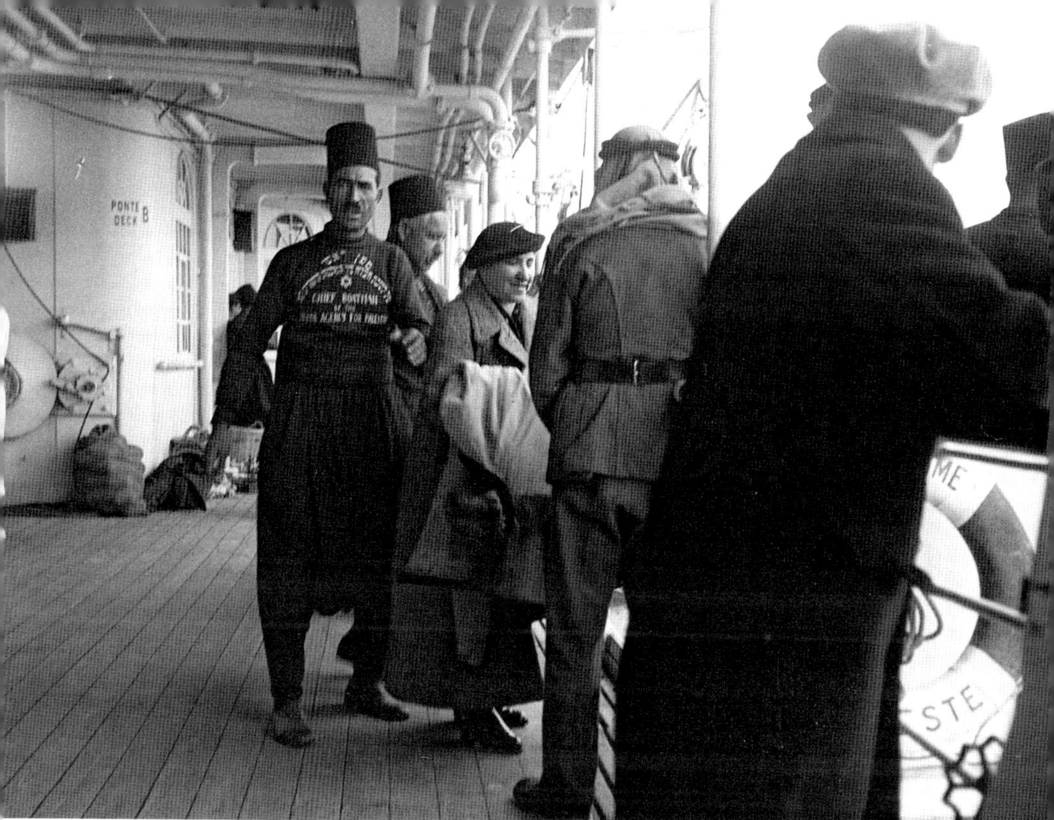

German immigrants arriving at Jaffa, 1933   Zoltan Kluger

come together to coexist in a bi-national state. He was not indifferent to the Arabs' sense of injustice, but failed to see the consequences of presiding over the most dramatic increase in Jewish immigration since the start of the Mandate. The figures jumped from 9,500 in 1932 to 30,000 in 1933 and 42,000 in 1934, reaching a peak of almost 62,000 in 1935. The size of the Yishuv doubled from 180,000 to nearly 400,000.

Had the country been insulated from the outside world, the problem might have been less acute. But the Jews of Europe were now increasingly drawn to Palestine, willingly or unwillingly, because of the rise of Nazism in Germany. When Hitler became chancellor in January 1933, there were half a million

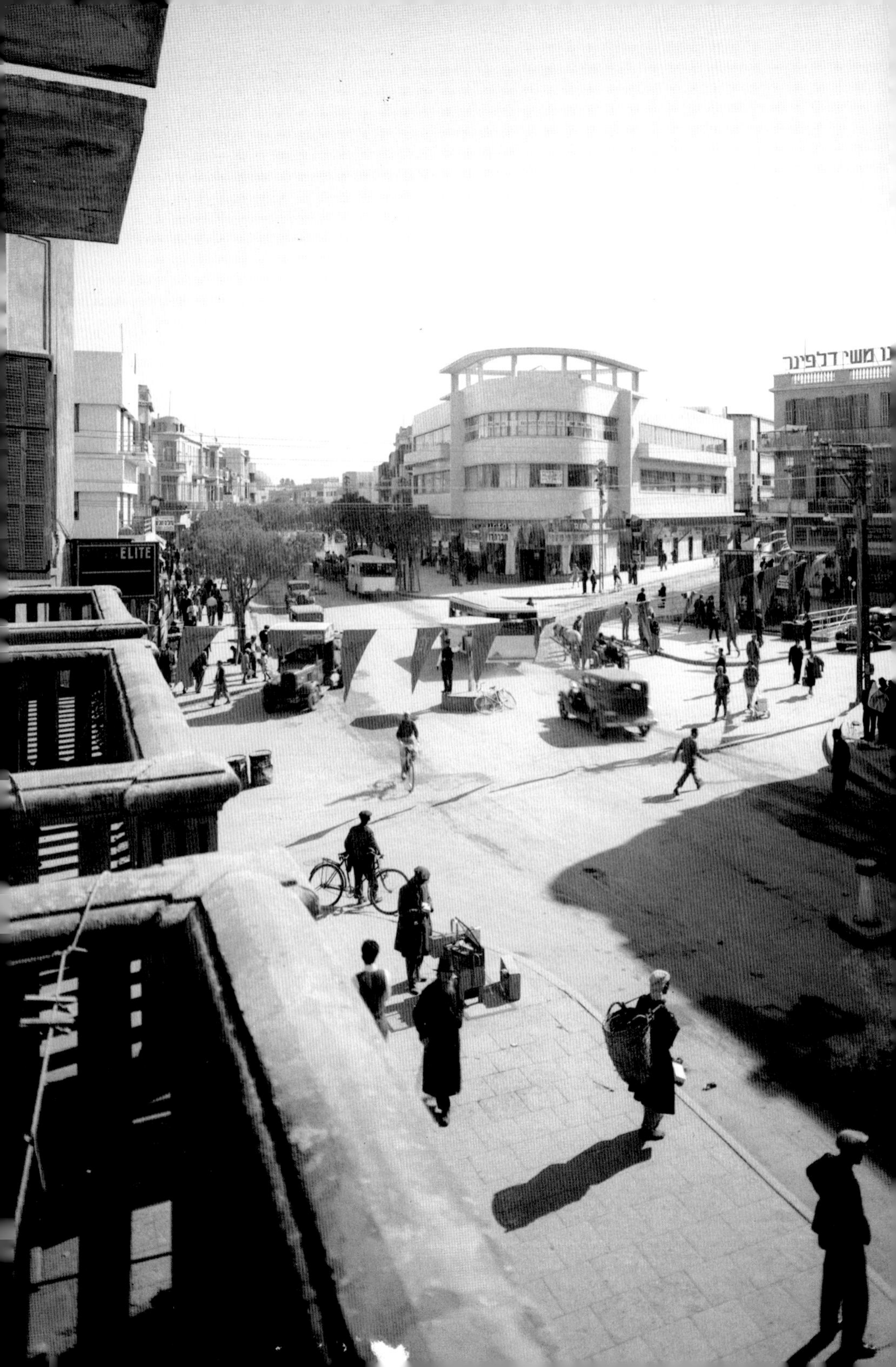

ELITE

Jews in Germany. Eight thousand of them were, like Lonya Gutmann, doctors. With the introduction of the Nazis' anti-Semitic laws, many of them were thrown out of work. Gutmann was a Russian Jew who had settled comfortably into the life of a successful middle-class doctor in Berlin. But he and his wife Lisa, a German Lutheran, were now in obvious danger. They left Germany in 1933, settling first in Italy. But Italy, like Britain and France, did not accept Gutmann's medical qualifications, and it was virtually impossible to get a visa for the United States. Although he was an atheist who felt neither Jewish nor Zionist, he chose to take his family to Palestine, where he could at least practise medicine. Lonya and Lisa set sail, accompanied by their two young daughters and a crate-load of furniture. Arriving in early 1934, they rented a flat on Balfour Street in the centre of Tel Aviv.[19]

Tel Aviv had grown into a sprawling European-style metropolis with 100,000 inhabitants. With its strikingly modern architecture it became known as the 'white city', and as it grew, its Arab neighbour, Jaffa, declined: 'one of the world's youngest cities … devoured one of its oldest'.[20]

Like many Jews from Germany, the Gutmanns suffered profound culture shock. Tel Aviv already had too many doctors and Lonya Gutmann struggled to find work—while stubbornly insisting on keeping up appearances as the head of a well-to-do bourgeois family. He spoke to his (few) patients in German or Russian, refusing to learn Hebrew. To make matters worse, the Jews of Tel Aviv were shocked to discover that he was married to a German Christian who celebrated Christmas and on Sundays took her daughters to a church in neighbouring Jaffa. The Gutmanns were not at all the immigrant material Ben-Gurion had envisaged. They were in Palestine not by choice but of

Left: *The White City: Tel Aviv, 1936*   American Colony

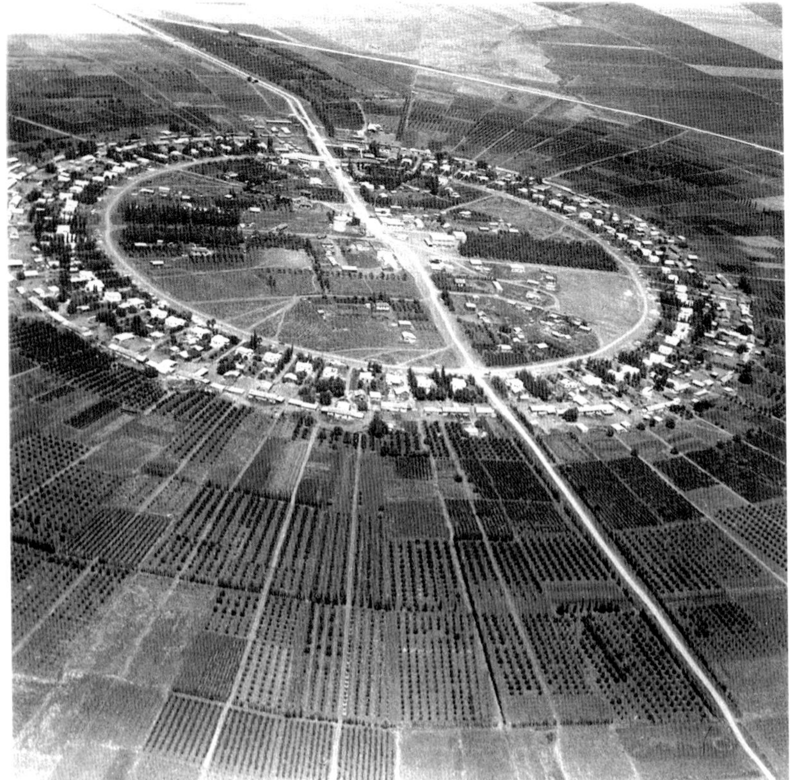

The settlement of Nahalal, late 1930s   Zoltan Kluger

necessity, hoping their stay would be temporary until things settled down in Europe.[21]

Their elder daughter, the beautiful and headstrong Assia, later to become a gifted writer and translator, was at first sent to an overcrowded school in Tel Aviv; but Lisa, a tough matriarch, was determined to find something better for her.[22]

Among the refugees from Hitler's Germany were Jewish photographers prevented from working by the Nazi régime. The Hungarian-born Zoltan Kluger, who arrived in Palestine from Berlin in 1933, helped create a new heroic iconography of the

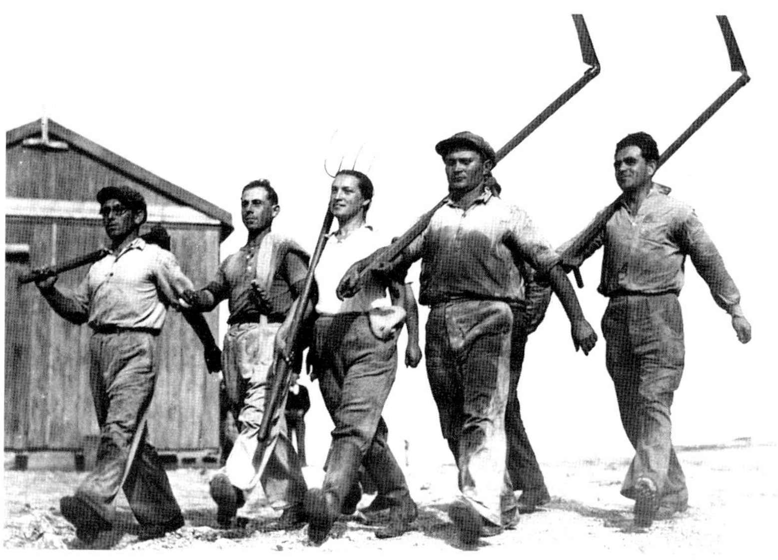

Jewish settlers returning from work, 1935   Zoltan Kluger

Zionist worker. His images glorified the land and the men and women of the kibbutz. Among the innovations he introduced were aerial photography and the use of montage. Kluger was employed by the Jewish National Fund to produce positive images of the life of the settlements. His pictures were often staged. He later told a friend, 'The pioneers here are dying from malaria; they live in poverty, are tired and morose, and I'm supposed to photograph them smiling. I'm sick of taking pictures of pioneers laughing.'[23]

The strike

In the spring of 1936, after almost two decades of British rule, an Arab rebellion broke out which lasted until 1939, finally shattering British complacency about Palestine's future. The first stirrings of revolt came, not from the Mufti or the Arab notables, but from a radical preacher in Haifa, Sheikh Izzedin al-Qassam, originally from Syria, whose uncompromising message and fiery blend of Islam and nationalism gave him a grass-roots following of a new kind. His short and violent career, leading to his death in November 1935 when British forces cornered and shot him, turned him into the first martyr of the Palestine revolt—and the harbinger of the nationwide insurgency which was to follow.

That same month the five normally feuding Arab political parties banded together to form an Arab Higher Committee which sent a delegation, led by the Mufti, to see Wauchope. They urged the high commissioner to pass on to London three demands—the formation of a democratic government (meaning one with an Arab majority), an end to Jewish land purchases, and the cessation of Jewish immigration.

In British eyes, such demands were unacceptable; but Wauchope was anxious not to appear immoveable. His counter-proposal was to offer the Arabs a political stake in decision-making, in the form of a legislative council—partly elected and partly nominated—in which Muslim and Christian Arabs would comprise a majority and would be able to press their demands through constitutional means rather than through protests, riots, and violence. In the 1920s Herbert Samuel's plan for a legislative council had been scuppered by the Arabs. Now it was the turn of the Zionists, who feared that such a body would work against their interests. The proposed council's powers were, to be sure, limited. But Wauchope set great store by it, and regarded it as a personal setback when the scheme was thwarted in the British parliament and then abandoned by the British government.

In April 1936, amid sporadic acts of inter-communal violence, the Arab Higher Committee endorsed a call for a general strike and formed 'national committees' to work at the local level to organise and enforce it. Not everyone complied: Palestine's railway workers, who were government employees, declined to

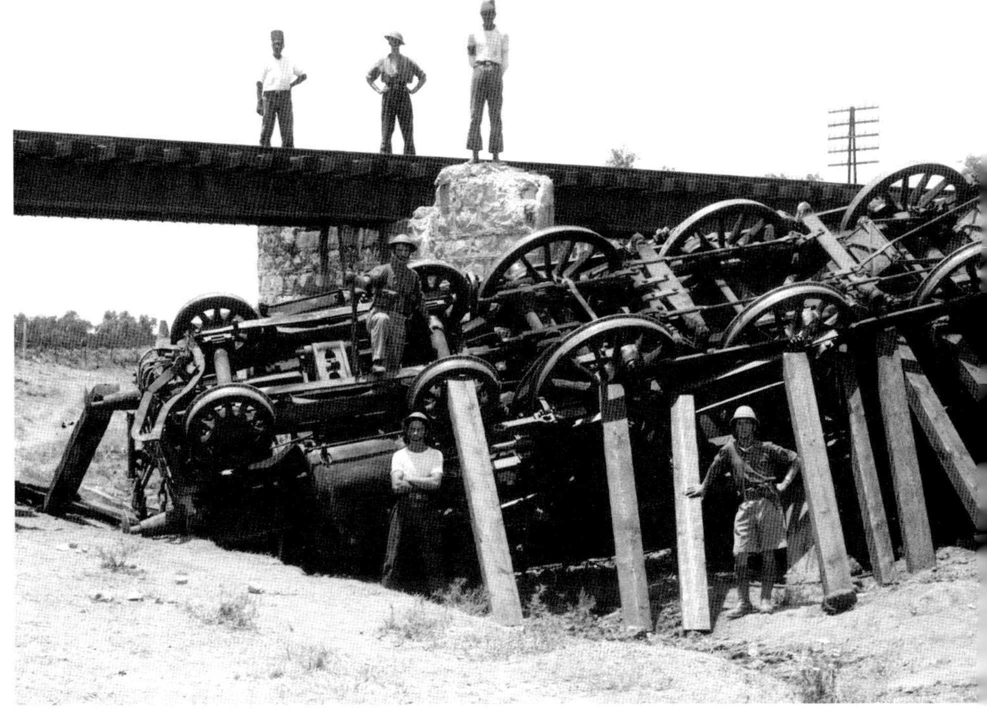

Train derailed by rebels, 1936   American Colony

do so; as did the dockers of Haifa, fearful that their jobs would be taken by Jewish workers. Nevertheless the strike took hold, and as it did so bands of men took to the hills to begin an armed insurgency which was to last, with peaks and troughs, until 1939. The rebels sought to paralyse the economy by blocking or mining roads, derailing trains, and cutting the pipeline which crossed northern Palestine bringing oil from Iraq.

The administration, the army, and the police were caught off guard. Troop reinforcements were rushed in, but at Wauchope's insistence their role was purely defensive. He was sure the strike would collapse, and that precipitate military action would be counterproductive.

The strike and the accompanying unrest forced members of the Arab élite to take sides. Tawfiq Canaan actively supported the revolt, wrote two books (in English) putting forward the

Arab case, and was promptly ostracised by the British establishment. Arabs working for the government were in an especially difficult position. Their response was to pay a hefty tax (ten per cent of their income) to the rebels, and to issue a memorandum—drawn up by Musa Alami, who had become Wauchope's adviser on Arab affairs—which expressed their lack of confidence in government policy. This remarkable document, signed by all senior Arab civil servants and judges, was presented to Wauchope in June 1936.

The onset of the rebellion spelt the end of Thomas Hodgkin's brief career in the Mandate administration. He sent a lengthy (anonymous) critique of government repression to a left-wing publication in London, and then handed in a letter of resignation. When he asked to remain in Palestine to watch the drama unfold, he was expelled.

A social worker in the Old City

The rebels' principal target was the British, but they also attacked Jews and Jewish settlements, burning crops and trees and damaging factories. Ben-Gurion's official policy was one of restraint. The Jews had little interest in attacking the Arabs, but every interest in helping the British suppress the revolt. The British, conscious that they were unprepared for the scale of the rebellion, came to value the Zionists' intelligence reports. They, in return, demanded British help in strengthening their defence force, the Haganah, which was technically illegal but quietly tolerated. With vivid memories of the bloodshed of 1929, the Yishuv was anxious that vulnerable Jewish communities should be protected.

A young social worker, Sylva Gelber, a Jewish immigrant who had arrived from Canada in 1932, found herself bringing food rations to the Jews of the Old City. It was dangerous work, since Arab snipers operated there. As the violence persisted,

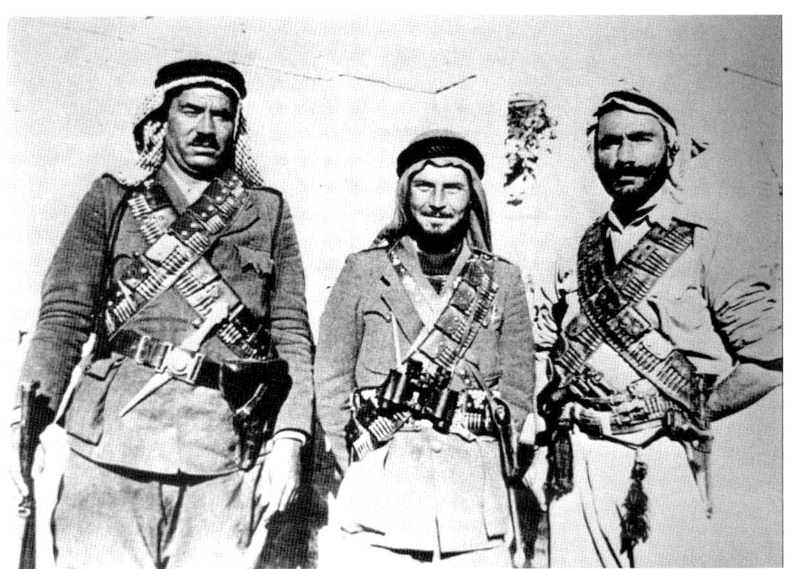

Abdul-Qader al-Husseini, centre, with other rebel leaders, 1936

the Jewish quarter became increasingly isolated; 'a sense of claustrophobia seemed to take hold of the whole community'. In May 1936, after the city was placed under a dusk-to-dawn curfew, and right through the summer, Gelber would enter it every morning, supposedly accompanied by a British policeman but sometimes venturing out on her own. 'On several occasions we would pass a spot where, a little earlier in the morning, an innocent passer-by had been shot from ambush, the blood still staining the roadway over which we had to walk.'[24]

A peasants' revolt

The rebellion was a grass-roots insurrection without formal leadership. At its height, there were some 10,000 rebels, of whom perhaps a quarter were full-time fighters. The Mufti sought to provide overall political direction, and his cousin Abdul-Qader al-Husseini was one of the most respected commanders. For a few months in 1936, the local rebels were joined by some 200 volunteers from Iraq, Syria, and Transjordan under the Lebanese-born Fawzi al-Qawuqji. There was often fierce rivalry among the rebel leaders.

A key battleground was Jaffa, where the army decided to clear a way into the old Arab quarter, a maze of narrow alleyways which provided a refuge for rebels and a haven for snipers. In June 1936 soldiers destroyed a large part of the area, blowing up more than 200 houses and leaving many of the residents homeless. To make matters worse, the operation was dressed up as an urban-improvement project. When Palestine's chief justice, Sir Michael McDonnell, took the unusual step of publicly upbraiding the government for its dishonesty, he was dismissed.

By September 1936, British officials were becoming increasingly alarmed. Realising that more drastic measures were called for, they threatened to introduce martial law if the strike and the unrest were not brought to an end. This threat, and the mediation efforts of Arab leaders outside Palestine, led to the announcement of a ceasefire the following month. The ceasefire came at Wauchope's insistence. The military—given the means to crush the revolt but denied a green light to do so— were furious that the rebels had not been punished or disarmed but allowed to disperse, ready and able to fight another day. But in Wauchope's mind the ceasefire was designed to produce a breathing space in which a royal commission under Lord Peel could examine not only the immediate factors behind the unrest but the underlying causes of the Palestine problem itself.

During the eight months of the commission's deliberations, normal life largely resumed. *Time* magazine reported that the Jews of Tel Aviv flocked to hear the country's first symphony orchestra—under the baton of Arturo Toscanini—playing Brahms, Schubert, and ('partly as a taunt to Nazi Germany') a

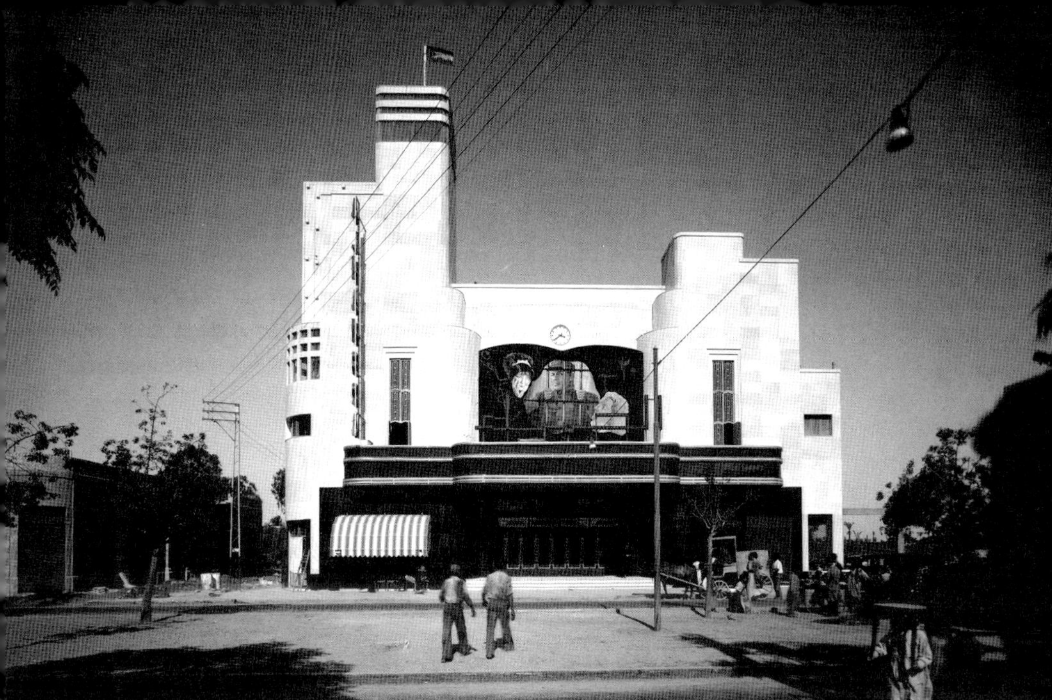

scherzo by the Jewish composer Felix Mendelssohn. The walls of the auditorium, it noted, were 'still pitted by Arab bullets'.[25]

A few months later, the *Palestine Post* announced the opening of a palatial new cinema in Jaffa. Designed in white and black marble by a Lebanese architect, the Alhambra had 1,200 seats. 'The construction … has been going on for over a year,' the newspaper reported, 'with a pause of a few months during the disturbances.' (The *Post*, a staunchly Zionist English-language newspaper, followed the official terminology in describing the rebellion.)[26]

The girl in the café

Meanwhile, the pressures from immigration, both legal and illegal, were inexorable. On a stormy winter evening in 1936, a young British journalist was sitting in the inviting warmth of a café in Jerusalem, filled with Jewish émigrés, where the orchestra was playing Strauss. Suddenly a girl walked in, wet and dishevelled, her face pale. She hesitated for a moment, and then blurted out:

> 'Will someone marry me?' The question is so blunt that for a moment the men have nothing to say … 'The police are looking for me. I have overstayed my permit. I am frightened. I don't want to go back to Germany.' … After a pause one of the men speaks … 'I will marry you,' he says, 'let's go to the Rabbi.'

In an hour's time the couple returned to the café, where a cheer went up. The next day they went back to the rabbi and got a divorce. It was not an isolated occurrence.[27]

The journalist was the 20-year-old Barbara Board, who had arrived in Palestine in 1936 and for much of the next decade reported from Jerusalem for the *Daily Sketch* and the *Daily Mirror*. When she turned her experiences into a book the following year, she chose not to focus on politics and violence—the day-to-day fare of her journalism—but, unusually, on the lives of women. She visited the women's prison in Bethlehem, housing both Arabs and Jews, and was shocked that Jewish illegal immigrants were kept side by side with women accused of theft or murder. She talked to Henrietta Szold, founder of the Hadassah hospital, whose work she admired, and to the women who produced the Children's Hour programmes for the Palestine Broadcasting Service (including Flora Moody, who wrote radio plays). A Jewish woman, Ruth, a loyal Zionist, recounted her life as a prostitute in Tel Aviv.

One evening the journalist walked through the narrow alleyways of Mea Shearim, the ultra-orthodox quarter of Jerusalem. She was impressed by its spirit of religious devotion but shocked by the poverty and destitution. Here she met Mrs Allpert from Leeds, who invited her into the small, neat house where she

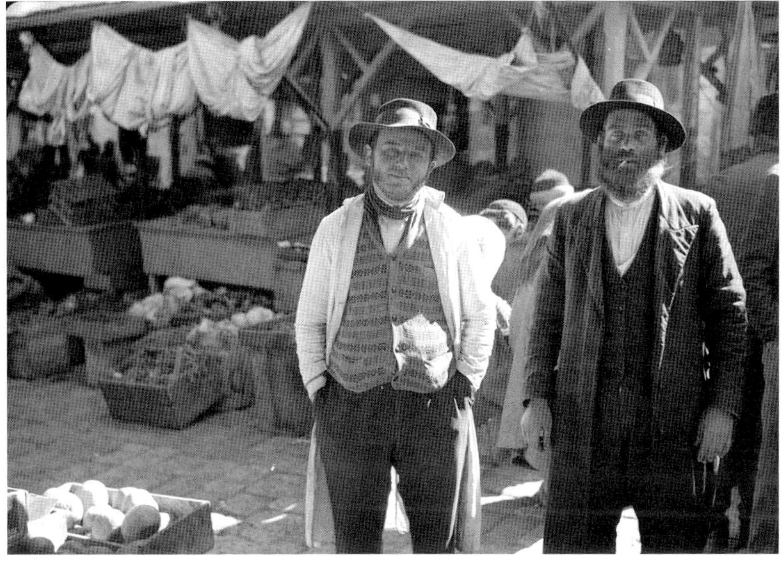

American Colony

Market in the ultra-orthodox quarter of Mea Shearim, 1930s

lived with her scholarly, Yiddish-speaking husband and five chil-dren—and where she still made Yorkshire pudding.

Later, Board crossed into neighbouring Transjordan and entered Emir Abdullah's harem—the first Western journalist to do so, she noted proudly. But never unduly impressed by people of wealth and privilege, as she travelled across the desert her sharp eye noticed the tears streaming down the faces of barefoot peasant women as they queued for water in the wintry cold.

Judgement of Solomon

From a journalist's point of view, Abdullah's kingdom provided relief from the pressure-cooker politics of Palestine, where after months of hearings the royal commission's work was drawing to a close. The Zionists, with their political acumen and mastery

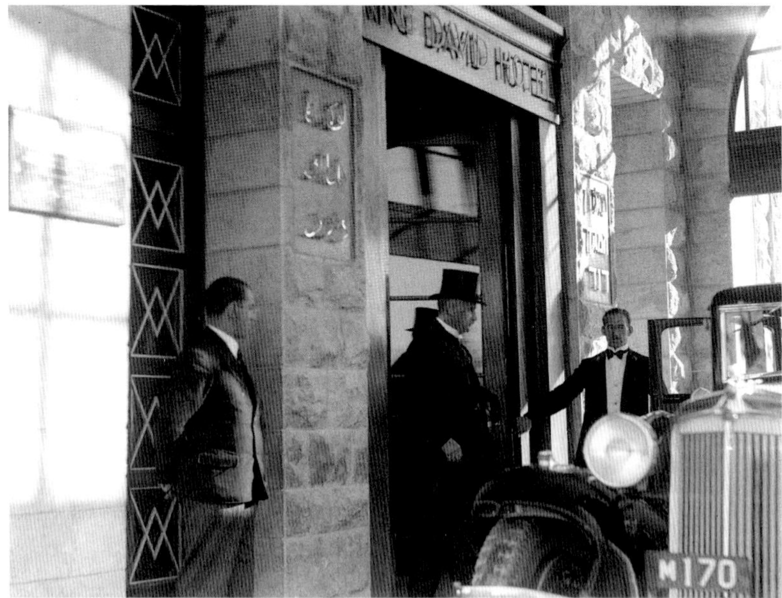

Lord Peel leaving the King David Hotel, 1936   American Colony

of public relations, had taken the commission seriously (to the point of bugging its private meetings). The Mufti, on the other hand, had initially boycotted its proceedings and only decided to testify at the last minute; he was, as usual, uncompromising.

Lord Peel's findings were published in July 1937. Of the nineteen reports produced by successive commissions of inquiry in the course of British rule, Peel's was the most thorough and the most eloquent. 'An irrepressible conflict has arisen,' the report declared, 'between two national communities within the narrow bounds of one small country. There is no common bond between them. Their national aspirations are incompatible.' The report's conclusion was that the Mandate had failed—and that the roots of that failure had been inherent in it from the very beginning. Like the child in the fable, Peel blurted out that the emperor had no clothes.[28]

But if his diagnosis was compelling, his remedy was controversial. He proposed a judgement of Solomon: the partition of Palestine into an Arab state (linked with Transjordan), a Jewish state, and an international zone under continuing British rule. The Zionists were unhappy with the plan but kept their options open. The Arabs rejected it outright. The government in London initially backed partition, but changed its mind when it realised the high cost, in money and men, of implementing it.

A by-product of the report was that it sabotaged the career of Musa Alami. It concluded that, in his handling of the unrest as a government lawyer, he had made errors of judgement. He was abroad at the time and given no chance to defend himself. On his return, he found his post had been abolished and he was forced to leave Palestine for exile in Beirut.[29]

Police using a Dobermann to track rebels, 1937   American Colony

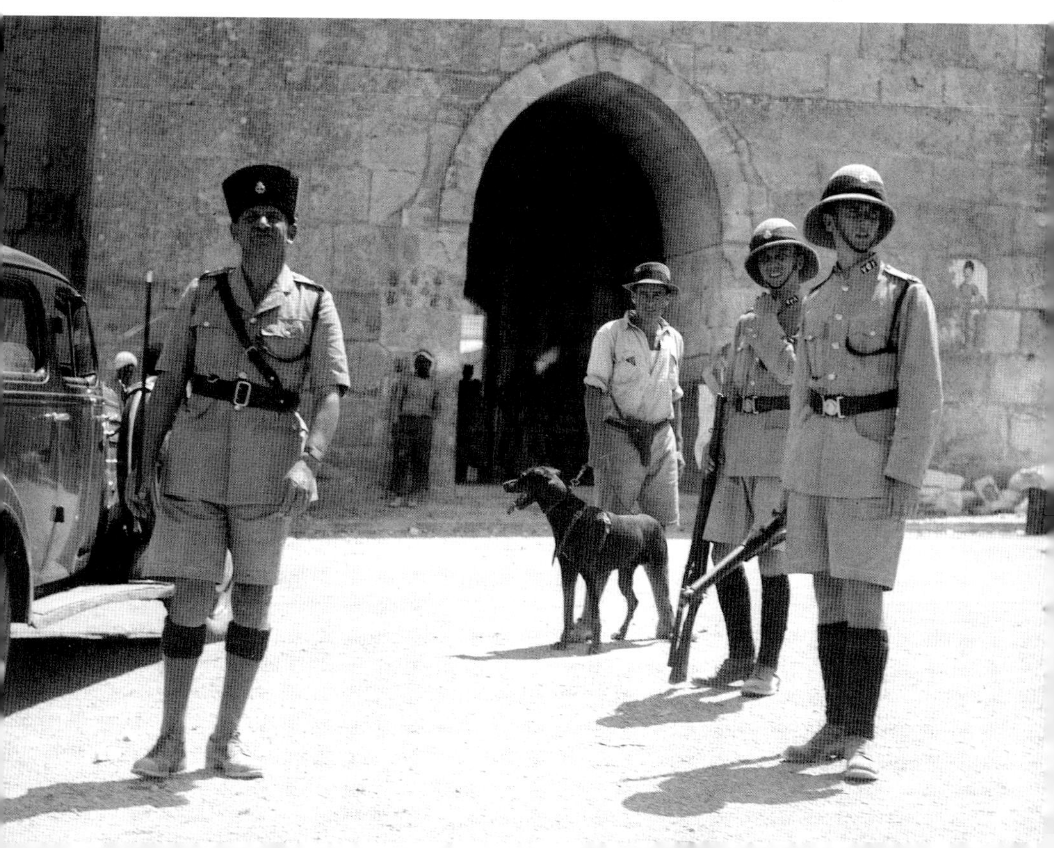

Repression

The rebellion flared up again with new intensity. Its final phase was heralded in September 1937 when gunmen—apparently loyal to Izzedin al-Qassam—shot dead a senior British official, Lewis Andrews, as he was leaving a church service in Nazareth. This crossed a line: no senior British figure had been assassinated before. In response, the authorities outlawed the Arab Higher Committee and removed Hajj Amin from his position as Mufti. He fled to neighbouring Lebanon, from where he continued his efforts to direct the revolt—and to organise death squads to eliminate his enemies and rivals.

Britain flooded Palestine with additional troops—eventually totalling some 30,000—and issued emergency regulations which gave the army new powers to suppress the revolt. At the suggestion of Sir Charles Tegart, who was brought in to advise the security forces, a fortified barbed-wire fence, known as the Tegart wall, was completed in August 1938 in an effort to seal off the border with Lebanon. (The work was given to Solel Boneh, the construction arm of the Histadrut.)[30] He also called for the building of fortified police stations known as Tegart forts. Military courts were introduced. In interrogating prisoners, security officials resorted to torture (including a form of water-boarding). Dobermanns were sent from South Africa to help track rebels. The worst of many well-documented excesses occurred in al-Bassa, a village near the Lebanese border, where in September 1938, after some of their comrades were blown up by a rebel mine, British soldiers killed some twenty Arabs and burnt the village to the ground.[31]

In June 1938 Orde Wingate, a maverick 35-year-old army officer and fervent Zionist, took command of a counter-insurgency force known as the Special Night Squads, made up of British soldiers and members of the Haganah (one of whom was Moshe Dayan). Captain Wingate—nicknamed Lawrence

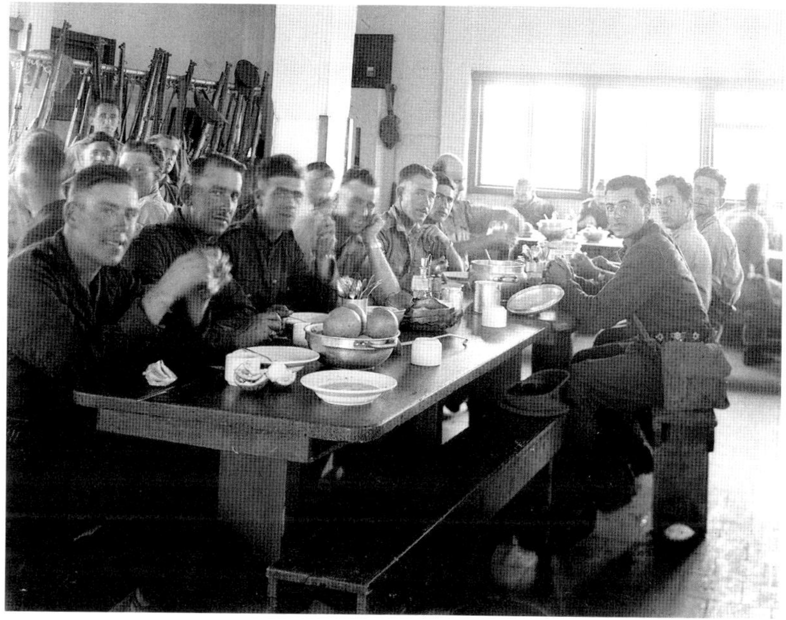

Members of the Special Night Squads, Ein Harod, 1938   Zoltan Kluger

of Judea—was given a virtually free hand in pacifying Galilee, the northern stronghold of the rebellion. In night-time raids his squads executed rebels, threw grenades into houses, and inflicted grim forms of torture and punishment. Many of the top brass were uncomfortable with the squads' existence, and after six months they were disbanded. [32]

Wauchope had retired, exhausted and dispirited, in March 1938. His successor was Sir Harold MacMichael, an Arabic speaker who had spent many years as a senior colonial official in Sudan. In contrast to the gregarious Wauchope, MacMichael was a figure of 'Olympian inaccessibility'.[33] Under the new high commissioner, there was now martial law in all but name, and the rebellion was crushed through the sustained and single-minded targeting of rebel areas and the intimidation

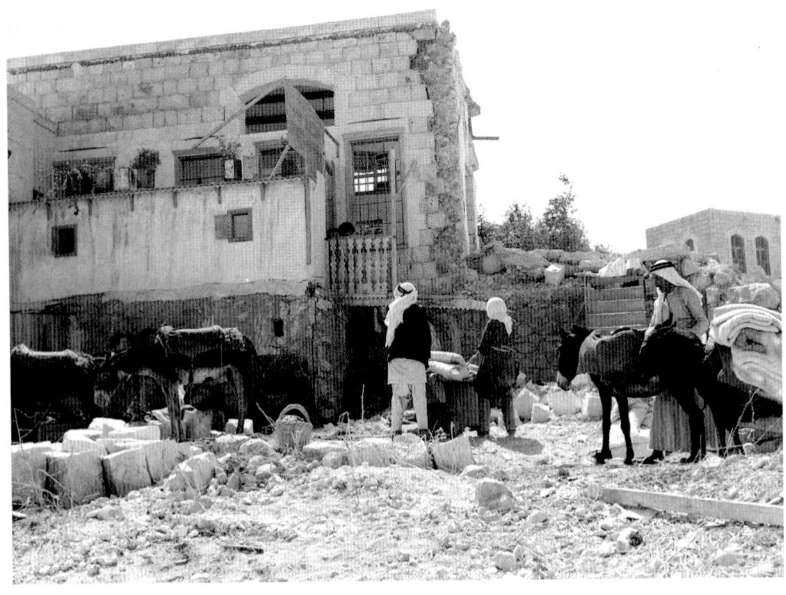

American Colony

Collective punishment: demolition of houses in Jenin, 1938

of civilians through demolition of houses and other forms of collective punishment.

Understanding the revolt

In 1938, the climactic year of the rebellion, George Antonius published his book *The Arab Awakening*. It was the first historical account in English of the origins and early development of Arab nationalism. But its last pages were devoted to Palestine and a critique of the Peel commission's proposals and a refutation of commonly-held ideas about the rebellion—in particular the notion that it was 'the result of an engineered agitation ... variously attributed to the intrigues of the *effendi* class, to the political ambitions of the Grand Mufti, to the agents and the subsidies of Italy and Germany, to Communist machinations ...'

On the contrary, he argued, this was a 'revolt of villagers' who were deeply disenchanted with their leaders:

> Far from its being engineered by the leaders, the revolt is in a very marked way a challenge to their authority and an indictment of their methods. The rebel chiefs lay the blame for the present plight of the peasantry on those Arab landowners who have sold their land, and they accuse the leaders of culpable neglect for failing to prevent the sales.

As for the persecution of Europe's Jews, this was 'a disgrace to its authors and to modern civilisation'. But, he went on:

> To place the brunt of the burden upon Arab Palestine is a miserable evasion of the duty that lies upon the whole of the civilised world. No code of morals can justify the persecution of one people in an attempt to relieve the persecution of another.

At a time when the case of Palestine's Arabs usually went by default, this was the most eloquent defence of their rights that had yet appeared. Published as it was on both sides of the Atlantic, *The Arab Awakening* exerted a certain influence on decision-makers, if not on wider public opinion.[34]

Soldiers and students

In late 1938, Hilda Wilson, a young British schoolteacher, got a lift into Jerusalem in a lorry full of British soldiers:

> 'Ow far've you walked, Miss?' asked one.
> 'Four miles.'
> 'Cripes! Just like our route marches at 'ome.'
> They went on to inform me that they were aged sixteen and seventeen. I didn't believe it, but they certainly looked no older. I told them that I was teaching boys of that age in an Arab school. They stared and one of them remarked cheerfully, 'I killed a couple of Arabs yesterday.'

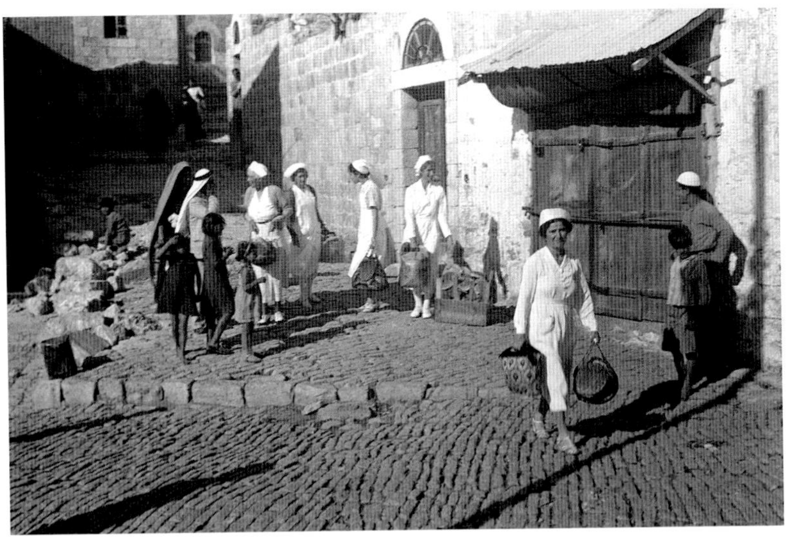

American Colony

Bertha Spafford Vester, left, and her nurses distribute bread, 1938

The Englishwoman had arrived in the Arab world almost a decade earlier when, at the age of only twenty-five, she had become principal of a girls' school in Sudan. After moving to Palestine, she was now teaching English at a private Arab school in Bir Zeit, a village north of Jerusalem. Sharp-eyed and intelligent—she was later to become an editor, a published poet, and a committed Quaker—she was conscious of her unusual vantage point, witnessing the rebellion through the eyes of bored young British soldiers and at the same time through the eyes of her vociferously nationalist students. One night the school would be visited by rebels, the next by soldiers. On one occasion she witnessed a rebel court, held at the school at night to deal with a local dispute. In Bir Zeit and neighbouring villages, there were frequent stories of how soldiers hunting for rebels and weapons would ransack homes, knock over jars of olive oil, and steal jewellery or money.[35]

At the height of the rebellion, in October 1938, the rebels managed to seize the Old City of Jerusalem and hold it for five days: a singular affront to the imperial power. After British forces had regained control, Bertha Spafford Vester and her nurses delivered bread to a grateful population.

In early 1939, two of the male teachers at the Bir Zeit school were detained by soldiers in a night-time operation and taken to join scores of other suspects lined up in the village. Hilda Wilson and a colleague hurried out into the night to witness the scene.

> Soldiers and lorries were everywhere. The men of the village, most of them wearing the peasant's long robe and headcloth, were being marshalled in single file … One by one they were led forward and halted in a strong beam of light projected from an armoured car. A soldier pulled back the man's headcloth and held his head from behind so that the beam shone full in his face, while another standing by the car with a paper in his hand shouted 'Shu ismak?' ('What's your name?'). The man's answer was compared with the paper, and a whispered conversation followed with the most important actor in the drama, a well-guarded personage invisible inside the armoured car. This was an Arab spy. Rumour next day said that he was a member of the Nashashibi party … (The Nashashibis were the Arab political faction hostile to the Mufti's party. Bir Zeit was solid for the Mufti.)

In the end, seventeen men were detained and taken to a prison in the nearby town of Ramallah. The rest were released. Not long afterwards, amid signs that a large-scale man-hunt was under way, a plane dropped pink notices announcing that the village was under curfew. (Hilda kept one, which can be found with her papers in Oxford.) When news came that a popular rebel leader, Abdul-Rahim al-Hajj Muhammad, had been killed in an engagement with the British, the boys of the school went into mourning. Hilda's class read a poem by Rupert Brooke.

The White Paper

MacMichael was a law-and-order man, out to rectify what he and others saw as Wauchope's excessive moderation. But he realised that, while the rebellion had to be stamped out, there also had to be a change of political direction. He went to London in late 1938 and worked out a new policy with Whitehall officials. There was a conviction that, with war looming in Europe, Arab opinion in the Middle East had to be appeased. British officials invited Arab and Jewish representatives to a conference in London. In his last act of mediation, despite being in poor health, George Antonius served as secretary to the Arab and Palestinian delegations.

When the conference ended in failure, the British government announced its own solution in the form of the White Paper of May 1939. This offered the Arabs the prospect of an independent, bi-national Palestine, with an Arab majority, in ten years. In the meantime there would be stringent limits on Jewish immigration and land purchases. This was the most significant shift in British policy since the issuing of the Balfour Declaration two decades earlier. Despite fierce opposition, not least from Churchill, the White Paper was approved by the House of Commons. The Zionists were aghast: they denounced what they saw as betrayal and organised mass protests in Jerusalem and Tel Aviv. But at the same time they badly needed Britain to emerge victorious from the looming struggle against Hitler.

Some Arab figures (Musa Alami among them) thought the White Paper probably represented the best offer they were likely to get, but the Mufti and his allies flatly rejected it. (Hajj Amin knew that whoever might lead any future Arab Palestine, the British would make sure it would not be him.) Hilda Wilson in Bir Zeit recorded that Arab opinion regarded the White Paper, with a touch of pride, as 'a concession won by Arab arms'. But by now, especially among the rural population, exhaustion had set in, which the army exploited in order to get information and recruit collaborators. The English schoolteacher left Palestine in July 1939, her affection for it undimmed. She returned to Britain, where her efforts to get her account published were unsuccessful.

By late 1939, on the eve of the Second World War, the revolt had been crushed. Some 6,000 Arabs had lost their lives—and 1,000 more had been killed by fellow Arabs in the bitter internal feud between supporters and opponents of the Mufti.[36]

The rebellion produced two very different results. It finally destroyed Britain's imperial complacency, forcing it into a significant reversal of policy. But its suppression left Arab Palestine shattered, demoralised, and leaderless—and fatally ill prepared for the struggle that lay ahead.

Tel Aviv, 1939: young Zionists protest at the British White Paper

Zoltan Kluger

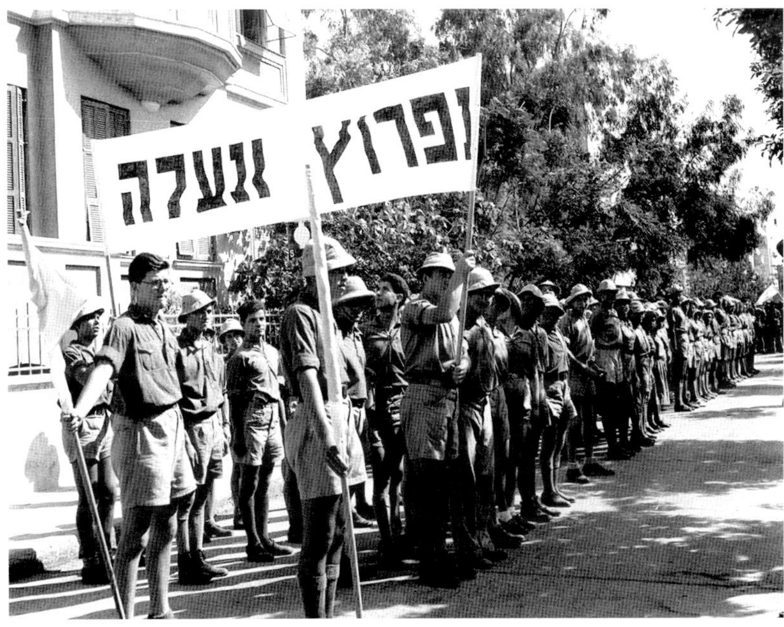

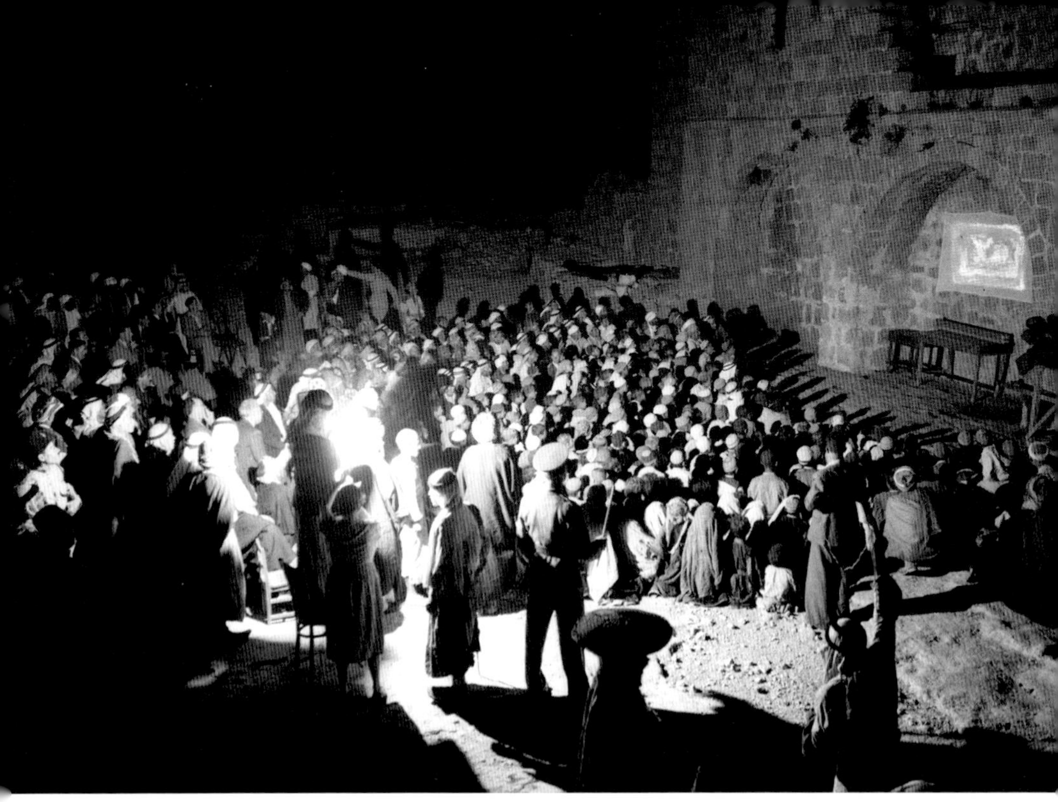

War-time film show in Halhul, a village near Hebron, 1940

4

An interlude of war, 1939–1945

'We ought to get a radio station going for the Arabs.'

Air Commodore Kenneth Buss, 1941

O N 3 SEPTEMBER 1939, the day Britain declared war on Germany, Tawfiq Canaan was arrested, together with his German wife Margot and his sister Badra. He suspected that he and Badra were on the police black-list, as nationalists critical of Britain. Tawfiq was indeed a nationalist, but he had no sympathy for Nazism. But the British establishment had not forgotten his open support for the Arab rebellion of the 1930s. His friends lobbied to secure his release, and he was never convicted of any offence. He was released after spending two months in Acre prison. But Margot and Badra were kept—with 'criminals, Bolsheviks, [and] harlots', as Tawfiq put it—in the women's prison in Bethlehem. They were then transferred to Wilhelma, a former Templer colony near the coast which now served as an internment camp, where conditions were better. Margot was detained for nine months, Badra for four years: she was not released until 1943.[1]

Britons and Jews

For Palestine, the war was a curious hiatus in which the local conflict between Arabs and Jews was eclipsed by the bigger, global conflagration. For most of the war, the country was an oasis of calm.

Ben-Gurion and the Zionists found themselves in a deeply ambivalent relationship with the British. The White Paper of 1939, so detested by the Zionists, had been the product of a Labour government. In the early months of the war, relations were badly strained between the Zionist leadership and Labour ministers—in particular the architect of the White Paper, the colonial secretary Malcolm MacDonald (son of the former prime minister Ramsay MacDonald). The Zionists were anxious to play an active part in the war, but were rebuffed. The British did not trust them, and feared the Arab reaction if they were seen to be playing a prominent role. Emblematic of the British attitude was that, in October 1939, some forty members of the Haganah (including Moshe Dayan) were arrested for carrying arms. MacDonald argued that he couldn't punish Arabs for this offence (which during the rebellion had carried the death penalty) and turn a blind eye if the Jews did the same. Dayan and his colleagues were sentenced to ten years in Acre prison.[2]

The situation changed dramatically when, in May 1940, Winston Churchill became prime minister at the head of a coalition government. The Zionists now had a powerful ally in Downing Street who was a fierce critic of the White Paper policy. For the time being, preoccupied with fighting the war, Churchill allowed the policy to stand, but quietly he did what he could to unpick it.[3]

The ambivalence felt by the Jews towards Britain was summed up in Ben-Gurion's much-quoted phrase that they should fight the war as if there were no White Paper, and the White Paper as if there were no war. This meant that the Zionists on the one hand gave active support to the British war effort, and on the other did everything they could to build up an autonomous army and to facilitate the illegal entry into Palestine of Jewish refugees from Europe.

The plight of Europe's Jews was a human tragedy exploited by politicians and racketeers alike. Germany was not alone in seeking to expel its Jews. So too did the anti-Semitic régimes in Poland and Romania, closely followed by Hungary. There was illegal immigration into Palestine by sea as well as land, across the border with Syria. But it was the fate of the immigrant ships which caught the Western public's imagination. As the Zionists were quick to grasp, the spectacle of Europe's unwanted Jews struggling to cross the sea to the Promised Land was a potent symbol and rallying-cry for their cause. For the British, limiting immigration was crucial to the success of their White Paper policy, and hence to their strategy for securing the war-time Middle East. For their critics, talk of quotas and legality and Palestine's 'absorptive capacity' seemed the pettifogging obstructionism of heartless bureaucrats. It was a battle Britain was bound to lose.[4]

In the early phase of the war the expulsion of the Jews from Germany and German-controlled territory was official Nazi policy: Adolf Eichmann's office was responsible for implementing it. In Poland, Romania, and Hungary, meanwhile, Jews desperate to escape turned to

> corrupt foreign consuls … who for handsome remuneration were willing to supply dubious visas and landing permits … In open collusion with the Polish, Romanian, and Hungarian authorities, a host of smugglers, ship brokers, captains, shadowy middlemen of all kinds then took over, participating in the highly lucrative clandestine traffic that brought thousands of Jews to Palestine waters, many after voyages that began in sealed trains departing after nightfall from stations in Warsaw, Bucharest, or Vienna.[5]

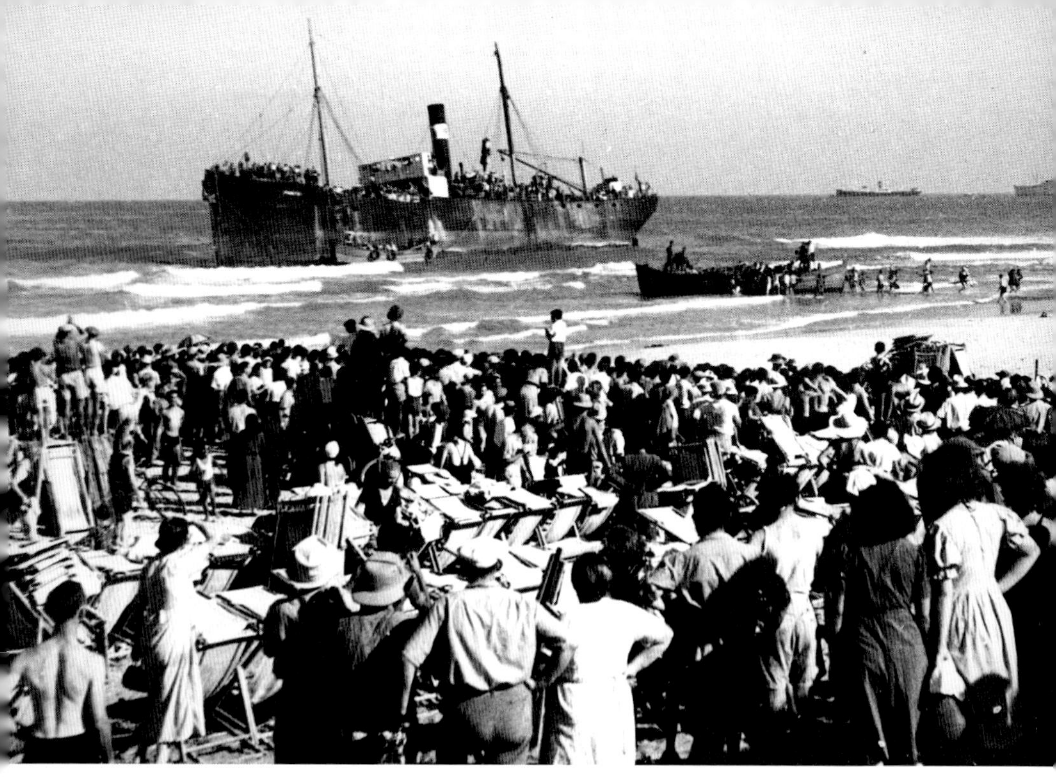

The Parita, *beached at Tel Aviv, August 1939*   Zoltan Kluger

When the refugees reached ports on the Black Sea or the Aegean, Zionist organisations herded them onto overcrowded and unseaworthy vessels they had purchased for exorbitant sums. During this initial phase, from 1939 to 1941, some two-dozen ships brought an estimated 13,000 refugees to Palestine.[6] Typical of many was the *Parita*, which in July 1939 sailed from Romania with some 850 immigrants on board. After weeks of zig-zagging round the Mediterranean, and being turned back from port after port, the vessel managed to beach on sand-banks near Tel Aviv. Some of the passengers managed to evade capture while the rest were sent to the Athlit detention camp near Haifa.

In one case, that of the *Patria* in November 1940, the

Haganah attached a bomb to the side of the vessel, in a bungled attempt to disable the ship and prevent the immigrants from being deported; more than 250 drowned. In public the Zionists maintained that the refugees had, in despair, committed mass suicide; only years later did the truth come out.

In December 1941, the *Struma*—an old cattle ship carrying more than 700 Romanian Jews—became the focus of a protracted row between Britain, Turkey, and the Yishuv. The vessel eventually limped out of the Bosphorus and was sunk, possibly by a Soviet mine or torpedo; only one of the passengers survived. Zionist posters denounced MacMichael, the high commissioner, as a murderer.

For Britain, the ships, and the unwelcome publicity they attracted, posed 'a dilemma with no solution and no end until after 1941, when the Nazi occupation [of much of Europe] and the decision to exterminate, not expel, the Jews effectively sealed off all escape routes from what would become the killing grounds of Eastern Europe'.[7] But the issue of the immigrant ships—which more than any other poisoned relations between Britain and the Yishuv—was to return with a vengeance towards the end of the war.

Off-duty in Tel Aviv

Even as Britain's policies were being excoriated by the Jews, its soldiers were being greeted by 'hospitality committees' in Tel Aviv. Zionist officials urged citizens to welcome their British and Allied guests, especially in shops and restaurants. The city needed Allied protection. In 1940, after Mussolini's Italy had entered the war on the side of Germany, Italian planes had bombed the coast of Palestine, targeting the oil installations of Haifa and, in the deadliest attack, striking Tel Aviv and killing over a hundred civilians.

Jewish families frowned on liaisons between their girls and

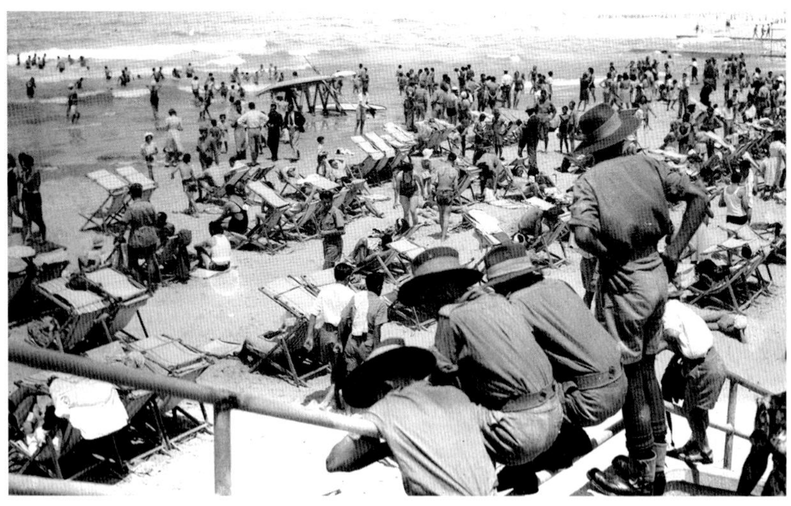

Australian soldiers in Tel Aviv, c. 1940   Matson Photo Service

British soldiers. But, undeterred, Assia Gutmann, by now an attractive and wilful teenager, started dating a string of admiring British soldiers. Her parents, Lonya and Lisa, had been unwilling to send her to the Balfour Elementary School in Tel Aviv, whose curriculum seemed to them 'too Zionist, alien, and constricting, detached from the richness of European culture'.[8] So in 1941 they took the highly unusual step of sending her to a Christian school in neighbouring Jaffa. This was the Tabeetha School, founded in 1863 by a Scottish missionary from Glasgow, Jane Walker-Arnott, and originally designed to teach Arab girls from poor families. (Among Miss Arnott's early supporters was the travel agent Thomas Cook.) When she died in 1911, the school was taken over by the Church of Scotland, which turned it into a fee-paying establishment—run on traditional British lines—for the children of wealthy Arabs. The school was a 'haven of Little Britain in the Middle East'. The girls wore pink dresses and blue sweaters. They played tennis and netball and performed Shakespeare plays. Assia, the only Jewish student, quickly mastered English as she had earlier mastered German, Russian, and Hebrew. Now, in addition to her elegant demeanour, she acquired a cut-glass English accent. The other girls thought her beautiful but haughty.

For British and Allied soldiers in the Middle East, Tel Aviv was a place to rest and relax and meet the opposite sex. The hospitality committees arranged dances and concert tickets for the soldiers and trips to shops and schools. Families signed up to invite them home for tea and cakes. Lisa was quick to put her name down, and among her guests was a young RAF sergeant, John Steele, who immediately fell for Assia. She for her part regarded this tall public-school boy as the embodiment of the English gentleman. Her mother, fearing her German ancestry made her vulnerable, encouraged the relationship, hoping that if the couple married the Gutmanns would be able to settle in Britain.[9]

Steele was on leave from his base in Egypt. But later in the war he was transferred to Palestine. Aware that she was dating a string of other men—including officers of higher rank—he nevertheless continued to see her. They frequented the Café Nussbaum and went to concerts given by the Palestine Philharmonic Orchestra. Some Jews actively campaigned against such liaisons. Assia received hate mail.

Hearts and minds

British officials devoted a great deal of money and effort to winning the active support of the Arabs, or at least their passive neutrality. They were alarmed at the single-mindedness of German and Italian radio propaganda, which fed on Arab grievances over British rule and—still a raw wound—the harsh suppression of the Arab rebellion. Senior officials who had maintained good contacts with the *mukhtars* (village leaders)

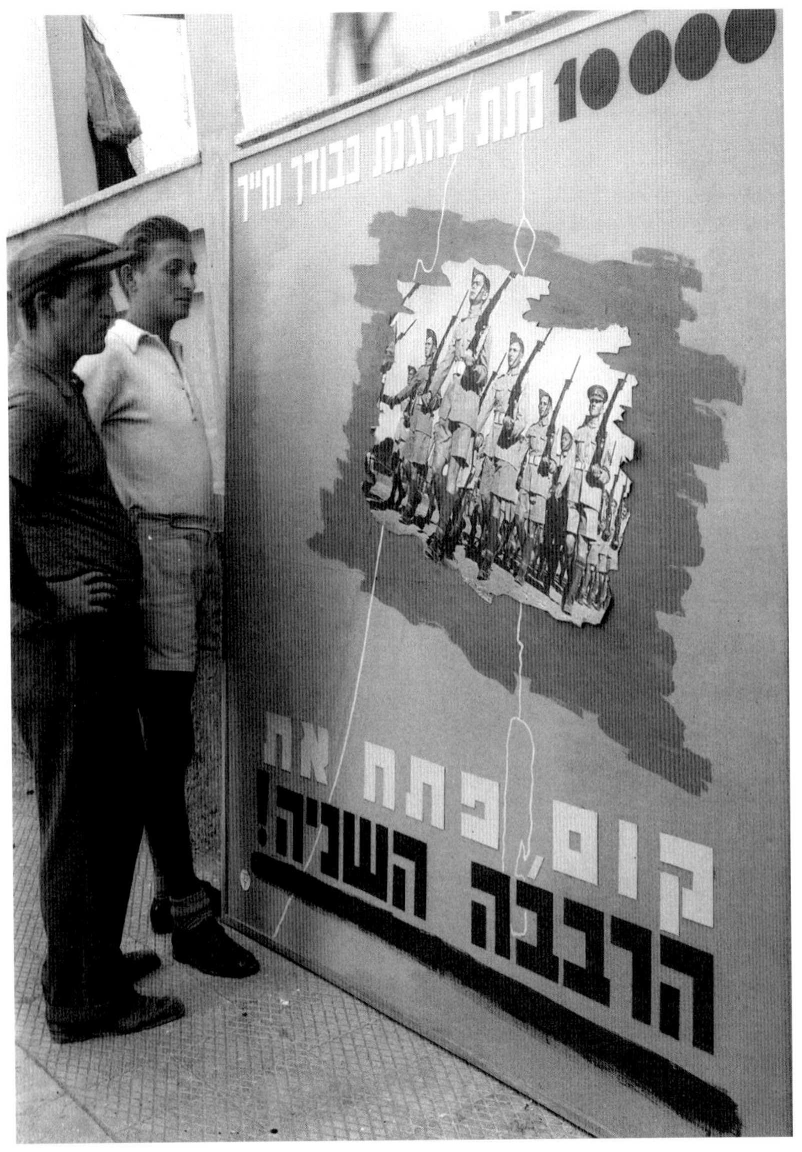

War-time recruitment poster, Tel Aviv, 1941   Zoltan Kluger

held a series of 'loyalty' meetings throughout the country. These were publicised in the Arabic newspaper *Filastin*, which supported the British war effort and was hostile to the Husseini faction led from exile by the Mufti, Hajj Amin.[10] In addition, mobile units brought films and war-time newsreels to rural areas without access to cinemas. Where there was no screen, the film would be beamed onto the wall of a school or a mosque.

Officials started campaigns to recruit Jews and Arabs into the British army. The Zionists, for all their hostility to British policy, urged able-bodied men and women to sign up. But they wanted the recruits to serve in a separate Jewish Brigade, under their own flag, and this idea, although supported by Churchill, aroused strong opposition from his civilian and military colleagues. The dispute, sometimes presented as a purely logistical problem, was at root political. The British believed that the presence of mixed Palestinian battalions, in which both Arabs and Jews served, would send a signal that the two communities had a common goal and that there was no discrimination between them. The Zionists, on the other hand, wanted to send the message that they were a nation like the other nations united in the war-time alliance against Hitler, and believed this would strengthen their case for statehood. Weizmann lobbied tirelessly to this end, but it was only in the last months of the war that Churchill finally pushed through the decision to establish a Jewish Brigade, in the teeth of considerable opposition.

In the meantime, some 30,000 members of the Yishuv had joined up. These included 5,000 women who served in the ATS (Auxiliary Territorial Service), the women's branch of the British army, although this occasioned some debate over the ethical as well as the political implications of women playing such roles.[11]

The Zionist leaders put all their weight behind the recruitment campaign. But as with the campaign for Jewish-only

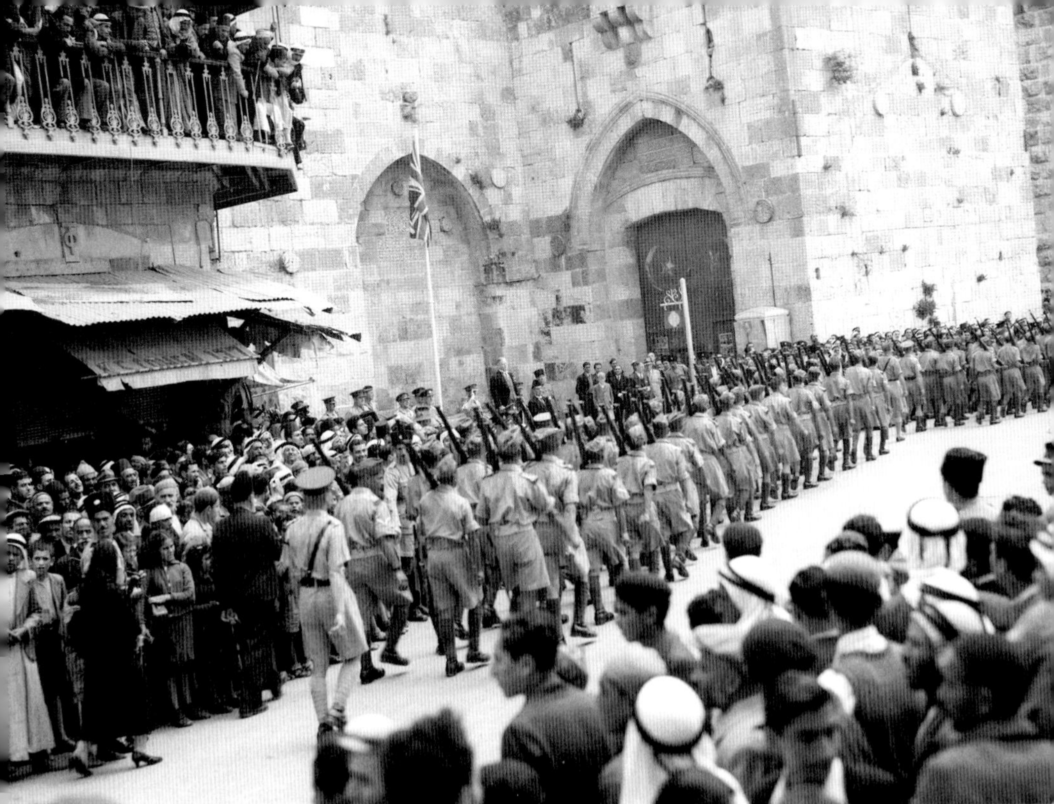

Arab recruits marching through Jerusalem, 1941   Matson Photo Service

labour, there was a coercive element in their efforts to mobilise the Yishuv. The British journalist Barbara Board reported on desertions by Jews who claimed they had been pressured into signing up, threatened with the loss of their jobs, and even beaten up.[12]

The shadow of the Mufti

British officials were anxious to show that Arabs, too, were being recruited, but here they encountered a different set of problems. Some 8,000 Arabs did sign up, but many young Arabs and their families regarded as abhorrent the idea of fighting for the power which was occupying their country. The Mufti—who was

164

soon to ally himself openly with Hitler—vehemently opposed any form of collaboration with Britain, and much of Arab Palestine remained loyal to him. But after the crushing of the rebellion of the 1930s, Hajj Amin and his clan, the Husseinis, were a much weakened force—and their opponents, the Nashashibis, were sufficiently emboldened to openly promote Arab recruitment. At the same time, the main motive for joining up, especially for young men from the villages, seems to have been economic.[13]

Some 200 Arab women served in the ATS. It was not easy to recruit women in a conservative, predominantly Muslim society, and those who joined up tended to be urban and middle-class, many of them Christians. Among them was Asia Halaby, who became a British army driver. The Halaby sisters, Asia and Sophie, daughters of a Christian Arab father and a Russian mother, had received a thoroughly British education at an Anglican mission school, the Jerusalem Girls' College, run by Mabel Warburton, whom they revered. The school, founded in 1918 after the start of the British occupation, brought together Muslim, Christian, and Jewish girls from well-to-do families. Miss Warburton fostered an ethos of self-confidence, hard work, and tolerance. In 1929, a few years after graduating from the college, Sophie Halaby won a scholarship to study art in Paris—a rare achievement for a young Arab woman at the time.[14]

Asia, meanwhile, became the first Arab woman in Palestine to own and drive a car. The ATS was quick to spot her unusual talents. She could repair army vehicles from the smallest jeep to the largest three-ton truck. The recruits were initially sent for training to the British base at Sarafand, near the coast. Here, fluent in English, French, Russian, and Arabic, Asia served as a translator. At the end of the course she was made an officer. The recruits were then transferred to Egypt, where they worked as drivers, nurses, and in other non-combat roles. Driving army

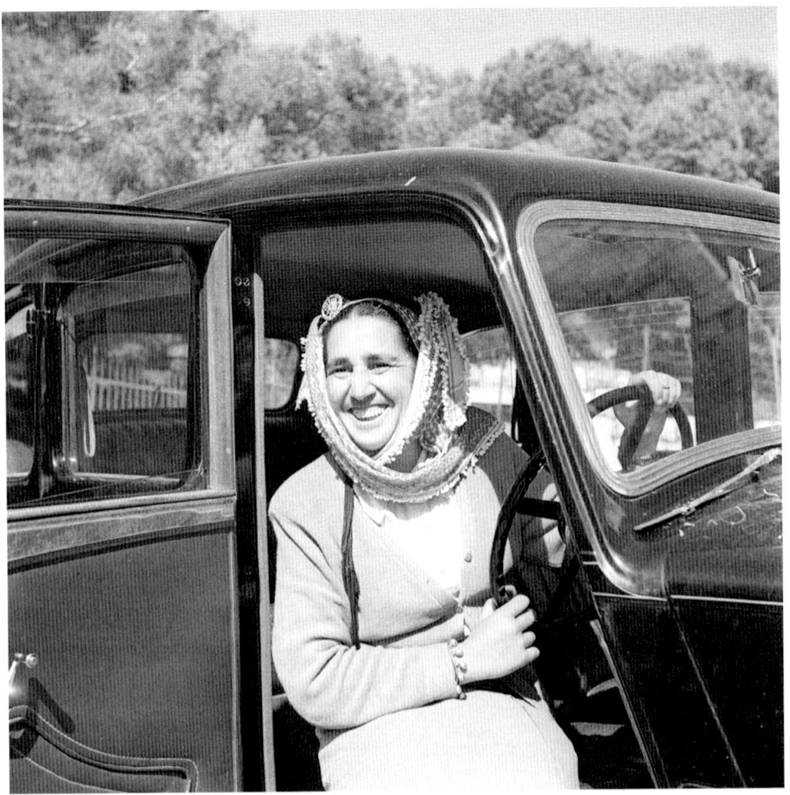

Asia Halaby, 1948   Willem van de Poll

vehicles in a desert war, in fierce heat and sandstorms, was tough work. On leave, still in uniform, Asia would drive through the streets of Jerusalem in her jeep, something that might normally have provoked hostility; but the Halaby sisters, while decidedly unconventional, were respected for their patriotism and their strength of character. They admired British culture and the values they had imbibed from Miss Warburton, but had no doubt that British rule and Zionist colonisation should end and that the Arabs of Palestine should be independent.[15]

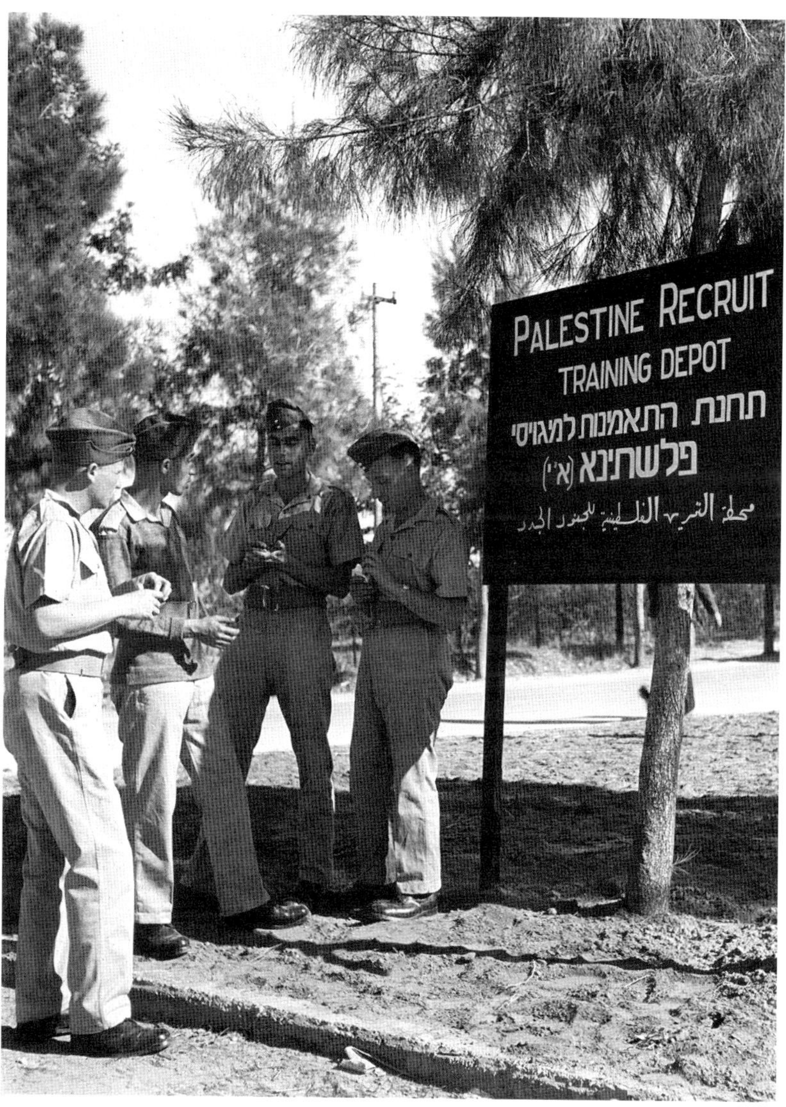

Jewish recruits at a British army base, Sarafand, 1940   Zoltan Kluger

Subversion, sabotage, propaganda

'We ought to get a radio station going for the Arabs,' remarked Air Commodore Kenneth Buss one afternoon in the summer of 1941. Buss ran the newly-created Jerusalem Bureau of the Special Operations Executive (SOE), the secret organisation created by Churchill in July 1940 to wage covert war against the Germans and their allies by means of subversion, sabotage, and propaganda. The person Buss was addressing was the young Jack Robertson, who spent the next few frantic weeks setting up a secret Arabic radio station.

Captain Robertson had arrived in the Middle East in April 1941 after a five-week voyage from Glasgow to Cape Town, and thence by plane and train to Cairo. He was thirty-one. At the start of the war, during the Blitz, he had manned an anti-aircraft battery on the edge of London, but had then been recruited into a 'hush-hush' job with SOE.[16] At its inception Churchill had famously instructed its head, Hugh Dalton, to 'set Europe ablaze'; but as the war continued, SOE's scope extended well beyond the European theatre.

The centre of British operations in the Middle East, both overt and covert, was Cairo, which became so important to the war effort that a minister of cabinet rank—the Minister Resident in the Middle East—was installed there. From Egypt, British officials ran the Middle East Supply Centre, which controlled the production and supply of essential goods throughout the region. And, to add to the mix, Cairo also played host to a plethora of secret or semi-secret organisations which were frequently at loggerheads with the military and political chiefs, and with one another. SOE's work, by its very nature, involved breaking the rules. The Germans were a ruthless adversary: Churchill was convinced they could not be defeated if the British waged war like gentlemen. In the Middle East, as elsewhere, this meant the covert—and therefore deniable—use of sabotage, assassination, and bribery.[17]

This was the clandestine world into which Jack Robertson was plunged. Himself a writer—before the war he had been a leader writer on the London *Evening News*—he now found himself rubbing shoulders with a cast of often colourful and eccentric characters that included the travel writer Freya Stark and her future husband Stewart Perowne, the archaeologist Seton Lloyd, Edward Hodgkin (brother of Thomas), and a charismatic former monk, Adrian Bishop. All contributed to SOE's propaganda effort in the Middle East. Their task was to counter German and Italian broadcasts and convince the Arabs that Britain would win the war—which at that point was by no means self-evident.

Jack was sent from Egypt to Palestine to work for Air Commodore Buss. He felt an immediate affection for the country, for the staff he inherited from Bishop (who had been posted to Baghdad), and for the Arab house near Herod's Gate which he acquired from the young Steven Runciman, who went off to Istanbul to further his career as a historian. Buss's almost casual remark set in train the remarkable and little-known story of the Near East Arab Broadcasting Station, better known as Sharq al-Adna. Whereas Palestine's own radio station, the Palestine Broadcasting Service, set up by Wauchope in the 1930s, had a local purpose and a local audience, Sharq al-Adna's brief was to reach the widest possible Arab audience and thereby play a role in the war-time battle for hearts and minds. British-controlled Palestine was a handy place to locate such a station.

According to Jack's own account, he got the new station up and running in just over three weeks. He knew no Arabic. He needed staff, equipment, and a site. The head of the Arab College, Ahmad Samih al-Khalidi—that 'maker of men', as Jack called him—helped him with the first. A transmitter was, with some difficulty, wrenched from the Free French in Beirut, to

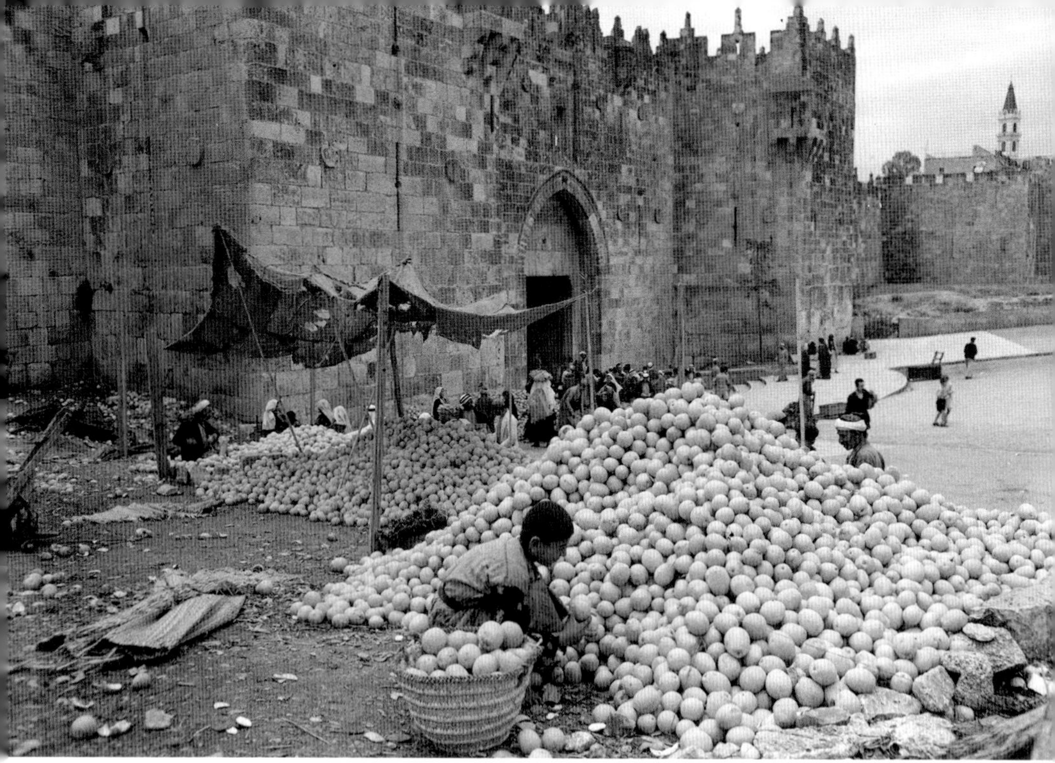

Oranges at Damascus Gate, 1944   Matson Photo Service

whom it had been loaned. And the chosen location was Jenin, a small town in northern Palestine. In September 1941, at the start of Ramadan, the Muslim month of fasting—and to the surprise of everyone, including Jack—the new station went on air.

It was an Arab station, as Buss had wanted, in the sense that its journalistic staff were Arab and it made no attempt to maintain the kind of balanced approach to news and current affairs of the BBC. (One observer remarked that, if the BBC's Arabic Service was *The Times*, Sharq al-Adna was the *Daily Mail.*) It was a populist, pro-Arab radio station, and with its blend of wartime news, music, and readings from the Quran, together with generous funding, it gained a wide audience.[18]

Jack's affection for Palestine was intense. To fall in love with the country, its mix of people, the unique quality of the light, the brief and memorable arrival of spring—this was commonplace. But Jack was a sentimentalist as well as an aspiring poet:

> Jerusalem is white stone walls against a sky of deep, unquenchable blue … Jerusalem is sunlight against the pinewoods … Jerusalem is the heaped-up, dazzling, tawny glow of oranges on stalls outside the Damascus Gate. Jerusalem is bells and the feet of old pious men shuffling off to prayer.

He called it the 'enchantment' of Palestine, and believed it had changed him. 'You cannot go and work in Palestine and be untouched by it; all the rest of your life you move and work in the echo and the reflection of what you had in Palestine.'[19]

The country worked its strange alchemy in another way, too. Under the influence of Ruth Belkine of the Palestine Broadcasting Service, who introduced him to war-time broadcasting and was later to become his wife, Jack was converted from Arabism to Zionism.[20]

Strange bedfellows

At the same time, and with the knowledge of only a handful of British officials, SOE reached a secret agreement with the Haganah. By 1941 Dayan and his colleagues had been released, after spending more than a year in Acre prison, and SOE was running a training camp for Haganah members on Mount Carmel, overlooking Haifa, where they were supplied with weapons and radio sets and trained in covert warfare. In return, the Haganah sent teams of agents into the Balkans and the Arab Middle East, and provided the British with valuable war-time intelligence.[21]

It was an improbable relationship, maintained in strict secrecy and marked by mistrust on both sides. Britons and Jews not only had their political differences; there was a clash of cultures. This was well expressed by David Hacohen, a senior Haganah official closely involved in the war-time relationship, and himself a graduate of the London School of Economics.

> [The British] had never met natives of our sort. The best doctors in the country were Jews. The best architects were Jews ... We paid taxes, but we never went to the government schools. We went to our own schools ... There were more English books in our houses than in their houses ... They couldn't come to terms with us.[22]

But wars make strange bedfellows, and during the darkest hours of 1941-42 the partnership endured. British officers helped the Haganah create an élite force, the Palmach, which played a role in June 1941 when Britain and its allies invaded Syria and Lebanon to dislodge the pro-German Vichy French. It was during the fighting that Dayan lost an eye. His colleague Yigal Allon was meanwhile rebuked for insubordination by his British officer, Major J. M. Collard, and replaced.[23] (After the war Jack Collard was to write a string of books on the Middle East, including two on the Palestine Mandate, using the pen-name John Marlowe.)

The British were even ready on occasion to co-operate with the extremists of the Irgun, the militant offshoot of the Haganah. Following a coup in Baghdad by pro-German army officers, Irgun members were released from jail in Palestine—including the group's leader, David Raziel—and sent to Iraq to carry out sabotage and, if possible, kidnap or kill the Mufti, Hajj Amin, who had taken refuge there. The mission was unsuccessful and Raziel was killed.[24] There were other casualties. On a mission to destroy oil refineries in Tripoli, on the Lebanese coast, all twenty-three members of a Palmach team were killed.

Syria and Iraq were denied to the Germans and their allies, but the danger was not over. By June 1942, with Rommel's tanks sixty miles from Alexandria, it seemed possible that

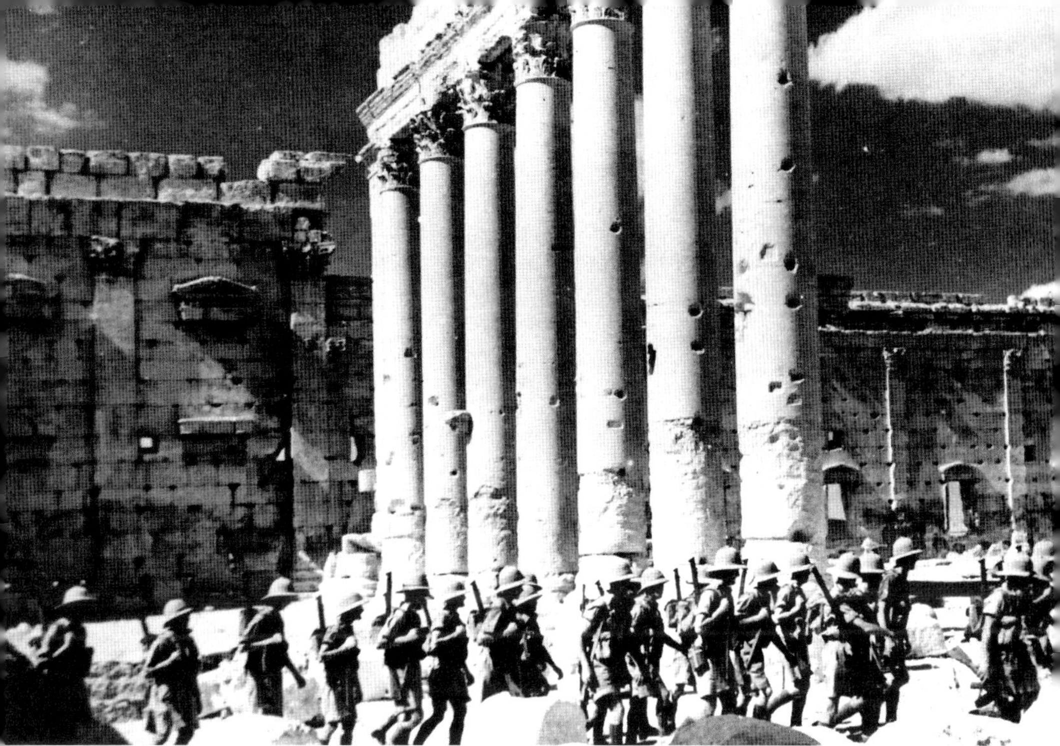

British troops in Palmyra, Syria, 1941   Photographer unknown

Egypt—which Churchill regarded as the bedrock of Britain's position in the Middle East—might fall to the Germans. Britain and the Yishuv were gripped by fear that Palestine might follow suit. SOE and 'the Friends'—the codename for their Haganah allies—devised desperate contingency measures, including the withdrawal of their teams to the mountains of Lebanon, from where they would wage a sustained guerrilla war against the German occupiers, and the sabotage of Haifa's oil installations and the pipeline from Iraq.[25] Some officials opted to leave Palestine, but Jack was determined to stay, and chose a secluded cave by a waterfall as a potential hide-out. On German radio Hajj Amin, now in Berlin, proclaimed in Arabic that the mighty British empire was finished.[26]

Only after the British victory at El-Alamein in October-November 1942 did the panic subside: the Middle East was safe. SOE ended its co-operation with the Haganah and took back the weapons it had handed out—though, in a final act of defiance, Allon and the Palmach raided a British store and recaptured them.[27]

As the year ended, it was clear that Britain's position in the Middle East had been transformed. But at the same time reports of the Nazi programme to exterminate the Jews of Europe could no longer be dismissed as rumour or exaggeration. From the Zionists' point of view, Britain's role in the defeat of Hitler was essential; but they could no longer rely on it to secure the success of the Zionist project. It was time to change horses.

The Biltmore programme

Before the war, the United States had not been a significant actor in the Palestine drama. This was about to change. The five million American Jews, though divided into Zionist and non-Zionist camps, were united in their outrage over the plight of the Jews of Europe and Britain's refusal to allow large numbers of them to enter Palestine. (The irony, not lost on British officials, was that the United States was also barring the door to large-scale Jewish immigration.) American Jews raised money for the refugees and for Zionist organisations. The artist Arthur Szyk produced posters supporting the campaign for a Jewish army. And party leaders, both Democrat and Republican, began to realise that events in far-away Palestine could have an impact on how Jews chose to vote.

In May 1942 Weizmann and Ben-Gurion—whose rivalry had become increasingly acrimonious—attended a congress of American Zionists at the Biltmore Hotel in New York.

Right: *Poster, New York, 1940*   Arthur Szyk

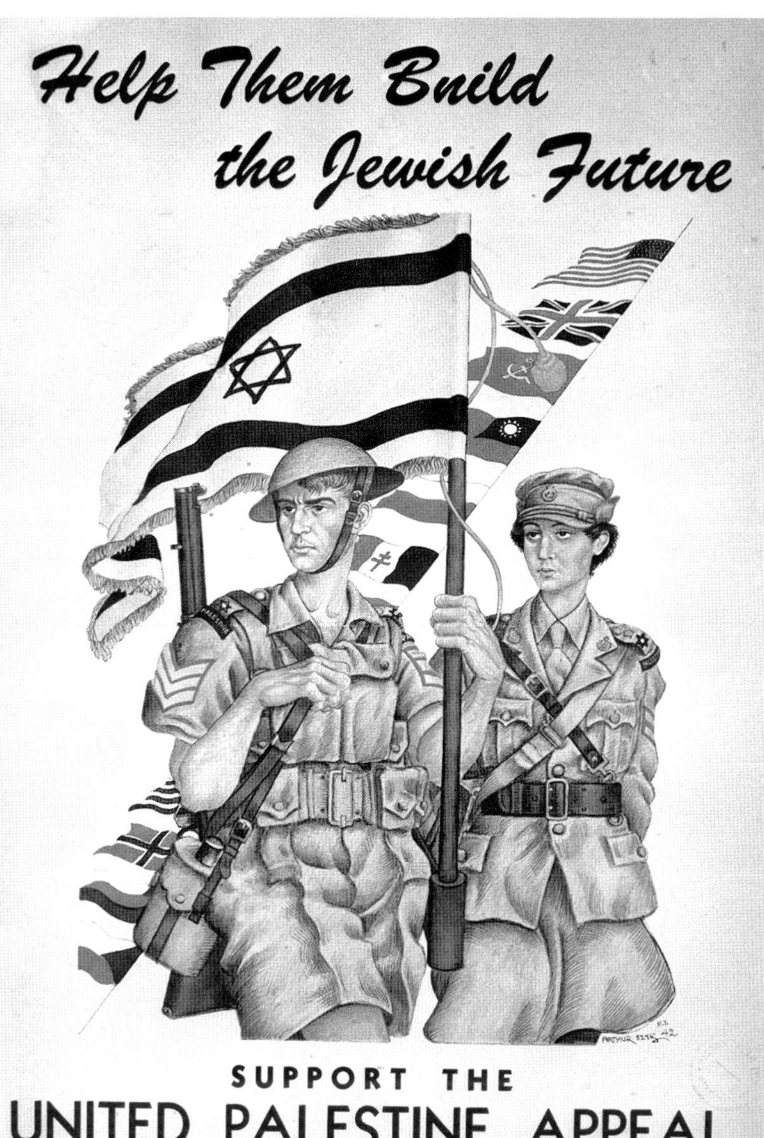
Help Them Build
the Jewish Future
SUPPORT THE
UNITED PALESTINE APPEAL
41 EAST 42 STREET · NEW YORK
A Constituent Agency of the United Jewish Appeal for Refugees, Overseas Needs and Palestine

Its programme—subsequently endorsed by the Zionists in Palestine—called for Palestine to be transformed into a 'Jewish Commonwealth' (meaning a Jewish state), for the Jewish Agency to take control of immigration, and for the creation of a Jewish army. This marked a distinct break with the caution and gradualism of the past, when Weizmann had insisted that the movement do nothing to jeopardise its relations with Britain. What's more, it indicated that the Zionists now intended to utilise to the full the influence that the United States and American Jewry could exert in money, propaganda, and political clout.

A soldier's war

When Private Norman Dannatt arrived in Palestine early in the war, he found himself in the Augusta Victoria compound, on the Mount of Olives, which was now serving as a military hospital. He had caught an infection on the long voyage from Britain, and now whiled away the time admiring the massive stone structure, conceived by Kaiser Wilhelm in the late nineteenth century, with its carved double-eagle emblems and its beautiful grounds with olives, figs, and pomegranates, and a profusion of spring flowers.

One day a group of soldiers were invited for tea and cucumber sandwiches at Government House with the high commissioner, Sir Harold MacMichael, and his wife and two daughters. They arrived by coach and were allowed to roam through the elegant grounds.

> There was a scruffy old Arab there pruning the roses. We went up to him and, in our coarse soldierly way, spoke to him, teasing him and addressing him as 'George'. We had learnt that we call all Arabs 'George' as a generic name … The gardener smiled gently at us and continued with his pruning. Later we found out, to our embarrassment, that 'George' was, in fact, the high commissioner himself, indulging his favourite hobby of gardening.

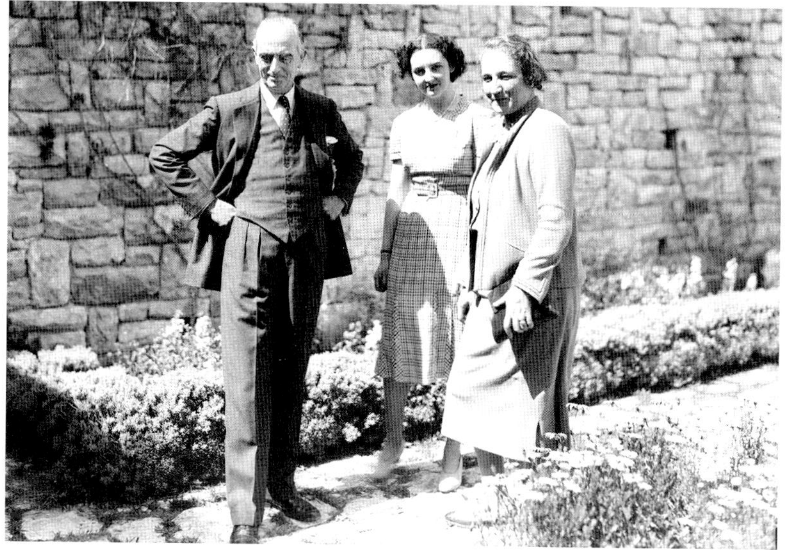

MacMichael with his wife and daughter, c. 1939   Matson Photo Service

Dannatt, a keen musician, accompanied MacMichael's daughter Araminta as she sang Noël Coward songs. His job, in the army pay corps, was dull, but the young soldier found compensation in Jerusalem's musical life.

[The city] lived and breathed music. During the week I could go from house to house where there were musical performances of some sort—string quartets, song recitals, and solo instrument recitals. There was even a house with a long upper room with, unusual for Jerusalem, a wooden floor, in which complete ballets were performed. The musicians and dancers were all amateurs— but really gifted amateurs at that.

Dannatt performed as an accompanist for the Palestine Broadcasting Service—working for Ruth Belkine—and began giving weekly organ recitals of popular music at the YMCA, for a fee of £1 a performance.[28]

For soldiers who wanted distraction from the war, Palestine offered another advantage: the chance to travel. Through a Zionist women's organisation, Dannatt arranged a holiday on a kibbutz, all expenses paid. (The Zionists, too, were in the hearts-and-minds business.) He visited half a dozen kibbutzim during his stay in Palestine and, like most visitors, admired the energy of the settlers and was intrigued by what he regarded as their 'communist' way of life. But he formed no opinion as to the rival claims of Arab and Jew; he was happy to have friends on both sides of the divide. Meanwhile an enterprising sergeant organised a subsidised trip to Lebanon and Syria, which were by now at peace and under the joint rule of Britain and the Free French. Conductors on the Damascus trams would receive the breezy assurance that 'Churchill will pay'.

An invisible war

War-time Jerusalem existed in a kind of bubble. Despite rationing and shortages, it was not difficult to have a good time. A cosmopolitan cast of characters—soldiers, spies, journalists, exiled royalty—gravitated to the King David Hotel, whose bar was a hotbed of news and gossip. Meanwhile members of the Anglo-Arab élite enjoyed the parties of Katy Antonius, the wife (and, after his sudden death in 1942, the widow) of George Antonius. Ordinary soldiers, who could not afford the prices of the smarter hotels and restaurants, frequented the city's cafés, clubs, bars, and brothels. Norman Dannatt and his mates found cheap liquor in an unexpected place: in the ultra-orthodox quarter of Mea Shearim, where Issy's Bar ('a seedy little dive') sold them locally-made red wine at a piastre a glass.[29]

The economic impact of the war had at first been catastrophic, especially for Jaffa's citrus industry. With exports to Europe no longer possible, thousands of tons of oranges had to be dumped. 'The stench of rotting fruit hung over the

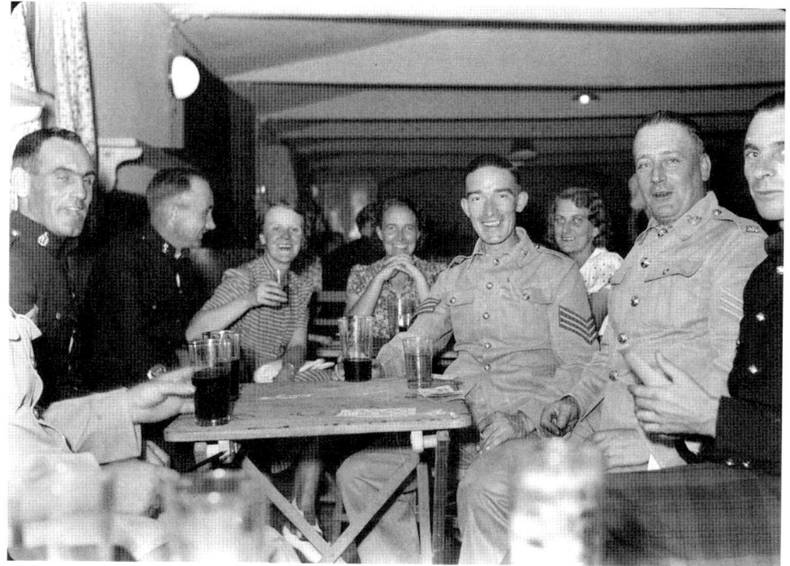

Officers' club, Jerusalem, 1940 Matson Photo Service

city.'[30] There was a sharp increase in unemployment among both Arabs and Jews. But as the war expanded into the eastern Mediterranean and tens of thousands of British and Allied troops poured into Palestine, the situation changed dramatically. The British army, with its huge appetite for goods and services of every kind, and its need to recruit large numbers of Arab and Jewish workers, became the motor of Palestine's economy. The army employed 42,000 civilians, two-thirds of whom were Arabs. Agricultural and industrial production increased. Jewish businesses were especially well placed to win contracts to build the roads, bridges, hospitals, and army installations needed by the British military.[31]

Arab women benefitted from the new demand for labour. By the 1940s rural women, who had traditionally worked in agriculture, 'had begun to enter the industrial workforce, albeit to

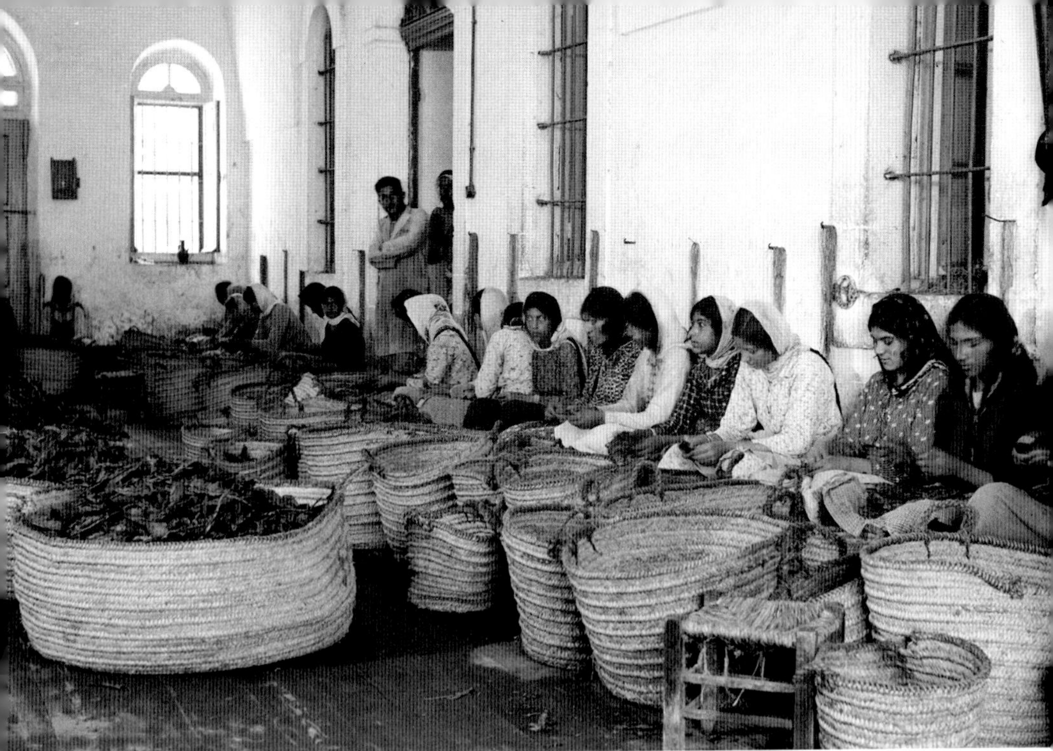

Nazareth, 1940: Arab women working in a tobacco factory

a modest degree'. Educated women who had previously worked as teachers or in government offices now found new opportunities opening up, especially in Haifa with its oil refinery, harbour, banks, and industry. 'Women worked in all these sectors … six thousand Arab women were employed in the Haifa area alone in 1946.' There were efforts to establish an Arab women's trade union.[32]

An administration which had on the whole favoured non-intervention now interfered in virtually every aspect of the life of the country—from the rationing of food and fuel to censorship of the press and the banning of strikes. Even the ownership and use of vehicles was strictly controlled. Despite all this, fuel shortages and the rise in food prices caused hardship among

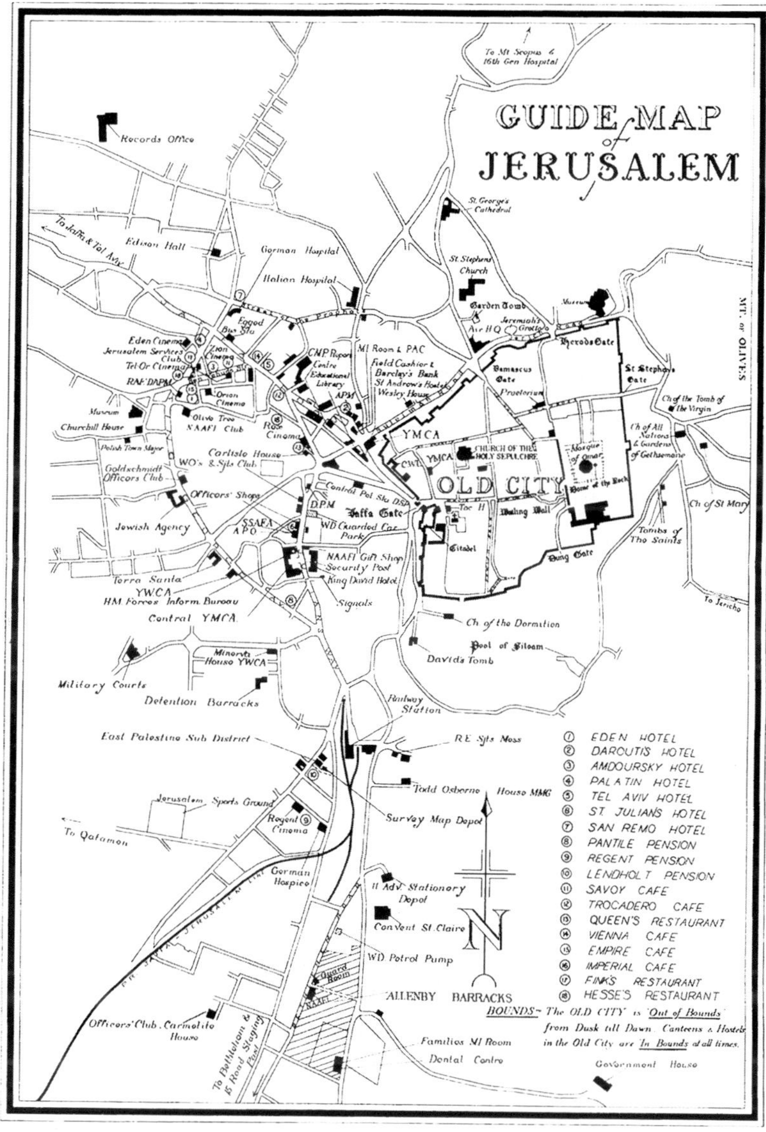

Map showing hotels, restaurants and areas out of bounds, 1946

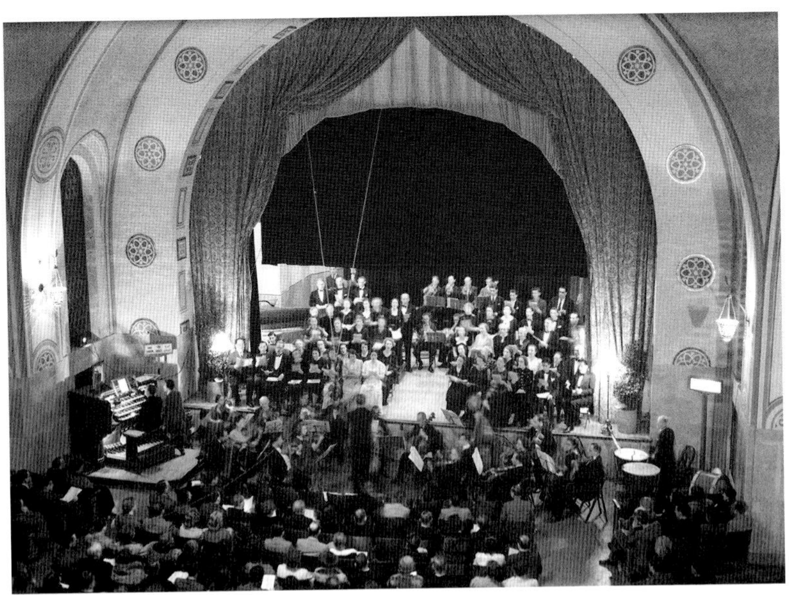

Choral concert at the YMCA, 1938   Matson Photo Service

poorer Arab and Jewish families. There was a thriving black market. When the social worker Sylva Gelber went with friends to dine at Max Hesse's fashionable restaurant, she discovered that the tender roast beef was in fact camel meat.[33]

Cultural life

Despite war-time hardships, there was no let-up in Jerusalem's cultural life. In 1944 Jabra Ibrahim Jabra returned from Cambridge to play an active role in the city's lively literary and artistic scene. He organised talks at the YMCA by leading Arab figures including Khalil Sakakini and Musa Alami and distinguished visitors from Cairo such as the blind writer Taha Hussein. His friend Afif Boulos ran the Orpheus Choir, which performed in the YMCA's well-appointed 600-seat auditorium.

Jewish artists and musicians still tended to dominate cultural life. Nevertheless the work of young Arab artists such as Sophie Halaby began to be noticed: she produced a series of landscape paintings of Jerusalem and its surrounding hills, censoring out the foreign buildings she considered out of place. Jack Robertson, together with the novelist Olivia Manning and her husband Reggie Smith (who worked as a producer for the Palestine Broadcasting Service), edited a war-time magazine, the *Jerusalem Forum*, to which Jabra contributed.[34]

Among the newcomers to the city was Albert Hourani, a frequent visitor from Cairo, where he worked for British officials as an adviser on Arab affairs. (His Jewish opposite number was the young Aubrey Eban, later better known as Israel's foreign minister Abba Eban.) Not yet thirty, Hourani came from a Lebanese family which had settled in Manchester. When he was in Jerusalem he joined a group of men and women—secular, liberal, mostly Oxbridge graduates—who would meet regularly at the bar of the King David Hotel. They included Walid Khalidi, son of Ahmad Samih al-Khalidi; Jabra Ibrahim Jabra and Afif Boulos; Luli Abul Huda, a Transjordanian working in war-time propaganda; and their British friends, several of whom belonged to the Mandate administration. The only Jewish member of the group was the non-Zionist Wolfgang Hildesheimer. Khalidi and Hourani would go on to become distinguished historians; Jabra, a writer, artist, and translator; Hildesheimer, an authority on Mozart. The Arabs in the group were, self-consciously, an élite within an élite, cut off from the wider Arab society, critical of British policy on Palestine, yet imbued with a deep love of English culture and literature. (Khalidi remembered one evening at Luli Abul Huda's flat 'where we all sat around on the floor listening to Albert read T. S. Eliot's *Waste Land* by candlelight'.)[35]

Hourani himself, with the detachment of hindsight, recalled the Jerusalem of the 1940s as 'a small town with small-town intellectuals, with small-town politics'. For him and his group of friends, in those war-time 'years of fragile tranquillity', 'Jerusalem was a dream. It was too good to go on.'[36]

The forgotten Jews

The journalist Barbara Board had spent the early part of the war in Hadera, near the coast, but in the summer of 1943 she decided to move to Jerusalem. On the way she stopped off in Tel Aviv and was struck by the contrast between appearance and reality.

> The skyline of Tel Aviv looks like a miniature Manhattan… but Tel Aviv is not prosperous. Its economy is as brittle as its tenements… The price of land in the city has rocketed to more than three hundred per cent of its pre-war value. The main streets are lined with chromium-plated shops, expensively dressed windows, modern stores and cinemas. Behind, in the narrow ways leading down to the seafront … there are cheap houses, cracked and crumbling; and slum blocks where garbage is thrown in the gutters and the people live in a physical misery made bearable only by the perpetual brightness and warmth of the sun.[37]

When she reached Jerusalem, she found a city shrouded in darkness under a war-time black-out. Food was expensive, taxis cheap, the cafés full. Board had come to know Palestine well. She was not unsympathetic to Zionism, but was moved by the stories she heard from non-Zionist Jewish friends whose apartments were full of the furniture, paintings, and musical instruments they had brought with them from Vienna—to which they dreamed of returning. They were in Palestine because they were stuck there. They lived in fear of the strong-arm fund-raising tactics of the extremists. Board saw them as the unseen, unheard victims of a problem she had come to regard as hopelessly intractable.[38]

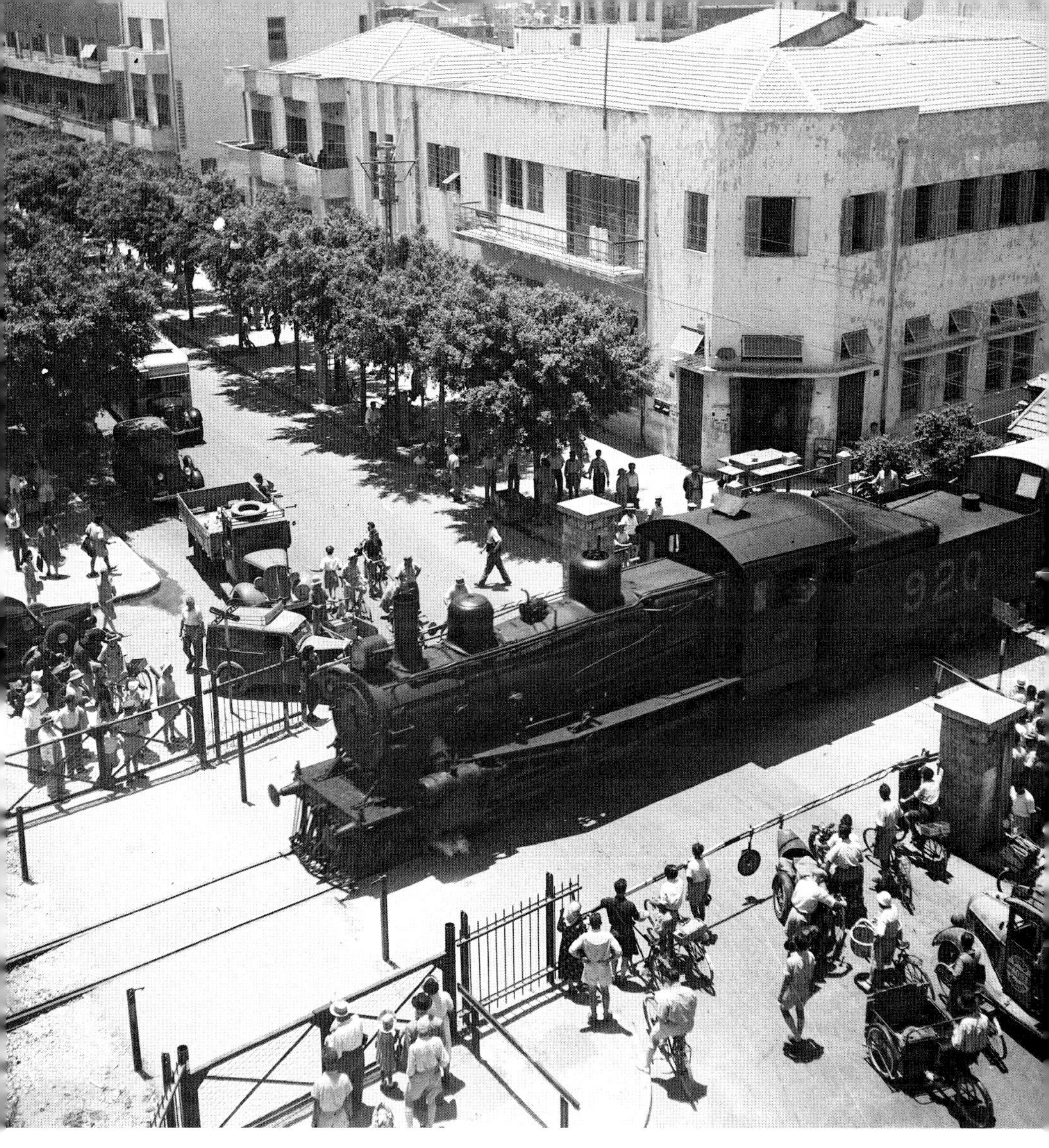

Tel Aviv, 1946   Zoltan Kluger

A new partition plan?

But Churchill had not forgotten the problem of Palestine. In April 1943, in conditions of secrecy, he set up a cabinet committee tasked with coming up with a new policy. Eight months later it produced a report which ditched the White Paper—hitherto the cornerstone of British policy in the Middle East—and came out in favour of partition. The proposal was not made public, for fear of upsetting the Arabs, but Weizmann got wind of it and was jubilant: with Churchill's backing, Jewish statehood appeared to be back on the agenda.[39]

In October 1944 the committee produced a revised report, together with a partition plan. Churchill and senior figures including MacMichael (who had hitherto opposed partition) backed the proposal; the Foreign Office disliked it but was overruled. However, it was decided that nothing would be published until the war was over. Had such a plan been imposed by Britain and the United States after they emerged victorious from the war, might it have worked? Would the Arabs have accepted partition, however reluctantly? Would the Zionists have accepted the boundaries of the state which the plan allotted to them? In the event, a combination of circumstances—a determined rearguard action by the Foreign Office, the shift of power within the Zionist movement from Weizmann to Ben-Gurion, and a dramatic unforeseen event in the Middle East—put paid to such hopes.

Rise of the extremists

In February 1944 Menachem Begin, leader of the Irgun, declared war on Britain. The Irgun had emerged during the Arab rebellion of the 1930s when, to show its opposition to Ben-Gurion's policy of restraint, its members had set off bombs in crowded Arab streets and markets. The militants were followers of Vladimir Jabotinsky, who had established his Revisionist

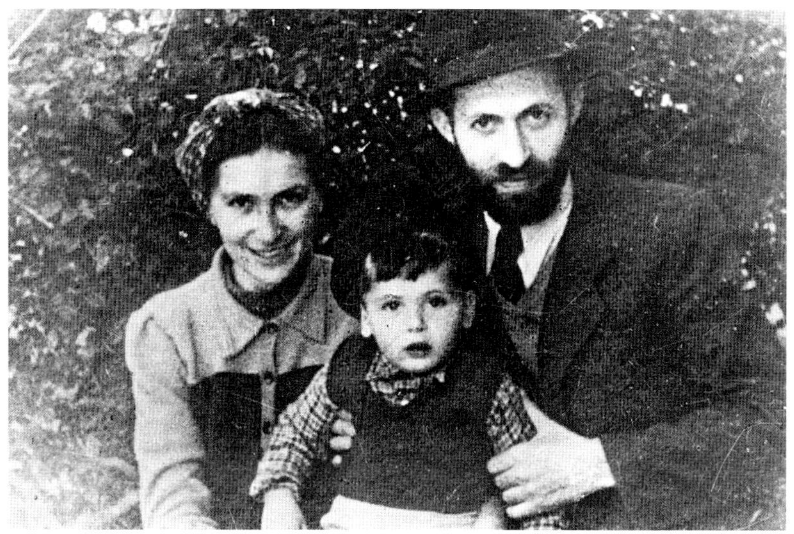

Menachem Begin, disguised as a rabbi, 1946   Photographer unknown

movement as a radical alternative to mainstream Zionism. Their goal was a Jewish state which embraced Transjordan as well as Palestine, and they believed that violence was the only way to get it.

In 1940 a charismatic young Polish poet, Abraham Stern, broke away from the Irgun. His group—which the British dubbed the Stern Gang—modelled itself on the Irish Republican Army. Bizarrely, Stern favoured striking a deal with the Germans and the Italians, on the grounds that they had a common interest in getting the Jews out of Europe. In British eyes, this made him guilty of collaboration as well as terrorism. In 1942 he was tracked down to an apartment in Tel Aviv, where he was hiding in a cupboard. When he made a dash for the window, a British policeman shot him dead. His cadre of dedicated followers survived, and now had a martyr.[40]

The Irgun was much the larger of the two groups. Now,

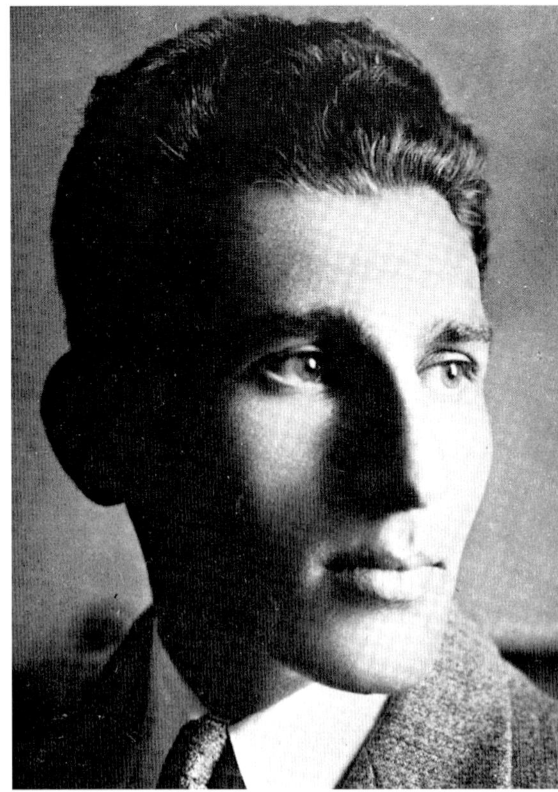

Abraham Stern,
1942
Photographer
unknown

under Begin, it ended the three-year truce it had declared in 1941 and launched a new campaign of violence to drive Britain out of Palestine. Begin loathed the Germans and the British in almost equal measure. Both his parents had died at the hands of the Nazis. Now, as Britain barred the gates to Palestine, it became in his conspiratorial mind an accomplice of the Germans in perpetuating Jewish suffering. The Irgun decided that, as long as the war continued, it would not attack military targets and instead struck at government buildings and police stations. In March 1944 it targeted three police stations simultaneously, killing six policemen. This led to a sharp escalation of tension. The extremists presented a challenge both to the Zionist leaders, who were reluctant to inform on fellow Jews, and to British officials, who found it frustratingly hard to get good intelligence on them. Repeated searches in Tel Aviv and in the Jewish settlements came up with little, and Begin himself always managed to evade capture.

The Stern Gang's speciality was assassination. In October 1944, as MacMichael was preparing to leave Jerusalem at the end of his term, its members tried unsuccessfully to gun him down. Then in November they struck again, this time in Cairo, where two of their members shot dead Lord Moyne, the Minister Resident in the Middle East—and a personal friend of Churchill's. The extremists had at a stroke alienated one of Zionism's most loyal and most powerful supporters.

> If our dreams of Zionism [the prime minister declared in the House of Commons] are to end in the smoke of assassins' pistols and our labours for its future to produce only a new set of gangsters worthy of Nazi Germany, many like myself will have to reconsider the position we have maintained so consistently and so long in the past.[41]

The Zionists were stung. Henceforth Churchill lost his ardour for Zionism and came to regard the question of Palestine with weary disillusion. Control of policy reverted to the Foreign Office, and the partition plan, which it had always opposed, was shelved.[42]

The two assassins were put on trial in Cairo and hanged. Ben-Gurion and his colleagues, despite their reluctance to trigger a civil war within the Yishuv, felt obliged to act decisively against the extremists. Declaring that 'the terrorists constitute a greater danger to us than they do to the authorities and the police', Ben-Gurion launched what became known as the *saison* (hunting season). The Haganah used harsh methods, including

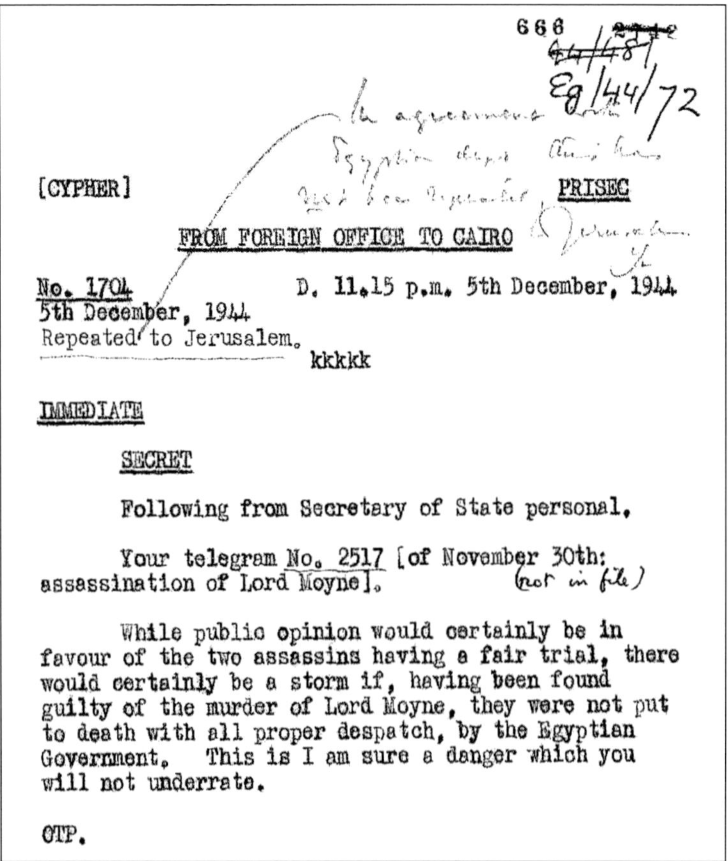

Foreign Office telegram, December 1944   Wikimedia Commons

torture, against the Irgun. The police rounded up more than 200 Irgun members, and in addition found arms, forged identity cards, and a printing-press.[43]

MacMichael had by now been succeeded as high commissioner by a distinguished war-time general, Lord Gort. He was welcomed as a breath of fresh air after the aloof MacMichael, whom the Zionists had vilified for his hard line on immigration. On his arrival, Gort asked officials in London what policy he

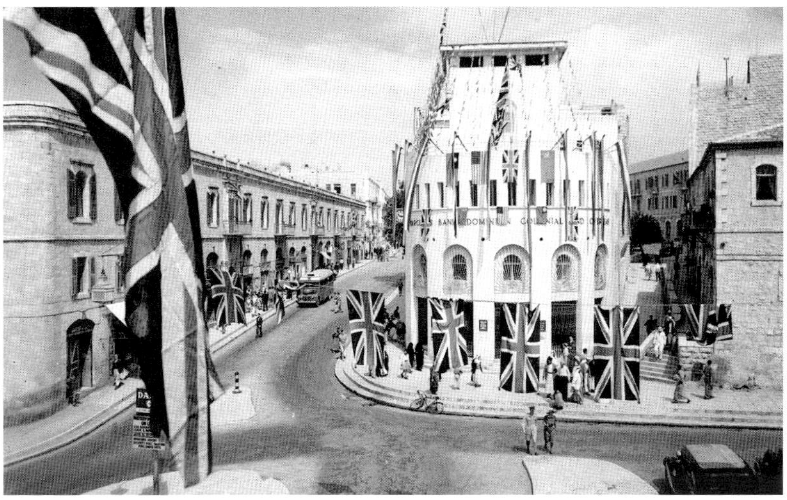

Barclays Bank, Jerusalem, May 1945   Matson Photo Service

should pursue. The answer, when it came, was that the war had left an abundance of problems in its wake and that a new policy on Palestine would have to wait.[44]

In May 1945 the Jerusalem branch of Barclays Bank— designed in the 1930s by Clifford Holliday—was swathed in Union Jacks to mark VE (Victory in Europe) Day. The city resounded to church bells. 'The notes of the National Anthem,' wrote Sylva Gelber, 'played by the Palestine Police Force Band echoed across the great expanse which separated the Judaean hills from the hills of Moab clearly visible on the other side of the Jordan.'[45]

But while one war was over, another was just beginning: a war between Britain and the Yishuv that was to determine the fate of Palestine.

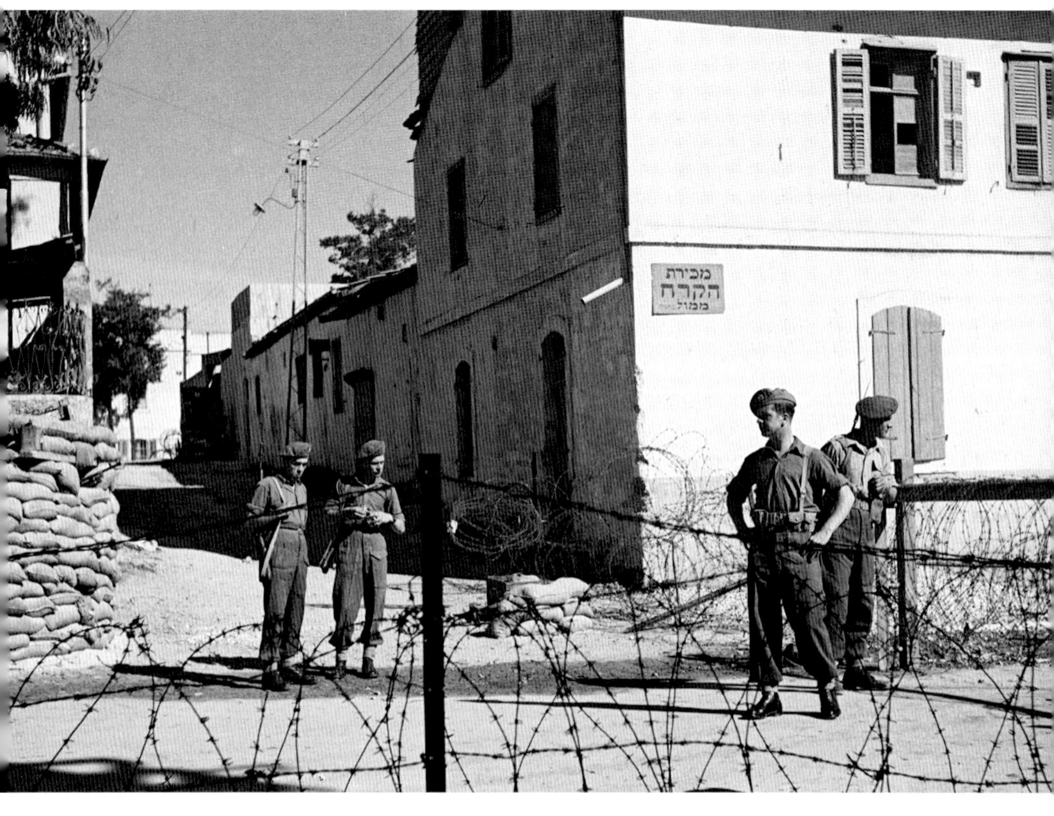

Lockdown in Tel Aviv, March 1947   Zoltan Kluger

5

Things fall apart, 1945–1948

'The outer stone walls bulged, swayed, convulsed inward and, with a thunderous roar, vanished into sheets of flame and clouds of smoke.'

Thurston Clarke, By Blood and Fire: The Attack on the King David Hotel *(1981)*

AS BRITISH RULE entered its final phase, the conflict in Palestine had become more complex and more violent. In Britain, the problem fell into the lap of the new Labour government under Clement Attlee which came to power following Churchill's resounding defeat in the post-war election of July 1945. The architect of Britain's policy on Palestine, in the crucial years from 1945 to 1948, was Attlee's unexpected choice as foreign secretary, Ernest Bevin. Bevin was a large, gruff, working-class trade unionist who had grown up in rural poverty, received little formal education, and made his name as the forceful leader of the Transport and General Workers' Union. When Churchill had become prime minister in 1940 he had made Bevin minister of labour, with sweeping powers to organise the workforce to meet the needs of a war-time economy. It was a shrewd choice. For all their obvious differences, both

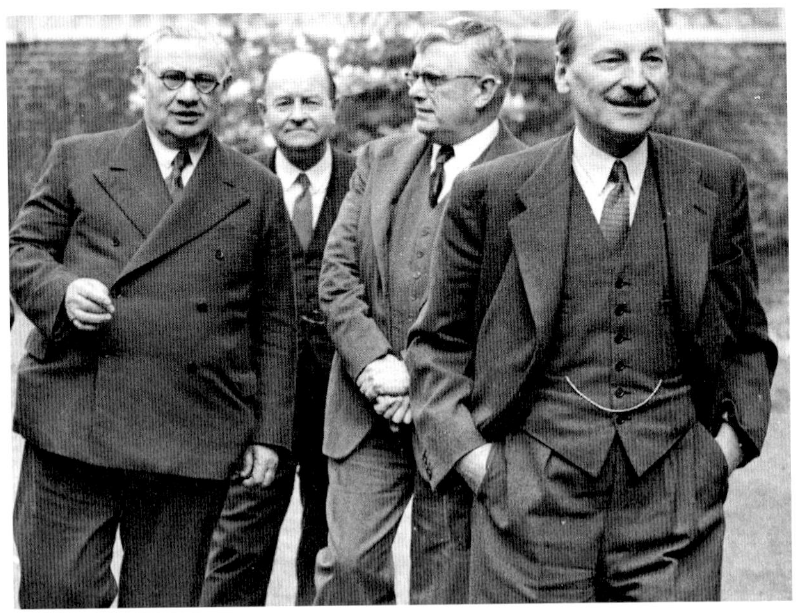

Ernest Bevin, left, with Clement Attlee, right, 1946   Photographer unknown

were old-fashioned patriots. Both were suspicious of communism and the Soviet Union. Both smoked, ate, and drank too much. These two British bulldogs formed an unlikely but effective partnership.[1]

After the war, Bevin—aged sixty-four and in poor health—had intended to retire. Instead he found himself dealing with the Foreign Office mandarins (in his eyes, effete aristocrats) and with the myriad problems of the post-war world. Palestine was a distraction. As he began to grapple with it—unburdened, by all accounts, by any fixed opinion—he discovered it was no longer the old triangular dispute between Britain, the Arabs, and the Jews. The stage had become more crowded.

The first and most important new actor was the United States. After the sudden death of Roosevelt in April 1945, his vice-president, Harry Truman, had found himself parachuted into the White House—which meant that, in electoral terms, he had yet to prove himself. With regard to Palestine, Truman confronted a fundamental contradiction (which in one guise or another has haunted all of his successors): while his officials, in both the State Department and the Pentagon, were increasingly conscious of Washington's stake in Middle East oil and Middle East bases, public opinion was increasingly supportive of Zionism.

The second new actor was the Arab League, created under British patronage during the war. While Britain hoped to build up a bloc of states well disposed towards its interests, the priority of the Arab rulers was to bring an end to colonial rule in the Middle East, including British rule in Palestine. The third was the fledgling United Nations, which as the successor to the League of Nations took over responsibility for global peace and security—and for supervision of the mandated territories. And finally there was the Soviet Union, emerging as a superpower and beginning to look for opportunities in a region where the Western imperialists had established such a strong bridgehead.

'Information work'

Edward Hodgkin's office in Jaffa looked out on 'five or six well-stocked cemeteries'.

> Much the largest was the Muslim one, which stretched for three or four hundred yards and occupied all the land shelving down from the road to the sea. It was a tangled mass of horizontal slabs and weeds ... On feast days this neglected site was transformed; family parties invaded it, putting up palm branches by the resting place of the departed, and picnicking for most of the day, chattering and eating their cheese sandwiches and drinking their soft drinks.[2]

This was July 1945. During the war Hodgkin had helped

produce propaganda—'information work', he called it—for SOE in Egypt and Iraq. Now, almost a decade after his brother Thomas had been expelled by the Mandate authorities, he was returning to Palestine to run Sharq al-Adna, the SOE radio station Jack Robertson had created four years earlier. He gladly accepted the posting, partly from affection for Palestine and partly from the conviction that Sharq al-Adna had an important post-war role to play as 'much the most powerful broadcasting station in the Middle East'. Based originally in Jenin, it had now moved to Jaffa, which he found a congenial base.

It was good to live a few yards from the Mediterranean, to go in the winter for long walks on the deserted beach which stretched all the way to Egypt, and in summer to swim or take out to sea small canvas-covered boats which were sometimes pursued by porpoises.

The beach at Jaffa (date uncertain)   American Colony

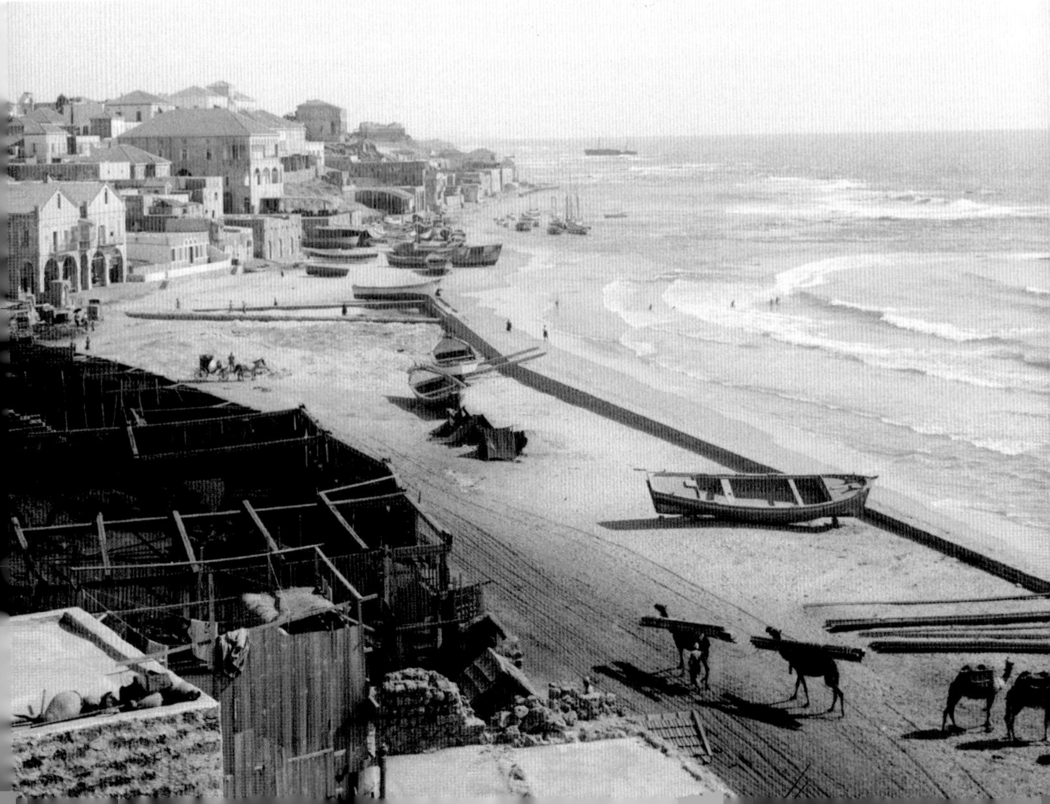

The war might have come to an end, but much of Britain's war-time military infrastructure remained in place. Sharq al-Adna was officially a military unit, directed from SOE's Middle East headquarters in Cairo; and Colonel Hodgkin, although he did not wear military uniform, was its General Staff Officer (GSO). The fiction was maintained that it was an independent radio station, but in Palestine and probably elsewhere everyone knew it was run by the British. After SOE was closed down, it was handed over to the intelligence service MI6.

In an unpublished memoir, Hodgkin describes his experiences with affection and humour—and only the occasional hint of his concern that the station might be attacked by Zionist extremists. He was constantly surprised at the dedication of his Arab colleagues to an organisation run by a resented foreign power. But nationalism was sometimes tempered by opportunism: 'I am certainly a patriot, Colonel Hodgkin,' remarked one of his staff who had sold land to the Zionists, 'but not a blind patriot.'

Much of the station's appeal lay in its music, feature programmes, and readings from the Quran. To these Hodgkin added a women's programme—overcoming the objections of some of his Arab colleagues—which proved popular. But, given Palestine's political and security situation, its news bulletins, covering regional and local developments, were both important and sensitive.

'Many in Whitehall,' Hodgkin recalled, 'would have liked Sharq to be more overtly propagandist—to angle and suppress the news. But we resisted all pressure of this sort, and, indeed, were left almost entirely on our own, to do and say what we liked.' There were four fifteen-minute news bulletins a day, in addition to a five-minute commentary, written by Hodgkin or a British colleague, which he conceded 'naturally expressed a mildly propagandist point of view'.

Every week there was a live broadcast of Friday prayers at the al-Aqsa Mosque in Jerusalem, including the sermon that traditionally followed. This was politically sensitive: the broadcast 'was very closely monitored, some responsible person listening with his finger on the control knob ready to switch it off if the rhetoric against Zionism or the British government became too violent'.[3]

'Disperse or we fire'

Despite the bitterness engendered by the *saison*—the crackdown on the Irgun the previous year—in October 1945 the Zionist militias secretly entered into a marriage of convenience. The Haganah, the Irgun, and the Stern Gang decided that their operations would be planned jointly and carried out in the name of the Jewish Resistance Movement. Although there was lingering mistrust and co-ordination was less than complete, the alliance lasted for ten months.

In November Barbara Board's bosses in Fleet Street sent her back to Palestine ahead of a much-anticipated statement by Bevin in the House of Commons. The Arabs feared that, under pressure from the Zionists in Palestine and the United States, the Attlee government would abandon the White Paper policy which Britain had maintained since 1939. The Zionists' priority was the fate of tens of thousands of European Jews who had survived the Holocaust and were now in displaced-persons camps in Germany and Austria. They pressed for them to come to Palestine but feared that, under the influence of his Foreign Office advisers, Bevin would stick to the White Paper policy, abandoning the commitment to a Jewish state which Labour had proclaimed so loudly and so often when in opposition.

The Zionists were closer to the mark. Bevin began by acknowledging the magnitude of the plight of Europe's Jews, but argued that Palestine could not provide a home for all of

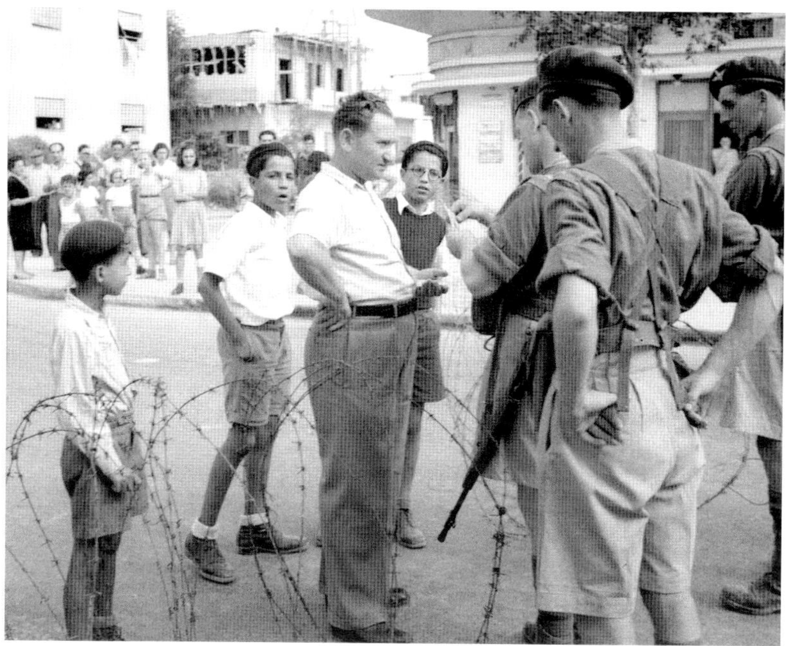

Tel Aviv, November 1945   Sgt F. Meek, army photographer

them. The two issues—Palestine and the refugees—would be considered by an Anglo-American Committee of Inquiry. This decision—a response to pressure from President Truman to allow 100,000 Jews into Palestine—was an attempt to persuade the Americans to take responsibility for solving the issue, rather than merely carping from the wings. The committee was to report in 120 days.[4]

The statement provoked a shocked reaction in the Yishuv, and Zionist indignation increased when, in talking to journalists about the displaced persons, Bevin warned the Jews not to try to 'get to the head of the queue'. Attlee had already said something similar, but coming in the wake of the Commons statement the remark caused offence.

The next day Tel Aviv erupted. A crowd of 30,000 gathered to hear speeches denouncing British policy, after which a smaller throng—made up of young people and, according to Barbara Board, supporters of the Irgun and the Stern Gang—started attacking government buildings. The journalist watched a crowd advancing on the red-bereted troops of the 6th Airborne Division, who had only recently been fighting in Europe. (The Yishuv nicknamed them 'poppies' because of their red heads and supposedly black hearts.)

In an unpublished memoir, the journalist described the scene.

> A banner with the inscription 'Disperse or we fire', printed in the three official languages of Palestine—Hebrew, Arabic, and English—was hoisted in front of the barricade as the troops pointed their Stens. The mob leaders and the younger terrorist members [of the Irgun and the Stern Gang] jeered at the warning and led the crowd on towards the barrier. A moment later, as the mob, armed only with stones, charged the barrier, the order to fire was given. Two rounds, aimed at the legs of the rioters, were discharged by one of the soldiers. There were screams, and a temporary surging backwards: then, with renewed fury, the mob came on again. The major in charge ordered two more rounds. This time one of the ring-leaders fell mortally wounded. The crowd swayed and halted, then slowly, amid the debris and smashed glass in front of the blazing building, retreated down the street.

Although she was aware that the soldiers were not trained for crowd control, Board found herself secretly admiring the 'stupid courage' of the rioters.

When she returned the following day, she found that the trouble was not over.

> Shortly after dawn a 50-year-old Jewish milkman, who mistakenly believed the curfew had lifted, started off on his bicycle to go his normal round in the Hatikvah quarter. He was shot dead, while

riding, by one of the Airborne soldiers. The incident provoked mass demonstrations.

In two days of riots, six Jews were killed and dozens injured, including children. People had been warned not to go out onto their balconies during the night-time curfew, but some had done so and been shot. Dozens of soldiers were also wounded.[5]

The Anglo-American Committee

The twelve members of the Anglo-American Committee of Inquiry began work in early 1946. They started in the United States, moved on to Europe, where some of them visited the displaced-persons camps, and then travelled to Cairo. They were due to reach Palestine in March.[6]

As they awaited the arrival of yet another fact-finding committee, the Arabs of Palestine were weak, divided, and dispirited. The pre-war Arab rebellion, although it had given public expression to their grievances and forced the imperial power to change its policy, had left Arab society drained. The economic cost of the uprising had been high, the political cost even higher. Their leaders were either dead, in prison, or in exile. From his successive places of exile—Beirut, Baghdad, Tehran, Berlin, Paris, and eventually Cairo—Hajj Amin al-Husseini retained his grip on Palestinian politics. However much his political rivals might want to take his place, they did not dare to. The result was political deadlock.

The British were adamant that Hajj Amin should not be permitted to return to Palestine. But in February 1946 they allowed his cousin Jamal to do so. Arriving overland from Lebanon, he was greeted by large crowds as a conquering hero and made a triumphal procession from the coast to Jerusalem. It was the clearest possible sign that, like it or not, the Husseinis were still a force to be reckoned with. As soon as he was installed in Jerusalem, Jamal al-Husseini took charge of a reconstituted

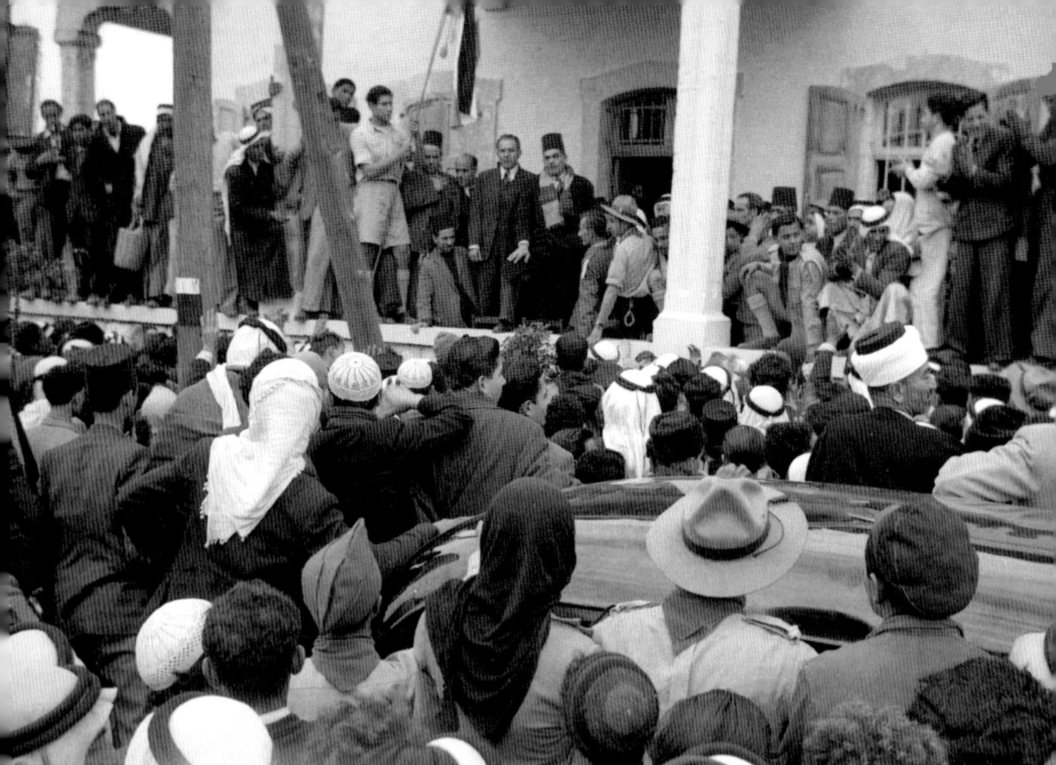

Jamal al-Husseini (with scarf) on his return to Palestine, 1946

Arab Higher Committee, which debated how to respond to the visiting commission.[7]

At this point Musa Alami returned to the political fray. He was determined that, with the Palestine problem at a critical juncture, the Arabs should not make the mistake they had made in 1936, when they had initially boycotted the hearings of the Peel commission. This time they should be better prepared and should present their case more effectively. To this end he recruited a team of young Arabs—including Albert Hourani and Walid Khalidi—to help him write a set of presentations and research papers. Independently, Tawfiq Canaan prepared a report on Arab health.

Alami's great asset—that he did not belong to any of the Arab political parties—was also his great liability. The other factions resented him and intrigued against him, and for his part, while his integrity was beyond doubt, he had an innate distaste for the wheeler-dealing of politics and did not always respond well to criticism. He has been described as an Arab Hamlet.[8]

In the event, of the four Arabs who spoke before the committee, it was Hourani who made the greatest impact. As the voice of reason, presenting the Arab case with skill and sensitivity, he seemed the natural successor to George Antonius.

The six Americans and six Britons on the committee found it hard to reach agreement. But in the end they rejected partition and made a number of interlocking recommendations including the immediate admission of the 100,000 Jews into Palestine. Truman seized on this last point, ignoring the rest. Attlee and Bevin insisted that the 100,000 could be admitted only if illegal armies in Palestine (meaning the Haganah) were disarmed. The committee's report satisfied no one: it failed to offer the Zionists a Jewish state or the Arabs an Arab state, or to secure for Bevin the American co-operation he so badly needed. Far from easing transatlantic tensions, the committee's work exacerbated them.

The price of loyalty

Atallah Mantoura prided himself on his appearance. 'He was very elegant,' recalled his daughter Doris, 'always well-dressed, his shoes well-polished, and always had a hat on.' He carried a beautifully-made fly-whisk of long white horsehair with a carved ivory handle. Mantoura was the second most senior Arab official in the Mandate administration. Born in Jaffa to a family with roots in Lebanon, he was a Christian Arab who in the First World War had avoided Ottoman conscription by escaping to Egypt, where he worked for British army censors decoding secret telegrams.

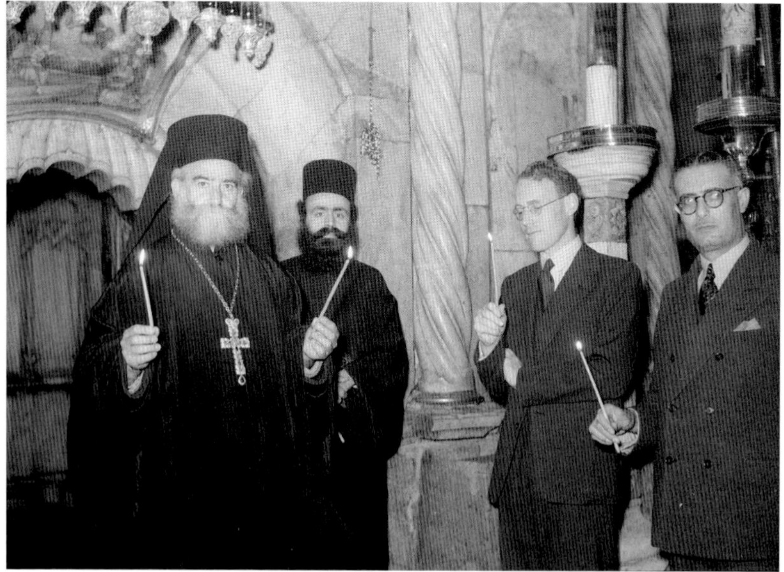

Atallah Mantoura, right, Easter 1941   Matson Photo Service

On his return to Palestine he married an Italian Catholic whose family had settled in Jaffa in Ottoman times. He began his career as a Mandate official in Jaffa but was soon transferred to Jerusalem, where he became assistant chief secretary responsible for finance and for the sensitive issue of relations between the government and the different religious communities. Among the Mantouras' friends and neighbours in Musrara, just outside the Old City walls, were the Canaans. As a reward for loyal service to Britain, Mantoura was given British citizenship and an MBE. In the eyes of some of his compatriots this made him a traitor. After his life was threatened, he went to work every morning at his office in the King David Hotel accompanied by two armed guards. Now in his mid-fifties, tired and disillusioned, he was planning to retire and settle in the south of France.[9]

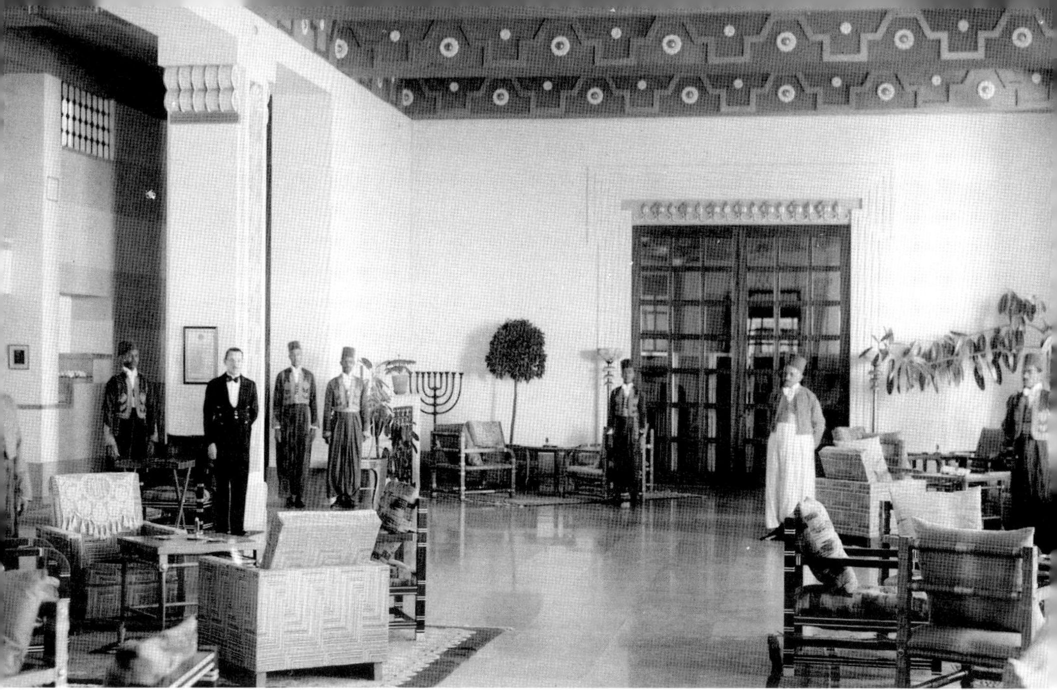

Lobby of the King David Hotel, 1930s

The target

No longer simply the epitome of elegance, the King David Hotel had become a symbol of power. The massive six-storey structure—made from local stone and reinforced to withstand earthquakes—had been built in eighteen months by a Swiss architect, Emile Vogt, and completed in December 1930. It was a piece of Hollywood Orientalism, a blend of modern luxury and biblical fantasy. The grand lobby, with its white marble floors, whitewashed pilasters, and Etruscan-style armchairs, was like an 'enormous jewellery box'.[10]

Originally conceived as a neutral space, a meeting-ground for the cosmopolitan well-to-do, the hotel found its neutrality compromised when, during the Arab rebellion of the 1930s, the army requisitioned the fourth floor and the civil administration took over the south wing. The arrangement was supposed to be temporary but continued during the war and beyond. The Swiss manager, the unflappable Max Hamburger, discovered that his world-famous hotel had become the civilian and military headquarters of the British administration. Together with Government House, the home of the high commissioner and his staff, it was the most prominent symbol of the British presence in Palestine. This made it a tempting target.[11]

Lord Gort had been obliged to resign for health reasons after only a year as high commissioner. He was succeeded by General Sir Alan Cunningham, who arrived in November 1945. Like his fellow-Scot Arthur Wauchope, Cunningham was a bachelor and a seasoned military man whose term in office was bedevilled by the challenges of putting down an insurgency. (The friendship between the two Scotsmen was cut short only by Wauchope's death in 1947.) Cunningham's difficulties were compounded by disagreement with Bevin over the political objective (partition, which Cunningham favoured, or a bi-national state, the Foreign Office's preferred solution) and with the Chief of the Imperial General Staff, General Bernard Montgomery, over the response to Zionist violence. Cunningham understood, as Monty did not, that there had to be a political solution: force by itself would be counterproductive. Monty was to harass the high commissioner mercilessly throughout his term in office.[12]

The British suspected that, despite its denials, the Jewish Agency—the main official Zionist institution—was hand in glove with the extremists. These suspicions were confirmed when they broke the code used by the agency in communications between Jerusalem and London. Some officials favoured dismantling it, but Cunningham needed an interlocutor: his goal was to try to shock the Zionist leadership into abandoning violence.[13]

A series of attacks carried out in the name of the Jewish Resistance Movement reached its climax when, on the night

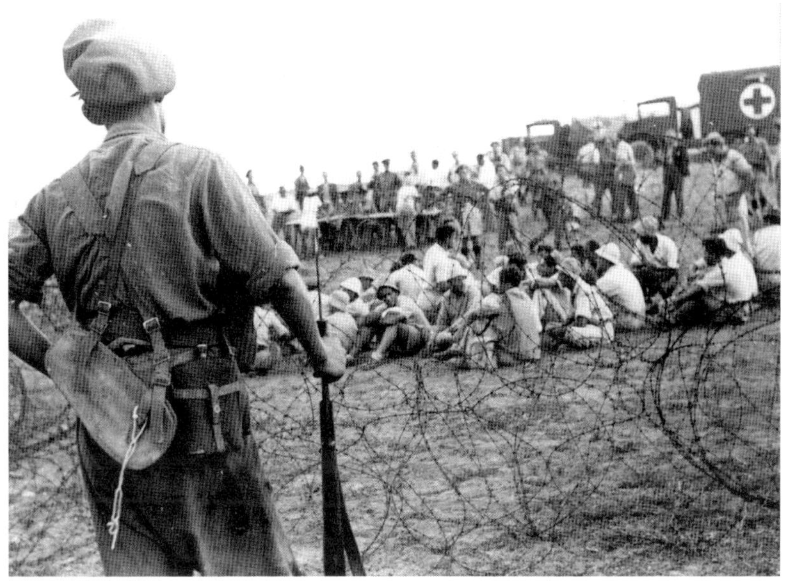

Operation Agatha: rounding up suspects, 1946   Photographer unknown

of 16-17 June 1946, the Haganah blew up ten road and rail bridges linking Palestine to its neighbours. The attacks were both audacious and skilfully executed. Cunningham, feeling he had no choice but to abandon his habitual restraint, authorised a country-wide crackdown on the Jewish Agency and the Haganah. The operation, unprecedented in scope, began before dawn on Saturday, 29 June. Over the next twelve days the country's cities, towns, and settlements were flooded with 100,000 soldiers and 10,000 police. They arrested some 2,700 Jews, including hundreds designated as VIJs (Very Important Jews), seized a mass of documents from the Jewish Agency, and raided two dozen Jewish settlements, at one of which they found, hidden underground, a large hoard of arms and ammunition.

The operation, codenamed Operation Agatha but which the Yishuv dubbed Black Sabbath, failed to net key figures such as

Ben-Gurion, who was in Paris, or to find compelling evidence of the agency's collaboration with the extremists. Part of the problem was that the British had few Hebrew speakers to translate the seized documents. They brought in Jewish policemen who, according to one of them, flushed anything that looked incriminating down the toilet.[14] The operation nevertheless had the effect of signalling that British patience had snapped. The Yishuv was stunned. Its leaders had to decide whether to run the risk of further escalation or, as Cunningham hoped, resume a political dialogue with the administration.

But most of the leadership regarded dialogue as futile. The Haganah high command approved a series of operations including an attack proposed by the Irgun on an unnamed government building (generally understood to be the King David Hotel). Begin believed he now had a green light. But Weizmann got wind of what was afoot. Old and sick and struggling to assert his moral authority, he summoned a group of Zionist leaders to his home and threatened to resign unless the planned operations were called off. They agreed, with misgivings, and the message was passed to Begin. But the Irgun leader, having already delayed the attack, decided it must now go ahead.

Rendezvous in the garden

On 22 July 1946, without her father's knowledge, the 18-year-old Leila Canaan was about to go on a date and drink her first gin. The location was the Winter Garden of the King David Hotel, and the man she was to meet was a dashing young Jordanian officer, Wasfi Tall, who had not yet been demobilised from the British army.[15]

After the trauma of the war, Tawfiq Canaan had resumed his work as a doctor and had invested heavily in the education of his four children. He considered Leila bright but headstrong. In addition to Arabic, she spoke German, English, French, and

Yiddish. She had grown up with Jewish friends (among them Moshe Dayan's future wife, Ruth) and enjoyed Jerusalem's new amenities, in particular the sports facilities and American-style soda fountain at the YMCA. Politics played little part in her life.

It was a stiflingly hot day. As Wasfi and Leila sat down, he told her he had been asked by Musa Alami to set up an Arab information office in New York. He wanted Leila to join him. She liked the idea but doubted whether her father would permit it.

Suddenly, at 12:37, the hotel was rocked by a massive explosion.

> The outer stone walls [of the secretariat] bulged, swayed, convulsed inward and, with a thunderous roar, vanished into sheets of flame and clouds of smoke. The roof shot into the air and plummeted to earth like an elevator out of control … crushing those on whom it landed.[16]

The street outside the hotel was showered with debris. 'Large concrete blocks flew into the air at speeds of up to a hundred miles an hour … chunks of cement crashed into pedestrians; bodies were blown into the street.'

A group of Irgun members, disguised as Arabs, had smuggled seven milk churns, packed with explosives, into the hotel basement. The explosion destroyed the south-east wing. Leila and Wasfi were lucky to escape with cuts. Among the missing were members of the administration, including two senior Jewish officials, Julius Jacobs and Victor Levi, and several Arab officials, including Atallah Mantoura. In the sweltering heat, Mantoura's son Jacques waited to find out if his father was alive or dead.

Leading the search was the chief secretary, Sir John Shaw, who was in charge of the administration while Cunningham was in London. Shaw had survived the blast but was deeply traumatised by it. Six feet seven inches tall, he was an unmistakable figure

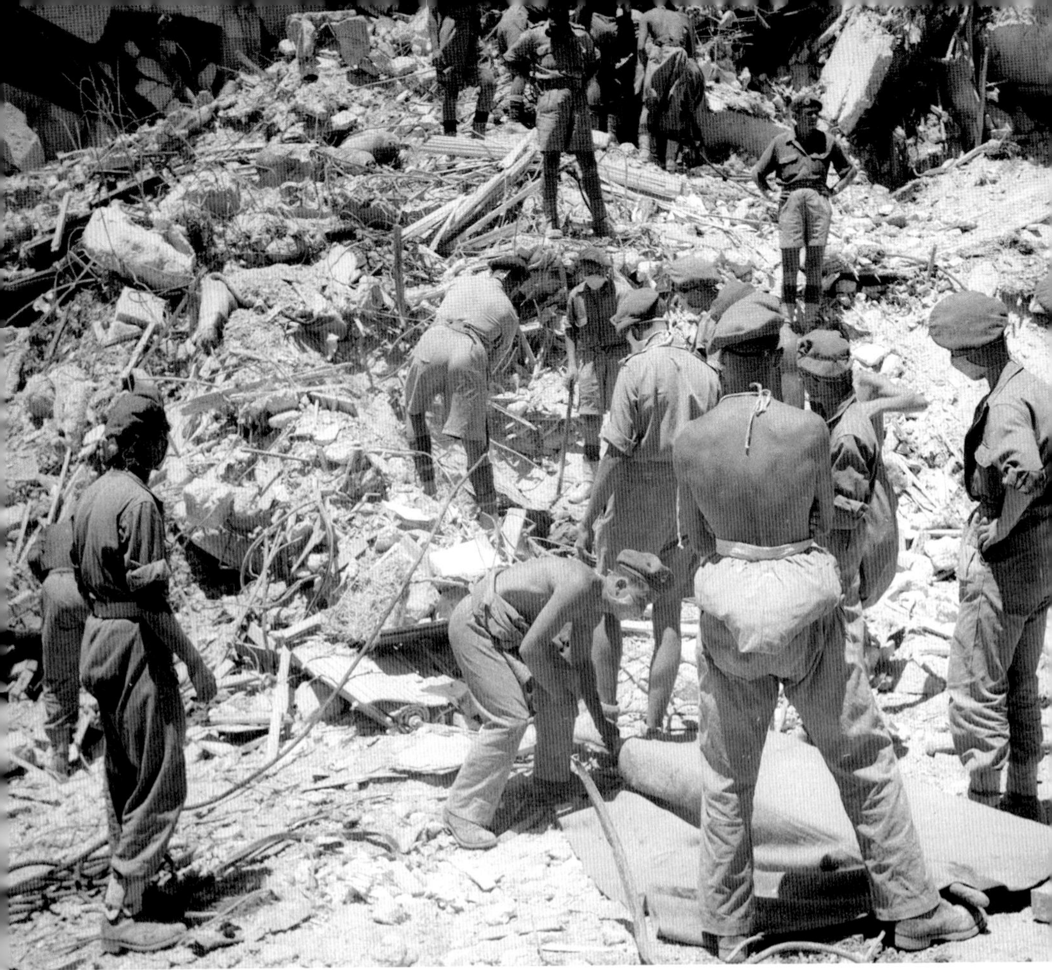

Searching for survivors: King David Hotel, 1946   Matson Photo Service

standing with his wife amid the debris. He dug out some of the survivors with his own hands. On the second day, as Jacques kept watch, a body was found alive. 'Are you a wog?' asked a police officer. 'Yes,' came the reply. 'A wog named Thompson.' Downing Thompson, assistant secretary in the administration, had been buried for thirty-one hours without food or water. He seemed unhurt, but the following day died of shock.[17]

It was not until three days after the bombing that Shaw called

Jacques over to look at the remains of a body. The brown suit, the brown shoes, the small round glasses were distinctive: it was his father. Jacques had previously been something of a playboy; now he wanted to know why his father had died.[18]

In early August the *Palestine Gazette*, the official Mandate newspaper, published a partial list of those who had been killed. More than half were junior employees—typists, messengers, drivers, secretaries, hotel staff. The rest were civil servants, soldiers, policemen, and intelligence officials. The final death toll was ninety-one: forty-one Arabs, twenty-eight Britons, seventeen Jews (including Jacobs and Levi), and five others.

One of those who had witnessed the bombing, sitting in a café nearby, was Assia Gutmann. Shortly afterwards she left Palestine, which held little appeal for her, to study in Britain.

Aftermath

During the recriminations that followed, the Irgun insisted that there had been warnings—phone calls to the hotel, to the French consulate, and to the *Palestine Post*. But the warnings had come too late. Even if the hotel had been evacuated, such was the force of the blast that more people would have died in the street than died in the hotel. The Irgun also insisted that the Haganah had known all along about the planning of the operation and had, at least in principle, authorised it. The Zionist leaders, thrown onto the defensive, vehemently denounced the bombing. But then Palestine's most senior army officer, General Evelyn Barker, scored a spectacular own goal by ordering his troops to boycott all Jewish businesses, with the aim, he declared, of 'punishing the Jews in a way the race dislikes—by striking at their pockets and showing our contempt for them'.

Amid the ensuing uproar there were calls for Barker's dismissal. These were resisted, but some months later he was quietly transferred out of the country. Before boarding the

The Palestine Gazette

Published by Authority

NOTICE.

THE HIGH COMMISSIONER announces with regret the deaths of the following members of the public service who lost their lives in the execution of their duty at the Secretariat on the 22nd July, 1946:—

MR. F. ABLA,
Clerk, Secretariat.

MISS C. ANTIPPA,
Clerk, Secretariat.

MISS H. AZZAM,
Typist, Secretariat.

MR. B. A. ABU LAHLUB,
Driver, District Administration,
Lydda District.

No. 706 F.P.C., M. A. ABDUL RAZEK,
Palestine Police Force.

MR. A. I. BADER,
Messenger, Secretariat.

MR. I. BADER,
Doorkeeper, Secretariat.

MR. L. J. BADER,
Messenger, Secretariat.

MISS L. BACHRACH,
Clerk, Secretariat.

MISS G. BARAMKI,
Secretary Stenographer,
Secretariat.

MR. L. BAUM,
Administrative Assistant,
Secretariat.

MISS M. BAWARSHI,
Typist, Secretariat.

MR. F. W. G. BLENKINSOP,
Assistant Secretary, Secretariat.

MR. B. G. BOURDILLON,
Assistant Secretary, Secretariat.

MR. E. G. BROWN,
Administrative Officer,
Secretariat.

MR. G. T. FARLEY,
Assistant Secretary, Secretariat,
and Commissioner on Special Duty.

MR. I. E. FARRADJ.
Clerk, Secretariat.

MR. B. C. GIBBS,
Assistant Secretary,
Secretariat.

MR. J. C. GRESS,
Assistant Accountant General,
Accountant General's Office.

MR. W. GOLDSCHMIDT,
Assistant Legal Draftsman,
Attorney General's Office.

MR. A. HISAIN,
Messenger, Secretariat.

MR. S. HOFFMANN,
Electrician, Public Works Department.

MR. I. M. ISSIS,
Messenger, Secretariat.

MR. J. JACOBS, O.B.E.,
Under Secretary, Secretariat.

No. 1777 2ND B/SGT. W. N. JENNINGS,
Palestine Police Force.

MR. G. D. KENNEDY,
Postmaster General.

MR. E. W. KEYS,
Assistant Secretary,
Secretariat.

MR. D. KHADDER,
Messenger, Secretariat.

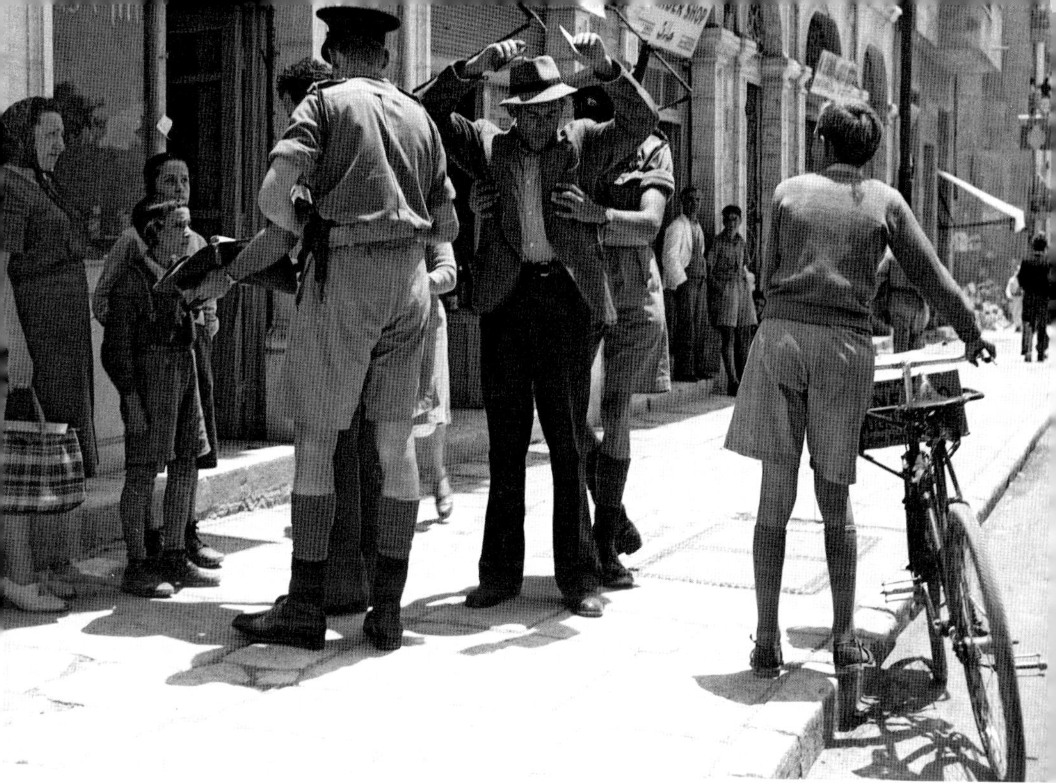

Above: *Police search in Jerusalem, 1947*   Hans Pinn
Left: *Recording the dead, 1946*   Wikimedia Commons

plane, he expressed his feelings for Palestine by urinating on its soil.[19]

Eight days after the bombing—a delay that many thought inexplicable—the army clamped down on Tel Aviv, conducting a four-day house-to-house search. During Operation Shark, 800 arrests were made. But most of those responsible for the attack were never caught.[20] As the violence continued, official buildings in central Jerusalem were encased with barbed wire and some 2,000 personnel deemed 'non-essential'—among them, Barbara Board—were sent home; a tacit admission by the occupying power that it could no longer safeguard the lives of its own citizens.

One of the consequences of the bombing of the hotel was to drive still deeper the wedge of mistrust and hostility between Britain and the Yishuv. For the social worker Sylva Gelber, postwar Palestine was no longer the country she had known since her arrival there in the 1930s. Having lived through the Arab rebellion, she had stayed on during the Second World War and in 1942 joined the department of labour of the Mandate administration, housed in the former German consulate. Lively and gregarious, she was valued not only for her social work but as a translator and conciliator.

She witnessed just how poisonous the atmosphere had become when she visited Tel Aviv shortly after the Irgun had killed three British policemen during an attack in nearby Sarona.

> Suddenly, there arrived in the city a couple of dozen heavily armed British constables. They burst into a number of cafés and other business establishments that they proceeded to wreck. They overturned private cars and motorcycles, beat up civilians with rifle butts, injured others by kicking and beating them, and took potshots at [passers-by]. I could not believe that these young British law-enforcement officers had gone berserk. Eventually, the military police managed to put a stop to the wild rampage.[21]

Gelber was sympathetic to Judah Magnes and the bi-nationalists. But moderate Zionism had been eclipsed. At the Zionist Congress in Basle at the end of 1946, Weizmann stood down, using the occasion to issue a ringing condemnation of terrorism. But by now events on the ground had acquired a dynamic of their own.

On 2 March 1947, following an attack by the Irgun on the British officers' club in Jerusalem which left twenty dead, Cunningham felt obliged to take an action he had hitherto resisted: the imposition of martial law. Operation Elephant involved the lockdown of parts

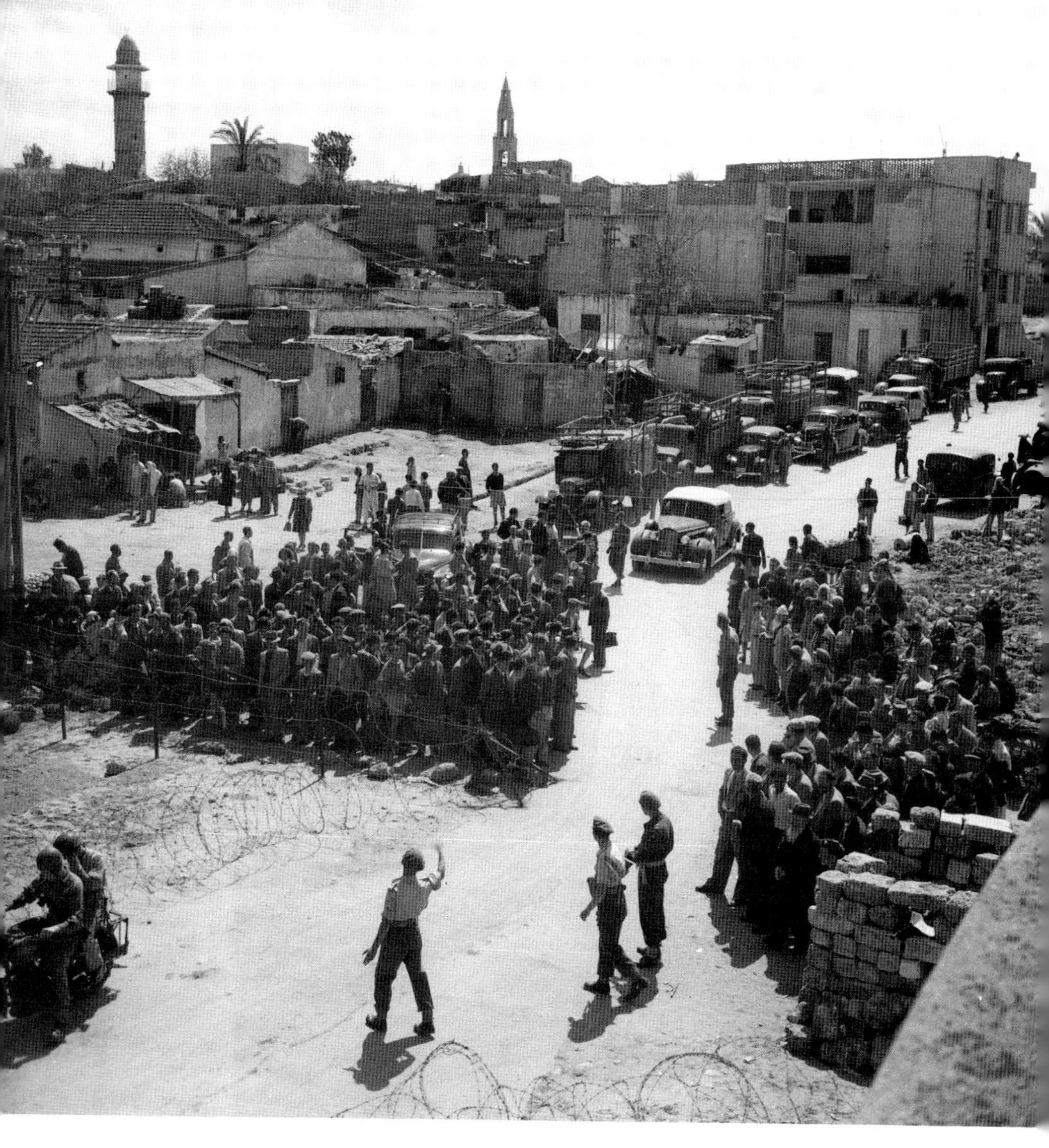

Operation Elephant, Tel Aviv, 1947　　　　　　　　Hans Pinn

of Jerusalem and most of Tel Aviv. But maintaining martial law in Tel Aviv, a city of 170,000, was virtually impossible for an already over-stretched military and caused hardship for the population and damage to the local economy. The operation lasted sixteen days, with meagre results: sixty arrests at a cost of twenty-four lives (ten Jews and fourteen Britons).[22]

Handing over to the UN

Even now, with the odds against him, Bevin did not give up the desperate search for a solution. In February he had come up with a variant of the bi-national formula: a plan for a Palestine state, divided into cantons, into which the 100,000 refugees could be absorbed. But the Bevin plan was rejected by both sides, and in April 1947 Britain referred the whole issue to the United Nations. Bevin's aim at this point was not to withdraw from Palestine but to force others to share responsibility for the problem. Many in Britain now believed the territory was a liability that should be shuffled off—among them Churchill, who could not understand why Britain was expending so much blood and treasure on what he derisively termed these 'wars of mice'. Between 1945 and 1947 the number of British troops in Palestine had doubled from 50,000 to 100,000. One-tenth of the armed forces of the British empire occupied a country the size of Wales. Palestine was costing the British exchequer close to £40 million a year.[23]

In July 1947, in an incident which further inflamed British public opinion, the Irgun kidnapped and hanged two British sergeants in retaliation for the execution of three of its members. The *Daily Express* splashed a gruesome picture of the men across its front page, under the headline 'Hanged Britons: Picture that will Shock the World'.

Despairing of a solution, Bevin declared that Britain would withdraw the following year. Even now, with the clock ticking, the United Nations responded slowly and uncertainly to the

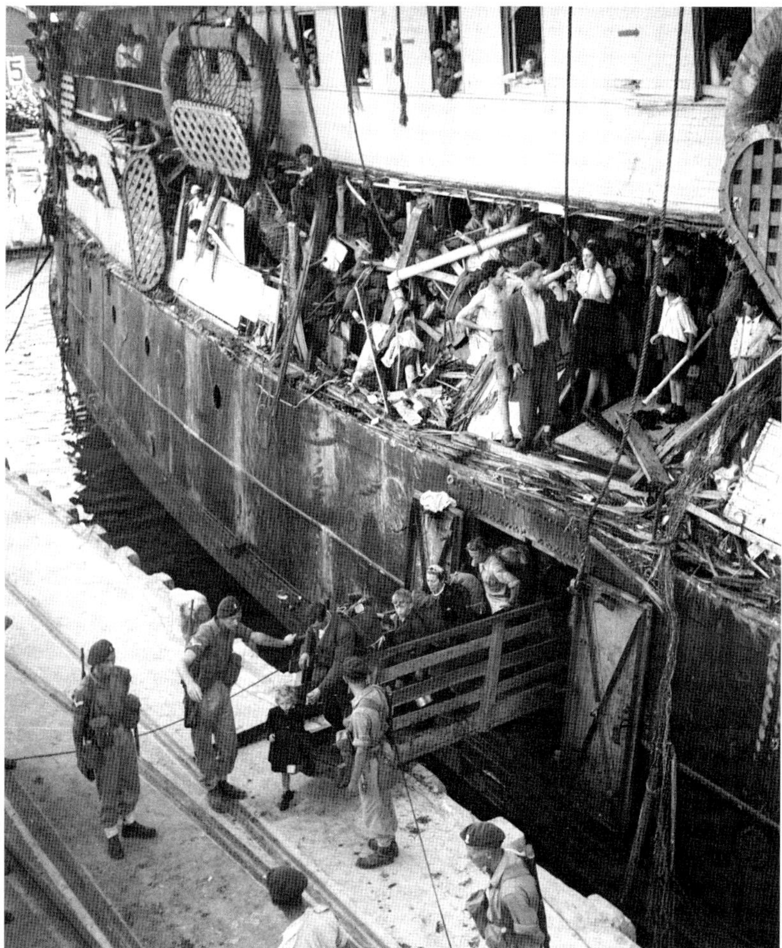

Haifa, 1947: children disembark from the Exodus   Hans Pinn

new responsibility thrust upon it. The members of a UN special committee (UNSCOP) travelled to Jerusalem and held their proceedings in the impressive rooms of the YMCA. The Zionists testified before it; the Arabs refused to do so.

Even as UNSCOP's work was under way, the Zionists staged a

propaganda coup. They had bought an old Mississippi steamer, the *President Warfield*—which they renamed the *Exodus*—and, after packing it with some 4,500 refugees, organised its passage from France to Palestine, in the constant glare of world publicity. British diplomats failed to persuade the French authorities to prevent the ship from sailing. As it approached Palestine, but still in international waters, the vessel was boarded by the Royal Navy and brought, battered and bruised, into Haifa. Here women and children disembarked. With the detention camps in Cyprus full, Bevin then took the fateful decision to send the ship to Hamburg, in the British-occupied zone of Germany— the last country the refugees wanted to be sent to. He had set out to make an example of the ship by showing he would not be browbeaten into accepting illegal immigration into Palestine. Instead, Britain suffered international vilification.[24]

The girl from Brooklyn

UNSCOP, in its majority report, recommended partition. This was something Bevin and his advisers had convinced themselves the UN would never endorse, since they felt sure the Arab states and the Soviet Union would vote against it. But in November 1947, after intense lobbying, the UN General Assembly—with Soviet backing—approved the proposal. This was a turning-point for Zionism, giving it the stamp of international legitimacy. But if the resolution increased the chances that the Zionists would win their state, it also made war in Palestine more likely. Britain refused to implement it in the teeth of Arab opposition and withheld co-operation from the UN as it struggled to do so.

Among the revellers who gathered in the centre of Jerusalem to celebrate the UN partition resolution was a 23-year-old American student, Zipporah ('Zippy') Borowsky. A few weeks earlier, she had boarded a liner to travel to Palestine, for what was supposed to be a year of study at the Hebrew University. She

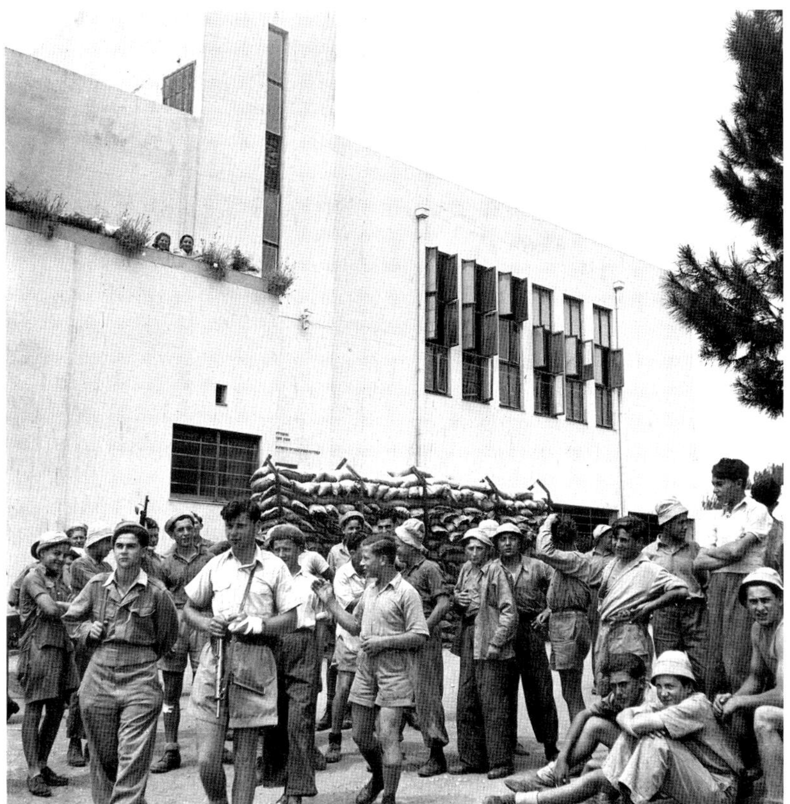

Young Zionists training with the Haganah, 1948   Zoltan Kluger

had never left home before. The voyage took seventeen days. The students arrived at Haifa and travelled by bus to a *pension* in Jerusalem. There was an initial culture shock. Zippy, a city girl from Brooklyn, found it hard to adapt to new food and a new climate—and clothes that were dowdy and casual by New York standards. Then there was the violence, which led most of the other students to go home. But Zippy stayed, dreaming at night of 'American ice cream sodas and tile bathrooms with hot and cold running water'.[25]

Without the knowledge of her parents back home in New York, she was inducted into the Haganah. The initiation took place secretly in a darkened room in a school. Her studies now largely abandoned, Zippy took a first-aid course and learned how to carry 'hand grenades stuffed into my blouse' and '[eavesdrop] on telephone conversations at British HQ'. She discovered that the Haganah had a stock of 'British Army overcoats, false identity papers, rifle permits, rifles and ammunition', for use if its fighters were stopped by a British patrol.[26]

The Zionists were preparing for war. They had built up supplies of arms—many of them bought or stolen during the Second World War—and, believing statehood might at last be within their grasp, were well organised and highly motivated. In contrast, the Arabs of Palestine were wholly unprepared and, in their weakness and division, continued to hope that someone else—Britain, the Arab states, the United Nations—would come to their rescue. The Mufti's cousin, Abdul-Qader al-Husseini, renowned for his role in the rebellion of the 1930s, began to organise resistance in the Jerusalem area. But there was no central command, and old divisions and rivalries persisted.

Meanwhile Arab foreign ministers, meeting in Cairo, created the Arab Liberation Army, under Fawzi al-Qawuqji, tasked with saving Palestine from partition.

Cycle of violence

On a stormy night in January 1948, while she was asleep at her boarding-house in Qatamon, a middle-class district of Jerusalem, Sylva Gelber heard, 'as though it were next door, the blast of a terrible explosion'. The Haganah had attacked the Semiramis Hotel, mistakenly believing it to be the headquarters of local Arab forces. Twenty-six civilians were killed, most of them members of a single Christian Arab family, together with the Spanish consul. To Gelber, this was further proof of the hardening of Jewish hearts. Her office in the old German consulate had already come under attack and now, disillusioned with all sides, she decided to leave. After making a hazardous car journey to the airport at Lydda, she returned to Canada. 'Suddenly, not yet forty, I felt very old.' [27]

A few weeks later, Abdul-Qader's men, helped by two British deserters, attacked the *Palestine Post*, the country's main English-language Zionist newspaper. 'The sky was blood-red,' recalled one eye-witness, 'and blazing stars were drifting over the buildings. The flames were pouring out of the ground-floor windows and the crackling of wooden frames sounded like the crunching of bones.' The paper's editor, Gershon Agronsky, was away in Tel Aviv, but eight of his compositors had 'dreadful face wounds from flying machinery or glass'. Two were blinded. In an act of defiance, the staff worked through the night to produce the next morning's edition.[28]

In February 1948, in an even more dramatic sign that they could strike at the heart of Jerusalem, Abdul-Qader's men bombed Ben Yehuda Street, the city's main Jewish residential and shopping district, this time using four British deserters and killing fifty-four people.[29] Tightening the screw, Abdul-Qader managed to cut Jerusalem's lifeline—the road linking it to Tel Aviv. With the city under siege, supplies of food, water, and ammunition ran low. Ben-Gurion, anxiously following events from Tel Aviv, was desperate to open the road to Jerusalem, so that convoys carrying food (and smuggled weapons) could get through to the city.

Enter Abdullah

Bevin had always clung to the goal of a bi-national state, believing partition to be an admission of failure—and, in any case, impossible to achieve without a large infusion of money and men. But now it seemed likely that partition would occur

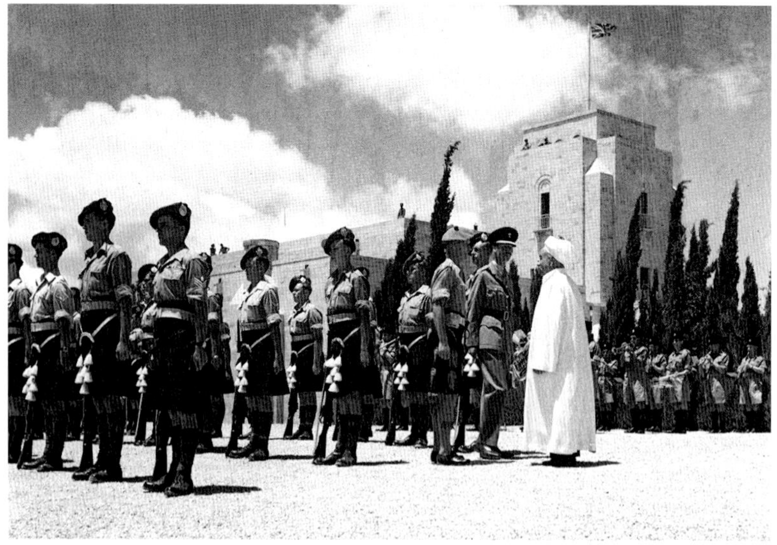

King Abdullah at Government House, Jerusalem, 1947   Hans Pinn

whether he liked it or not. He was aware of the ambition of Britain's loyal ally, Emir (now King) Abdullah of Transjordan, to absorb Palestine—or as much of it as he could—into his kingdom. In November 1947, in the run-up to the UN partition resolution, Abdullah had had a secret meeting with an envoy from the Jewish Agency, Golda Meir. She had told him that the Zionists would accept his takeover of those parts of Palestine that the UN had allotted to the Arabs—provided he did nothing to prevent the establishment of the Jewish state. Here were the makings of a deal: the two sides had a shared interest in avoiding conflict between them and preventing the birth of a Palestinian Arab state under their common enemy, Hajj Amin al-Husseini.

The king was careful to seek British approval. At a meeting in London in February 1948, Bevin told Abdullah's prime minister confidentially that, provided the king's forces kept out of the areas the UN had allotted to the Jews, he had no objection to military intervention by the Arab Legion—the British-officered, British-funded army which was the backbone of Transjordan's defence force.

Massacre and flight

Gradually the Zionists' superior organisation and motivation began to tell. On 8 April 1948, Abdul-Qader, the Arabs' one outstanding commander, was killed in a battle near Jerusalem. His funeral was marked by an outpouring of grief. Even as it was under way, news began to filter through that the Irgun and the Stern Gang had entered Deir Yassin, a hitherto peaceful Arab village near Jerusalem, and, after meeting resistance, had killed over a hundred people, including women and children. Word of the massacre spread swiftly, giving new impetus to the exodus of the Arabs from their homes and land which was already under

Funeral of Abdul-Qader al-Husseini, 1948　　　Photographer unknown

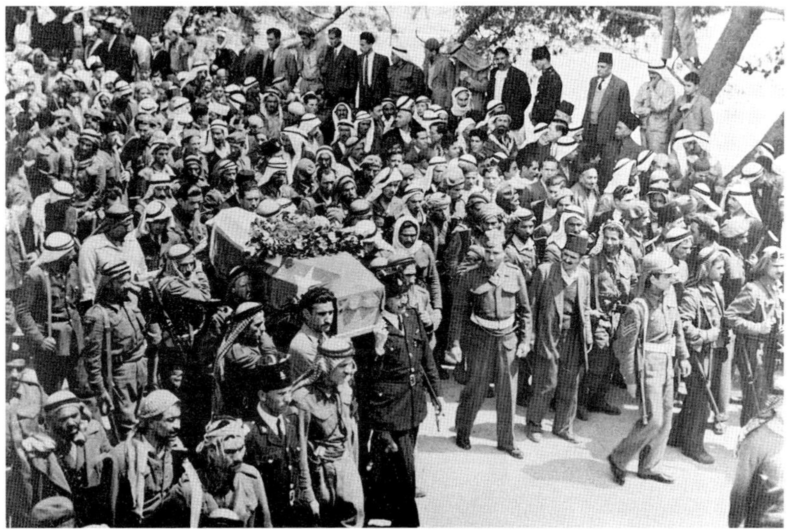

way. In retaliation, seventy-four Jews were killed—most of them doctors and medical personnel—when their convoy was attacked on its way to Jerusalem's Hadassah hospital. The Zionists were furious that the British did not intervene until six hours after the start of the attack, when it was too late to save lives.

Quite by chance, Zippy Borowsky witnessed the aftermath of the Deir Yassin massacre. She was on first-aid duty at a base the Haganah had set up in the village, and watched as its soldiers were clearing up:

> [They] were dragging out household items and articles of clothing … They hurried to eradicate the symbols of the dead, the remnants of things that no longer had owners, to bury them, burn them, to rid their noses of the smell, their eyes of the sight and their hearts of the knowledge.

She felt an overwhelming need to escape from 'this haunted Arab village'.[30]

Leaving Jaffa

Towards the end of April 1948, the 15-year-old Hasan Hammami left Jaffa with his family. The Hammamis had been respected members of the city's business community, active in trade and in the citrus industry. They had been part of the old cosmopolitan Jaffa where Christian and Muslim Arabs and Sephardi and Ashkenazi Jews had shared a common existence in a city that had been tolerant as well as prosperous. Now the communities had been torn apart, and violence was escalating. The family decided to leave for Lebanon, for what they thought would be a short holiday.

They took a taxi to the port. The young Hasan was shocked to see how different it was from the place where he had spent idyllic summers watching the boats go by. Now it was a scene of chaos and confusion. 'People were crammed into boats of

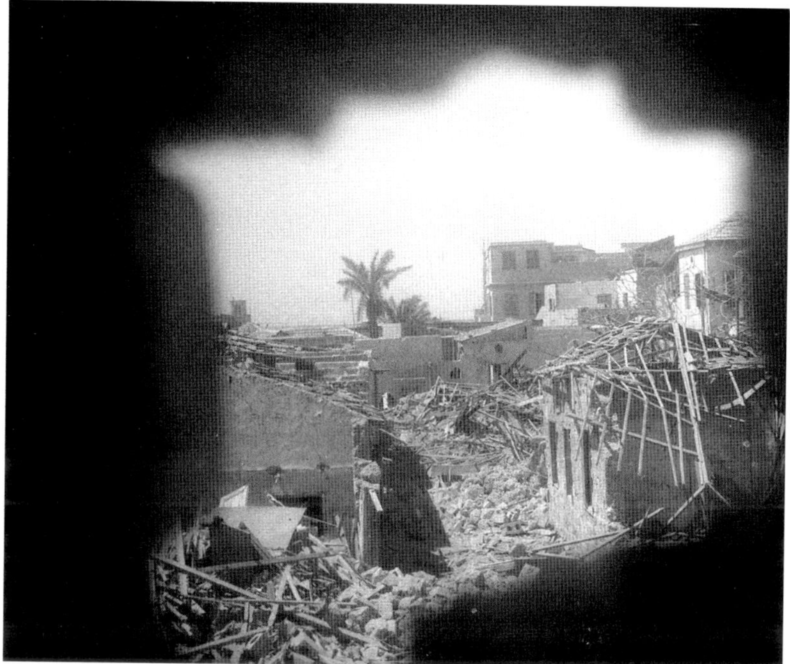

The border area between Jaffa and Tel Aviv, 1948   Beno Rothenberg

every size and shape,' he recalled later. 'Feluccas with their sails, launches, tugs, and lighters were all full and all heading out to the open sea.' The Hammami family squeezed onto a crowded vessel with hundreds of others. But the boat ran into a storm. The food ran out. An old man died, and a woman gave birth; the baby did not survive. After three days at sea, the Hammamis reached the Lebanese port of Tyre, to begin a life of exile.[31]

Breakdown

In the countdown to the British departure, there were scenes of chaos as violence spread and basic services broke down. There were also flashes of black humour. Palestine's spin doctor, Richard Stubbs—who ran the Public Information Office, where journalists would gather to receive official briefings, drink at the bar, and eat egg and chips—found that his car had been stolen, a not uncommon occurrence at the time. It was a maroon Ford saloon that he was fond of. When he made enquiries through Arab contacts to see if he could recover it, he received an unexpected reply from the Arab commander Fawzi al-Qawuqji in Nablus. He could have the car back in return for advice on how to improve Arab propaganda. While readily acknowledging that Arab public relations left much to be desired, Stubbs declined the offer.[32]

By this time many people had already left. Jacques Mantoura had married Leila Canaan, and, after he was detained and threatened by a Zionist militia, they escaped to Beirut before eventually settling in London, where they were to spend the rest of their lives. Leila's father, Tawfiq Canaan, lost his home in Musrara which, with his extensive library, was looted. He had managed to put his collection of amulets and talismans in a safe place. Sophie Halaby managed to safeguard her paintings before she, too, left Musrara to seek refuge in the Old City. Edward Hodgkin got married and took his wife back to Britain, where he was later to become foreign editor of *The Times*. Jabra Ibrahim Jabra left Palestine for Iraq, where he worked as a teacher, writing novels, painting, and translating Shakespeare (and Dylan Thomas) into Arabic.

Some stayed. Fadwa Tuqan remained in her native Nablus. She watched the refugees flee eastwards, finding shelter in mosques and schools and in caves in nearby hills. The disaster had an unexpected consequence. 'When the roof fell in on Palestine in 1948,' she wrote later, 'the veil fell off the face of the Nablus woman.'[33]

Asia Halaby, too, stayed on and in the early morning of 14 May 1948 braved the snipers' bullets to say goodbye to the last batch of British officials to leave—the only one of their employees to do so. It was a melancholy scene.

[T]he lobby of the King David Hotel was almost deserted. Yellow dust covers shrouded its heavy armchairs and sofas. Its usually immaculate floor was littered with scrap paper. Half a dozen filing cabinets, their locks sealed with red wax, waited at the door ...[34]

The officials shook her hand and boarded their bus. She found it hard to believe that it was all over. Shortly afterwards, the last high commissioner, Sir Alan Cunningham, left Government House in a bullet-proof Daimler to drive to the airstrip at Qalandia, from where he flew to Haifa to board a waiting ship. In a brief ceremony, the Union Jack was lowered and 'with the speed of an execution and the silence of a ship that passes in the night British rule in Palestine came to an end'.[35] As one eye-witness later recalled, the Mandate had dissolved in a moment, 'like salt in water'.[36]

That afternoon, in a museum in Tel Aviv, Ben-Gurion had

In Herzl's shadow: the birth of a state Photographer unknown

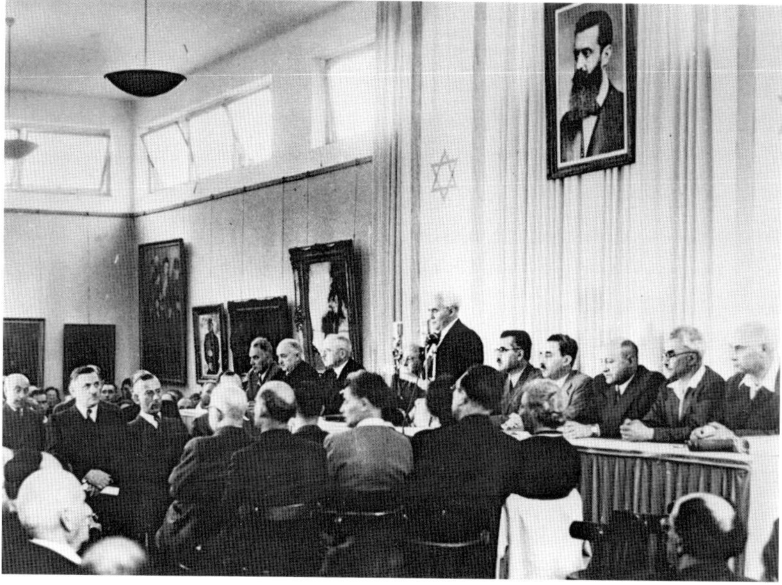

proclaimed the birth of the state of Israel. Truman was quick to recognise it, and a few days later the Soviet Union followed suit.

Invasion and war

At a few minutes to midnight, King Abdullah and members of his staff stood at the eastern end of the Allenby Bridge which spanned the river Jordan, waiting for the formal end of the Palestine Mandate.

> At twelve o'clock precisely the King drew his revolver, fired a symbolic shot into the air and shouted the word 'forward'. The long column of Jordanian troops which stretched down the road behind the bridge already had the engines of their cars ticking over and, as they moved off at the word of command, the hum of their motors rose to a roar.[37]

At the moment British rule ended, the Arab states sent their armies into Palestine: Transjordan and Iraq from the east, Syria and Lebanon from the north, and Egypt from the south. Egyptian planes bombed Tel Aviv. The Zionists were armed and prepared, but even so Ben-Gurion's advisers estimated their chances of success at fifty-fifty.[38]

The Arab Legion's British commander, John Glubb, had no illusions about the balance of forces. He had only 4,500 men at his disposal, and was unwilling to throw them into a battle he feared they might lose. As his troops took up positions on the West Bank, he was well aware that, for Arabs and Jews alike, the great prize was the Old City of Jerusalem with its holy places. He was reluctant to advance towards the city, but after repeated orders from Abdullah had no choice but to do so.

A ten-day battle for Jerusalem, from 18 to 28 May, with heavy casualties, ended with the Arab Legion in control of the Old City.

There followed a four-week truce, from 11 June to 9 July,

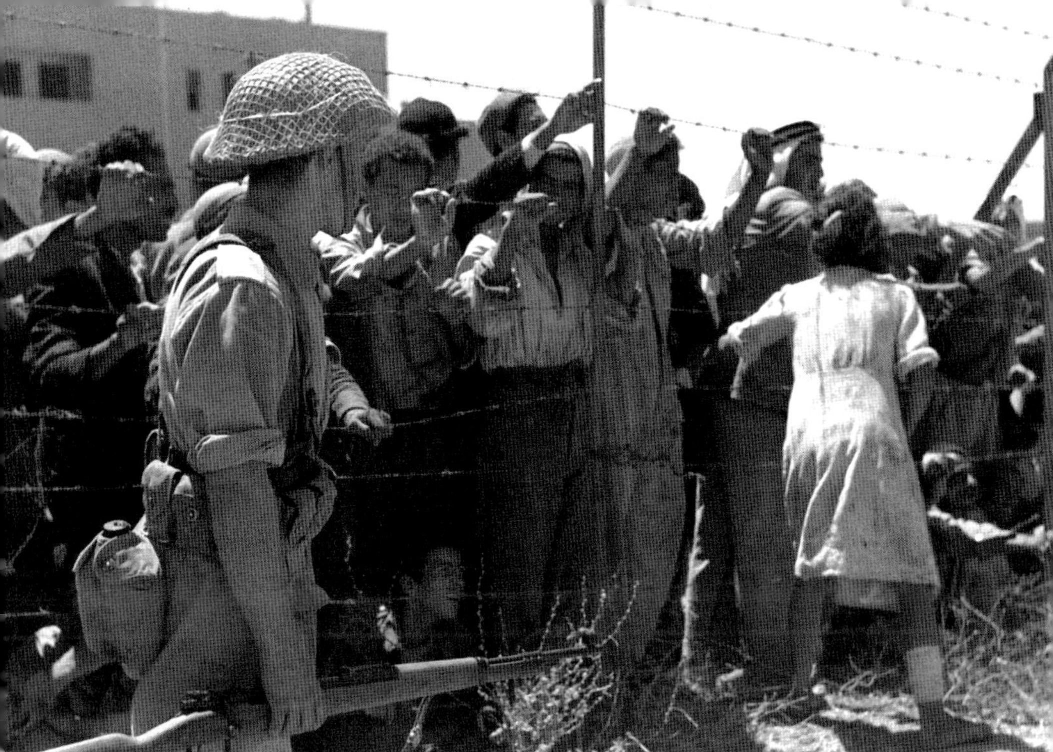

Ramleh, 1948   David Eldan

*The original caption describes the men as prisoners of war; in fact they were
civilians penned up prior to their eventual expulsion.*

engineered by the UN's Swedish mediator, Count Folke
Bernadotte. The Israelis used the truce to re-arm with weapons
obtained in the United States and Czechoslovakia. But, under
strong American pressure, Britain announced it was removing
British officers from the Arab Legion and stopping arms supplies
to Transjordan, leaving Glubb's forces desperately short of arms
and ammunition.

Having done well in round one, the Arab Legion fared
badly in round two. The focus of the fighting was in the area
between Jerusalem and Tel Aviv, and in particular the towns of
Lydda and Ramleh. When Glubb decided he had no choice
but to withdraw his forces from the area, these towns fell to

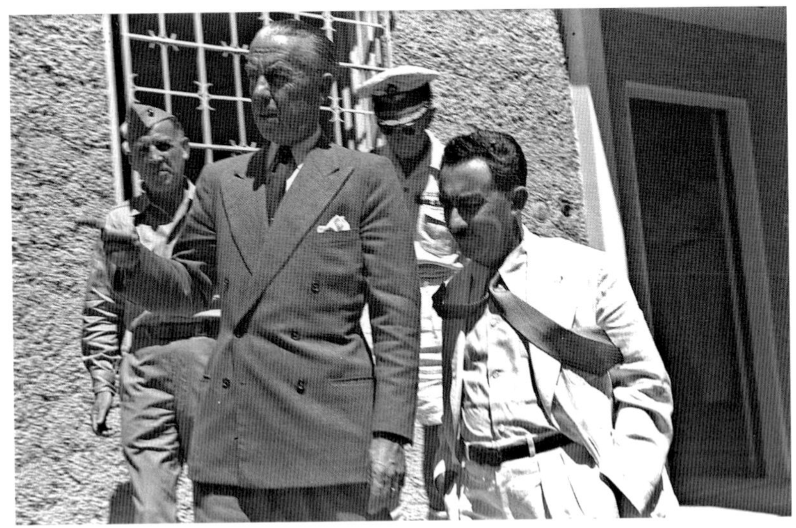

Photographer unknown

Bernadotte in September 1948, shortly before his assassination

the Israelis. What followed was one of the worst atrocities of the war. Mistakenly believing that they were under attack by the Arab Legion, Israeli troops opened fire indiscriminately, killing an estimated 250 of Lydda's Arab inhabitants. They then expelled the rest. Loudspeaker vans were used to order them to leave, and soldiers fired shots over their heads. In broiling heat a column of refugees, carrying only the possessions they had hastily gathered, made their way over rocks and scrub on the long journey to Ramallah, which was in the hands of the Arab Legion. Many died before they got there. From the two towns over 40,000 Arabs were expelled.[39]

Bitter legacy

Count Bernadotte produced a plan to end the fighting, block the Israelis' attempt to gain control of Jerusalem, and safeguard the refugees' right of return. This earned him the wrath of the Stern

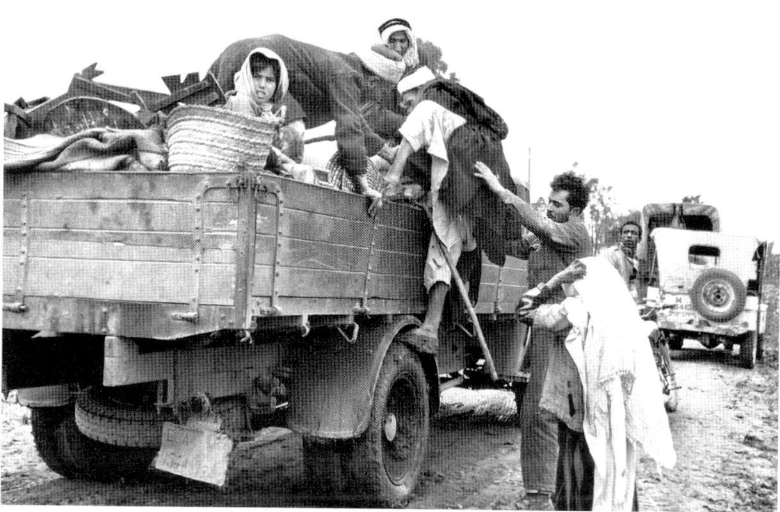

Fleeing from Faluja, north of Gaza, 1949   Photographer unknown

Gang, which assassinated him in Jerusalem in September 1948. His role was taken by his American assistant, Ralph Bunche. By early 1949 the Israelis' victory was assured. The Arab rulers, hobbled by incompetence and rivalry, had failed to prevent them from taking over more than three-quarters of Palestine. Abdullah gained the West Bank and the Old City of Jerusalem, which he absorbed into his domain, renamed the Hashemite Kingdom of Jordan. Egypt took control of the Gaza Strip.

The first Arab-Israeli war ended, not with a peace settlement, but with a series of armistice agreements signed in Rhodes between January and July 1949. More than 6,000 Israelis had been killed and over twice as many Palestinian Arabs (and smaller numbers of Egyptians, Iraqis, Jordanians, and Syrians). The Israelis now controlled the western part of Jerusalem and the Jordanians the eastern part. The two sides glared at one another across the armistice line which separated them. The Arab College, which Ahmad Samih al-Khalidi had built up so lovingly in the Mandate years, stood forlornly in no-man's land, looted and derelict.

In all, some 700,000 refugees, roughly half the Arab population of Palestine, either fled or were driven from their homes.[40] Many escaped to the West Bank, whose population doubled, swelling the size of Abdullah's kingdom. Others fled to the Gaza Strip, whose population quadrupled. United Nations refugee camps were set up in these two areas and in neighbouring Arab states.

Intended to be temporary, the camps exist to this day.

Flight or expulsion?

Why the refugees fled was for several decades the subject of fierce contention. Successive Israeli governments maintained they had left of their own accord or at the behest of Arab leaders. But beginning in the 1980s, a group of Israeli scholars who became known as the 'new historians' began to call into question this and other myths surrounding the birth of the Jewish state. Benny Morris, in his seminal book *The Birth of the Palestinian Refugee Problem* (1987), used newly-discovered Israeli sources to argue that, while a number of factors had been at work, expulsion was clearly one of them. Morris disputed the claim that Ben-Gurion had put into effect a pre-prepared plan for their expulsion, but made it clear that in specific cases he had instructed Haganah officers to clear (or 'cleanse') towns or villages of Arabs. Morris also argued that the idea of 'transfer'—a euphemism for expulsion—was 'inevitable and inbuilt into Zionism'. How else to turn a Jewish minority in Palestine into a Jewish majority other than by reducing the size of the Arab population, either peacefully or otherwise? [41]

No less important than the exodus of the Arab refugees was

Per-Olow Anderson

Right: *Gaza, 1956: a blind refugee with her grand-daughter*

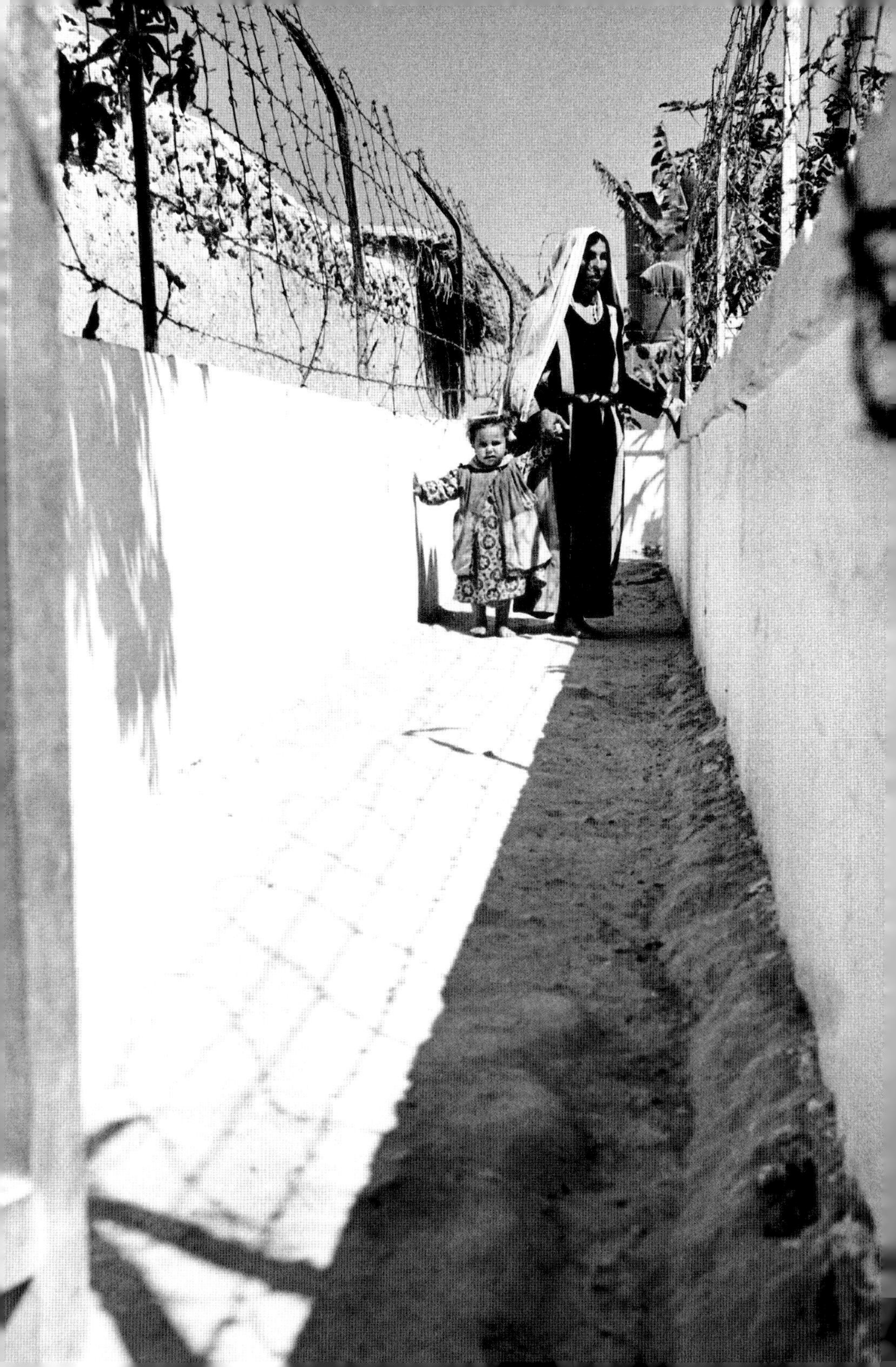

the fact that, with only minor exceptions, Israel firmly barred the door to prevent their return—despite international pressure (including from the United States) and a string of UN resolutions which upheld their right to return to their homes and land, or receive compensation if they chose not to do so. A special UN body, the United Nations Relief and Works Agency (UNRWA), was created to run the refugee camps. Israeli officials argued that the perpetuation of the refugee problem was a cynical ploy designed to put pressure on them, and that the refugees should be dispersed. But the refugees themselves refused to be dispersed, and the United Nations and the Arab governments were unwilling to act against their wishes. For the Palestinians, the camps are an enduring symbol of their plight and their cause.[42]

Arab intellectuals sought to draw lessons from the Palestine débâcle. Musa Alami wrote a scathing critique of the failings of the Arab governments, calling for unity and root-and-branch reform.[43] Abdullah Tall, the Arab Legion officer whose troops had captured Jerusalem's Old City, told an American journalist in 1949, 'I honestly don't know whether we hate the Jews more than we do each other. Egypt hates Transjordan, Transjordan hates Syria, Syria hates Iraq. With unity and without British interference we could have won this war.'[44]

But Arab divisions and poor leadership were not the whole story. A series of factors during the period of British rule—migration from the land to the towns and cities, the loss of power and authority of the old landowning élite, the weakness (or absence) of Arab institutions and the Arabs' consequent dependence on the British for essential services such as health and education—led to the eventual collapse of a traditional Arab society. An old world was vanishing, and a new world did not yet exist. To be sure, the departure of the British and the war that followed were the proximate causes of Palestine's destruction; but the seeds of its dissolution had been sown much earlier.[45]

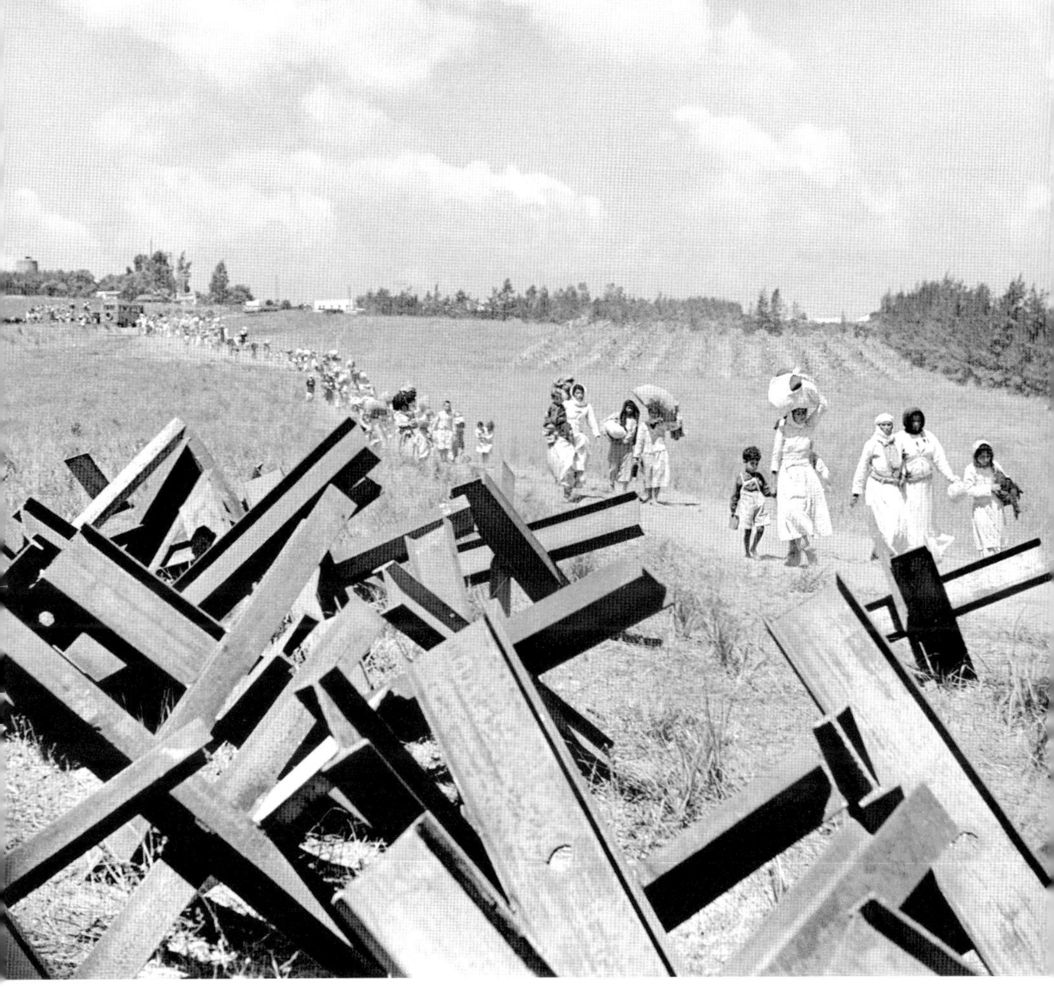

Paul Goldman

Women and children expelled from Bir Burin, 1948

Bir Burin was a village near the border with the Jordanian-controlled
West Bank, to which the villagers were expelled. In 1949 the settlement
of Be'erotayim was established on their land. When the photograph was
published in the weekly Davar Hashavua *in June 1948, the caption was*
changed to read: 'Arab women and children were returned to Arab territory'.[46]

235

Photographers at war

Throughout 1948 and 1949 the job of the official Israeli photographers had been to record heroism and struggle. Their employers had wanted life-affirming pictures of the men and women who were fighting in what Israelis regard as their war of independence. But in recording the war they also recorded the Nakba—the Catastrophe—the name the Palestinian Arabs give to the events of these fateful years. Outside Israel the names of these photographers—Zoltan Kluger, Paul Goldman, Beno Rothenberg, David Eldan, Hugo Mendelson, and others—are not well known. (Even in Israel, younger generations may be scarcely aware of them.)

The photographers saw it all: the expulsions as Arab villages were conquered and emptied; the looting, which was widespread and seldom punished; the Arabs behind barbed wire, whether Egyptian soldiers in the south or civilians in Ramleh, penned up prior to their expulsion. As professional photojournalists they faithfully recorded what they saw; but they were pragmatic enough to know that those who received their pictures—whether government agencies or newspaper or magazine editors—would accept some and reject others. As a result, much of their work was not published and either disappeared or lay hidden in files for decades—until a new generation of Israelis, curious about their country's past, discovered them. Museums held exhibitions rediscovering and celebrating the work of Rothenberg, Goldman, and Kluger. The catalogues that accompanied them showed the range and skill of their work and the almost matter-of-fact way in which they recorded the Nakba. 'I am a Zionist,' declared Rothenberg, '[but] I am not in favour of blurring the evidence.'[47]

At the same time, as the world entered the digital age, official archives put some of their photographs into the public domain. The result is patchy.[48] Some archives continue to withhold both

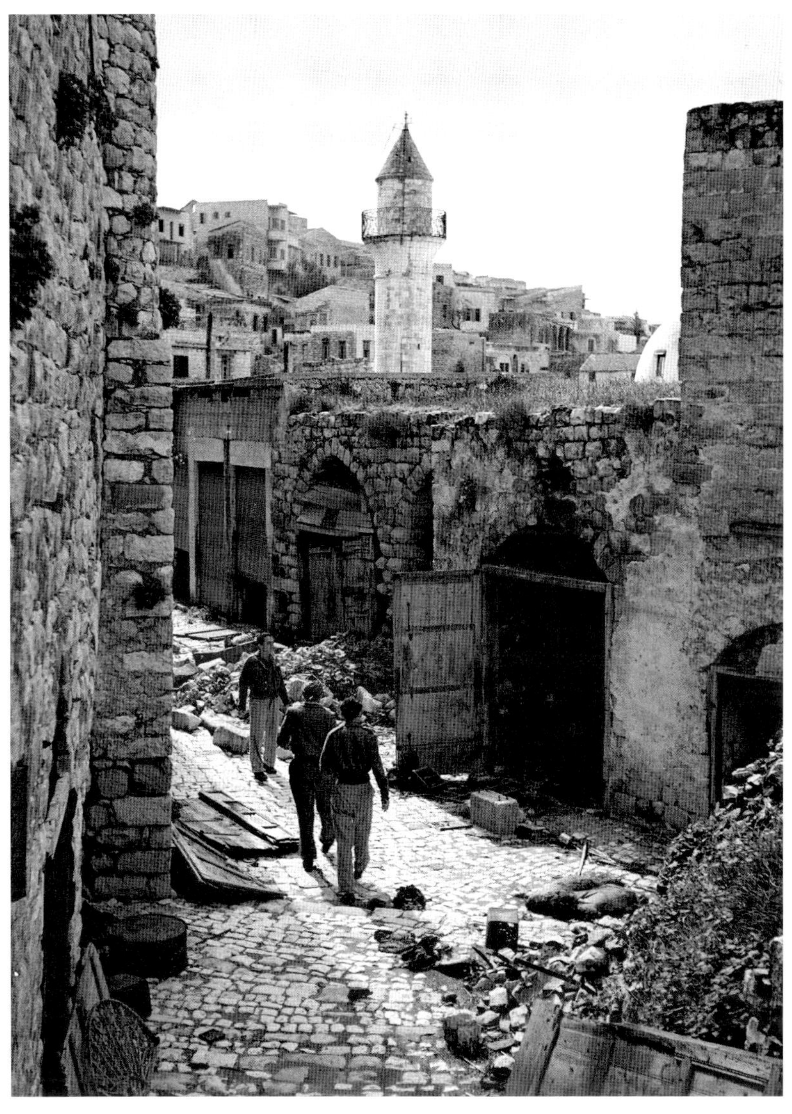

237

documents and photographs. In 2019, in a remarkable piece of investigative journalism, the newspaper *Ha'aretz* uncovered a sustained and continuing attempt by the ministry of defence to force archivists to put sensitive material under lock and key.[49]

The archaeology of the Nakba

In the aftermath of the war, Zoltan Kluger, the Hungarian-born refugee from Nazi Germany who had celebrated the pioneers of Jewish settlement, was as prolific as ever. He revisited Safad, in the north, its buildings scarred and crumbling. He photographed the remains of Arab villages—described in his captions as 'abandoned'—whose houses had either been destroyed or were occupied by new Jewish immigrants from Eastern Europe or from Arab countries (Iraq, Yemen, Morocco).[50]

Kluger's employers at the Government Press Office regarded the influx of Jews after 1948 as a success story to be celebrated. But he and the other photographers were aware that the situation was not quite so simple. For one thing, the process of absorbing large numbers of immigrants in a short period of time proved extremely challenging. (The airlifting of Yemeni Jews in 1949-50, mythologised at the time as Operation Magic Carpet, was in reality a tale of chronic mismanagement and considerable suffering.)[51] For another, there could be no disguising the fact—however much it might be downplayed—that new communities were taking the place of old.

Kluger was the master of the staged scene. One can only wonder how far he was concerned solely with producing propaganda pictures and how far he was aware of the subtext lying just below the surface of his images. In the new settlement of Elkosh—the former Arab village of Deir al-Qassi, near the border with Lebanon—he photographed a group of immigrant schoolchildren dancing in a ring. The shot is carefully framed, with the children and their teachers in the foreground and,

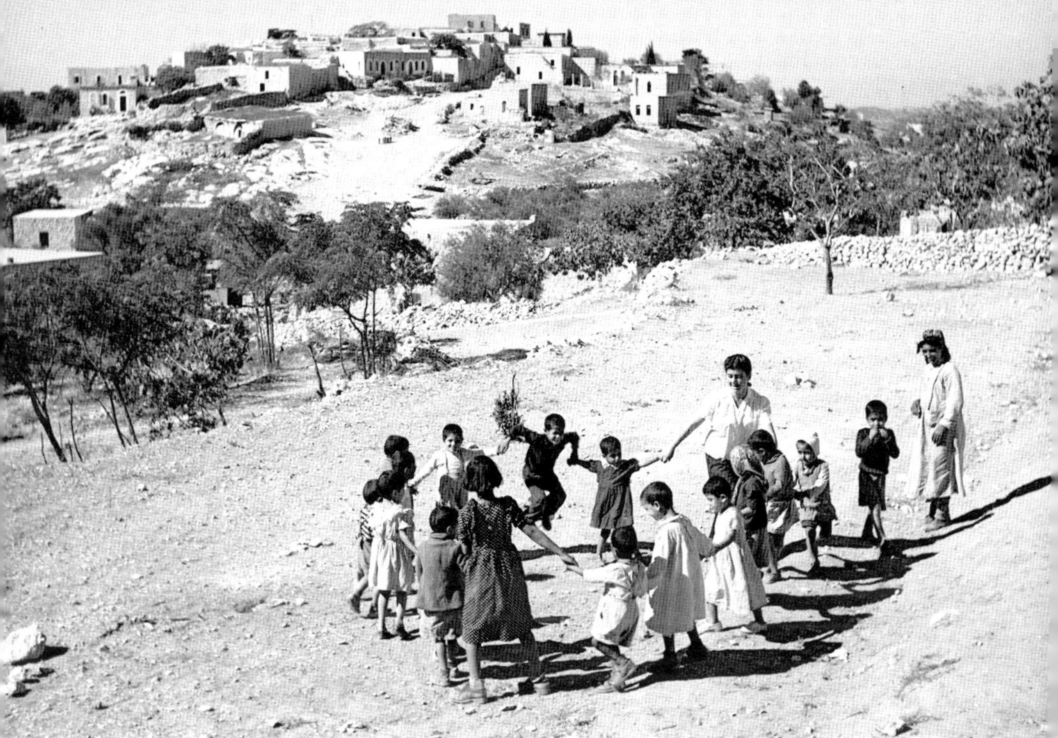

Immigrant Kurdish children dancing in Elkosh, 1949　　　　　Zoltan Kluger

above them on a hilltop, the houses of the old Arab village. New immigrants dancing in new settlements had been a staple of Kluger's work. In the past they had been Russians or Poles. Now, in Elkosh, they were from Kurdistan.

A refugee from Nazi Germany was photographing newly-arrived Kurdish refugees in a village whose former inhabitants were now refugees in United Nations camps.

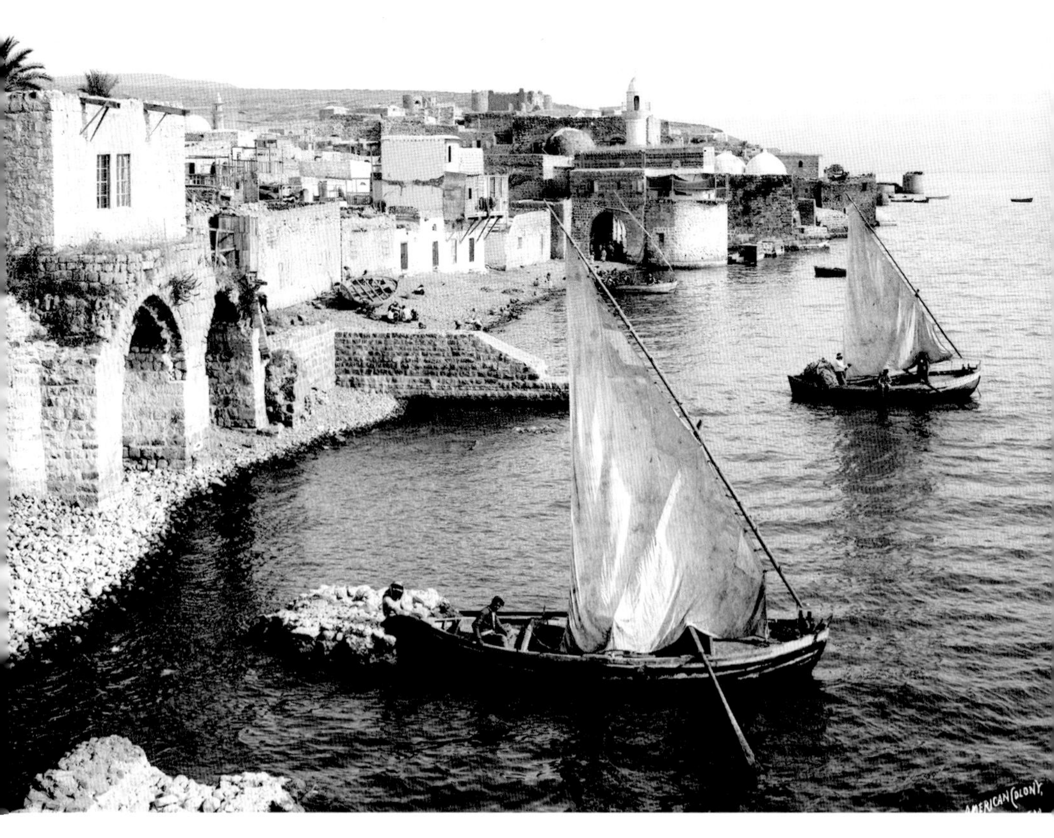
AMERICAN COLONY

Epilogue: the land and the people

'Memory can speak truth to power.'[1]

THE METAMORPHOSIS OF Palestine was not pre-ordained; it was man-made. It did not begin in 1948, or even in 1917. It unfolded from the middle of the nineteenth century when Western powers intensified their interest and involvement in the Holy Land, drawing it into a tightening web of political and economic interests.[2] These powers, and in particular their consuls in Jerusalem, became in effect quasi-colonial rulers. This was not imperialism in its conventional form: it was encroachment rather than conquest, and involved not one imperial actor but several working in competition. What's more, while these powers were ready to challenge and erode Ottoman authority in Palestine, they were careful not to go too far: for geostrategic reasons, they were committed to preserving the integrity of the Ottoman empire, essentially as a buffer against Russian expansion.

The consuls were a mixed bunch, ranging from the benign to the lunatic, but they had in common an adherence to the colonial attitudes of the age. They viewed Arabs and Turks with barely disguised contempt: first, because they were deemed utterly incapable of governing, let alone modernis-ing, Palestine; and, second, because they were predominantly

Left: *Tiberias and the Sea of Galilee, c. 1900*　　　　American Colony

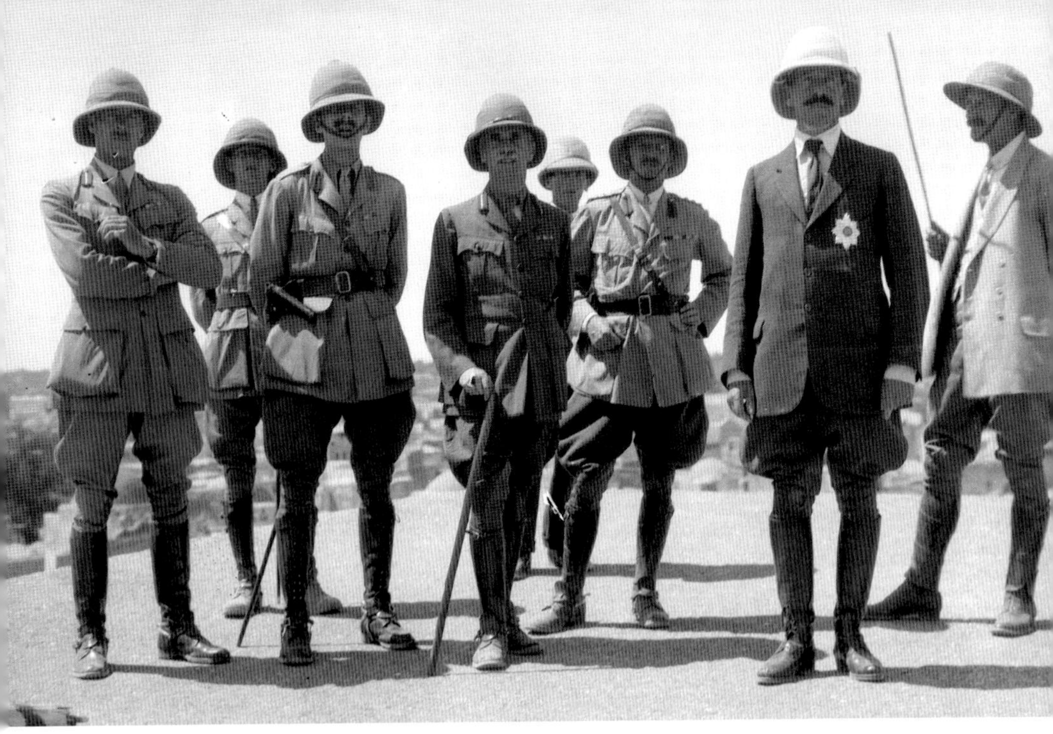

Sir Herbert Samuel and military escort, 1921 American Colony

Muslim. Only Western Christians were capable of performing this God-given mission (albeit with the tiresome complication that the Christians in Palestine, both indigenous and foreign, were constantly at one another's throats, with corrosive relations between Protestant and Catholic, and between the Western and Eastern traditions).

Palestine's 'international' character

A new phase was ushered in by an accident of war: the defeat and collapse of the Ottoman empire in the First World War. From 1917 Palestine was governed not by a weak Ottoman authority constantly harried by a gaggle of foreign consuls, but by a single all-conquering imperial power—one moreover which had just emerged bloodied but triumphant from a global war. British officials brought to Palestine the colonial preconceptions they had imbibed in India, Africa, or elsewhere, which were deeply ingrained but ill suited to the country's special conditions. Some of these preconceptions were shared, despite their avowedly progressive ideals, by the Zionist leaders. Ben-Gurion admired imperial Britain as a force for modernisation—as well as a necessary instrument for the success of Zionism—and felt the same instinctive sense of superiority and condescension towards the Arabs that the British felt towards 'subject' peoples.[3] Weizmann, too, while he could turn on the charm when dealing with such figures as Emir Faisal, privately regarded Arabs in general as irredeemably backward and ignorant, and their leaders as eminently corruptible.

These were not just cultural prejudices; they had political consequences. Consistently throughout British rule, officials in both Jerusalem and London refused to accept that the Arabs of Palestine were a nation with the same right to statehood and national sovereignty as other nations. Not one of Britain's proposals for Palestine's future—from the White Paper of 1922 and the Peel commission report of 1937, to the pre-war White Paper of 1939, the unpublished Churchill proposal of 1944, and the Bevin plan of 1947—envisaged the emergence of an independent Palestinian Arab state.[4] Such a state was regarded with horror by British officials as a 'Mufti state'—in other words, one which would be under the thumb of their arch-enemy, Hajj Amin al-Husseini. The most they could swallow was the union of Palestine (or part of Palestine) with Transjordan under their loyal ally, Emir Abdullah.

Time and again officials would invoke Palestine's 'international' character—meaning that the Palestinian Arabs were only one of several parties with a claim to the Holy Land, and not necessarily the most important one. The other claimants included the Zionists (as a result of Britain's commitment in the

Balfour Declaration) and the various powers—Britain, France, Russia, the Vatican, and others—whose stake in Palestine was either religious or political or both. The role of British officials was to act as impartial arbiters of these different claims and interests, while always making sure that British interests came first.

Claim and counter-claim

The Zionists, for their part, had an obvious motive in presenting the Arabs' claim to Palestine as morally, politically, and legally inferior to their own. Broadly speaking, they used four lines of argument: that the Arabs did not work the land, drain the marshes, and combat malaria as the Zionist settlers did; that they were merely Arabs, indistinguishable from other Arabs, and thus not a proper nation; that they were backward and uncivilised, and therefore disqualified from rule; and, finally, that their leaders were corrupt, incompetent, and so deeply hypocritical that they secretly sold land to the Zionists at exorbitant prices.

How far do such arguments hold water? A people's rights are not determined by their own or their leaders' capabilities. The Zionists may have used more modern agricultural methods, but the Arabs' attachment to their land was fierce and deep-rooted. Palestinian Arabs, certainly by the 1920s as British rule got under way, were not Egyptians or Iraqis or even Syrians—though, for some, an old identification with a Greater Syria persisted—but were in the process of forming a distinct national identity of their own. The notion of ignorant, feckless Arabs, lazy and fatalistic, is an Orientalist trope, part and parcel of the language used in the age of empire to denigrate people deemed inferior. And, finally, the Arab leaders were indeed, with few exceptions, corrupt and ineffectual, and many of them did indeed sell land to the Zionists; but, fortunately for large

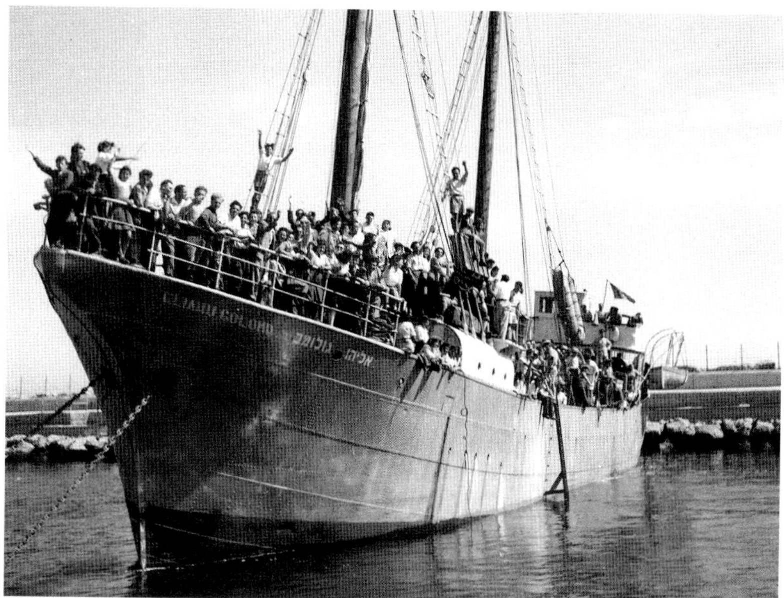

An immigrant ship arriving at Haifa, 1946   Hans Pinn

parts of the world, a badly-led nation is not a nation without rights. In short, the Palestinian Arabs had (and have) as much right to statehood as any of the other nations which emerged from colonial rule.

The more thoughtful Zionist leaders knew this perfectly well, and understood that the arguments they deployed had more propagandistic than legal or political force. But, taken together, they were a convenient and often effective means of discrediting Arab claims. The Zionist claim, on the other hand, while invoking a historical right to Palestine, nevertheless rested largely on its moral validity. Indeed one might argue that the essence of the Zionist case was moral, and that the principles of international law took distinctly second place. (In a revealing remark, Balfour declared that it would not always be practicable, from Britain's point of view, to make self-determination the decisive principle in shaping the post-1918 world—Palestine being a case in point.)[5]

At the heart of Zionism's moral case was (and is) the suffering of the Jews, particularly during two periods of horrific persecution—the Russian pogroms of the late nineteenth and early twentieth centuries, and the Nazi campaign of anti-Semitism starting in the 1930s and culminating in the Holocaust. The Zionist movement accordingly saw itself as being much more than a state-building project: it was in essence a rescue mission,[6] an instrument for saving those Jews who had survived the pogroms and the Holocaust. It was this which transformed the significance of Palestine after the defeat of Hitler, to a degree that Bevin never fully grasped.

In this final and decisive phase, when the Zionists—emboldened by the backing of Harry Truman's America—took on Britain, the argument was essentially whether rescue lay only in Palestine, as Ben-Gurion insisted, or was an international responsibility, as Bevin tried vainly to argue. Western opinion tended to side with the Zionists, and to see Britain as an insensitive bully. In the end, the contentious issue of illegal immigration, on which the Zionists focused their considerable propaganda skills, together with the pressure exerted by the single-minded violence of the Irgun and the Stern Gang, fatally eroded the support of the British public for maintaining the Mandate, which in turn helped precipitate Britain's final, humiliating withdrawal.

As for the Palestinian Arabs, their response to Jewish suffering was to ask, not unreasonably, why they should be expected to pay the price for the sins of Europe.

'Memory is right'

Questioned at the Paris peace conference after the First World War about the basis of the Zionist claim to Palestine, Weizmann

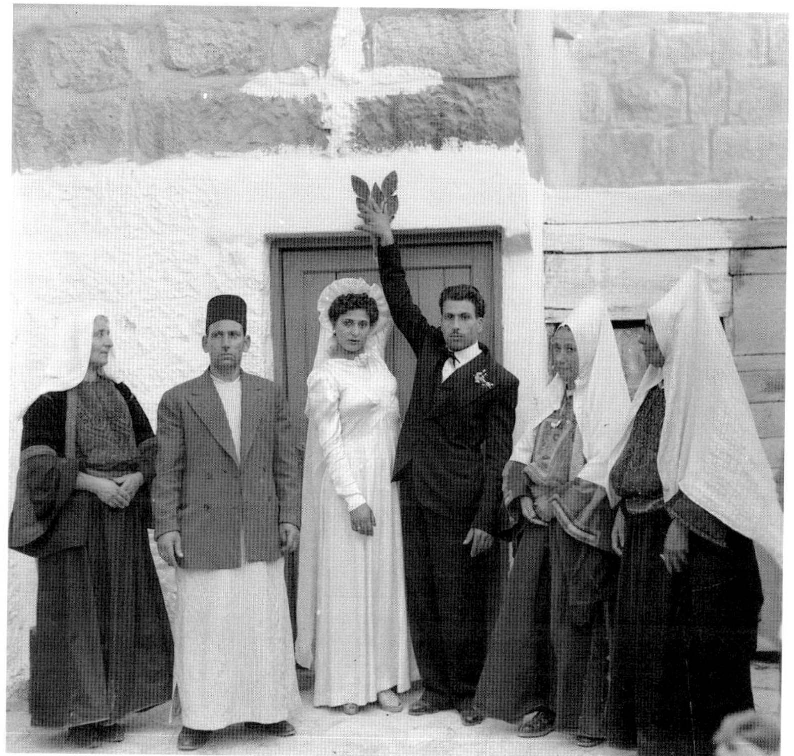

American Colony

Bride and groom in Bethlehem, blessing their new home, 1940s

gave an unusual reply: 'Memory is right.'⁷ Skilful diplomatist
that he was, he was giving expression to the age-old Jewish
saying 'Next year in Jerusalem', a sentiment nurtured during
the millennia of exile. But today, more than seven decades after
the creation of the state of Israel, the Palestinian Arabs have at
least as much justification for saying the same. For them, too,
'Memory is right.' They, too, have not forgotten Jerusalem. Many
of the refugees in the United Nations camps still keep the keys,
rusty with age, to the homes from which they or their parents
or grandparents fled or were expelled in 1948. And, unlike

247

the Jews, who after their long exile 'returned' to Palestine—it was, to be sure, a metaphorical return—the Palestinian Arabs had been in continuous possession of their land and homes for centuries before the first wave of Zionist settlement got under way in the 1880s.

In the end, the Zionists won their state not through the force of argument but through the force of arms. And the Palestinians lost their homes and land, despite the fact that their moral and legal case was strong, because they were weak and divided and because the Arab states were unable to rescue them. There are Zionists whose consciences are troubled by the events of 1948, which created a moral ambiguity at the heart of Israel's existence.[8] Ben-Gurion's most recent biographer records that until the end of his life he was, in private, haunted by the Palestinian exodus.[9] Other Zionists effectively shrug their shoulders and say, *'C'est la guerre.'*

The bride was bought and sold—by Crusader knights and Ottoman pashas, by the pilgrims and predators of the nineteenth century, and by British imperialists and Zionist settlers in the twentieth. She was abused by those who sold her and those who bought her. During the three decades of British rule, the Palestinian Arabs consistently voiced their demand for independence and sovereignty. Equally consistently, their rights were denied.[10]

Notes

Chapter 1

1   I am grateful to the Palestine Exploration Fund for making available the full record of the meeting. For the work of the fund, and much else, I have drawn on Naomi Shepherd, *The Zealous Intruders: The Western Rediscovery of Palestine*, London: William Collins, 1987. (The archbishop was born 'Thompson' but decided to drop the 'p' as he thought this less plebeian: *Dictionary of National Biography*.)

2   Quoted in Shepherd, *The Zealous Intruders*, p. 107.

3   The statistics are taken from Alexander Schölch, *Palestine in Transformation, 1856-1882: Studies in Social, Economic, and Political Development*, tr. William C. Young and Michael C. Gerrity, Washington, DC: Institute for Palestine Studies, 1993; paperback edition, 2006, p. 284.

4   Bernard Wasserstein, *Divided Jerusalem: The Struggle for the Holy City*, London: Profile, 2001. A valuable account of the nineteenth-century background can be found in Gudrun Krämer, *A History of Palestine: From the Ottoman Conquest to the Establishment of the State of Israel*, tr. Graham Harman and Gudrun Krämer, Princeton: Princeton University Press, 2008; paperback edition, 2011.

5   Wasserstein, *Divided Jerusalem*, p. 14.

6   Elizabeth Anne Finn, *Reminiscences of Mrs Finn*, London: Marshall, Morgan and Scott, 1929, p. 246.

7   Quoted in Shepherd, *The Zealous Intruders*, p. 109. The governor was speaking to the French poet Gérard de Nerval.

8   Schölch, *Palestine in Transformation*, pp. 91-92.

9   *Illustrated Christian Weekly*, New York, 29 April 1871, quoted in Sue Rainey, 'Illustration

"Urgently Required": The *Picturesque Palestine* Project, 1878-1883', *Prospects*, New York, Vol. 30, October 2005.

10 Mahmoud Yazbak, 'Templers as Proto-Zionists? The "German Colony" in Late Ottoman Haifa', *Journal of Palestine Studies*, Vol. 28, No. 4, summer 1999.

11 Shepherd, *The Zealous Intruders*, pp. 175-177.

12 See the informative chapter on *The Land and the Book* in Heleen Murre-van den Berg, *New Faith in Ancient Lands*, Leiden: Brill, 2007. Thomson's work was published in many different editions; for quotations I have used the one-volume edition of Thomas Nelson, London, 1872: bananas (p. 111), tax gatherers (p. 320).

13 For Bonfils and Orientalism, see Yeshayahu Nir, *The Bible and the Image: The History of Photography in the Holy Land, 1839-1899*, Philadelphia: University of Pennsylvania Press, 1985, pp. 141-160. Also useful is Ritchie Thomas, 'Bonfils and Son, Egypt, Greece, and the Levant, 1867-1894', *History of Photography*, Vol. 3, No. 1, January 1979.

14 Stephen Sheehi, *The Arab Imago: A Social History of Portrait Photography, 1860-1910*, Princeton: Princeton University Press, 2016, p. 9.

15 See Nir, *The Bible and the Image*. For Abdul-Hamid's fascination with photography, see Sheehi, *The Arab Imago*; and for details of his collection, Muhammad Isa Waley, 'Images of the Ottoman Empire: The Photograph Albums Presented by Sultan Abdülhamid II', *British Library Journal*, autumn 1991; and William Allen, 'The Abdul Hamid II Collection', *History of Photography*, Vol. 8, No. 2, April-June 1984.

16 Quoted in Shepherd, *The Zealous Intruders*, p. 127.

17 Charles Warren, *Underground Jerusalem*, London: Richard Bentley, 1876, p. 82. Later in life, as London's police chief, Warren was involved in the hunt for Jack the Ripper.

18 Mia Gröndahl, *The Dream of Jerusalem: Lewis Larsson and the American Colony Photographers*, Stockholm: Journal, 2005, p. 50; a richly illustrated volume which restores Larsson to his rightful place as the colony's foremost photographer.

19 Jane Fletcher Geniesse, *American Priestess: The Extraordinary Story of Anna Spafford and the American Colony in Jerusalem*, New York: Doubleday, 2008, p. 148;

and Gröndahl, *The Dream of Jerusalem*, p. 46.

20 On the life and work of the American Colony, in addition to the two sources mentioned above, I have drawn on Odd Karsten Tveit, *Anna's House: The American Colony in Jerusalem*, tr. Peter Scott-Hansen, Nicosia: Rimal Publications, 2011, and, for the Spaffords' own vivid but self-serving account, Bertha Spafford Vester, *Our Jerusalem: An American Family in the Holy City*, New York: Doubleday, 1950.
For the religious beliefs of the Spaffords, see Yaakov Ariel and Ruth Kark, 'Messianism, Holiness, Charisma, and Community: The American-Swedish Colony in Jerusalem, 1881-1933', *Church History*, Vol. 65, No. 4, December 1996.

21 Joan Haslip, *The Sultan: The Life of Abdul Hamid*, London: Cassell, 1958, pp. 234-250. The most recent biography is Francis Georgeon, *Abdülhamid II: Le sultan calife*, Paris: Fayard, 2003.

22 Derek Hopwood, *The Russian Presence in Syria and Palestine, 1843-1914*, Oxford: Clarendon Press, 1969, pp. 9, 51.

23 Stephen Graham, *With the Russian Pilgrims to Jerusalem*, London: Thomas Nelson, 1913, p. 17. The book—which has been reprinted many times—was Graham's first popular success. Part of its appeal lay in its thirty-eight black-and-white photographs, taken with a simple Kodak camera. The author's subsequent efforts to justify the attitudes of the Russian Orthodox Church led to accusations of anti-Semitism. Michael Hughes, *Beyond Holy Russia: The Life and Times of Stephen Graham*, Cambridge: Open Book Publishers, 2014, pp. 99-100.

24 Graham, *With the Russian Pilgrims*, p. 16.

25 Graham, p. 13.

26 Graham, pp. 12-13.

27 Graham, pp. 84-85.

28 Tom Segev, *A State at Any Cost: The Life of David Ben-Gurion*, tr. Haim Watzman, New York: Farrar, Straus and Giroux, 2019, pp. 21ff and 55ff.

29 Segev, p. 58.

30 Noah Lucas, *The Modern History of Israel*, London: Weidenfeld and Nicolson, 1974, p. 58.

31 Theodor Herzl, *The Jewish State: An Attempt at a Modern Solution of the Jewish Question*, tr. Sylvie d'Avigdor, London: Henry Pordes, 1972, p. 15.

32 Lucas, *The Modern History of Israel*, p. 44.

33 Mitri Raheb (ed.), *Tawfiq Canaan: An Autobiography*, Bethlehem: Diyar Publisher, 2020, pp. 31ff.

34 Raheb (ed.), *Tawfiq Canaan: An Autobiography*, pp. 45ff.

35 See Rashid Khalidi, *Palestinian Identity: The Construction of Modern National Consciousness*, New York: Columbia University Press, 1997; and Neville J. Mandel, *The Arabs and Zionism before World War I*, Berkeley: University of California Press, 1976.

36 Philippe Bourmaud, '"A Son of the Country": Dr Tawfiq Canaan, Modernist Physician and Palestinian Ethnographer', in Mark LeVine and Gershon Shafir (eds.), *Struggle and Survival in Palestine/Israel*, Berkeley: University of California Press, 2012.

37 Nir, *The Bible and the Image*, p. 4.

38 *National Geographic*, Vol. 25, No. 3, March 1914. The 65-page essay is entitled 'Village Life in the Holy Land', with photographs by Lewis Larsson and text by his American colleague John D. Whiting.

39 Eugene Rogan, *The Fall of the Ottomans: The Great War in the Middle East*, London: Allen Lane, 2015, p. 24.

40 Salim Tamari, *Year of the Locust: A Soldier's Diary and the Erasure of Palestine's Ottoman Past*, Berkeley: University of California Press, 2011; paperback edition, 2015.

41 Vester, *Our Jerusalem*, pp. 240-243.

42 Gröndahl, *Dream of Jerusalem*, pp. 222ff.

43 Raheb (ed.), *Tawfiq Canaan: An Autobiography*, pp. 72ff.

44 Tamari, *Year of the Locust*, p. 56.

Chapter 2

1 Bertha Spafford Vester, *Our Jerusalem: An American Family in the Holy City*, New York: Doubleday, 1950, pp. 277-278.

2 Vester, p. 280.

3 Chaim Weizmann, *Trial and Error*, London: Hamish Hamilton, 1949, p. 207. Motelle is the Yiddish form of Motol, a town in what is today Belarus.

4 Ronald Storrs, *Orientations*, London: Ivor Nicholson & Watson, 1937, p. 487.

5   Simon Sebag Montefiore, *Jerusalem: The Biography*, London: Weidenfeld and Nicolson, 2011, p. 410, which quotes the full exchange between them.

6   The argument is made by Tom Segev, *One Palestine, Complete: Jews and Arabs under the British Mandate*, tr. Haim Watzman, New York: Henry Holt, 2000; paperback edition, 2001, pp. 40, 43; and by Naomi Shepherd, *Ploughing Sand: British Rule in Palestine, 1917-1948*, London: John Murray, 1999; paperback edition, 1999, pp. 10ff.

7   Elizabeth Monroe, *Britain's Moment in the Middle East*, London: Chatto & Windus, 1963, p. 43.

8   Emphasis added. For the text of the first draft, see footnote 9, below. For Weizmann's reaction, see *Trial and Error*, p. 260.

9   Weizmann, *Trial and Error*, p. 262. For an analysis of the two drafts, quoted in full, see John Marlowe, *The Seat of Pilate: An Account of the Palestine Mandate*, London: Cresset Press, 1959, p. 26.

10   Weizmann, *Trial and Error*, p. 302.

11   For the story of the prolonged post-war haggling, and its outcome, see Margaret MacMillan, *Peacemakers: The Paris Peace Conference of 1919 and Its Attempt to End War*, London: John Murray, 2001.

12   Storrs, *Orientations*, p. 335.

13   Storrs, p. 516.

14   Roberto Mazza, 'The Preservation and Safeguarding of the Amenities of the Holy City without Favour or Prejudice to Race or Creed: The Pro-Jerusalem Society and Ronald Storrs, 1917-1926', in Angelos Dalachanis and Vincent Lemire (eds.), *Ordinary Jerusalem, 1840-1940: Opening New Archives, Revisiting a Global City*, Leiden: Brill, 2018. Mazza argues that, while proclaiming a non-sectarian intent, Storrs achieved precisely the opposite, turning a mixed, cosmopolitan city into a divided one.

15   Storrs, p. 394.

16   Bernard Wasserstein, *The British in Palestine: The Mandatory Government and the Arab-Jewish Conflict, 1917-1929*, London: Royal Historical Society, 1978, Ch. 4.

17   Jennifer Glynn (ed.), *Tidings from Zion: Helen Bentwich's Letters from Jerusalem, 1919-1931*, London: I. B. Tauris, 2000, p. 50.

18 Ofer Aderet, 'This Founding Father of the Jewish State was a Serial Cheater Who Hated Israel', *Ha'aretz*, 12 September 2020. The article quotes Motti Golani, co-author of a new Hebrew-language biography of Weizmann: 'He was ready to lay down his life for the country—but to live [there] was a different matter.'

19 Storrs, *Orientations*, p. 394.

20 Glynn (ed.), *Tidings from Zion*, p. 11. For the story of Annie Landau, see Laura S. Schor, *The Best School in Jerusalem: Annie Landau's School for Girls, 1900-1960*, Waltham, Mass.: Brandeis University Press, 2013.

21 Tom Segev, *A State at Any Cost: The Life of David Ben-Gurion*, tr. Haim Watzman, New York: Farrar, Straus and Giroux, 2019, p. 182.

22 Wasserstein, *The British in Palestine*, p. 91.

23 Ari Shavit, *My Promised Land: The Triumph and Tragedy of Israel*, Melbourne and London: Scribe, 2014; paperback edition, 2015, pp. 29ff. Shavit, an Israeli journalist, is Norman Bentwich's grandson.

24 Storrs, *Orientations*, p. 500.

25 *Tidings from Zion*, p. 105.

26 Ruth Oren, 'Zionist Photography, 1910-41: Constructing a Landscape', *History of Photography*, Vol. 19, No. 3, Autumn 1995. For portraits of the early Jewish photographers, and impressive examples of their work, see Vivienne Silver-Brody, *Documentors of the Dream: Pioneer Jewish Photographers in the Land of Israel, 1890-1933*, Jerusalem: Magnes Press, 1998.

27 Segev, *A State at Any Cost*, p. 158. On Zionist attitudes to the Arabs, see Noah Lucas, *The Modern History of Israel*, pp. 142-143.

28 Wasserstein, *The British in Palestine*, pp. 103ff.

29 Weizmann, *Trial and Error*, p. 361.

30 Fadwa Tuqan, *A Mountainous Journey: A Poet's Autobiography*, tr. Olive Kenny, Saint Paul, Minnesota: Graywolf Press, 1990, pp. 1-16.

31 Quoted in Roger Owen (ed.), *Studies in the Economic and Social History of Palestine in the Nineteenth and Twentieth Centuries*, London: Macmillan, 1982, pp. 48-49.

32 Tuqan, *A Mountainous Journey*, pp. 51, 71, 78.

33 Quoted in Benjamin Hyman, 'British Planners in Palestine, 1918-1936', PhD thesis, London School of Economics, 1994, p. 362. Hyman examines in detail the work of five town planners, including Clifford Holliday.

34 I am grateful to Sarah Holliday, Eunice's grand-daughter, for allowing me to read and quote from Eunice's original letters. For her published comments on Ashbee and the Pro-Jerusalem Society, see Eunice Holliday, *Letters from Jerusalem: During the Palestine Mandate*, ed. John Holliday, London: Radcliffe Press, 1997, p. 12.

35 Holliday, *Letters from Jerusalem*, p. 16.

36 Holliday, p. 20.

37 From the author's correspondence with Tim Holliday in 2018, in what turned out to be the last months of his life.

38 Richard Cork, *David Bomberg*, New Haven: Yale University Press, 1987, p. 146.

39 Holliday, *Letters from Jerusalem*, pp. 39-40.

40 Cork, *David Bomberg*, p. 154.

41 Storrs, *Orientations*, p. 495.

42 John Marlowe, *Rebellion in Palestine*, London: Cresset Press, 1946, p. 74.

43 *Palestine Civil Service List*, Jerusalem, 1931. The list was published annually. I am grateful to Debbie Usher, archivist at the Middle East Centre, Oxford, for making several volumes of the list available to me. Hajj Amin's date of birth is uncertain but seems to have been either 1893 or 1895. For the life of this controversial figure, see Philip Mattar, *The Mufti of Jerusalem*, New York: Columbia University Press, 1988.

44 Wasserstein, *The British in Palestine*, p. 129.

45 *Tidings from Zion*, p. 67.

46 Geoffrey Furlonge, *Palestine is My Country: The Story of Musa Alami*, London: John Murray, 1969; and Wasserstein, *The British in Palestine*, pp. 190ff.

47 Jane Fletcher Geniesse, *American Priestess: The Extraordinary Story of Anna Spafford and the American Colony in Jerusalem*, New York: Doubleday, 2008, pp. 274ff.

48 Vester, *Our Jerusalem*, p. 297.

49 Philippe Bourmaud, '"A Son of the Country": Dr Tawfiq Canaan, Modernist Physician and Palestinian Ethnographer', in Mark LeVine

and Gershon Shafir (eds.), *Struggle and Survival in Palestine/ Israel*, Berkeley: University of California Press, 2012.

50 Jabra I. Jabra, *The First Well: A Bethlehem Boyhood*, tr. Issa J. Boullata, Arkansas: University of Arkansas Press, 1995; paperback edition, London: Hesperus Press, 2012, pp. 3-4, 27-28, 47.

51 Jabra, *The First Well*, p. 17.

52 Storrs, *Orientations*, p. 507.

53 Marlowe, *The Seat of Pilate*, p. 3.

54 *Tidings from Zion*, p. 133.

55 Vester, *Our Jerusalem*, p. 319.

56 *Tidings from Zion*, p. 136.

57 *Tidings from Zion*, p. 145, and Shavit, *My Promised Land*, pp. 44-47.

58 Jabra, *The First Well*, p. 85.

59 *Tidings from Zion*, p. 156.

60 *Tidings from Zion*, p. 171.

61 Holliday, *Letters from Jerusalem*, p. 101.

62 Holliday, pp. 101-102.

63 *Tidings from Zion*, p. 177. The Hebron massacre is described in graphic detail in Tom Segev, *One Palestine, Complete*, Chapter 14.

64 Flora Moody, letters of 30 August and 1 September 1929; Moody Papers, Rhodes House, Oxford. I am grateful to Judith David for granting me permission to quote from her mother's letters. An account of events in Safad (often spelt Safed) by Mrs Semple appeared in the *Glasgow Herald* on 14 September 1929, under the headline 'Reign of Terror in Safed: Victims Seek Sanctuary in Scots College' (accessed online).

65 Holliday, p. 105.

66 Holliday, p. 96.

67 Hillel Cohen, *Year Zero of the Arab-Israeli Conflict: 1929*, tr. Haim Watzman, Waltham, Massachusetts: Brandeis University Press, 2015.

Chapter 3

1 Elizabeth Monroe, 'The Origins of the Palestine Problem', in Peter Mansfield (ed.), *The Middle East: A Political and Economic Survey*, Oxford; Oxford University Press, 1973, pp. 56-57.

2 Bernard Wasserstein, *The British in Palestine: The Mandatory Government and the Arab-Jewish Conflict, 1917-1929*, London: Royal Historical Society, 1978, pp. 214-215.

3   Jane Fletcher Geniesse, *American Priestess: The Extraordinary Story of Anna Spafford and the American Colony in Jerusalem*, New York: Doubleday, 2008, p. 301.

4   Eunice Holliday, *Letters from Jerusalem*, ed. John Holliday, London: Radcliffe Press, 1997, p. 123.

5   Holliday, *Letters*, p. 123. The story of the Scottish church is told in Walter T. Dunlop, *Faith Rewarded: The Story of St Andrew's Scots Memorial, Jerusalem*, Peterborough: Fastprint Publishing, 2014.

6   Tim Holliday, 'Memories of Palestine', an unpublished essay on his childhood in the 1930s in Palestine. (The essay is undated but seems to have been written in the 1990s.) I am grateful to members of the Holliday family who put me in touch with Tim, with whom I corresponded until his death in 2019.

7   *Dictionary of National Biography*, citing private information.

8   E. C. Hodgkin in the introduction to his brother's letters: Thomas Hodgkin, *Letters from Palestine, 1932-36*, London: Quartet, 1986, p. xvi.

9   Norman and Helen Bentwich, *Mandate Memories*, London: Hogarth Press, 1965, p. 152.

10   Hodgkin, *Letters from Palestine*, p. 22. The film was the 1925 version of Ben Hur.

11   May Seikaly, *Haifa: Transformation of an Arab Society, 1918-1939*, London: I. B. Tauris, 1995; paperback edition, 2002, pp. 2ff.

12   Holliday, *Letters*, pp. 159-160.

13   The translation is from an unpublished anthology of Palestinian poetry compiled and translated by Faris Glubb. Umayya is a reference to the Umayyads, a ruling dynasty during the heyday of the Arab empire.

14   Fadwa Tuqan, *A Mountainous Journey: A Poet's Autobiography*, tr. Olive Kenny, Saint Paul, Minnesota: Greywolf Press, 1990, p.78.

15   Jabra Ibrahim Jabra, *The First Well: A Bethlehem Boyhood*, tr. Issa J. Boullata, Arkansas: University of Arkansas Press, 1995; paperback edition, London: Hesperus Press, 2012, p. 180.

16   Isaiah Berlin, *Flourishing: Letters 1928-1946*, ed. Henry Hardy, London: Chatto & Windus, 2004; paperback edition, London: Pimlico, 2005, pp. 105-106.

17   Thomas Hodgkin, 'Antonius,

Palestine, and the 1930s', a lecture delivered at the Middle East Centre, Oxford, in June 1981, and first published in *Gazelle Review*, No. 10, London: Ithaca Press, 1982. The officials' names are not pseudonyms: John Patrick Domvile, for example, was indeed a senior intelligence official. See Matthew Hughes, *Britain's Pacification of Palestine: The British Army, the Colonial State, and the Arab Revolt, 1936-1939*, Cambridge: Cambridge University Press, 2019, p. 406.

For the life and work of Antonius, see Susan Silsby Boyle, *Betrayal of Palestine: The Story of George Antonius*, Boulder, Colorado: Westview Press, 2001, and Albert Hourani's essay, '*The Arab Awakening* Forty Years After', in his book *The Emergence of the Modern Middle East*, London: Macmillan, 1981.

18 Andrea L. Stanton, *This is Jerusalem Calling: State Radio in Mandate Palestine*, Austin, Texas: University of Texas Press, 2013, p. 20.

19 This section is based on Yehuda Koren and Eilat Negev, *Lover of Unreason: Assia Wevill, Sylvia Plath's Rival and Ted Hughes's Doomed Love*, New York: Carroll & Graf, 2007, pp. 1-19, which reconstructs Assia's remarkable life. (Wevill was her married name.)

20 Laura Francis, 'Ornament is Crime: The White City of Tel Aviv', *Port*, 25 November 2017; www.port-magazine.com/architecture/ornament-is-crime-the-white-city-of-tel-aviv.

21 For a fuller picture of German immigration to Palestine, see Claudia Sonino, *German Jews in Palestine, 1920-1948: Between Dream and Reality*, Lanham: Lexington Books, 2016, and Thomas Sparr, *German Jerusalem: The Remarkable Life of a German-Jewish Neighbourhood in the Holy City*, tr. Stephen Brown, London: Haus Publishing, 2021.

22 Koren and Negev, *Lover of Unreason*, pp. 19ff.

23 Ruth Oren and Guy Raz, *Zoltan Kluger, Chief Photographer, 1933-1958*, Tel Aviv: Eretz Israel Museum, 2008, p. 44. I am grateful to Ruth Oren for making the catalogue available to me.

24 Sylva M. Gelber, *No Balm in Gilead: A Personal Retrospective of Mandate Days in Palestine*, Ottawa: Carleton University Press, 1989, p. 90.

25 *Time*, 4 January 1937.

26 *Palestine Post*, 19 May 1937.

27 Barbara Board, *Newsgirl in Palestine*, London: Michael Joseph, 1937, pp. 194-195.

28 John Marlowe, *The Seat of Pilate: An Account of the Palestine Mandate*, London: Cresset Press, 1959, p. 152.

29 Geoffrey Furlonge, *Palestine is My Country: The Story of Musa Alami*, London: John Murray, 1969, pp. 111-113, and Wasserstein, *The British in Palestine*, pp. 190ff.

30 Hughes, *Britain's Pacification of Palestine*, pp. 173ff.

31 Hughes, pp. 330ff.

32 Hughes, pp. 281ff.

33 John Marlowe, *Rebellion in Palestine*, London: Cresset Press, 1946, p. 254.

34 George Antonius, *The Arab Awakening: The Story of the Arab National Movement*, London: Hamish Hamilton, 1938; paperback edition, New York: Capricorn Books, 1965, pp. 405-411. (Italy and Germany did indeed support the rebellion with funds and propaganda, but there is little reason to believe that their help made much difference.)

35 Hilda Wilson papers, Middle East Centre Archive, St Antony's College, Oxford. Her account of the school year 1938-39 is a text of over 30,000 words which publishers rejected because of its description of the behaviour of British soldiers. Further extracts can be found in Derek Hopwood, *Tales of Empire: The British in the Middle East, 1880-1952*, London: I. B. Tauris, 1989.

For information about her, I am grateful to St Hugh's College, Oxford, where she studied, and to the Quakers of Barnstaple, Devon, who shared their memories of this independent-minded woman in her later years. The Palestinian school where she taught is today Birzeit University.

36 The estimates are those of Matthew Hughes, who believes the toll was higher than previously thought: see Hughes, *Britain's Pacification of Palestine*, pp. 376ff. He records that fewer than 300 British soldiers and police were killed, a low figure given that at the height of the revolt 30,000 troops, one-sixth of the British army's total strength worldwide, were deployed in a territory the size of Wales.

Chapter 4

1   Mitri Raheb (ed.), *Tawfiq Canaan: An Autobiography*, Bethlehem: Diyar Publisher, 2020, pp. 113ff.

2   Nicholas Bethell, *The Palestine Triangle: The Struggle between the British, the Jews and the Arabs, 1935-1948*, London: André Deutsch, 1979; paperback edition, London: Futura Publications, 1980, pp. 79-80. Moshe Dayan, *Story of My Life*, London: Weidenfeld and Nicolson, 1976, pp. 31ff.

3   Bethell, *The Palestine Triangle*, pp. 89-90.

4   For more on the immigrant ships, see Bethell, *The Palestine Triangle*, and Christopher Sykes, *Crossroads to Israel*, London: William Collins, 1965.

5   A. J. Sherman, *Mandate Days: British Lives in Palestine, 1918-1948*, London: Thames & Hudson, 1997, p. 129.

6   Bethell, *The Palestine Triangle*, p. 95.

7   Sherman, *Mandate Days*, p. 131.

8   Yehuda Koren and Eilat Negev, *Lover of Unreason: Assia Wevill, Sylvia Plath's Rival and Ted Hughes's Doomed Love*, New York: Carroll & Graf, 2007, pp. 19-20.

9   *Lover of Unreason*, pp. 20-22.

10 Mustafa Abbasi, 'Palestinians Fighting against Nazis: The Story of Palestinian Volunteers in the Second World War', *War in History*, 2019, Vol. 26, No. 2.

11 Daphna Sharfman, *Palestine in the Second World War: Strategic Plans and Political Dilemmas*, Brighton: Sussex Academic Press, 2015.

12 Barbara Board, *Reporting from Palestine, 1943-1944*, ed. Jacqueline Karp, Nottingham: Five Leaves Publications, 2007, p. 193.

13 Abbasi, 'Palestinians Fighting against Nazis', gives higher estimates.

14 Laura S. Schor, *Sophie Halaby in Jerusalem: An Artist's Life*, Syracuse, NY: Syracuse University Press, 2019, pp. 25-30.

15 Schor, *Sophie Halaby*; and Ellen L. Fleischmann, *The Nation and Its 'New' Women: The Palestinian Women's Movement, 1920-1948*, Berkeley: University of California Press, 2003, p. 193.

16 John Connell, *The House by Herod's Gate*, London: Sampson Low, Marston, 1947, pp.

11ff. (John Connell was Jack Robertson's pen-name.)

17 Bickham Sweet-Escott, *Baker Street Irregular*, London: Methuen, 1965, a memoir by a former banker who worked for SOE in the Balkans and the Middle East. For a detailed account of what can be gleaned from official papers and other sources, see Saul Kelly, 'A Succession of Crises: SOE in the Middle East, 1940-45', *Intelligence and National Security*, March 2005, Vol. 20, No. 1.

18 Connell, *The House by Herod's Gate*, pp. 97-109.

19 Connell, pp. 51, 62.

20 The story is told in Robin Bryer, *Jack: A Literary Biography of John Connell (John Henry Robertson, 1909-1965)*, Milton Keynes: Author House, 2010.

21 M. R. D. Foot, *SOE: The Special Operations Executive*, London: British Broadcasting Corporation, 1984, pp. 1-19, 30; and Bethell, *The Palestine Triangle*, p. 102.

22 Quoted in Bethell, p. 122.

23 Anita Shapira, *Yigal Allon: Native Son*, tr. Evelyn Abel, Philadelphia: University of Pennsylvania Press, 2008, pp. 120-121. The incident was

in late 1942. Allon and his colleagues insisted they were answerable to the Haganah, not to the British.

24 Philip Mattar, *The Mufti of Jerusalem: Al-Hajj Amin al-Husayni and the Palestinian National Movement*, New York: Columbia University Press, 1988, pp. 86ff.

25 Bethell, *The Palestine Triangle*, p. 134; Sharfman, *Palestine in the Second World War*, pp. 24-25.

26 Connell, *The House by Herod's Gate*, pp. 180-182.

27 Kelly, 'A Succession of Crises', p. 133 (see footnote 17); cf. Bethell, p. 139.

28 Norman Dannatt, 'The War (I Did It My Way)', an illustrated memoir published at www.memoriesofwar.org.uk.

29 Dannatt, p. 35.

30 Adam LeBor, *City of Oranges: An Intimate History of Arabs and Jews in Jaffa*, London: Bloomsbury, 2006; 2nd edition, London: Head of Zeus, 2017, p. 83.

31 Sharfman, *Palestine in the Second World War*, pp. 44-45.

32 Fleischmann, *The Nation and Its 'New' Women*, pp. 196-198.

33 Sylva M. Gelber, *No Balm in Gilead: A Personal Retrospective of Mandate Days in Palestine*, Ottawa: Carleton University Press, 1989.

34 Schor, *Sophie Halaby*; Jabra I. Jabra, *Princesses' Street: Baghdad Memories*, tr. Issa J. Boullata, Fayetteville: University of Arkansas Press, 2005; and Kamal Boullata, *Palestinian Art, 1850-2005*, London and Beirut: Saqi Books, 2009.

35 Walid Khalidi, 'On Albert Hourani, the Arab Office, and the Anglo-American Committee of 1946', *Journal of Palestine Studies*, Vol. 35, No. 1, autumn 2005, p. 61.

36 Quoted in Hadara Lazar, *Out of Palestine: The Making of Modern Israel*, New York: Atlas, 2011, p. 96. (Among her other interviewees is Wolfgang Hildesheimer.)

37 Board, *Reporting from Palestine*, pp. 85-86.

38 Board, pp. 101-103.

39 Bethell, *The Palestine Triangle*, pp. 148-151, and Gavriel Cohen, 'Harold MacMichael and Palestine's Future', *Studies in Zionism*, 1981, Vol. 2, No. 1.

40 Bethell, pp. 127-129.

41 His words, often misquoted, are recorded in Hansard, 17 November 1944.

42 Bethell, pp. 181-199.

43 Bethell, pp. 189-191; Cohen, 'Harold MacMichael'.

44 Bethell, pp. 199-200.

45 Gelber, *No Balm in Gilead*, p. 195.

Chapter 5

1 Chris Wrigley, 'Ernest Bevin, 1881-1951', *Dictionary of National Biography*, 2008; accessed online.

2 Edward Hodgkin, 'Sharq al-Adna', p. 1. This forty-one-page chapter is part of an unpublished memoir written for his family. I'm grateful to his daughter Joanna for access to the manuscript and permission to quote from it.

3 Hodgkin, pp. 15, 35.

4 Hansard, 13 November 1945.

5 Barbara Board, *This Land is Mine*, an unpublished account of her experiences in Palestine in 1945-46. I am grateful to her daughter, Jacqueline Karp-Gendre, for making the manuscript available to me and allowing me to quote from it.

The fullest account of Board's life and work is Jacqueline Karp, 'Editing My Mother: The Journalist Barbara Board', Seattle, Washington: *Bridges*, Vol. 13, No. 1, 2008.

This was not the only occasion in November 1945 when the British army used live fire on protesters. A series of incidents led to thirteen Jewish fatalities. See Giora Goodman, '"Troops Were Then Forced To Fire": British Army Crowd Control in Palestine, November 1945', *Small Wars & Insurgencies*, Vol. 26, No. 2, 2015.

6   The committee's work and the tensions it produced between London and Washington are described in detail in Wm. Roger Louis, *The British Empire in the Middle East, 1945-1951*, Oxford: Oxford University Press, 1984, pp. 397ff.

7   Walid Khalidi, 'On Albert Hourani, the Arab Office, and the Anglo-American Committee of 1946', *Journal of Palestine Studies*, Vol. 35, No. 1, Autumn 2005.

8   Bernard Wasserstein, *The British in Palestine: The Mandatory Government and the Arab-Jewish Conflict, 1917-1929*, London: Royal Historical Society, 1978, p. 192.

9   Doris Mantoura Sherif, *My Family*, Montreux: privately printed, 2013. I'm grateful to Dr Fauzi Mantoura for lending me his aunt's memoir.

10   Daniella Ohad Smith, 'Hotel Design in British Mandate Palestine', *Journal of Israeli History*, Vol. 29, No. 1, March 2010.

11   Thurston Clarke, *By Blood and Fire: The Attack on the King David Hotel*, New York: G. P. Putnam's, 1981.

12   For an account of Monty's experiences in Palestine, in 1938 and then after the Second World War, see James Barker, 'Monty and the Mandate in Palestine', *History Today*, Vol. 59, No. 3, March 2009. For his bitter dispute with Cunningham, see Motti Golani, *Palestine between Politics and Terror, 1945-1947*, tr. Ralph Mandel, Waltham, Massachusetts: Brandeis University Press, 2013. Also valuable, as an overview of Cunningham's time in office, is Wm. Roger Louis, 'Sir Alan Cunningham and the End of British Rule in Palestine', *Journal of Imperial and Commonwealth History*, Vol. 16, No. 3, 1972.

13   Golani, *Palestine between Politics and Terror*, pp. 64ff.

14   Nicholas Bethell, *The Palestine*

Triangle: The Struggle between the British, the Jews, and the Arabs, 1935-48, London: André Deutsch, 1979; paperback edition, London: Futura Publications, 1980, p. 251.

15 Clarke, *By Blood and Fire*, pp. 170ff.

16 Clarke, p. 221.

17 Clarke, pp. 244-245.

18 Clarke, p. 252.

19 Gregory Blaxland, *The Regiments Depart: A History of the British Army, 1945-1970*, London: William Kimber, 1971, p. 44.

20 Clarke, p. 251, and Bethell, pp. 269-271.

21 Sylva M. Gelber, *No Balm in Gilead: A Personal Retrospective of Mandate Days in Palestine*, Ottawa: Carleton University Press, 1989, p. 221.

22 Golani, *Palestine between Politics and Terror*, pp. 193-196.

23 Wm. Roger Louis and Robert W. Stookey (eds.), *The End of the Palestine Mandate*, London: I. B. Tauris, 1985, pp. 19-20.

24 Bethell, *The Palestine Triangle*, pp. 269-271.

25 Zipporah Porath, *Letters from Jerusalem, 1947-1948*, Jerusalem: Association of Americans and Canadians in Israel, 1987, p. 68. (Porath was her married name.)

26 Porath, pp. 76-77, 123.

27 Gelber, *No Balm in Gilead*, pp. 272-277. For a graphic account of the attack on the Semiramis Hotel, see Larry Collins and Dominique Lapierre, *O Jerusalem!*, London: Weidenfeld and Nicolson, 1972; paperback edition, London: Pan, 1973, pp. 110-115.

28 Monica Wilson (née Dehn), in a letter from Jerusalem to her parents in London. Wilson papers, Middle East Centre Archive, St Antony's College, Oxford. (I have written more about Monica's experiences in Palestine in *The Poisoned Well: Empire and its Legacy in the Middle East*, London: Hurst, 2016; revised edition, 2018.)

29 On the role of British deserters, see Christopher Caden and Nir Arielli, 'British Army and Palestine Police Deserters and the Arab-Israeli War of 1948', *War In History*, Vol. 28, No. 1, January 2021.

30 Porath, *Letters from Jerusalem*, p. 162.

31 Adam LeBor, *City of Oranges: An Intimate History of Arabs and Jews*

in Jaffa, London: Bloomsbury, 2006; second edition, London: Head of Zeus, 2017, pp. 116ff. Hammami's own account, written in September 2015, can be found at https://memoriesofpalestine.com/portfolio/hasan-hammami/.

32 Richard Stubbs, *Palestine Story: A Personal Account of the Last Three Years of British Rule in Palestine*, Brettenham, Suffolk, privately printed, 1995.

33 Tuqan, *A Mountainous Journey*, p. 113.

34 Collins and Lapierre, *O Jerusalem!*, p. xvii.

35 Jon Kimche, *Seven Fallen Pillars*, *London*: Secker & Warburg, 1950, pp. 235-236.

36 Hazem Zaki Nusseibeh, who was working at the time for the Palestine Broadcasting Service, in a remark to the British historian Nigel Ashton. I am grateful to Professor Ashton for this information. For background, see Nusseibeh's memoir *Jerusalemites: A Living Memory*, Nicosia: Rimal Publications, 2009.

37 Sir Alec Kirkbride, *From the Wings: Amman Memoirs, 1947-1951*, London: Frank Cass, 1976, p. 28.

38 Benny Morris, *The Birth*

of the Palestinian Refugee Problem Revisited, Cambridge: Cambridge University Press, 2004, p. 35.

39 Morris, *The Birth of the Palestinian Refugee Problem Revisited*; and Ari Shavit, *My Promised Land*.

40 Morris, *The Birth of the Palestinian Refugee Problem Revisited*. Some of the documents Morris used were subsequently removed by defence ministry officials; Hagar Shezaf, 'Burying the Nakba', *Ha'aretz*, 5 July 2019.

41 Morris, p. 60.

42 Milton Viorst, *Reaching for the Olive Branch: UNRWA and Peace in the Middle East*, Washington, DC: Middle East Institute, 1989.

43 Musa Alami, 'The Lesson of Palestine', *Middle East Journal*, Vol. 3, No. 4, October 1949.

44 Kenneth W. Bilby, *New Star in the East*, New York: Doubleday, 1950, p. 80.

45 See Baruch Kimmerling and Joel S. Migdal, *The Palestinian People: A History*, Harvard: Harvard University Press, 2003, especially pp. 138-141.

46 Yeshayahu Nir, writing in the introduction to *Paul Goldman, Press Photographer, 1943-1961*, Tel Aviv: Eretz Israel Museum,

2004, p. 16 (the catalogue of an exhibition, with text in Hebrew and English).

47 Galia Gur Zeev, *Beno Rothenberg: Photographed and Reported, 1947-1957*, Tel Aviv: Eretz Israel Museum, 2007 (the catalogue of an exhibition, with text in Hebrew and English).

48 Many graphic photographs of 1948-1949 can be found in Ariella Azoulay, *From Palestine to Israel: A Photographic Record of Destruction and State Formation, 1947-1950*, tr. Charles S. Kamen, London: Pluto Press, 2011.

49 Shezaf, 'Burying the Nakba' (see note 40). For the visible and invisible legacies of the Nakba in post-1948 Israel, see Ofer Ashkenazi, 'Hidden in Plain Sight: The Nakba and the Legacy of the Israeli Historians' Debate', *Zeithistorische Forschungen/ Studies in Contemporary History*, 2019 (https:// zeithistorische-forschungen. de/3-2019/5796).

50 Rona Sela, 'Presence and Absence in "Abandoned" Palestinian Villages', *History of Photography*, Vol. 33, No. 1, 2009.

51 Esther Meir-Glitzenstein, 'Operation Magic Carpet: Constructing the Myth of the Magical Immigration of Yemenite Jews to Israel', *Israel Studies*, Vol. 16, No. 3, October 2011. For Israel's rapid demographic expansion after 1948—and the treatment of its Arab minority—see Tom Segev, *1949: The First Israelis*, New York: The Free Press, 1986.

Epilogue

1 Dina Matar, *What It Means to Be Palestinian: Stories of Palestinian Peoplehood*, London: I. B. Tauris, 2011, p. 10.

2 See Alexander Schölch, *Palestine in Transformation 1856-1882: Studies in Social, Economic, and Political Development*, tr. William C. Young and Michael C. Gerrity, Washington, DC: Institute for Palestine Studies, 1993; and other sources cited in Chapter One.

3 Tom Segev, *One Palestine Complete: Jews and Arabs under the British Mandate*, trs. Haim Watzman, New York: Henry Holt, 2000, pp. 150-153.

4 The White Paper of 1939 did envisage an independent, bi-national state with an Arab majority, although its constitutional terms were vague, suggesting that the Zionists would have a veto on the country's political

development. It was nevertheless as close as Britain ever came to acknowledging Palestinian Arab rights, and as such was denounced by the Zionists as an out-and-out betrayal of the Balfour Declaration. Whether its proposals could ever have been realised, given the lack of support for bi-nationalism on both sides, and the momentum Zionism had acquired by 1939, is moot.

5　Doreen Ingrams, *Palestine Papers: 1917-1922: Seeds of Conflict*, London: John Murray, 1972; paperback edition, London: Eland, 2009, pp. 61, 73.

6　John Marlowe, *The Seat of Pilate: An Account of the Palestine Mandate*, London: Cresset Press, 1959, p. 167.

7　Quoted in Margaret MacMillan, *Peacemakers: The Paris Peace Conference of 1919 and Its Attempt to End War*, London: John Murray, 2001; paperback edition, 2003, p. 423.

8　See, for example, Ari Shavit, *My Promised Land: The Triumph and Tragedy of Israel*, Melbourne and London: Scribe, 2014; paperback edition, 2015.

9　Tom Segev, *A State at Any Cost: The Life of David Ben-Gurion*, tr. Haim Watzman, New York: Farrar, Straus & Giroux, 2019, p. 450.

10　Seth Anziska, *Preventing Palestine: A Political History from Camp David to Oslo*, Princeton: Princeton University Press, 2018.

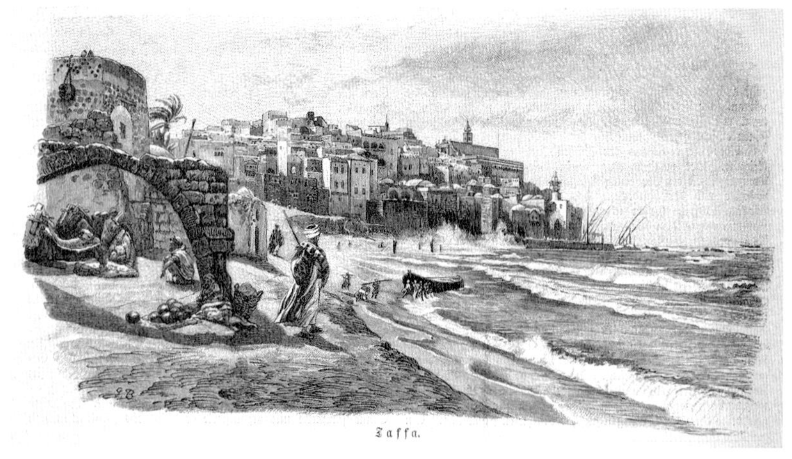

Jaffa, 1893   Gustav Bauernfeind

Select bibliography

Alshaer, Atef (ed.), *A Map of Absence: An Anthology of Palestinian Writing on the Nakba*, London: Saqi Books, 2019

Alterman, Nathan, *Little Tel Aviv*, tr. Yishai Tobin, Tel Aviv: Hakibbutz Hameuchad Publishing Company, 1981

Amichai, Yehuda, *Selected Poems*, tr. Assia Gutmann, London: Cape Goliard, 1968; Penguin, 1971

Anderson, Per-Olow, *They Are Human Too… A Photographic Essay on the Palestine Arab Refugees*, Chicago: Henry Regnery, 1957

Antonius, George, *The Arab Awakening: The Story of the Arab National Movement*, London: Hamish Hamilton, 1938

Arad, Shlomo, *Paul Goldman, Press Photographer, 1943-1961*, Tel Aviv: Eretz Israel Museum, 2004

Azoulay, Ariella, *From Palestine to Israel: A Photographic Record of Destruction and State Formation, 1947-1950*, tr. Charles S. Kamen, London: Pluto Press, 2011

Bentwich, Norman and Helen, *Mandate Memories: 1918-1948*, London: Hogarth Press, 1965

Berlin, Isaiah, *Flourishing: Letters, 1928-1946*, London: Pimlico, 2005

Bethell, Nicholas, *The Palestine Triangle: The Struggle between the British, the Jews, and the Arabs, 1935-1948*, London: André Deutsch, 1979

Black, Ian, *Enemies and Neighbours: Arabs and Jews in Palestine and Israel, 1917-2017*, London: Allen Lane, 2017

Board, Barbara, *Newsgirl in Palestine*, London: Michael Joseph, 1937

Board, Barbara, *Reporting from Palestine, 1943-1944*, ed. Jacqueline Karp, Nottingham: Five Leaves Publications, 2008

Boullata, Kamal, *Palestinian Art, 1850-2005*, London and Beirut: Saqi Books, 2009

Broadhurst, Joseph F., *From Vine Street to Jerusalem*, London: Stanley Paul, 1936

Bryer, Robin, *Jack: A Literary Biography of John Connell (John Henry Robertson, 1909-1965)*, Milton Keynes: Author House, 2010

Cesarani, David, *Major Farran's Hat: Murder, Scandal and Britain's War against Jewish Terrorism, 1945-1948*, London: Heinemann, 2009

Clarke, Thurston, *By Blood and Fire: The Attack on the King David Hotel*, New York: G. P. Putnam's, 1981

Cohen, Hillel, *Year Zero of the Arab-Israeli Conflict: 1929*, tr. Haim Watzman, Waltham, Massachusetts: Brandeis University Press, 2015

Collins, Larry, and Dominic Lapierre, *O Jerusalem!* New York: Simon & Schuster, 1972

Connell, John, *The House by Herod's Gate*, London: Sampson Low, Marston, 1947

Cork, Richard, *David Bomberg*, New Haven: Yale University Press, 1987

Darwish, Mahmoud, *Selected Poems*, introduced and translated by Ian Wedde and Fawwaz Tuqan, Cheadle, Cheshire: Carcanet Press, 1973

Dayan, Moshe, *Story of My Life*, London: Weidenfeld and Nicolson, 1976

Dunlop, Walter T., *Faith Rewarded: The Story of St Andrew's Scots Memorial, Jerusalem*, Peterborough: FastPrint Publishing, 2014

Elston, D. R., *No Alternative: Israel Observed*, London:

Hutchinson, 1960

Engle, Anita, *The Nili Spies*, London: Hogarth Press, 1959

Fieldhouse, D. K., *Western Imperialism in the Middle East, 1914-1958*, Oxford: Oxford University Press, 2006

Fergusson, Bernard, *The Trumpet in the Hall*, London: Collins, 1970

Fleischmann, Ellen L., *The Nation and Its 'New' Women: The Palestinian Women's Movement, 1920-1948*, Berkeley: University of California Press, 2003

Furlonge, Geoffrey, *Palestine is My Country: The Story of Musa Alami*, London: John Murray, 1969

Gelber, Sylva M., *No Balm in Gilead: A Personal Retrospective of Mandate Days in Palestine*, Ottawa: Carleton University Press, 1989

Geniesse, Jane Fletcher, *American Priestess: The Extraordinary Story of Anna Spafford and the American Colony in Jerusalem*, New York: Random House, 2008

Golani, Motti, *The End of the British Mandate for Palestine, 1948: The Diary of Sir Henry Gurney*, Basingstoke: Palgrave Macmillan, 2009

Golani, Motti, *Palestine between Politics and Terror, 1945-1947*, Waltham, Massachusetts: Brandeis University Press, 2013

Goren, Arthur A. (ed.), *Dissenter in Zion: From the Writings of Judah L. Magnes*, Cambridge, Massachusetts: Harvard University Press, 1982

Graham-Brown, Sarah, *Palestinians and Their Society, 1880-1946*, London: Quartet, 1980

Gröndahl, Mia, *The Dream of Jerusalem: Lewis Larsson and the American Colony Photographers*, Stockholm: Journal, 2005

Hazkani, Shay, *Dear Palestine: A Social History of the 1948 War*, Stanford: Stanford University Press, 2021

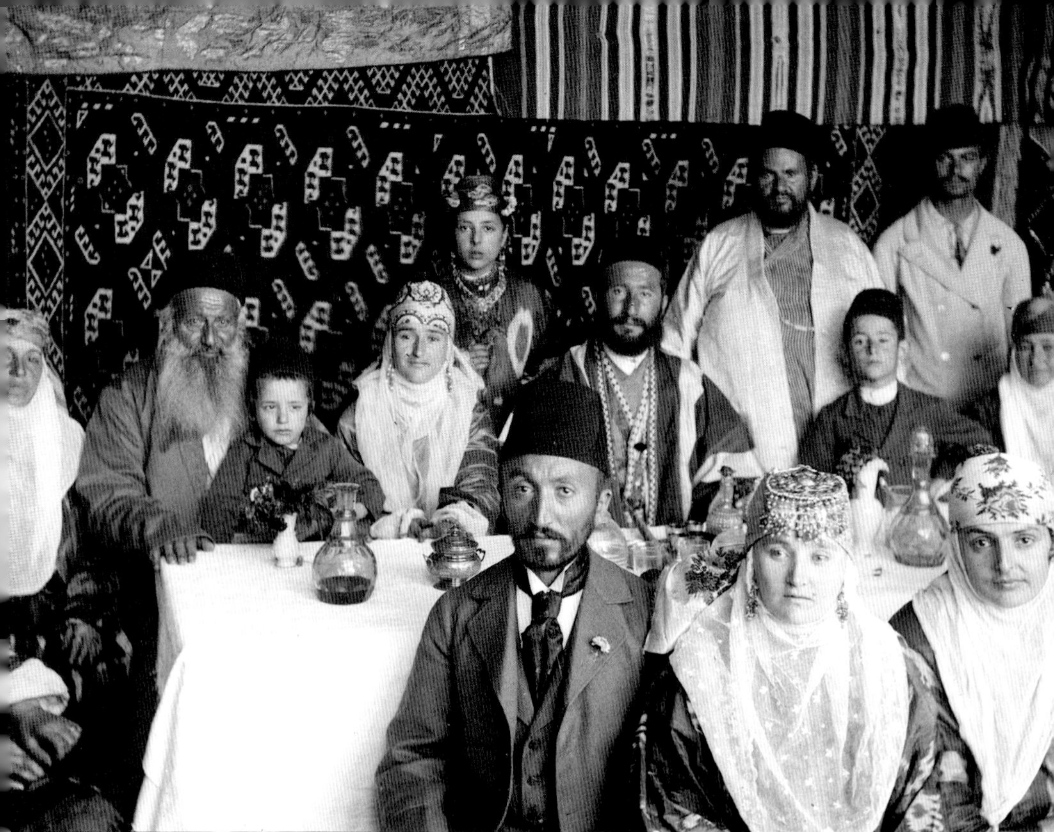

Jerusalem, early 1900s: Bukharan Jews celebrate the festival of Sukkot

Hertzberg, Arthur (ed.), *The Zionist Idea: A Historical Analysis and Reader*, New York: Atheneum, 1959

Hodgkin, Thomas, *Letters from Palestine, 1932-1936*, ed. E. C. Hodgkin, London: Quartet, 1986

Holliday, Eunice, *Letters from Jerusalem: During the Palestine Mandate*, ed. John Holliday, London: Radcliffe Press, 1997

Hopwood, Derek, *Tales of Empire: The British in the Middle East, 1880-1952*, London: I. B. Tauris, 1989

Hopwood, Derek, *The Russian Presence in Syria and Palestine, 1843-1914*, Oxford: Clarendon Press, 1969

Hourani, Albert, *A History of the Arab Peoples*, London: Faber, 1991

Hourani, Albert, *The Emergence of the Modern Middle East*, London: Macmillan, 1981

Hughes, Matthew, *Britain's Pacification of Palestine: The British Army, the Colonial State, and the Arab Revolt, 1936-1939*, Cambridge: Cambridge University Press, 2019

Ingrams, Doreen, *Palestine Papers, 1917-1922: Seeds of Conflict*, London: John Murray, 1972

Jabra, Jabra Ibrahim, *The First Well: A Bethlehem Boyhood*, tr. Issa J. Boullata, Arkansas: University of Arkansas Press, 1995

Jayyusi, Lena (ed.), *Jerusalem Interrupted: Modernity and Colonial Transformation, 1917-Present*, Northampton, Massachusetts: Olive Branch Press, 2015

Kanafani, Ghassan, *Palestine's Children*, tr. Barbara Harlow, London: Heinemann, 1984

Keith-Roach, Edward, *Pasha of Jerusalem: Memoirs of a District Commissioner underthe British Mandate*, London: Radcliffe Press, 1994

Khalidi, Anbara Salam, *Memoirs of an Early Arab Feminist*, tr. Tarif Khalidi, London: Pluto Press, 2013

Khalidi, Walid (ed.), *All That Remains: The Palestinian Villages Occupied and Depopulated by Israel in 1948*, Washington, DC: Institute for Palestine Studies, 1992

Khalidi, Walid, *Before Their Diaspora: A Photographic History of the Palestinians, 1876-1948*, Washington, DC: Institute for Palestine Studies, 1984

Khalidi, Walid (ed.), *From Haven to Conquest: Readings in Zionism and the Palestine Problem until 1948*, Washington, DC: Institute for Palestine Studies, 1971

Kirkbride, Sir Alec, *A Crackle of Thorns*, London: John Murray, 1956

Klein, Menachem, *Lives in Common: Arabs and Jews in Jerusalem, Jaffa, and Hebron*, tr. Haim Watzman, London: Hurst, 2014

Koren, Yehuda, and Eilat Negev, *Lover of Unreason: Assia Wevill, Sylvia Plath's Rival and Ted Hughes's Doomed Love*, New York: Carroll & Graf, 2007

Krämer, Gudrun, *A History of Palestine: From the Ottoman Conquest to the Founding of the State of Israel*, tr. Graham Harman and Gudrun Krämer, Princeton: Princeton University Press, 2008

Kurzman, Dan, *Genesis 1948: The First Arab-Israeli War*, London: Vallentine, Mitchell, 1970

Landau, Jacob, *Abdul-Hamid's Palestine*, London: André Deutsch, 1979

Larsson, Theo, *Seven Passports for Palestine*, Sutton, Sussex: Longfield, 1995

Lazar, Hadara, *Out of Palestine: The Making of Modern Israel*, New York: Atlas, 2011

LeBor, Adam, *City of Oranges: An Intimate History of Arabs and Jews in Jaffa*, London: Bloomsbury, 2006; second edition, London: Head of Zeus, 2017

Lees, G. Robinson, *Village Life in Palestine*, London: Longmans, Green, 1905

Lesch, Ann Mosely, *Arab Politics in Palestine, 1917-1939*, Ithaca: Cornell University Press, 1979

LeVine, Mark, and Gershon Shafir (eds.), *Struggle and Survival in Palestine/Israel*, Berkeley: University of California Press

Louis, Wm. Roger, *The British Empire in the Middle East, 1945-1951*, Oxford: Oxford University Press, 1984

Louis, Wm. Roger, and Robert W. Stookey (eds.), *The End of the Palestine Mandate*, London: I. B. Tauris, 1985

Louis, Wm. Roger, 'Sir Alan Cunningham and the End of British Rule in Palestine', *Journal of Imperial and*

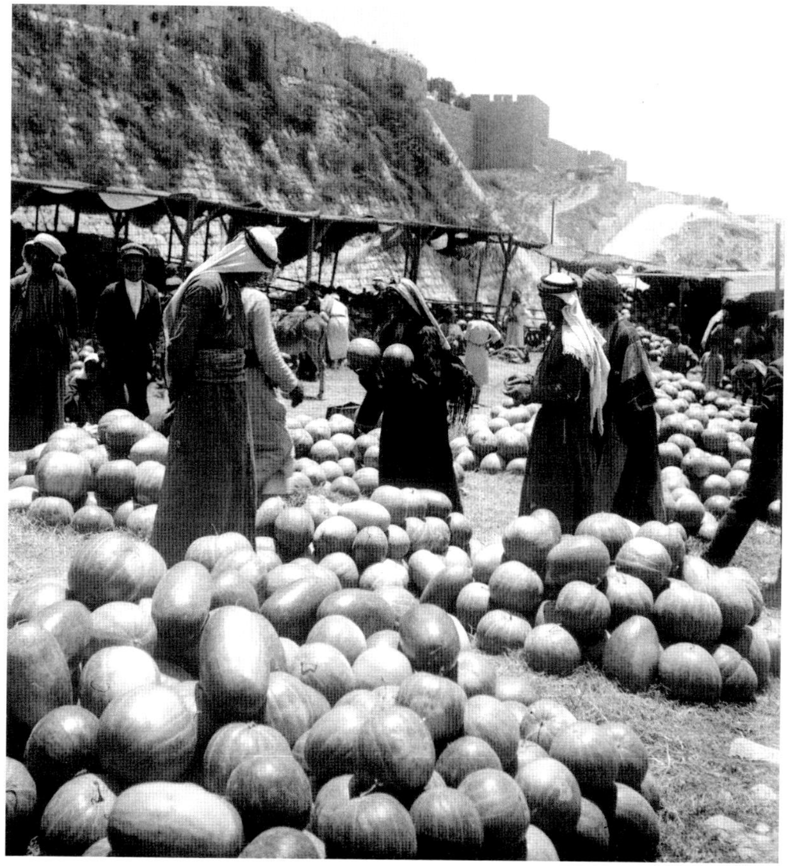

American Colony

Selling watermelons outside the walls of Jerusalem, c. 1900-1920

Commonwealth History, Vol. 16, Issue 3, 1988
Mackworth, Cecily, *The Mouth of the Sword*, London: Routledge
    & Kegan Paul, 1949
Mandel, Neville J., *The Arabs and Zionism before World War I*,
    Berkeley: University of California Press, 1976
Marlowe, John, *Rebellion in Palestine*, London: Cresset Press,
    1946

Marlowe, John, *The Seat of Pilate: An Account of the Palestine Mandate*, London: Cresset Press, 1959

Matar, Dina, *What It Means To Be Palestinian: Stories of Palestinian Peoplehood*, London: I. B. Tauris, 2011

Mattar, Philip, *The Mufti of Jerusalem: Al-Hajj Amin al-Husayni and the Palestinian National Movement*, New York: Columbia University Press, 1988

Milstein, Uri, *History of Israel's War of Independence, Vol. III*, tr. Alan Sacks, Lanham, Maryland: University Press of America, 1998

Monroe, Elizabeth, *Britain's Moment in the Middle East*, London: Chatto & Windus, 1963

Monroe, Elizabeth, 'The Origins of the Palestine Problem', in Peter Mansfield (ed.), *The Middle East: A Political and Economic Survey*, London: Oxford University Press, 1973

Morris, Benny, *The Birth of the Palestinian Refugee Problem*, Cambridge: Cambridge University Press, 1987

Morris, Benny, *The Birth of the Palestinian Refugee Problem Revisited*, Cambridge: Cambridge University Press, 2004

Morris, Benny, *1948: The First Arab-Israeli War*, Yale and London: Yale University Press, 2008

Nashef, Khaled (ed.), *Ya kafi, ya shafi … The Tawfik Canaan Collection of Palestinian Amulets*, Birzeit University, 1998

Nir, Yeshayahu, *The Bible and the Image: The History of Photography in the Holy Land, 1839-1899*, Philadelphia: University of Pennsylvania Press, 1985

Norris, Jacob, *Land of Progress: Palestine in the Age of Colonial Development, 1905-1948*, Oxford: Oxford University Press, 2013

Oren, Ruth, 'Zionist Photography, 1910-41', *History of*

Photography, Vol. 19, no. 3, Autumn 1995

Osman, Colin, *Jerusalem: Caught in Time*, Reading: Garnett, 1999

Oz, Amos, *A Tale of Love and Darkness*, tr. Nicholas de Lange, London: Chatto & Windus, 2004

Pappé, Ilan, *The Rise and Fall of a Palestinian Dynasty: The Husaynis 1700-1948*, London: Saqi Books, 2010

Perez, Nissan N., *Time Frame: A Century of Photography in the Land of Israel*, Jerusalem: The Israel Museum, 2000

Perowne, Stewart, *The One Remains*, London: Hodder & Stoughton, 1954

Perowne, Stewart, *Jerusalem and Bethlehem*, London: J. M. Dent, 1965

Porath, Zipporah, *Letters from Jerusalem, 1947-1948*, Jerusalem: Association of Americans and Canadians in Israel, 1987

Rogan, Eugene L., and Avi Shlaim (eds.), *The War for Palestine: Rewriting the History of 1948*, Cambridge: Cambridge University Press, 2001

Rogers, Mary Eliza, *Domestic Life in Palestine*, London: 1862; paperback edition, London: Kegan Paul International, 1989

Rose, John H. Melkon, *Armenians of Jerusalem: Memories of Life in Palestine*, London: Radcliffe Press, 1993

Rose, Norman, *'A Senseless Squalid War': Voices from Palestine 1890s-1948*, London: Bodley Head, 2009

Rothenberg, Beno, *Land of Israel: Photos by Beno Rothenberg*, Jerusalem and Tel Aviv: Schocken, 1958

Samuel, Edwin, *A Lifetime in Jerusalem*, London: Vallentine, Mitchell, 1970

Schölch, Alexander, *Palestine in Transformation, 1856-1882*, tr. William C. Young and Michael C. Gerrity, Washington, DC: Institute for Palestine Studies, 1993

Schor, Laura S., *Sophie Halaby in Jerusalem: An Artist's Life,*

Syracuse: Syracuse University Press, 2019

Schor, Laura S., *The Best School in Jerusalem: Annie Landau's School for Girls*, Waltham, Massachusetts: Brandeis University Press, 2013

Sebag Montefiore, Simon, *Jerusalem: The Biography*, London: Weidenfeld and Nicolson, 2011

Segev, Tom, *1949: The First Israelis*, New York: The Free Press, 1986

Segev, Tom, *One Palestine, Complete: Jews and Arabs under the British Mandate*, tr. Haim Watzman, New York: Henry Holt, 2000

Segev, Tom, *A State at Any Cost: The Life of David Ben-Gurion*, tr. Haim Watzman, New York: Farrar, Straus and Giroux, 2019

Seikaly, May, *Haifa: Transformation of an Arab Society, 1918-1939*, London: I. B.Tauris, 1995

Sharfman, Daphna, *Palestine in the Second World War: Strategic Plans and Political Dilemmas*, Brighton: Sussex Academic Press, 2015

Shepherd, Naomi, *The Zealous Intruders: The Western Rediscovery of Palestine*, London: William Collins, 1987

Shepherd, Naomi, *Ploughing Sand: British Rule in Palestine, 1917-1948*, London: John Murray, 1999

Sherman, A. J., *Mandate Days: British Lives in Palestine, 1918-1948*, London:Thames & Hudson, 1997

Shlaim, Avi, *Collusion across the Jordan: King Abdullah, the Zionist Movement and the Partition of Palestine*, Oxford: Oxford University Press, 1988

Silver-Brody, Vivienne, *Documentors of the Dream: Pioneer Jewish Photographers in the Land of Israel, 1890-1933*, Jerusalem: Magnes Press, 1998

Simson, H. J., *British Rule, and Rebellion*, Edinburgh: William Blackwood, 1937

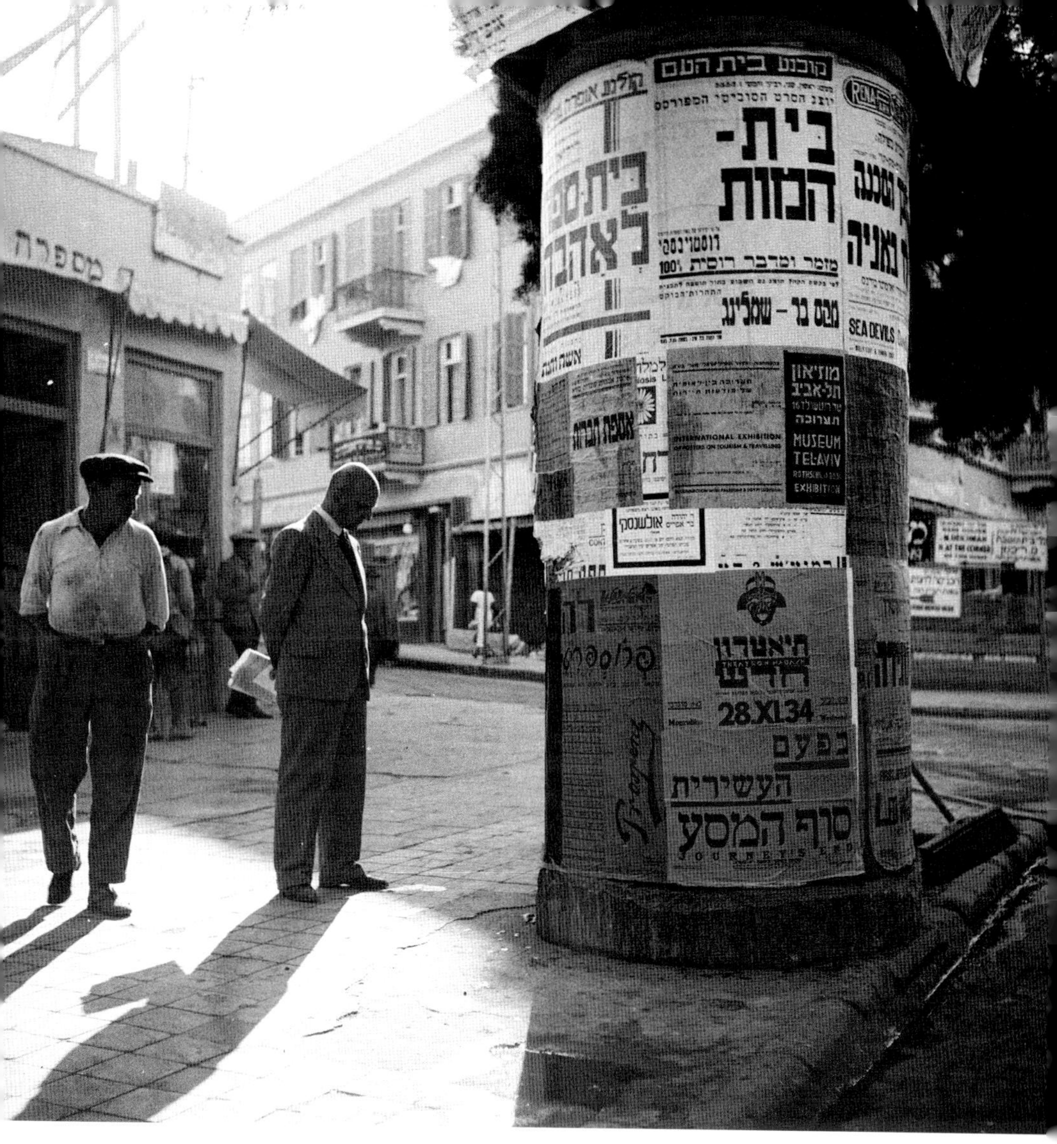

Posters in Tel Aviv, 1934   Zoltan Kluger

Smith, Colin, *The Last Crusade*, London: Sinclair-Stevenson, 1991

Sonino, Claudia, *German Jews in Palestine, 1920-1948: Between Dream and Reality*, Lanham: Lexington Books, 2016

Sparr, Thomas, *German Jerusalem: The Remarkable Life of a German-Jewish Neighbourhood in the Holy City*, tr. Stephen Brown, London: Haus, 2021

Stein, Kenneth W., *The Land Question in Palestine, 1917-1939*, Chapel Hill: University of North Carolina Press, 1984

Stubbs, Richard, *Palestine Story: A Personal Account of the Last Three Years of British Rule in Palestine*, Brettenham, Suffolk: privately printed, 1995

Summerer, Karène Sanchez, and Sary Zananiri (eds.), *Imaging and Imagining Palestine: Photography, Modernity, and the Biblical Lens*, Leiden: Brill, 2021

Swedenburg, Ted, *Memories of Revolt: The 1936-1939 Rebellion and the Palestinian National Past*, Minneapolis: University of Minnesota Press, 1995

Sykes, Christopher, *Crossroads to Israel*, London: William Collins, 1965

Tamari, Salim, *Year of the Locust: A Soldier's Diary and the Erasure of Palestine's Ottoman Past*, Berkeley: University of California Press, 2011

Tamari, Salim, *The Great War and the Remaking of Palestine*, Berkeley: University of California Press, 2017

Torday, J. C., *Towards a Visualisation of the Zionist Sabra, 1930-1967*, DPhil, University of Brighton, 2014

Tuqan, Fadwa, *A Mountainous Journey: A Poet's Autobiography*, tr. Olive Kenny, Saint Paul, Minnesota: Graywolf Press, 1990

Twain, Mark, *The Innocents Abroad*, American Publishing Company, 1869; London: Penguin Classics, 2002

Tveit, Odd Karsten, *Anna's House: The American Colony in Jerusalem*, tr. Peter Scott-Hansen; Nicosia: Rimal Publications, 2011

Vaughan, James R., *The Failure of American and British Propaganda in the Arab Middle East, 1945-1957,* London: Palgrave Macmillan, 2005

Viorst, Milton, *Reaching for the Olive Branch: UNRWA and Peace in the Middle East,* Washington, DC: Middle East Institute, 1989

Waley, Muhammad Isa, 'Images of the Ottoman Empire: The Photograph Albums Presented by Sultan Abdülhamid II', *British Library Journal,* 1991

Warren, Sir Charles, *Underground Jerusalem,* London: Richard Bentley & Son, 1876

Wasserstein, Bernard, *The British in Palestine: The Mandatory Government and the Arab-Jewish Conflict, 1917-1929,* London: Royal Historical Society, 1978; second edition, Oxford: Blackwell's, 1991

Wasserstein, Bernard, *Herbert Samuel: A Political Life,* Oxford: Clarendon Press, 1992

Wasserstein, Bernard, *Divided Jerusalem: The Struggle for the Holy City,* London: Profile, 2001

Wasserstein, Bernard, *Britain and the Jews of Europe, 1939-1945,* Oxford: Oxford University Press, 1979

Wasserstein, Bernard, 'The British Mandate in Palestine: Myths and Realities', in Martin Kramer (ed.), *Middle Eastern Lectures: Number One,* Tel Aviv: Moshe Dayan Center, 1995

Weizmann, Chaim, *Trial and Error,* London: Hamish Hamilton, 1949

Yizhar, S., *Khirbet Khizeh,* tr. Nicholas de Lange and Yaacob Dweck, New York: Farrar, Straus and Giroux, 2014

Yizhar, S., 'The Prisoner', tr. V. C. Rycus, in Jacob Sonntag (ed.), *New Writing from Israel,* London: Corgi Books, 1976

Yudkin, Leon I., *Escape into Siege: A Survey of Israeli Literature*

Today, London: Routledge, 1974

Zeev, Galia Gur, *Beno Rothenberg: Photographed and Reported, 1947-1957*, Tel Aviv: Eretz Israel Museum, 2007

Zerubavel, Yael, *Desert in the Promised Land*, Stanford, California: Stanford University Press, 2019

Acknowledgements

This book could not have been written without the help of friends, family members, librarians, and archivists. A number of fellow writers and journalists—Ian Black, Paul Taylor, Robin Lustig, Sarah Graham-Brown, and Zina Rohan—read the text and provided valuable comments and criticism. Peter Clark, with his eagle eye, spotted many errors and oddities. Edward Mortimer, although suffering from the cancer which was soon to end his life, read the manuscript and made helpful suggestions. Mia Gröndahl, with her unique knowledge of the American Colony photographers, helped me understand their work and answered a number of my queries. Two distinguished historians of the Palestine Mandate, Bernard Wasserstein and Naomi Shepherd, though taking issue with some of my conclusions, were generous with their time and gave me much food for thought.

The help of both the library and the archive of the Middle East Centre, St Antony's College, Oxford, was invaluable. Anyone with an interest in oral history will benefit from its uniquely rich archive, built up in the centre's early days by the historian Elizabeth Monroe. Its section on Palestine is without parallel.

A number of families helped me locate unpublished material. Fauzi Mantoura and his sister Patricia provided me with two family memoirs, and shared their memories of their grandfathers Tawfiq Canaan and Atallah Mantoura, and of their parents Leila and Jacques Mantoura. Judith David, born in Mandate Palestine, let me have copies of the letters written by her mother Flora Moody, as well as reminiscing about her father, Sydney Moody, and life in Palestine when she was growing up. Jacqueline Karp-Gendre told me about the life and work of her mother, Barbara Board, and allowed me to quote from an unpublished memoir. Sarah Holliday showed me the papers and photographs left by Clifford and Eunice Holliday. Tim Holliday corresponded with me from France in what turned out to be the last months of his life. My conversations with all of the above were enjoyable as well as rewarding.

In my long hunt for photographs, I received a good deal of help, while also hitting a number of dead-ends. Ruth Oren helped me understand the evolution of Zionist photography, as did John Tordai, himself a fine photographer. Lee Rotbart helped me navigate Israeli archives. The Eretz Israel Museum in Tel Aviv allowed me to use a photograph taken by Paul Goldman. UNRWA gave me permission to use pictures from their archive. Peter Anderson let me use a photo taken by his father, Per-Olow Anderson. The Palestine Exploration Fund made available documents and photographs in their keeping. I am grateful to Wikimedia Commons for putting so many images into the public domain, and to a number of archives whose websites proved valuable: these include the Rijksmuseum in Amsterdam, the Royal Collection in Britain, the Government Press Office in Israel, the Central Zionist Archives, and the Library of Congress, which houses the principal collection of American Colony photographs as well as other valuable historical material.

Jana Gough skilfully edited the manuscript, enhancing its clarity and consistency. For the design and production of the book I am indebted to Anthony Eyre.

My daughter Ania, constantly bemused by my technical

ignorance, has helped me understand how to choose, download, and edit or crop photos. Last but not least, my wife Jola has borne my preoccupation with this project for more than six years with a unique mixture of support, encouragement, and impatience.

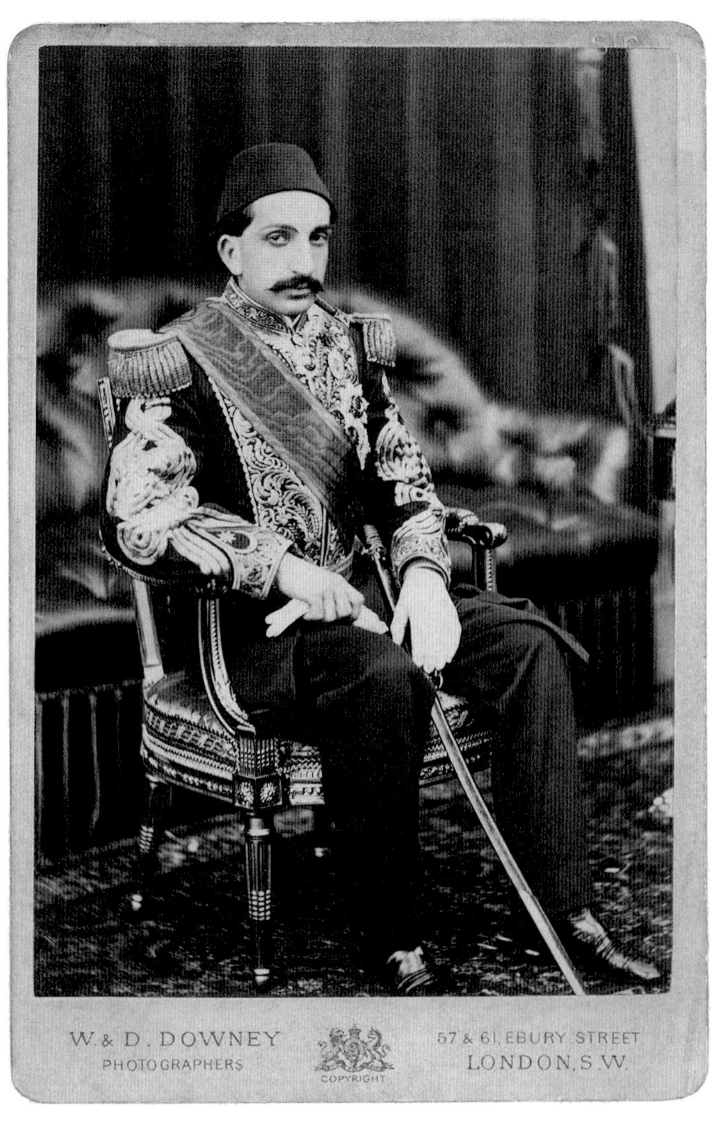

The young Abdul-Hamid, 1867   W & D Downey

Dramatis personæ

Abdul-Hamid II, Sultan (1842-1918)—Ottoman ruler, an autocrat but also a moderniser, who failed to halt his empire's decline and was eventually overthrown by the Young Turks in 1909; one of the first patrons of photography in the Middle East.

Abdul-Rahim Hajj Muhammad (1892-1939)—popular Palestinian rebel leader who was killed by British troops during the Arab rebellion of the 1930s.

Agronsky, Gershon (1894-1959)—Russian-born, American-educated editor of the *Palestine Post* who was close to the Zionist statesman Chaim Weizmann; after the birth of Israel in 1948, he became the mayor of Jerusalem.

Alami, Musa (1897-1984)—Palestinian nationalist from a distinguished Jerusalem family who, after studying law at Cambridge, joined the Palestine administration in 1925; served as adviser to the high commissioner Sir Arthur Wauchope, but was criticised in the Peel commission's report of 1937 and forced from office, thereafter acting as an independent nationalist and philanthropist.

Allenby, General Edmund (1861-1936)—British army officer who led the Middle East campaign in the First World War which led to the capture of Jerusalem in 1917; he was nicknamed 'The Bull'.

Andrews, Lewis Yelland (1896-1937)—Australian-born district commissioner in Galilee, assassinated by Arab gunmen leaving a church service in Nazareth, in September 1937; this ushered in the final, and bloodiest, phase of the Arab rebellion of 1936-39.

Antonius, George (1891-1942)—writer of Lebanese origin who joined the education department of the Palestine government, but resigned in protest at what he regarded as discrimination; author of *The Arab Awakening* (1938), an influential study of the origins of Arab nationalism; his wife Katy's soirées at their home in Jerusalem were popular with the Anglo-Arab élite.

Balfour, Arthur James (1848-1930)—British statesman who, as foreign secretary, signed the Balfour Declaration of November 1917 pledging British support for a Jewish 'national home' in Palestine.

Ben-Gurion, David (1886-1973)—son of a notary in Płonsk, in tsarist-ruled Poland, who emigrated to Palestine in 1906, becoming the head of the labour movement, a leading pioneer of Zionism, and Israel's first prime minister.

Bentwich, Norman (1883-1971)—British attorney-general in Palestine; a moderate Zionist; his wife Helen's letters, published posthumously as *Tidings from Zion*, provide a vivid description of their life in Jerusalem.

Bernadotte, Count Folke (1895-1948)—Swedish diplomat who, in May 1948, was appointed United Nations mediator in Palestine. He was assassinated in Jerusalem by members of the Stern Gang on 17 September 1948.

Bevin, Ernest (1881-1951)—post-war British foreign secretary, with a trade-union background, who played a crucial role in the closing years of the British Mandate, 1945-48, earning the undying hostility of Zionists.

Board, Barbara (1916-1986)—British journalist who reported from Palestine between 1936 and 1946 for the *Daily Sketch* and the *Daily Mirror*; author of *Newsgirl in Palestine* (1937), *Newsgirl in Egypt* (1938), and *Reporting from Palestine, 1943-1944* (published posthumously, 2008); a second manuscript, on Palestine in 1945-46, remains unpublished.

Cafferata, Raymond (1897-1966)—British police chief in Hebron during the Arab massacre of Jews in August 1929; he

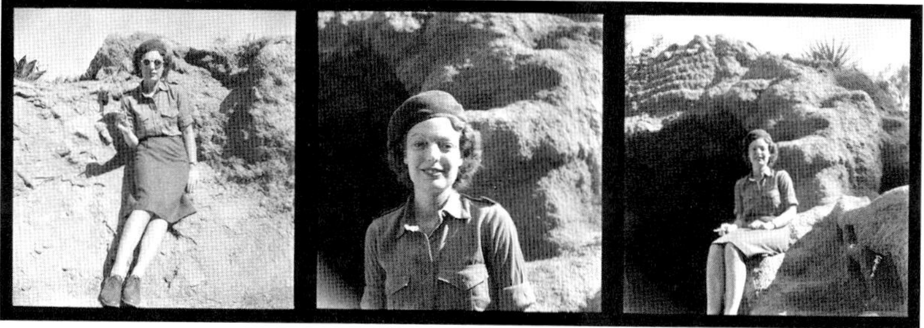

Barbara Board, c. early 1940s   Photographer unknown

later survived an assassination attempt by the Irgun; he resigned, embittered, and returned to England.

Canaan, Tawfiq (1882-1964)—Palestinian doctor, ethnographer, and nationalist; an authority on malaria and leprosy; on visits to Palestinian villages, he collected amulets and talismans which are today housed at Birzeit University, in the West Bank, and at the Pitt-Rivers Museum, Oxford; author of ethnographic studies and of an unfinished memoir; father of Leila Mantoura (see below).

Chancellor, Sir John (1870-1952)—British soldier and colonial governor in Africa who served as Palestine's third high commissioner from December 1928 to September 1931; he was never comfortable in the post and his last months were overshadowed by the violent unrest of 1929.

Churchill, Winston (1874-1965)—British statesman who played a central role in the emergence of the modern Middle East after the First World War, including the creation of the Palestine Mandate; a staunch supporter of Zionism.

Collard, Jack Marler (1909-1995)—British soldier, oil-company official, and writer who, using the pen-name John Marlowe, wrote a series of books about the Middle East, including *Rebellion in Palestine* (1946) and *The Seat of Pilate: An Account of the Palestine Mandate* (1959).

Cunningham, General Sir Alan (1887-1983)—distinguished British soldier who fought in both world wars and was Palestine's last high commissioner, from November 1945 until the end of the Mandate in May 1948.

Dannatt, Norman (1919-2017)—British soldier and musician who served in Palestine during the Second World War; his memoir *The War (I Did It My Way)* is published on-line (www.memoriesofwar.org.uk).

Gelber, Sylva (1910-2003)—Canadian, born into a Jewish family in Toronto, who lived in British-ruled Palestine, 1932-1948, becoming one of the country's first trained social workers. Her memoir of the period, *No Balm in Gilead* (1989), records her life during the Arab rebellion of the 1930s, her commitment to bi-nationalism, and her growing disillusionment, leading her to return to Canada, where she became a well-known writer and activist on social issues.

Gort, Field Marshal John Vereker, 6th Viscount (1886-1946)—British soldier who was high commissioner of Palestine from October 1944 to November 1945; he resigned because of ill health.

Graham, Stephen (1884-1975)—British writer and journalist, whose influential book *With Russian Pilgrims to Jerusalem* (1913) provided a vivid account of his journey to the Holy Land in 1912 with hundreds of devout Russian peasants.

Gutmann, Assia (1927-1969)—German-born writer and translator whose parents fled Nazi Germany and settled in Palestine; she grew up in Tel Aviv but eventually settled in Britain, where she became the lover of the poet Ted Hughes; in 1969 she killed herself and her young daughter. Among her translations was a selection of work by Israel's leading poet Yehuda Amichai.

Hacohen, David (1898-1984)—Russian-born Zionist official who studied at the London School of Economics and became a senior official of the Zionist trade-union federation, the

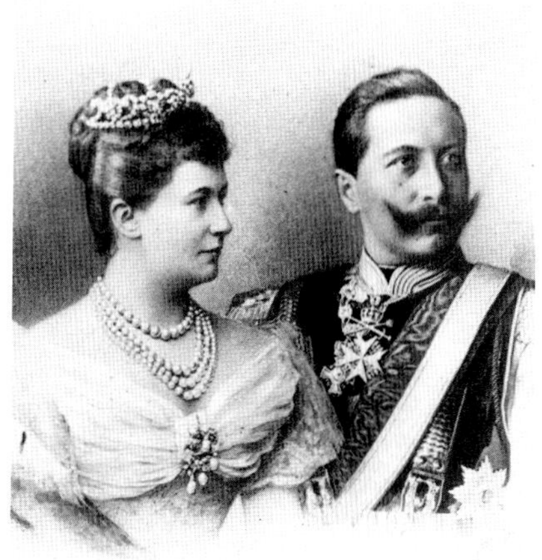

Kaiser Wilhelm II and Empress Augusta Victoria, 1898 Library of Congress

Histadrut, running its construction arm, Solel Boneh; after 1948 a member of the Israeli Knesset; author of a memoir, *Time to Tell.*

Halaby, Sophie (1906-1997)—Palestinian artist who was born in Jerusalem to a Christian Arab father and a Russian mother. She trained in Paris, after which she became a landscape painter. Her younger sister, **Asia** (Anastasia) **Halaby** (1909-1998), worked as a driver for the British army during the Second World War.

Hammami, Hassan (b. 1933)—Palestinian who grew up in Jaffa, where his father ran a citrus business; the family escaped by sea in April 1948; he became a businessman and settled in Florida.

Herzl, Theodor (1860-1904)—Hungarian-born Viennese journalist who was the founding father of Zionism, and whose booklet *The Jewish State,* written in German, helped launch the movement.

Hodgkin, Edward Christian (1913-2006)—British official (brother of Thomas; see below) who during the Second World War worked for the Special Operations Executive in Egypt and

Iraq, and after the war in Palestine as director of the Arabic radio station Sharq al-Adna, 1945-47; he subsequently became foreign editor of *The Times*.

Hodgkin, Thomas (1910-1982)—British writer who as a young man was secretary to the high commissioner in Palestine, Sir Arthur Wauchope, an experience brought to life in his *Letters from Palestine, 1932-36* (published posthumously, 1986).

Holliday, Clifford (1897-1960)—British architect who worked in Palestine in the 1920s and 1930s and, among other projects, designed St Andrew's Church, Jerusalem; husband of Eunice (see below).

Holliday, Eunice (1899-1992)—author of *Letters from Jerusalem* (published posthumously, 1997), which describes life in Palestine during the early days of the Mandate and the rebellion of the 1930s.

Hourani, Albert (1915-1993)—British historian of Lebanese descent who as a young man advised British officials on Middle East policy and testified before the Anglo-American Committee of Inquiry; author of such classic studies as *Arabic Thought in the Liberal Age* (1962) and *A History of the Arab Peoples* (1991).

al-Husseini, Abdul-Qader (1908-1948)—Palestinian commander, a cousin of Hajj Amin (see below); regarded as a natural leader of men, he fought as a commander in the Arab rebellion of 1936-39 and in the first Arab-Israeli war of 1947-48, in which he was killed.

al-Husseini, Hajj Amin (1897-1974)—Palestinian from a leading family in Jerusalem who became the leading Arab politician during British rule in Palestine; he was forced into exile during the Arab rebellion of 1936-39 and spent the Second World War in Baghdad and Berlin supporting the Nazi cause.

Jabotinsky, Vladimir (1880-1940)—Russian-born Zionist who created the Jewish Legion which fought alongside the British army in the First World War, and went on to found the

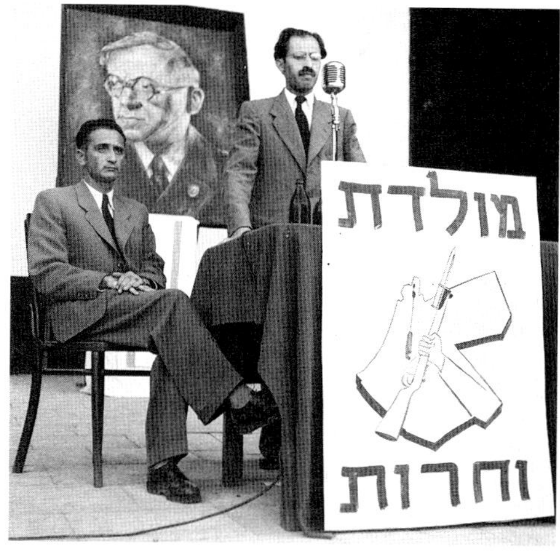

Menachem Begin, August 1948, with poster of Vladimir Jabotinsky
Hans Pinn

right-wing breakaway faction of the Zionist movement known as the Revisionists.

Jabra Ibrahim Jabra (1920-1994)—Palestinian writer from an impoverished Christian family who described his early life in a memoir, *The First Well: A Bethlehem Boyhood* (English translation, 1995); after 1948 he settled in Iraq, becoming a distinguished writer, critic, and translator.

al-Khalidi, Ahmad Samih (1896-1951)—Palestinian scholar and educationalist who ran the Arab College in Jerusalem from 1925 until the end of the British Mandate; he left Palestine in 1948 and died in Beirut three years later.

Landau, Annie (1873-1945)—British schoolteacher who ran the highly-regarded Evelina de Rothschild school for girls in Jerusalem; her parties were very popular; she was an Orthodox Jew and a non-Zionist.

Larsson, Lewis (1881-1958)—Swedish-born member of the American Colony in Jerusalem and its leading photographer; he later became the Swedish consul in Jerusalem.

MacMichael, Sir Harold (1882-1969)—British colonial official who spent many years in Sudan, and served as high commissioner in Palestine from March 1938 to August 1944; considered remote and aloof.

Magnes, Judah Leon (1877-1948)—American writer, rabbi, and peace activist who served as president of the Hebrew University of Jerusalem after its inauguration in 1925; a prominent supporter of Brit Shalom, a small group which advocated bi-nationalism.

Mantoura, Atallah (1891-1946)—Palestinian Christian official who worked for the British army in Egypt during the First World War and subsequently became the second-most senior Arab official in the Palestine administration; he was killed in the bombing of the King David Hotel, at the age of fifty-four.

Mantoura, Leila (1927-2000)—daughter of Tawfiq Canaan (see above) who survived the bombing of the King David Hotel in 1946 and subsequently married Atallah Mantoura's son Jacques.

McDonnell, Sir Michael (1882-1956)—British chief justice in Palestine from 1927 to 1936; an Irish Catholic, he was critical of government policy and was responsible for hounding Norman Bentwich (see above) from office; in later life he was active in the British fascist movement.

Moody, Sydney (1889-1979)—British official who spent twenty-two years in Palestine, from 1917 to 1939, as a soldier in Allenby's army, as district officer in Safad, and as a senior official in the secretariat in Jerusalem; the diaries of his Scottish wife Flora are in Rhodes House, Oxford.

Peel, Lord (William Robert Wellesley, 1867-1937)—British statesman, secretary of state for India, and chairman of the royal commission which in July 1937 recommended the partition of Palestine; the inquiry put great strain on his health and he died a few months later.

Perowne, Stewart (1901-1989)—British writer and colonial official; he was a schoolteacher at the government-run Arab

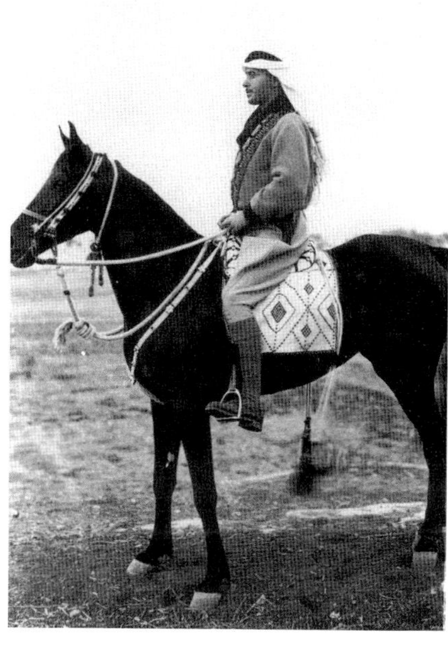

Fawzi al-Qawuqji, 1948
Palmach Archive

College in Jerusalem, 1927-29; during the Second World War he produced propaganda in Aden and Baghdad with Freya Stark, whom he later, briefly, married; author of a Palestine memoir, *The One Remains* (1954).

Plumer, Field-Marshal Herbert Plumer, 1st Viscount (1857-1932)—veteran of the First World War who served as Palestine's second high commissioner, from August 1925 to July 1928.

Qawuqji, Fawzi al- (1890-1977)—Arab soldier of fortune, born in Tripoli, Lebanon, who fought in Syria against the French, and in Palestine and Iraq against the British.

Rutenberg, Pinchas (1879-1942)—Russian Zionist who in 1923 founded the Palestine Electricity Company, a hydroelectric project, inaugurated in 1933, to harness the waters of the Jordan and Yarmuk rivers.

Sakakini, Khalil (1878-1953)—Palestinian educationalist, humanist, and author of a remarkable diary of life in Jerusalem

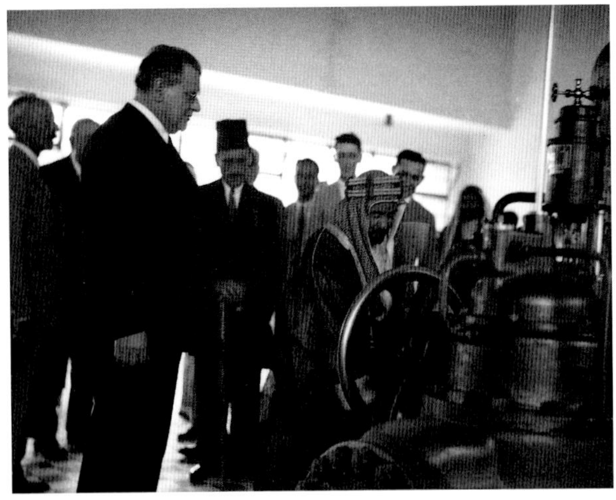

American Colony

*Pinchas Rutenberg with Emir Abdullah of Transjordan at the opening of the
Rutenberg hydroelectric project, 1933*

under Ottoman and British rule.

Samuel, Sir Herbert Louis (1870-1963)—British politician and
Zionist, the first high commissioner in Palestine, 1920 to 1925.

Spafford, Horatio (1828-1888)—lawyer from Chicago who
founded the American Colony in Jerusalem, which on his death
was taken over by his Norwegian-born wife Anna.

Storrs, Sir Ronald (1881-1955)—British governor of Jerusalem,
1917-26; a witty and cultivated man and patron of the arts whom
many found arrogant and egotistical.

Stubbs, Richard (1909-1996)—British spokesman in Palestine, 1946-
1948; author of a memoir, *Palestine Story* (privately published, 1995).

Szold, Henrietta (1860-1945)—American Zionist who, late
in life, founded the Hadassah hospital in Jerusalem; she was
highly regarded for her work in medical and social welfare and
was, politically, a bi-nationalist.

Tegart, Sir Charles (1881-1946)—British policeman, of Irish descent, who acted as a security adviser in Palestine, 1937-38, during the Arab rebellion; he recommended the building of a security fence along the northern border and a series of fortified police stations known as 'Tegart forts'.

Thomson, William McClure (1806-1894)—American Protestant missionary who settled in Beirut in the 1830s and travelled extensively in Palestine. His best-known work, *The Land and the Book*, was published in 1859.

Tuqan, Fadwa (1917-2003)—Palestinian poet and feminist who lived throughout her long life in Nablus, in the West Bank; author of an autobiography, *A Mountainous Journey* (English translation, 1990).

Tuqan, Ibrahim (1904?-1941)—Palestinian poet and broadcaster (brother of the above); he resigned from the Palestine Broadcasting Service after allegations of nationalist bias.

Twain, Mark (Samuel Langhorne Clemens, 1835-1910)—American writer whose first major book, *The Innocents Abroad* (1869), described a journey to Europe and the Holy Land. An irreverent satire on the religious package tour, the book was an instant success.

Walker-Arnott, Jane (1834-1911)—Scottish founder of the Tabeetha School in Jaffa, in 1863; after her death the school was taken over by the Church of Scotland. One of its students, in the 1940s, was Assia Gutmann (see above).

Warren, Sir Charles (1840-1927)—British Royal Engineers officer, an archaeologist for the Palestine Exploration Fund; author of, among other books, *Underground Jerusalem*. Later, as London's police chief, involved in the hunt for Jack the Ripper.

Wauchope, Sir Arthur (1874-1947)—a distinguished British general who served as high commissioner in Palestine from November 1931 to March 1938; a wealthy Scottish batchelor whose period in office was overshadowed by the Arab rebellion of 1936-39.

Weizmann, Chaim (1874-1952)—Russian-born scientist who

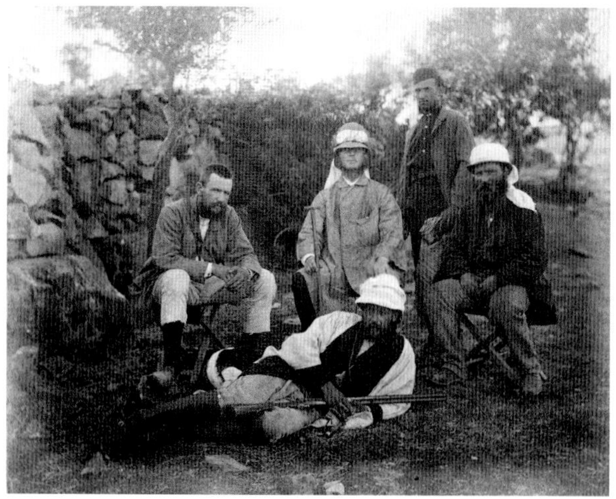

Sgt. Henry Phillips

Captain Charles Warren, seated left, with members of a Palestine Exploration Fund expedition, 1867

became one of the leading advocates of Zionism, helped bring about the Balfour Declaration of 1917, and in 1948 became Israel's first president.

Wilson, Sir Charles (1836-1905)—British archaeologist and author who worked in Jerusalem for the Palestine Exploration Fund; he edited the immensely popular *Picturesque Palestine.*

Wilson, Hilda Mary (1904-1990)—British writer and schoolteacher, born in Durham and educated at St Hugh's College, Oxford, who for ten years, 1929-39, worked as a schoolteacher in Sudan, Lebanon, and Palestine, where she wrote a diary of life at an Arab school during the rebellion of the 1930s. On her return to Britain she worked in publishing, became an active Quaker, published a volume of poems (*The Three-Sighted,* 1961) and eventually retired to Devon. Her account of life in Palestine is lodged at the Middle East Centre, Oxford.

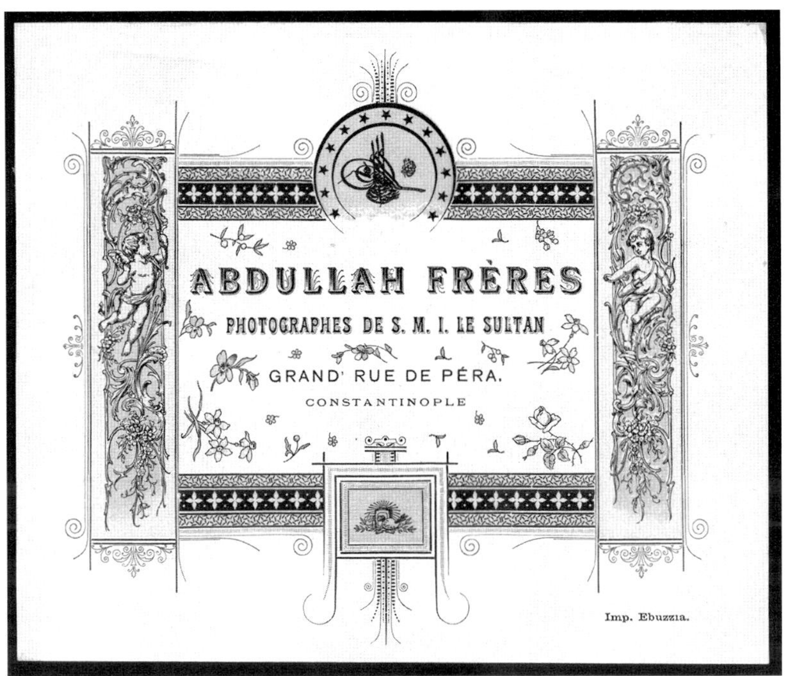

Illustrators

Abdullah Frères—Three Armenian brothers—Vichen (1820-1902), Hovsep (1830-1908), and Kevork (1839-1918) Abdullahyan—who in the late nineteenth century became the leading Ottoman photographers and the principal contributors to Sultan Abdul-Hamid's extensive collection.

Karimeh Aboud (1893-1940)—Born in Bethlehem the daughter of a Lutheran pastor, Aboud established a studio in Nazareth, becoming one of the very few Arab women photographers of the 1920s and 1930s.

One of Sultan Abdul-Hamid's photograph albums, c. 1880 Abdullah Frères

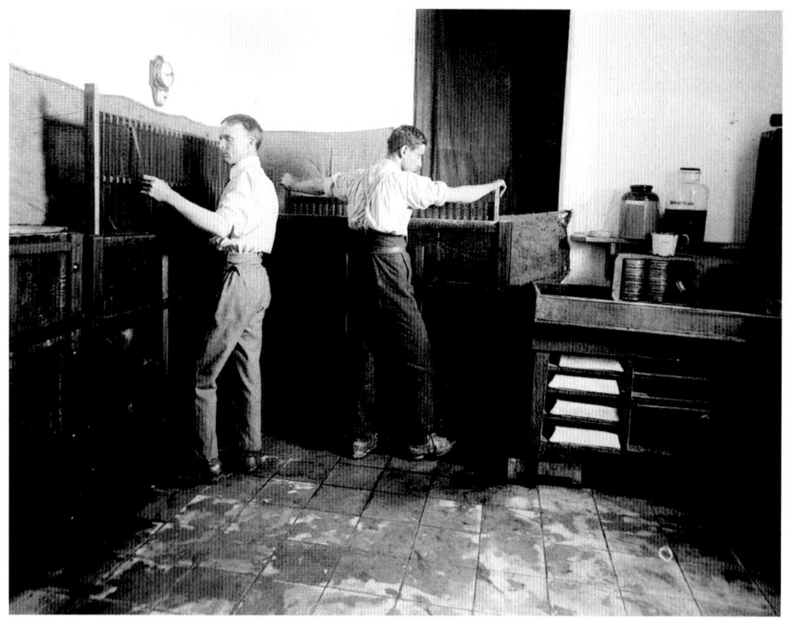

Lewis Larsson in his studio, c. 1920　　　　　　　　American Colony

Per-Olow Anderson (1921-1989)—Swedish photo-journalist who in 1956 visited Gaza to photograph refugees for his book *They Are Human Too...* (1957).

George Grantham Bain (1865-1944)—A photographer who in 1898 founded of one of the earliest news agencies in the United States. The extensive Bain collection of photographs is housed in the Library of Congress.

Gustav Bauernfeind (1848-1904)—German artist who visited the Middle East in 1880 and settled in Jerusalem in 1898, becoming one of the most celebrated Orientalist painters.

Francis Bedford (1815-1894)—British landscape photographer who, at Queen Victoria's bidding, accompanied the Prince of Wales on an Eastern tour, including Palestine, in 1862.

Yaacov Ben-Dov (1882-1968)—Photographer and film-maker,

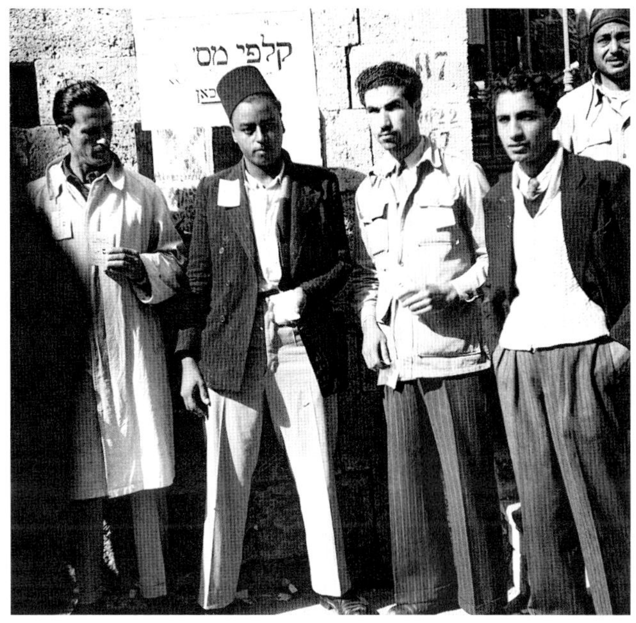

Hugo Mendelson

Nazareth, 1949: Arabs waiting to vote in Israel's first elections

originally from Ukraine, who emigrated to Palestine in 1907; considered the father of Zionist cinematography.

Félix Bonfils (1831-1895)—French photographer who, with his wife and son, set up a highly successful studio in Beirut, becoming one of the pioneers of Middle East photography; his studio portraits pandered to Orientalist prejudices, but his best work is brought together in the four-volume *Souvenirs d'Orient* (1877-78).

Harry Fenn (1837-1911)—An American illustrator of Scottish ancestry; one of the two artists who contributed to the immensely popular *Picturesque Palestine* (1881-83).

Paul Goldman (1900-1986)—Hungarian-born photographer who settled in Palestine, where he worked for Zionist institutions. He died penniless, leaving behind a collection of work which was restored and exhibited by the Eretz Israel Museum in Tel Aviv.

Harris & Ewing—George W. Harris (1872-1964) and Martha Ewing (1870-1959) opened a studio in Washington, DC, in 1905 and became known as portrait photographers. By the 1930s their company had become the biggest photographic agency in the United States.

Benjamin West Kilburn (1827-1909)—American photographer best known for his landscape images of the United States and Canada; a pioneer of stereo-photography in the 1860s.

Zoltan Kluger (1896-1977)—Hungarian-born photographer who settled in Palestine in the 1930s, working for official Zionist organisations. Among his projects was an aerial survey of the country. In the 1950s he emigrated to the United States, where he died.

Garabed Krikorian (1847-1918)—Armenian, born in Smyrna (modern-day Izmir), who in the 1880s became the first local photographer to establish a studio in Jerusalem; he specialised in portraits.

Lewis Larsson (1881-1958)—Member of a Swedish farming family which in 1896 emigrated to Palestine, where he eventually became the principal photographer of the American Colony in Jerusalem and the city's Swedish consul.

Eric Matson (1888-1977)—Swedish-born member of the American Colony. When it split up in the 1930s, he took over the photographic agency, which in 1934 was renamed the Matson Photo Service. He later moved to the United States, where he donated 20,000 of the colony's photographs to the Library of Congress.

Mendelson, Hugo (1918-2012)—German-born photographer who worked for Israel's Government Press Office, chronicling the first Arab-Israeli war and its aftermath.

Zvi Oron-Orushkes (1888-1980)—Polish-born photographer who in 1929 was made the official Mandate photographer, which evoked some criticism from within the Yishuv.

Hans Pinn (1916-1978)—Born in Berlin, Pinn settled in Palestine in 1930. He worked as a photographer for the British army during the Second World War, and later for official Zionist organisations.

Khalil (or Carl) Raad (1854-1957)—A Lebanese Christian who was the first Arab photographer to establish a studio in Jerusalem; in a long career he recorded events from the First World War to the Arab-Israeli war of 1948.

Beno Rothenberg (1914-2012)—Born in Germany, Rothenberg settled in Palestine in the 1930s, becoming an active photographer after the Second World War. He worked with the Haganah documenting the conflict of 1948–49, and in later life became better known as an archaeologist.

Samuel Joseph Schweig (1903-1984)—Russian-born photographer who arrived in Haifa in 1922 and specialised in photographing the early Zionist settlements for the Jewish National Fund.

Abraham Soskin (1882 or 1884-1965)—Russian-born photographer who settled in Palestine in 1905 and took some of the earliest pictures of Tel Aviv.

Arthur Szyk (1894-1951)—Polish-born American artist and cartoonist who produced a series of posters supporting the Jews of Palestine and highlighting Nazi atrocities.

Willem van de Poll (1895-1970)—A successful Dutch photojournalist who, starting in the 1930s, made several visits to the Middle East.

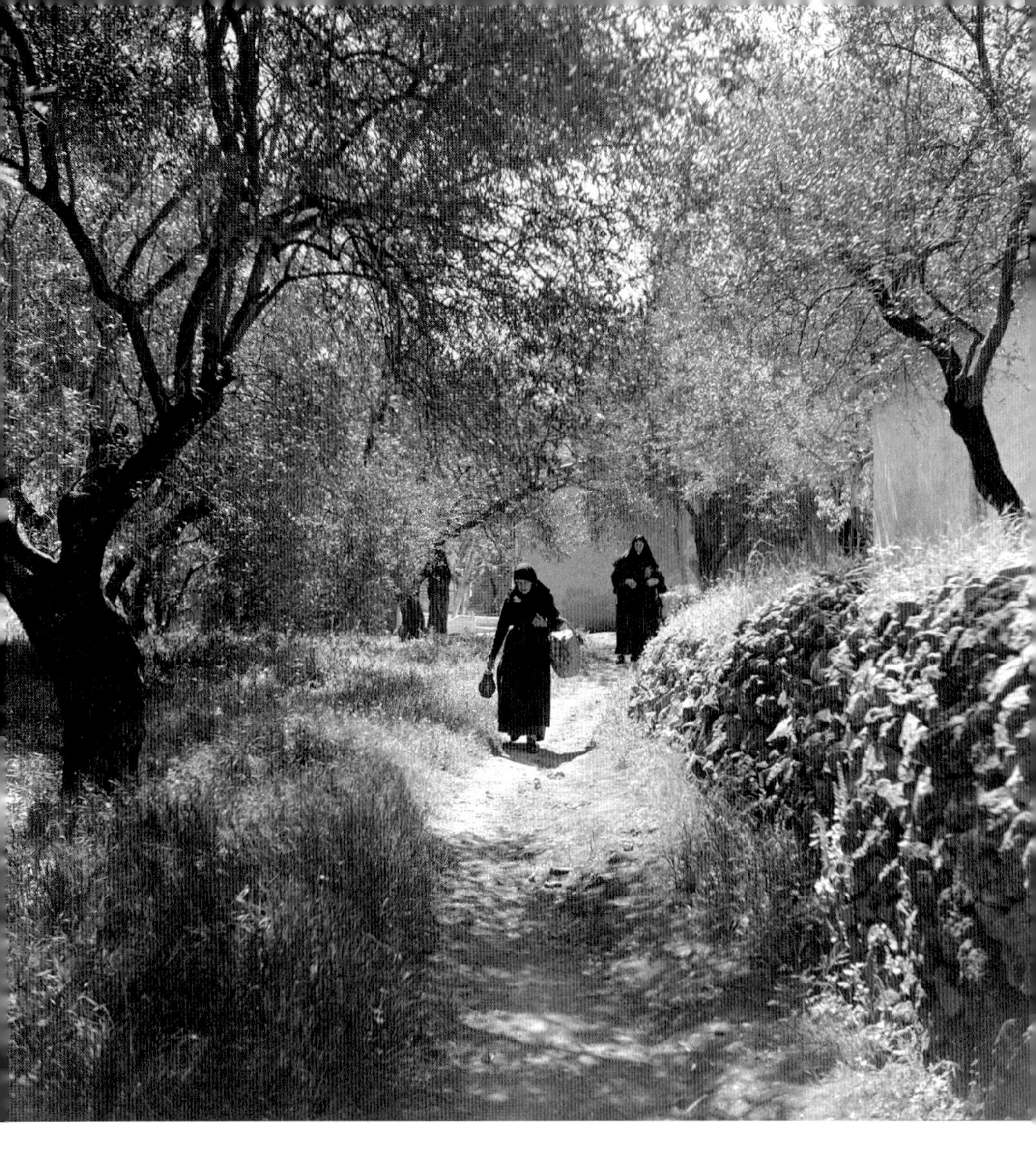

Russian nuns in Ein Karem, near Jerusalem, 1948   Willem van de Poll

Picture credits

Abbreviations

MATPC   Eric Matson Collection, Library of Congress [American Colony archive]
PPMSCA   Other collections, Library of Congress
GGBAIN   Bain Collection, Library of Congress
GPO   Government Press Office [Israel]

(Note: The American Colony studio worked as a collective; individual photographers were not named. Most of their prints were the work of a team led by Lewis Larsson; from the early 1930s, when the studio was renamed the Matson Photo Service, they were the work of Eric Matson and his colleagues.)

Front and back covers
1   Woman of Bethlehem, probably early 1900s. American Colony (MATPC 04644).
2   'Jerusalem, Looking to Mount Scopus', 1925. David Bomberg (Tate Gallery).

Frontispiece
    Via Dolorosa, early 1900s. American Colony (MATPC 06601).

Introduction
    Hills around Safad, northern Palestine, 1947. Zoltan Kluger (GPO D834-104).

Chapter 1: Pilgrims and predators, 1850-1917
1   Garden of Gethsemane, Jerusalem, c. 1880. Félix Bonfils (Rijksmuseum).
2   Family in Ramallah, c. 1900. American Colony (MATPC 06849).
3   The sea at Jaffa, c. 1898. American Colony (MATPC 06515).

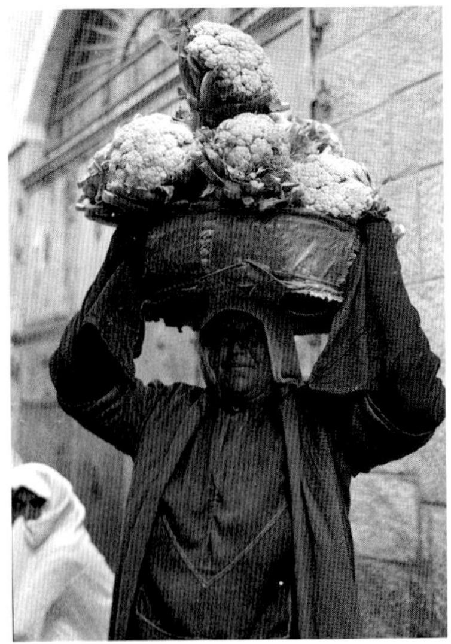

American Colony

Village woman selling cauliflowers, 1930s

4   The United States consul, William Coffin, c. 1910, with two kavasses, or guards. Photographer unknown. From the album 'Members of the American Colony (Jerusalem), friends, and associates' (PPMSCA 18883).

5   Pilgrims on the Via Dolorosa, early 1900s. American Colony (MATPC 05443).

6   The Western, or Wailing, Wall, c. early 1900s. American Colony (MATPC 12188).

7   Damascus Gate, Jerusalem, c. 1880. Harry Fenn, *Picturesque Palestine* (Wikimedia Commons).

8   The pulpit, Haram al-Sharif, Jerusalem, 1862. Francis Bedford (Royal Collection).

9   'Young Woman of Bethlehem', c. 1880. Félix Bonfils (PPMSCA 02776).

10 The entrance to the Armenian Convent, Jerusalem, early 1900s. American Colony (MATPC 06551).

11 The Russian church of St Mary Magdalene, Mount of Olives, c. 1870-1880. Félix Bonfils (PPMSCA 04154).

12 The sultan's railway, third-class carriage, 1908. Photographer unknown. Stereo-Travel Company, New York (LOT 13739).

13 The American Colony salon, c. 1900. On the right are Lewis Larsson and Anna Spafford. American Colony (PPMSCA 15830).

14 Kaiser Wilhelm passing the American Colony as he enters Jerusalem, 1898. American Colony (MATPC 04613).

15 Sultan Abdul-Hamid, 1909. Artist unknown. A commemorative postcard (Wikimedia Commons).

16 Russian pilgrims in the Jordan, 1899. Stereograph by B. W. Kilburn (PPMSCA 10650).

17 The early Jewish settlement of Degania, near the Sea of Galilee, 1912. Yaacov Ben-Dov (Israel Internet Association).

18 Inside Jaffa Gate. American Colony (MATPC 06546).

19 The 'biblical lens': young shepherd, early 1900s. American

Colony (MATPC 05673).

20 Village of Silwan, early 1900s. American Colony (MATPC 06744).

21 Villagers building a stone house, early 1900s. American Colony (MATPC 04638).

22 Jemal Pasha on horseback by the Dead Sea, c. 1916. Lewis Larsson, American Colony (PPMSCA 13709).

23 'Muslim volunteers setting out from Jerusalem', 1915. A postcard version of a photograph published in a Leipzig newspaper. Khalil Raad (Wikimedia Commons).

24 An orchard stripped bare by locusts, 1915. American Colony (MATPC 01898).

25 Tawfiq Canaan, left, in the uniform of an Ottoman medical officer, c. 1916. American Colony (LOT 13833). From the album 'World War I in Palestine and the Sinai', 1914-1917.

Chapter 2: Palestine Raj, 1917-1929

1 Jerusalem, December 1917: the two British sergeants who were the first to accept the city's flag of surrender. American Colony (LOT 13833).

2 Arthur Balfour, c. 1917. G. G. Bain (GGBAIN 02758)

3 The Balfour Declaration, 1917. (GPO, D748-072).

4 Ronald Storrs, 1923. Harris & Ewing (HEC 42763).

5 The arrival of the Zionist Commission, 1920. American

Colony (Israel State Archives).

6 Sir Herbert Samuel, 1920. American Colony (MATPC 02290).

7 Ben-Gurion addressing Jewish workers, 1924. Photographer unknown (GPO D684-003).

7a Map of settlement in Palestine, 1880-1917 (Wikimedia Commons).

8 Tel Aviv, 1920. Abraham Soskin (Israel Internet Association).

9 Peasant girl, Nazareth, 1920s. Karimeh Aboud (Wikimedia Commons).

10 The hills around Nablus, c. 1915-1920. G. G. Bain (GGBAIN 25945).

11 Clifford Holliday at the grave of Philip d'Aubigny, a Crusader knight, in front of the Church of the Holy Sepulchre, 1925. American Colony (MATPC 08519).

12 Hajj Amin al-Husseini leading the Nebi Musa procession, 1937. American Colony (MATPC 16971).

13 The young Musa Alami with his father and sister, c. early 1900s. Garabed Krikorian (PPMSCA 18411). From the album 'Studio Portraits of Members of the American Colony (Jerusalem), Friends, and Associates', 1870-1935.

14 An imported Dodge, 1920s. American Colony (MATPC 13609).

15 A street in Bethlehem, early 1900s. American Colony (MATPC 05109).

16 Opening of the Hebrew University, 1925. American Colony (MATPC 04712).

17 Lord Plumer with his grandson, during a visit to Jerusalem by Henry de Jouvenel, the French high commisioner for Syria and Lebanon, 1926. American Colony (MATPC 07323).

18 Aftermath of the earthquake of 1927. American Colony (MATPC 03030).

19 The unrest of 1929: Jews fleeing from the Old City. American Colony (MATPC 15716).

20 Arab leaders meeting at a school in Jerusalem to protest at British policy, 1929. Hajj Amin al-Husseini is in the front row, second from the left. American Colony (MATPC 03048).

21 Volunteers guarding the Old City, 1929. American Colony (MATPC 15734).

Chapter 3: Days of rage, 1929-1939

1 Arab riots in Jaffa, October 1933. American Colony (MATPC 15790).

2 The American Colony in happier times: Eric Matson's wedding, 1924. American Colony (MATPC 04682).

3 The King David Hotel and in the background the YMCA, 1930s. American Colony (MATPC 02581).

4 St Andrew's, the Scottish Memorial Church, Jerusalem, 1930s. American Colony (MATPC 03437).

5 The high commissioner, Sir Arthur Wauchope, with Annie Landau at her school, Jerusalem, 1935. Zvi Oron-Orushkes (Central Zionist Archives).

6 Arab and Jewish orange packers, Tel Aviv, 1930s. American Colony (MATPC 03595).

7 Sports Day at the Arab College, Jerusalem, 1940. American Colony (MATPC 20407).

8 Musicians performing for the Palestine Broadcasting Service, 1936-1946. Matson Photo Service (MATPC 14326).

9 German immigrants arriving at Jaffa, 1930s. Zoltan Kluger (GPO, D820-019).

10 Tel Aviv—the White City—in 1936. American Colony (MATPC 00775).

11 The settlement of Nahalal, seen from the air, 1937-1938. Zoltan Kluger (University of Haifa).

12 Settlers returning from work, 1935. Zoltan Kluger (GPO, D19-090).

13 Train derailed by rebels, 1936. American Colony or its successor, the Matson Photo Service (MATPC 18120).

14 Abdul-Qader al-Husseini with other rebel leaders, 1936. Photographer unknown (Institute for Palestine Studies).

15 Alhambra cinema, Jaffa, 1930s. American Colony (MATPC 03562).

16 A market in Mea Shearim, Jerusalem, 1930s. American Colony (MATPC 19041).

17 Lord Peel leaving the King David Hotel, 1936. American Colony (MATPC 18238).

18 Police with Dobermann, Herod's Gate, Jerusalem, 1937. American Colony (MATPC 16586).

19 Members of the Special Night Squads, Ein Harod, December 1938. Zoltan Kluger (GPO, D393-034).

20 Demolished house in Jenin, 1938. American Colony (MATPC 19130).

21 Bertha Spafford Vester with her nurses, after the ending of the siege of Jerusalem, 1938. American Colony (MATPC 18868).

22 Young Zionists in Tel Aviv protest at the British White Paper of 1939. Zoltan Kluger (GPO, D817-045).

Chapter 4: An interlude of war, 1939-1945

1 A war-time film show in Halhul, a village near Hebron, 1940. American Colony. (MATPC 20326).

2 The *Parita*, beached at Tel Aviv, 1939. Zoltan Kluger (Wikimedia Commons).

3 Australian soldiers, Tel Aviv, c. 1941. American Colony (MATPC 21382).

4 Recruitment poster, Tel Aviv, 1941. Zoltan Kluger (GPO, D403-131).

5 Arab recruits, Jerusalem, 1941. Matson Photo Service (MATPC 14522).

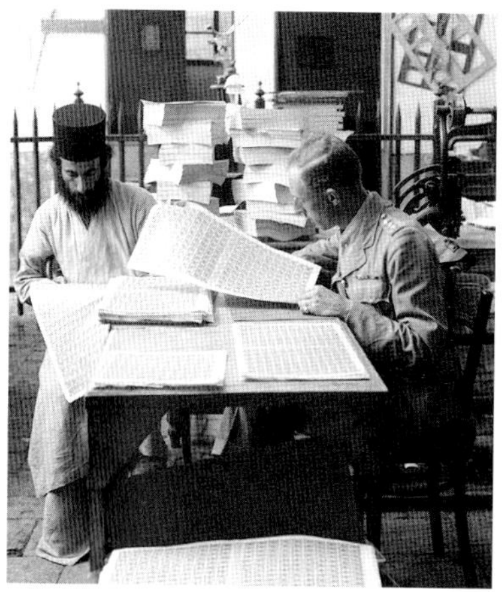

American Colony

Printing Palestine's first postage stamps (under military supervision), 1920

6 Asia Halaby, 1948. Willem van de Poll (Dutch National Archive).

7 Jewish recruits at a British base, Sarafand, 1940. Zoltan Kluger (GPO, D817-014).

8 Oranges near Damascus Gate, Jerusalem, 1944. Matson Photo Service (MATPC 00479).

9 British troops in Palmyra, August 1941. Photographer unknown (National Museum of the US Navy).

10 War-time poster, New York, 1940. Arthur Szyk (Wikimedia Commons).

11 MacMichael with his wife and daughter, c. 1939. Matson Photo Service (MATPC 03673).

12 Officers' club, Jerusalem, 1940.

Matson Photo Service (MATPC 20453).

13 Arab women at a tobacco factory, Nazareth, 1940. Matson Photo Service (MATPC 20711)

14 Official map of Jerusalem issued in 1946 to show soldiers hotels, restaurants, and areas out of bounds. (Wikimedia Commons)

15 Choral concert at the YMCA, 1938. Matson Photo Service (MATPC 22420).

16 Tel Aviv, 1946. Zoltan Kluger (GPO, D839-113).

17 Menachem Begin disguised as a rabbi. Photographer unknown (GPO, D705-079).

18 Abraham Stern. Photographer unknown (GPO, D193-062).

19 Foreign Office telegram, December 1944 (Wikimedia Commons).

20 Barclays Bank, Jerusalem, VE Day, 1945. Matson Photo Service (MATPC 12585).

Chapter 5: Things fall apart, 1945-1948

1 Lockdown in Tel Aviv, March 1947. British soldiers erect a barrier at the border of Jaffa and Tel Aviv. Zoltan Kluger (GPO, D814-047).

2 Bevin and Attlee, April 1946. Photographer unknown (Archive New Zealand).

3 The sea at Jaffa; date uncertain. American Colony (MATPC 06253).

4 Tel Aviv, November 1945. Sg. F. Meek, Army Film & Photographic Unit (Imperial War Museum).

5 Jamal al-Husseini in Jenin after his return from exile, 1946. Matson Photo Service (MATPC 21902).

6 Atallah Mantoura, celebrating Easter at the Church of the Holy Sepulchre, 1941. Matson Photo Service (MATPC 20992).

7 Lobby of the King David Hotel, 1930s. American Colony (MATPC 04812).

8 Operation Agatha, 1946: rounding up suspects. Photographer unknown (Palmach Archive).

9 Searching for survivors: King David Hotel, July 1946. Matson Photo Service (MATPC 21939).

10 *Palestine Gazette*, August 1946, recording those who had died in the bombing of the King David Hotel; the list was still incomplete. (Wikimedia Commons).

11 Police search, Jerusalem, 1947. Hans Pinn (GPO, D836-025).

12 Operation Elephant, Tel Aviv, 1947. Hans Pinn. (GPO, D836-038).

13 Haifa, 1947: children disembark from the *Exodus*. Hans Pinn (GPO, D820-100).

14 Young Zionists taking part in Haganah training, 1948. Zoltan Kluger (GPO, D819-092).

15 King Abdullah being received at Government House, Jerusalem, 1947. Hans Pinn (GPO, D813-094).

16 Funeral in Jerusalem of Abdul-Qader al-Husseini, April 1948. Photographer unknown (GPO, D282-119).

17 The border area between Jaffa and Tel Aviv, 1948. Beno Rothenberg (Meitar Collection/ National Library of Israel/ The Pritzker Family National Photography Collection).

18 Ben-Gurion proclaims the birth of the state of Israel, May 1948. Photographer unknown. (GPO, D662-055).

19 Ramleh, 1948. David Eldan (GPO, D277-026).

20 Count Folke Bernadotte, shortly before his assassination, with Israel's first foreign minister, Moshe Sharett, Jerusalem, September 1948. Photographer unknown (GPO, D159-114).

21 Fleeing from Faluja, north of Gaza, 1948. Photographer unknown (UNRWA).

22 Gaza, 1956: a blind refugee with her grand-daughter. Per-Olow Anderson, from his book *They Are Human Too...* (1957), by permission of his son, Peter Anderson.

23 Women and children expelled from Bir Burin, 1948. Paul Goldman (Eretz Israel Museum, Tel Aviv).

24 Scars of war: Safad, 1949. Zoltan Kluger (GPO, D839-085).

25 Elkosh, 1949: immigrant children from Kurdistan. Zoltan Kluger (GPO, D824-058).

Epilogue

1 Tiberias and the Sea of Galilee, c. 1898. American Colony (MATPC 07012).

2 Herbert Samuel with military escort, 1921. American Colony

(MATPC 22563).

3 Immigrant ship arriving at Haifa, 1946. Hans Pinn (GPO, D820-084).

4 Bride and groom blessing their new home, Bethlehem, 1940s. American Colony (MATPC 12961).

Bibliography

1 Jaffa, 1893. Gustav Bauernfeind (Wikimedia Commons)

2 Bukharan Jews celebrating the feast of Sukkot, early 1900s. American Colony (MATPC 05651).

3 Selling watermelons outside the walls of Jerusalem, c. 1900. American Colony (MATPC 05613).

4 Posters in Tel Aviv, 1934. Zoltan Kluger (GPO, D838-083).

Dramatis personae

1 Sultan Abdul-Hamid, 1867. W. & D. Downey (Bibliothèque nationale de France).

2 Barbara Board in the Second World War. Photograph supplied by her daughter Jacqueline Karp-Gendre.

3 Kaiser Wilhem II and the Empress Augusta Victoria (Library of Congress).

4 Begin, with a poster of Jabotinsky, August 1948. Hans Pinn (GPO).

5 Fawzi al-Qawuqji, 1948. Photographer unknown (Palmach Archive).

6 Pinchas Rutenberg with Emir Abdullah, 1933. At far left is the

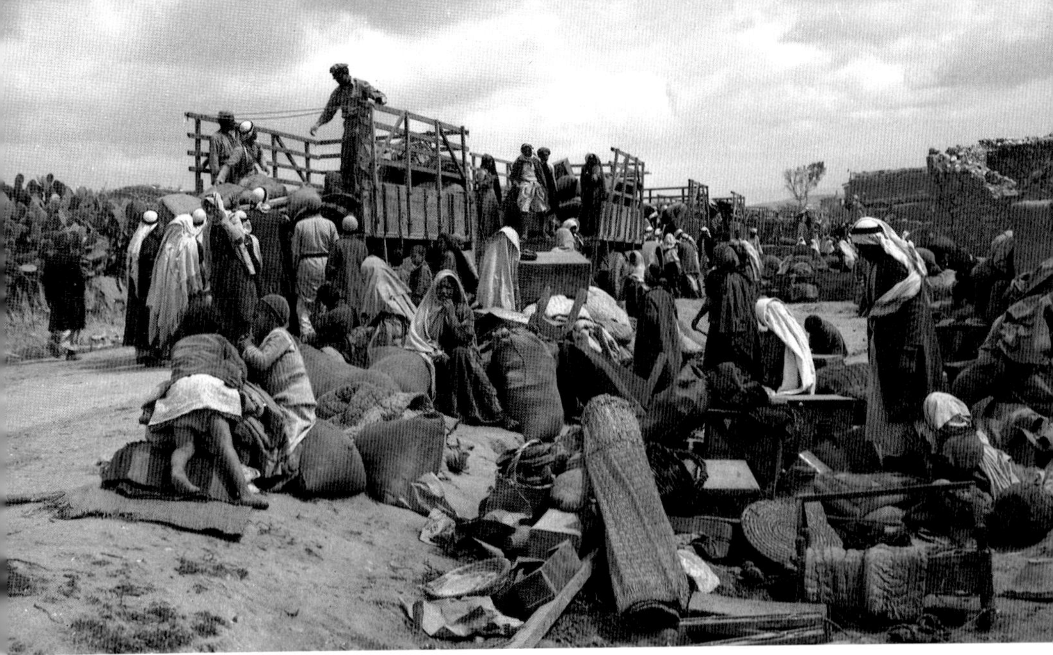

Expulsion of the villagers of Iraq al-Manshiya, southern Palestine, 1949

high commissioner, Sir Arthur Wauchope. American Colony (MATPC 15245).

7 Captain Charles Warren and colleagues in Palestine, 1867. Sgt. Henry Phillips (Palestine Exploration Fund).

Illustrators & picture credits

1 One of Sultan Abdul-Hamid's photograph albums, c. 1880s. Abdullah Frères (Library of Congress).

2 Lewis Larsson in his photographic studio, c. 1920. American Colony (MATPC 11636).

3 Nazareth, 1949: young Arabs waiting to vote in Israel's first elections. Hugo Mendelson

(GPO, D715-072).

4 Russian nuns in Ein Karem, near Jerusalem, c. 1948. Willem van de Poll (Dutch National Archive).

5 Village woman selling cauliflowers, c. 1930s. American Colony (MATPC 19398).

6 Printing Palestine's first postage stamps, 1920, under military supervision. American Colony (MATPC 04691).

7 Expulsion of the villagers of Iraq al-Manshiya, southern Palestine, 1949. Beno Rothenberg (Meitar Collection/National Library of Israel/The Pritzker Family National Photography Collection).

Index

A

Abdul-Hamid II 31, 32, 42, 43, 50, 56, 88, 250, 274, 286, 287, 299, 306, 311, 312
Abdullah, Emir 143, 221, 222, 228, 231, 232, 243, 296, 311
Abdullah Frères 32, 299, 312
Abdul-Mejid 23
Aboud, Karimeh 82, 299, 307
Abul Huda, Luli 183
Acre 16, 19, 21
Acre prison 155, 156, 171
Agronsky, Gershon 221
Alami, Faidi 94, 96
Alami, Musa 94, 95, 123, 138, 145, 152, 182, 202, 209, 234, 255, 259, 265, 271, 307
al-Aqsa Mosque 198
Albert, Prince (Edward VII) 28
Alhambra cinema 141, 308
Alice through the Looking-Glass 97
Ali, Muhammad 19
Allenby Bridge 228
Allenby, general 64-66, 72, 75, 97, 287, 294
Allon, Yigal 172, 174, 261
Allpert, Mrs 142
American Colony 4, 10, 15, 17, 22, 24, 33, 37-39, 41, 50, 55, 57-59, 61, 62, 64, 73, 75, 89, 92, 94, 96, 97, 99, 101, 102, 105, 107, 108, 111, 112, 115-118, 124, 126, 133, 137, 141, 143-145, 148, 150, 196, 205, 241, 242, 247, 250, 251, 255, 257, 271, 272, 275, 280, 283, 284, 293, 296, 300, 302, 305-312

American University of Beirut 52, 98
Anatolia 42
Andrews, Lewis 146, 287
Anglo-American Committee of Inquiry 199, 201, 292
Antonius, George 122, 123, 128, 148, 152, 178, 203, 257-259, 269, 288
Antonius, Katy 122, 123, 178, 288
Antwerp 37
Arab College 126, 127, 169, 231, 293, 294, 308
Arab Higher Committee 136, 146, 202
Arab League 195
Arab Legion 223, 228-230, 234
Arab Liberation Army 220
Argentina 48
Ashbee, C. R. 72, 87, 255
Ashkenazi Jews 49, 224, 266
Athlit castle 119
Athlit detention camp 158
ATS (Auxiliary Territorial Service) 163, 165
Attlee, Clement 193, 194
Augusta Victoria compound 42, 57, 61, 76, 106, 176
Augusta Victoria, empress 42, 291, 311
Austria 19, 198
Azhar, al- 17

B

Baghdad 42, 169, 172, 201, 262, 292, 295
Balfour, Arthur 66, 67, 71, 101, 102, 245, 288, 307
Balfour Declaration, the 9, 68, 69, 73, 74, 84, 86, 91, 152, 244, 267, 288,

298, 307
Balfour Elementary School 160
Balfour Street 133
Barclays Bank 191, 310
Barker, General Evelyn 211
Bassa, al- 146
BBC 129, 170
Bedford, Francis 28, 300, 306
Beethoven 126, 127
Begin, Menachem 186-189, 208, 293, 310
Beirut 16, 17, 27, 31, 34, 63, 78, 145, 169,
    201, 226, 262, 270, 293, 297, 301
Beit Jala 50
Beit Nassar 118
Belkine, Ruth 171, 177
Ben-Dov, Yaacov 49, 81, 300, 306
Ben-Gurion (see also David Gruen) 50, 77,
    78, 80, 81, 83, 102, 127, 133, 138, 156,
    174, 186, 189, 208, 221, 227, 228, 232,
    243, 246, 248, 251, 254, 267, 278, 288,
    307, 311
Bentwich, Helen 76, 77, 81, 94, 97, 101,
    104-106, 109, 253, 257, 269, 288
Bentwich, Norman 76, 91, 94, 96, 102,
    106, 114, 176, 178, 254, 257, 261, 269,
    277, 288, 290, 294
Ben Yehuda Street 221
Berlin 42, 44, 130, 133, 134, 173, 201,
    292, 303
Berlin, Isaiah 127, 257
Bernadotte, count 229, 230, 288, 311
Bethlehem 23, 30, 31, 99, 100, 105, 118,
    126, 142, 155, 247, 252, 256, 257, 260,
    273, 277, 293, 299, 305, 306, 307, 311
Bevin, Ernest 193, 194, 198, 199, 203,
    206, 216, 218, 221, 222, 243, 246, 262,
    288, 310
Bir Burin 235, 311
Bir Zeit 150, 151, 152
Bishop, Adrian 169
Black Sabbath 207
Board, Barbara 142, 143, 164, 184, 198,
    200, 213, 258, 260, 262, 263, 269, 270,
    284, 288, 289, 311
Bombay 40
Bomberg, Alice 90
Bomberg, David 90, 91, 255, 270, 305
Bonfils, Félix 12, 30-32, 35, 250, 301, 305,
    306

Borowsky, Zipporah ('Zippy') 218-220, 224
Boulos, Afif 182, 183
Brahms 140
Britain 4, 9, 14, 19, 21-24, 28, 32, 34, 43,
    44, 57, 62, 64, 66, 69-72, 75, 77, 93,
    94, 96, 117, 133, 146, 152, 153, 155-
    157, 159, 160, 161, 165, 169, 172-174,
    176, 178, 186, 188, 191, 193-195, 197,
    198, 204, 211, 214, 216, 218, 220, 222,
    226, 229, 243-246, 253, 258, 259, 267,
    270, 273, 276, 281, 284, 290, 298
Brit Shalom (Covenant of Peace) 102, 294
Brooke, Rupert 151
Buber, Martin 102
Bucharest 157
Bunche, Ralph 231
Buss, Air Commodore Kenneth 155,
    168-170

C
Café Nussbaum 161
Cafferata, Raymond 108, 288
Cairo 16, 17, 34, 168, 182, 183, 189, 197,
    201, 220
Cambridge 94, 96, 122, 127, 182, 251,
    258, 265, 271, 273, 276, 277, 287
Canaan, Badra 155
Canaan, Bishara 50, 52
Canaan, Leila, *see* Mantoura, Leila
Canaan, Margot 53, 155
Canaan, Tawfiq 50, 52, 53, 62, 77, 98, 137,
    155, 202, 208, 226, 252, 255, 260, 283,
    289, 294, 307
Chancellor, Sir John 106, 114, 119, 289
Chaplin, Charlie 100
Churchill White Paper, the 84
Churchill, Winston 67, 84, 114, 152, 156,
    163, 168, 173, 178, 186, 189, 193, 216,
    243, 289
Church of the Nativity, Bethlehem 23, 100
Clarke, Thurston 193, 263
Coffin, William 20, 306
Collard, Major J. M. 172, 289
Cook, Thomas 26, 41, 160
Coward, Noël 177
Cunningham, Sir Alan 206-209, 214, 227,
    263, 274, 290
Curzon, lord 69, 84
Cyprus 105, 218

Czechoslovakia 229

D

Daily Express 216
Daily Mail 170
Dalton, Hugh 168
Damascus 16, 27, 34, 36, 63, 94, 128, 170, 171, 178, 306, 309
Dannatt, Private Norman 176-178, 261, 290
Dardanelles 44
Darwin, Charles 14
Davar Hashavua 235
David, king 18
Dayan, Moshe 146, 156, 171, 172, 209, 260, 270, 281
Dayan, Ruth 209
Deedes, Wyndam 75
Degania 49, 81, 306
Deir al-Qassi 238
Deir Yassin 223, 224
Dictionary of National Biography 120, 249, 257, 262
Domaggi, Father 100
Dome of the Rock, the 18, 72
Downey, W & D 32, 286, 311
Dreyfus 48

E

East Africa 48
Eban, Aubrey (Abba) 183
Ecole des Frères 94
Egypt 19, 26, 28, 69, 86, 111, 116, 122, 161, 165, 168, 169, 173, 196, 203, 228, 231, 234, 250, 288, 291, 294
Eichmann, Adolf 157
Ein Harod 80, 104, 147, 309
El-Alamein 174
Eldan, David 229, 236, 311
Eliot, T. S. 183
Elkosh 238, 239, 311
Evelina de Rothschild School 76
Evening News, London 169
Exodus, SS 218

F

Faisal, Emir 83, 91, 243
Fenn, Harry 27, 28, 301, 306
Filastin 52, 163

Finn, Mrs Elizabeth Anne 21, 249
First World War 9, 24, 36, 56, 74, 78, 88, 90, 94, 104, 120, 122, 203, 242, 246, 287, 289, 292, 294, 295, 303
Fleet Street 198
Foreign Office 186, 189, 190, 194, 198, 206, 310
Forster, E. M. 122
France 19, 21, 23, 32, 34, 44, 57, 64, 71, 119, 133, 204, 218, 244, 284, 311
Free French 169, 178

G

Gaza Strip 16, 231, 232, 300, 311
Gelber, Sylva 138, 139, 182, 191, 214, 220, 258, 262, 264, 271, 290
German Colony, the 77, 250
Germany 9, 32, 43, 44, 56, 62, 131, 133, 134, 140, 142, 148, 155, 157, 159, 189, 198, 218, 238, 239, 259, 290, 303
Glubb, John 228, 229, 257
Goldman, Paul 235, 236, 265, 269, 284, 301, 311
Gort, lord 190, 206, 290
Government Press Office 238, 284, 302, 305
Graham, Stephen 45-47, 249, 251, 271, 274, 283, 290
Greater Syria 52, 83, 244
Gruen, David (see also Ben-Gurion) 47, 49, 50
Gutmann, Assia 134, 160, 161, 211, 258, 260, 269, 274, 290, 297
Gutmann, Lisa 133, 134, 160, 161
Gutmann, Lonya 133, 160, 211, 269, 290, 297

H

Ha'aretz 238, 254, 265
Hacohen, David 172
Hadassah hospital 102, 142, 224, 296
Hadera 184
Haganah 77, 138, 146, 156, 159, 171-174, 189, 198, 203, 207, 208, 211, 219, 220, 224, 232, 261, 303, 310
Haifa 16, 26, 78, 104, 118, 123, 124, 135, 137, 158, 159, 171, 173, 180, 217-219, 227, 245, 250, 257, 278, 303, 308, 310, 311
Halaby, Asia 165, 166, 226, 309

Halaby, Sophie 165, 183, 226, 260, 262, 277, 291
Hamburg 53, 218
Hamburger, Max 206
Hammami, Hasan 224
Harrison, Austen 106
Hatikvah, the 74, 200
Hatt-i Humayün 23
Hebrew University of Jerusalem 101, 102, 114, 218, 294, 308
Hebron 49, 57, 108, 109, 154, 256, 274, 288, 309
Heifetz, Jascha 104
Herod the Great 18
Herzl, Theodor 48, 49, 78, 227, 251, 291
Hesse, Max 182
Hildesheimer, Wolfgang 183, 262
Histadrut 77, 146, 291
Hitler 9, 131, 134, 152, 163, 165, 174, 246
Hodgkin, Edward 121, 169, 195, 197, 226, 257, 262, 272
Hodgkin, Thomas 121-123, 127, 128, 138, 169, 196, 257, 292
Holliday, Clifford 87-90, 102, 105-107, 111, 116-118, 123, 124, 191, 255-257, 272, 284, 292, 307
Holliday, Eunice 87, 88, 90, 102, 107, 111, 116, 117, 124, 255, 257, 272, 284, 292
Holliday, Tim 88, 118, 255, 257, 284
Holocaust 198, 246
Hourani, Albert 183, 202, 258, 262, 263
House of Commons 152, 189, 198, 199
Hungary 48, 157
Husseini, Abdul-Qader al- 139, 220, 221, 223, 292, 308, 310
Husseini, Hajj Amin al- 74, 91-93, 107, 108, 146, 152, 163, 165, 172, 173, 201, 222, 243, 255, 261, 276, 292, 307, 308
Husseini, Hajj Amin al-. *See also* Mufti, the
Husseini, Jamal al- 201, 202, 310
Husseinis, the 93, 165, 201
Hussein, Taha 182

I

Ibrahim Pasha 19
Imperial Orthodox Palestine Society 47
Iraq 42, 71, 123, 127, 137, 140, 172, 173, 196, 226, 228, 234, 238, 292, 293, 295, 312

Irgun 172, 186, 187, 188, 190, 198, 200, 208, 209, 211, 214, 216, 223, 246, 289
Irish Republican Army 187
Issy's Bar 178
Istanbul 17, 19, 34, 42, 43, 44, 45, 169

J

Jabotinsky, Vladimir 74, 186, 292, 293, 311
Jabra Ibrahim Jabra 99, 100, 105, 126, 127, 182, 183, 226, 256, 257, 262, 273, 293
Jacobs, Julius 209, 211
Jaffa 16, 17, 24, 26, 32, 34, 36, 37, 44, 52, 75, 81, 84, 88, 112, 121, 130, 131, 133, 140, 141, 160, 178, 195, 196, 203, 204, 224, 225, 261, 265, 268, 274, 291, 297, 305, 306, 308, 310, 311
Jazzar, Ahmad al- 19
Jemal Pasha 57, 58, 59, 60, 61, 62, 63, 64, 307
Jenin 148, 170, 196, 309, 310
Jerusalem 4, 10, 12, 14-24, 27, 28, 31-34, 36-41, 44, 46, 47, 49, 50, 53, 55, 57, 59, 60, 63-66, 72, 74-77, 87, 88, 90-94, 97, 98, 101, 102, 105-109, 116-118, 121, 122, 125, 126, 128, 130, 142, 149-152, 164-166, 168, 171, 177-179, 182-184, 189, 191, 198, 201, 204, 206, 209, 213, 214, 216-224, 228-231, 234, 241, 243, 247, 249, 250-258, 260, 261, 264, 265, 270-278, 280, 281, 287, 288, 290,-298, 300, 302-312
Jerusalem Forum 183
Jerusalem Girls' College 165
Jewish Agency 91, 176, 206, 207, 222
Jewish Brigade 163
Jewish National Fund 78, 81, 135, 303
Jewish Resistance Movement 198, 206

K

Khalidi, Ahmad Samih al- 127, 169, 183, 231
Khalidi, Husain 121
Khalidi, Walid 183, 202, 262, 263
kibbutzniks 80, 81, 104
King David Hotel 116, 117, 144, 178, 183, 193, 204, 205, 208, 210, 227, 263, 270, 294, 308, 309, 310
Kingsway development 123

Kluger, Zoltan 8, 131, 134, 135, 147, 153, 158, 162, 167, 185, 192, 219, 236, 237, 238, 239, 258, 279, 302, 305, 308, 309, 310, 311
Kol Eretz Israel (the Voice of the Land of Israel) 129
Krikorian, Garabed 34, 41, 95, 302, 307
Kurdistan 239, 311

L

Landau, Annie 76, 77, 120, 254, 274, 278, 293, 308
Larsson, Lewis 37, 38, 40, 55, 56, 60, 61, 97, 115, 116, 250, 252, 271, 274, 293, 300, 302, 305, 306, 307, 312
League of Nations 71, 195
Lear, Edward 26, 34
Lebanon 52, 71, 83, 146, 172, 173, 178, 201, 203, 224, 228, 238, 295, 298, 308
Levi, Victor 209, 211
Lloyd George, David 66, 69, 71, 74, 75, 114
Lloyd, Seton 169
London 13, 28, 32, 42, 44, 66, 69, 74, 76, 90, 94, 96, 99, 114, 136, 138, 145, 152, 168, 169, 172, 190, 206, 209, 222, 226, 243, 249-267, 269- 278, 280-282, 290, 297
London School of Economics 172, 255, 290
Lovers of Zion 48
Lydda 221, 229, 230

M

MacDonald, Malcolm 156
MacDonald, Ramsay 114, 156
MacMichael, Araminta 177
MacMichael, Sir Harold 147, 152, 159, 176, 177, 186, 189, 190, 262, 293, 309
Magnes, Dr Judah 101, 102, 128, 214, 254, 271, 278, 294
Manchester 66, 183
Manger Square 100
Manhattan 184
Manning, Olivia 183
Mantoura, Atallah 203, 204, 209, 283, 294, 310
Mantoura, Jacques 209-211, 226, 284
Mantoura, Leila (née Canaan) 208, 209,

226, 284, 289, 294
Marlowe, John. *See* Collard, Major J. M.
Matson, Eric 55, 115, 116, 129, 154, 160, 164, 170, 177, 179, 180, 182, 191, 202, 204, 210, 302, 305, 308, 309, 310
McDonnell, Sir Michael 114, 140, 294
Mea Shearim 142, 143, 178, 308
Mecca 36
Medina 36
Meek, Sgt F. 199
Meir, Golda 222
Mendelson, Hugo 236, 301, 312
Mendelssohn, Felix 141
Meyers, Elijah 40, 41
MI6 197
Middle East Supply Centre 168
Moab 191
Mohammedan Saints and Sanctuaries in Palestine 98
Monroe, Elizabeth 69, 253, 256, 276, 283
Montgomery, General Bernard 206
Moody, Flora 109, 142, 256, 284, 294
Moody, Sydney 109, 142, 256, 284, 294
Morocco 52, 238
Morris, Benny 232, 265, 276
Morris, William 72
Moscow 34, 44
Mosseris, family 117
Motelle 66, 252
Mount Carmel 171
Mount of Olives 34, 35, 42, 57, 76, 77, 91, 176, 306
Moyne, lord 189
Mozart 183
Mufti, the 91, 93, 107, 113, 123, 135, 136, 139, 144, 146, 148, 151, 152, 153, 163, 164, 172, 220, 243, 255, 261, 276
Muhammad, Abdul-Rahim al-Hajj 151, 287
Muhammad, prophet 18
Musrara 53, 204, 226
Mussolini 124, 159

N

Nablus 16, 57, 84, 86, 105, 125, 226, 297, 307
Nakba 236, 238, 265, 266, 269
Napoleon 19
Nås 37
Nashashibis, the 93, 151, 165

Nazism 9, 131, 134, 140, 155, 157, 159, 174, 189, 238, 239, 246, 290, 292, 303
Near East Arab Broadcasting Station. *See* Sharq al-Adna
Nicholas I, tsar 23
Notre Dame, hospice 34
Nuwayhid, Ajaj 130

O

Odessa 44, 45, 47
OETA, Occupied Enemy Territory Administration 73, 74, 76
Olives, mount of 34, 35, 42, 57, 76, 77, 91, 176, 306
Operation Agatha 207, 310
Operation Elephant 214, 215, 310
Operation Magic Carpet 238, 266
Operation Shark 213
Orpheus Choir 182
Oxford 11, 127, 151, 251, 255, 256, 258, 259, 263, 264, 271, 272, 274, 276, 278, 281, 283, 289, 294, 298

P

Pale of Settlement 66
Palestine Broadcasting Service 128, 129, 142, 169, 171, 177, 183, 265, 297, 308
Palestine Civil Service List 93, 255
Palestine Electric Corporation 123
Palestine Exploration Fund 13, 24, 28, 36, 53, 249, 284, 297, 298, 312
Palestine Gazette 211, 310
Palestine Philharmonic Orchestra 161
Palestine Police Force Band 191
Palestine Post 141, 211, 221, 258, 287
Palmach, the 172, 174, 295, 310, 311
Palmerston, lord 23
Paris 32, 44, 48, 71, 165, 201, 208, 246, 251, 253, 267, 291
Parita, SS 158, 309
Passfield White Paper 114
Patria, SS 158
Peel commission 148, 202, 243, 287
Peel, lord 113, 140, 144, 294, 309
Pentagon 195
Perowne, Stewart 169
Perrott, C. H. 116
Picturesque Palestine, Sinai and Egypt 28
Plain of Esdraelon 104

Płonsk 47, 288
Plumer, lord 102, 104, 106, 109, 295, 308
Poland 47, 49, 90, 157, 288
President Warfield, SS. See Exodus, SS
Pro-Jerusalem Society 72, 87, 88, 105, 253, 255
Public Information Office 225

Q

Qalandia 227
Qassam, Sheikh Izzedin al- 135, 146
Qatamon 220
Qawuqji, Fawzi al- 140, 220, 226, 295, 311

R

Raad, Khalil 34, 41, 60, 61, 303, 307
RAF 161
Ramallah 15, 151, 230, 305
Ramleh 229, 236, 311
Rashidiyya secondary school 127
Raziel, David 172
Revisionists, the 74, 293
Rhodes 231, 256, 294
Roberts, David 26
Robertson, Jack 168-171, 173, 183, 196, 261, 270
Romania 157, 158
Roosevelt, F. D. 194
Rothenberg, Beno 225, 236, 266, 277, 282, 303, 311, 312
Royal Navy 218
Runciman, Steven 169
Russia 15, 19, 21, 23, 24, 44, 46,-50, 57, 66, 67, 244, 251
Russian Compound 34, 47
Rutenberg, Pinchas 123, 124, 295, 296, 311

S

Safad 8, 49, 109, 237, 238, 256, 294, 305, 311
Sakakini, Khalil 59, 94, 182, 295
Saladin 18
Samuel, Sir Herbert 75, 76, 84, 91, 93, 94, 96, 97, 101, 102, 104, 114, 136, 242, 277, 281, 296, 297, 303, 307, 311
Sarafand 165, 167, 309
Sarona 214
Schubert 140

Schweig, Joseph 81, 303

Selim the Grim, sultan 17

Semiramis Hotel 220, 264

Sephardic Jews 49

Shakespeare 161, 226

Sharif, Haram al- 18, 24, 28, 306

Sharq al-Adna 169, 170, 196, 197, 262,
    292

Shaw, Sir John 209, 210

Shaw, Sir Walter 113

Simpson, Sir John Hope 113

Smith, Reggie 183

SOE (Special Operations Executive) 168,
    169, 171, 173, 174, 196, 197, 261

Solel Boneh 146, 291

Solomon 18, 143, 145

Soskin, Abraham 80, 81, 303, 307

Souvenirs d'Orient 31, 301

Soviet Union 194, 195, 218, 228

Spafford, Anna 37-40, 59, 61, 64, 94, 97,
    250, 251, 255, 257, 271, 280, 296, 306

Spafford, Horatio 37, 296

Special Night Squads 146, 147, 309

St Andrew's Church, Jerusalem 117, 118,
    257, 270, 292, 308

Stark, Freya 169, 295

State Department 195

Steele, John 161

Stern, Abraham 187, 188, 310

Stern Gang 187, 189, 198, 200, 223, 230,
    246, 288

St George's Cathedral 34

St Mary Magdalene, Church of 34, 306

Storrs, Ronald 70, 72, 74-77, 81, 87, 88,
    90, 91, 97, 102, 104, 252-256, 296, 307

Strauss 142

Street of the Prophets 107, 108

Struma, SS 159

Stubbs, Richard 225, 265

Suleiman the Magnificent 17

Supreme Muslim Council 92

Sursuq family 78, 80

Switzerland 48

Sykes, Mark 70, 260, 280

Syria 18, 19, 27, 52, 57, 62, 71, 83, 91,
    136, 140, 157, 172, 173, 178, 228, 234,
    244, 251, 272, 295, 308

Syrian Protestant College 52, 98

Szold, Henrietta 102, 142, 296

Szyk, Arthur 174, 303, 309

T

Tabeetha School 160, 297

Talbieh 98

Tall, Abdullah 234

Tall, Wasfi 208, 209

Tanzimat 23

Tegart forts 146, 297

Tegart, Sir Charles 146, 296, 297

Tegart wall 146

Tel Aviv 11, 80, 81, 84, 104, 118, 124, 127,
    130, 133, 134, 140, 142, 152, 153,
    158-162, 184, 185, 187, 189, 192, 199,
    200, 213-216, 221, 225, 227-229, 258,
    265, 266, 269, 277, 279, 281, 282, 284,
    290, 302, 303, 307-311

The Arab Awakening 123, 148, 149, 258,
    259, 269, 288

The Birth of the Palestinian Refugee Problem
    232, 265, 276

The Innocents Abroad 26, 280, 297

The Land and the Book 27, 250, 297

The Times 41, 170, 226, 292

Thomas, Dylan 226

Thompson, Downing 210

Thomson, Wiiliam McClure 27, 297

Thomson, William, archbishop of York 13,
    15, 44, 250

Tiberias 49, 241, 311

Toscanini, Arturo 140

Transjordan 71, 84, 121, 123, 140, 143,
    145, 187, 222, 223, 228, 229, 234, 243,
    296

Tripoli 172, 295

Truman, Harry 195, 199, 203, 228, 246

Tuqan, Fadwa 86, 125, 126, 130, 226, 254,
    257, 265, 270, 280, 297

Tuqan, Ibrahim 86, 125, 130

Turjman, Ihsan 57, 59, 63

Twain, Mark 26, 280, 297

Tyre 225

U

Underground Jerusalem 36, 250, 281, 297

United Nations 71, 195, 216-218, 220,
    222, 223, 229, 232, 234, 239, 247, 288

United States 15, 19, 24, 28, 32, 37, 39,
    47, 64, 67, 97, 133, 174, 176, 186, 194,

198, 201, 229, 234, 300, 302, 306
UNRWA (United Nations Relief and Works
    Agency) 234, 265, 281, 284
UNSCOP 217, 218

V

Vatican, the 244
VE Day 191, 310
Vester, Bertha, née Spafford 59, 61, 64,
    65, 97, 104, 115, 116, 150, 151, 251,
    252, 309
Vester, Frederick 59, 66, 115
Victoria, queen 13, 28, 32, 40, 300
Vienna 32, 48, 123, 157, 184
Vogt, Emile 205

W

Wailing Wall 106
Wales 16, 216, 259, 300
Walker-Arnott, Jane 160, 297
Warburton, Mabel 165, 166
Warren, Charles 36, 250, 281, 297, 298,
    312
Warsaw 47, 157
Washington 195, 249, 263, 265, 266, 273,
    277, 281, 302
Waste Land 183
Wauchope, Sir Arthur 120, 121, 123,
    128-130, 136-138, 140, 147, 152, 169,

206, 287, 292, 297, 308, 312
Weizmann, Chaim 66, 67, 69, 70, 71,
    73-77, 83, 84, 101, 114, 163, 174, 176,
    186, 208, 214, 243, 246, 252-254, 281,
    287, 297
Whitehall 152, 197
White House 195
Wilhelma 155
Wilhelm II, kaiser 40-44, 64, 176, 291, 306
Wilson, Hilda 149, 151, 152, 259, 298
Wilson, Sir Charles 28, 298
Wilson, Woodrow 71
Wingate, Orde 146
Woodward, John Douglas 28

Y

Yemen 238
Yiddish 47, 49, 143, 209, 252
Yildiz Palace 42
Yishuv, the 83, 101, 104, 128, 131, 138,
    159, 163, 164, 173, 189, 191, 199, 200,
    207, 208, 214, 303
YMCA 117, 177, 182, 209, 217, 308, 310
Young Turks, the 56, 57, 287

Z

Zionist Commission 73, 307
Zionist Congress, 1946 214
Zurich 31